FREQUENTLY UPDATED LISTINGS

Restaurants, bars and hotels change all the time. To ensure you get the most out of your guide, the app features all of our favourites, as well as the latest openings, and is updated regularly. Simply update your app when you receive a notification to access the most current listings available.

Shopping in Oman still revolves around the traditional souks that can be found in every town in the country – most famously at Mutrah in Muscat, Salalah and Nizwa, which serve as showcases of traditional Omani craftsmanship and produce ranging from antique khanjars and Bedu jewellery to halwa, rose-water and frankincense. Muscat also boasts a number of modern malls, although these are rare elsewhere in the country.

TRAVEL TIPS & DESTINATION OVERVIEWS

The app also includes a complete A to Z of handy travel tips on everything from visa regulations to local etiquette. Plus, you'll find destination overviews on shopping, sport, the arts, local events, health, activities and more.

HOW TO DOWNLOAD THE WALKING EYE

Available on purchase of this guide only.
1. Visit our website: www.insightguides.com/walkingeye
2. Download the Walking Eye container app to your smartphone (this will give you access to both the destination app and the eBook)
3. Select the scanning module in the Walking Eye container app
4. Scan the QR code on this page – you will be asked to enter a verification word from the book as proof of purchase
5. Download your free destination app* and eBook for travel information on the go

* Other destination apps and eBooks are available for purchase separately or are free with the purchase of the Insight Guide book

Contents

THE BEST OF SWEDEN: TOP ATTRACTIONS

Explore Sweden's attractive cities and fascinating history, laze on a beach, shimmy in the snow, snack on seafood, hike the spruce-filled forests or sit on a steamship and watch the world go by – make your visit memorable with a rundown of the very best Sweden has to offer.

△ **Stockholm**. Europe's first Green Capital floats on 14 islands: visit Gamla Stan, a medieval maze of alley-ways and enchanting architecture. See page 161.

▽ **Göteborg**. Thread your way through Sweden's second city by tram or boat, ride the rollercoasters at Liseberg amusement park, and dine on the day's catch at one of Göteborg's top seafood restaurants. See page 213.

△ **Bohuslän Coast**. Sun-worshippers flock to the sandy beaches of Bohuslän in summer, or take to sailing boats and kayaks to explore thousands of offshore islands, skerries, rocks and reefs. See page 230.

△ **Visby, Gotland**. Turreted walls encircle this medieval Hanseatic trading town, full of crooked houses, cobbled streets and rose-covered ruins. In August, troubadours and jousting knights bring the past to life during the Medeltidsveckan festival. See page 210.

△ **Inlandsbanan**. This historic railway runs from Sweden's heartland right into the Arctic Circle, stopping at tiny stations for meals, and to shoo reindeer off the tracks. See page 268.

△ **Kingdom of Glass**. In southern Sweden, Glasriket (the 'Kingdom of Glass') is a region full of historic glassworks. Stock up on glowing bowls and richly-coloured vases, watch the masters at work, or give glass-blowing a go yourself. See page 202.

▷ **Göta Kanal**. Slip into a slower gear and sail by steamship along the engineering marvel that is the Göta Kanal. The four-day coast-to-coast cruise passes through some unmissable towns and villages. See page 249.

◁ **Kungsleden Trail**. Sweden's most famous long-distance walking path wends its way through the mountains of Lapland, through dark forests and broad green valleys scattered with Alpine flowers. See page 281.

▽ **Sunken ships**. Sweden's mighty 17th-century empire is epitomised by the remains of two stunning warships. Kalmar Länsmuseum contains 30,000 objects recovered from the *Kronan*; while Stockholm's Vasamuseet contains the spectacular battleship *Vasa* herself. See pages 172 and 205.

△ **Sweden in winter**. Stay in the Ice Hotel, carved from crystal-clear blocks of river ice; visit the Sami market at Jokkmokk; or marvel at the eerie Northern Lights, billowing overhead like multicoloured smoke. See pages 280 and 283.

THE BEST OF SWEDEN: EDITOR'S CHOICE

Discover romantic castles, wild adventures, the best summer festivals, weird and wonderful food, and the secrets of the Swedish soul with our pick of the country's most unique attractions.

ONLY IN SWEDEN

Dala horses. A better-known symbol of Sweden than the Swedish flag, you can watch these shiny-red horses being carved and painted in Dalarna. See page 256.
Carl Larsson's house. The artist's beautiful riverside cottage is a humbling example of love, family life and Swedish design working in perfect harmony. See page 257.
Ice Hotel. Pack your warmest pyjamas for a stay in this wintry palace, filled with unique ice sculptures that melt away in spring. See page 280.
Gammelstad church town. This perfectly-preserved example of a Scandinavian 'church village', with 424 little wooden houses, is a Unesco World Heritage site. See page 293.
Tanum rock carvings. Bohuslän's *hällristningar* provide an enigmatic glimpse into the customs and beliefs of those who lived here 4,000 years ago. See page 232.
Vasaloppet. A powerful Swedish legend is celebrated at the gruelling Vasaloppet cross-country ski race, held each year between Sälen and Mora. See page 258.

Kalmar Slott.

BEST CASTLES AND PALACES

Drottningholm Palace. Inspired by the Palace of Versailles, this Unesco World Heritage site contains two unique 18th-century master-pieces in its theatre and Chinese pavilion. See page 180.
Kalmar Slott. A turreted Renaissance castle with moat, drawbridge and a secret passage in the privy, built by paranoid King Erik XIV. See page 205.
Gripsholm Slott. This beautiful royal residence on Lake Mälaren contains the Swedish National Portrait Gallery... and a fantastic 260-year-old stuffed lion. See page 194.
Borgholm Slott. On the island of Öland, the brooding ruins of Borgholm Slott make a dramatic backdrop to summer theatre performances and concerts. See page 206.
Läckö Slott. This gleaming Baroque castle is one of the stand-out sights on a steamship cruise along the Göta Kanal. See page 243.

Dalahästen, Sweden's famous wooden horses.

BEST OUTDOOR ADVENTURES

Sail the Stockholm archipelago. 24,000 islets and skerries lie on the city's doorstep: discover them on a historic schooner or modern luxury yacht. See page 186.

Build a raft. Drift down the River Klarälven on a home-made timber raft, eating, snoozing, fishing and keeping an eye out for beavers. See page 238.

Orsa Bear Park. See brown bears and their cuddly-looking cubs up close at the Orsa Bear Park. See page 255.

Snorkel trails. Explore the marine environment at Sweden's newest national park, Koster-havet, by swimming along marked snorkel routes. See page 233.

Dog-sledding. Hitch a team of ice-eyed Siberian huskies to your sled and race off into the Arctic Circle. See page 277.

Tour skating. Sweden's frozen lakes and rivers are a winter playground, where you can zip along for miles on a pair of skates. See page 125.

Rafting on the Klarälven River.

BEST FESTIVALS AND EVENTS

Midsummer. Wear flowers in your hair, swig schnapps and dance around a Mid-summer pole like a true Swede at Scandinavia's happiest celebration. See page 146.

Dalhalla Opera. In sum-mer, opera fans flock to this unique venue, a lime-stone quarry with fabulous acoustics, to hear some of the world's top artists. See page 254.

Medeltidsveckan. Jousters and jugglers entertain the crowds at

Visby's week-long medieval festival in August. See page 209.

Stockholm Pride. Scandinavia's biggest gay pride event is marked in July with lectures, films, theatre performances, partying and a 60,000-strong parade. See page 174.

Skansen Christmas market. Twinkling lights, gingerbread and mulled wine usher in the festive season at Stockholm's charming open-air museum. See page 173.

BEST FOOD

Crayfish parties. In July and August, a party hat and a bib are essential attire for the eating of crayfish and the drinking of schnapps. See page 142.

Smörgåsbord. The Swedish *smörgåsbord* elevates the humble buffet table to an art form, with its beautifully prepared hot-and-cold dishes. See page 139.

Fermented herring. An emergency gas-leak team was summoned to a block of flats in Södermalm in 2012. The source of the ghastly smell? A newly opened tin of *surströmming*...

See page 139.

New Nordic cuisine. The rise of New Nordic cuisine, devoted to showcasing the finest Scandinavian produce, has put Sweden firmly on the culinary map. See page 139.

Seafood restaurants. Head to Göteborg and the west coast for a taste of the freshest lobsters, shrimps, mussels and oysters. See page 142.

Fika. The *fika* is a cherished custom in Sweden, the chance to catch up with old friends over coffee and a cinnamon bun. See page 82.

Midsummer celebration in full swing.

Kayaking in Dyngön.

Traditional goose herding can be seen daily in Skanör from the end of June to mid-August.

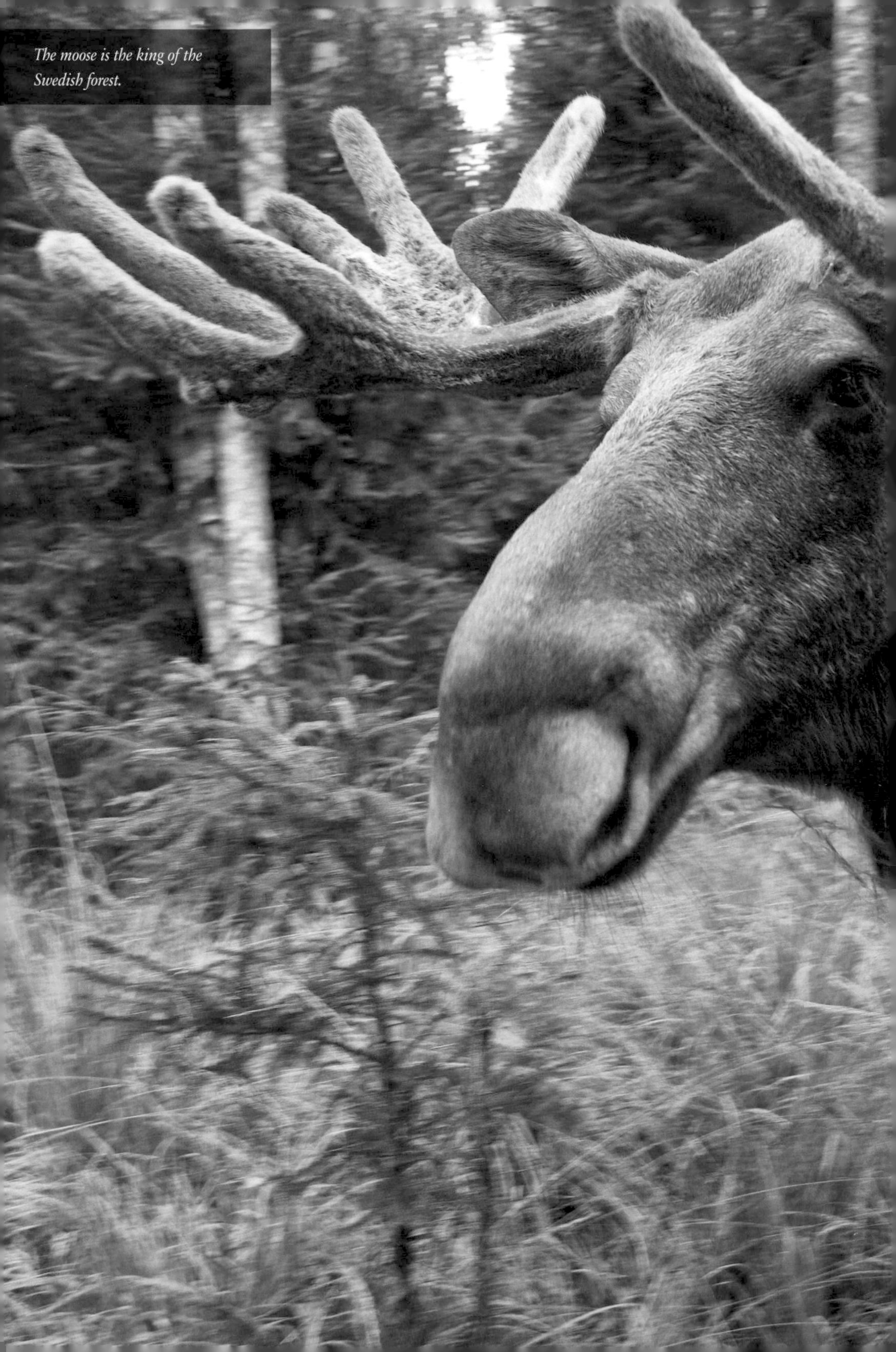

The moose is the king of the Swedish forest.

Dog-sledding with Siberian huskies in Lapland.

THE SPIRIT OF SWEDEN

A love of nature and tradition lies at Sweden's heart:
Swedes spend the lazy days of summer hiking, fishing
or picking berries, and winter skiing and skating.

Skasen window.

Not long ago, Sweden was an introverted place, perched uneasily on the edge of Western Europe. But attitudes have changed, and today Sweden has a new-found confidence. Part of this is down to the success of the country's cultural exports – think Stieg Larsson's wildly successful crime fiction, the fame of actors like *True Blood*'s Alexander Skarsgård, and the success of innovative companies like Skype.

Curious visitors are arriving in ever greater numbers to see just what else Sweden has been hiding, drawn not just to the bustling big cities of Stockholm, Göteborg (Gothenburg) and Malmö, but also to the rural regions and the vast wilderness areas of Lapland and the far north.

This is an ideal country for those who love the great outdoors – outside the cities, space and silence loom large. Sweden was the first country in Europe to create a national park system, which preserves its wild northern mountains, wriggling coastline and whispering forests of pine and spruce.

A love of nature is deeply rooted within the national psyche. It's fully expressed at Midsummer, when you'll find Swedes dancing around maypoles and bonfires; and in July and early August when every city-dweller abandons the office and heads for a red-painted *sommarstuga* (summer cottage) to fish and swim. Under the Midnight Sun, the long, lazy days of summer are literally endless – you can hike, play golf, or go horse-riding, sailing or canoeing all 'night' long if you choose.

Picking mushrooms.

Sweden is also a popular winter destination. The climate is much less harsh than people imagine and Christmas, with its traditional markets, brightly decorated streets and St Lucia processions, is a magical time of year. Skiing centres such as Åre rival the better-known Alpine resorts, and winter is also the time to marvel at the aurora borealis (Northern Lights), mush a dog sled, or track wolves and lynx on a snowy 'safari'.

The country has a wealth of cultural interest too. Well-preserved historical sites, like the enigmatic Bronze Age rock carvings in Bohuslän, the medieval walled town of Visby, and the remains of the old Viking capital Birka, tell the stories of lives long past. State-of-the-art museums and galleries display the country's artistic heritage. Sweden has even become a centre of gastronomic excellence, with restaurants in Stockholm, Göteborg and Malmö all boasting Michelin stars. Meanwhile in the far north, Scandinavia's indigenous Sami people still maintain their semi-nomadic way of life.

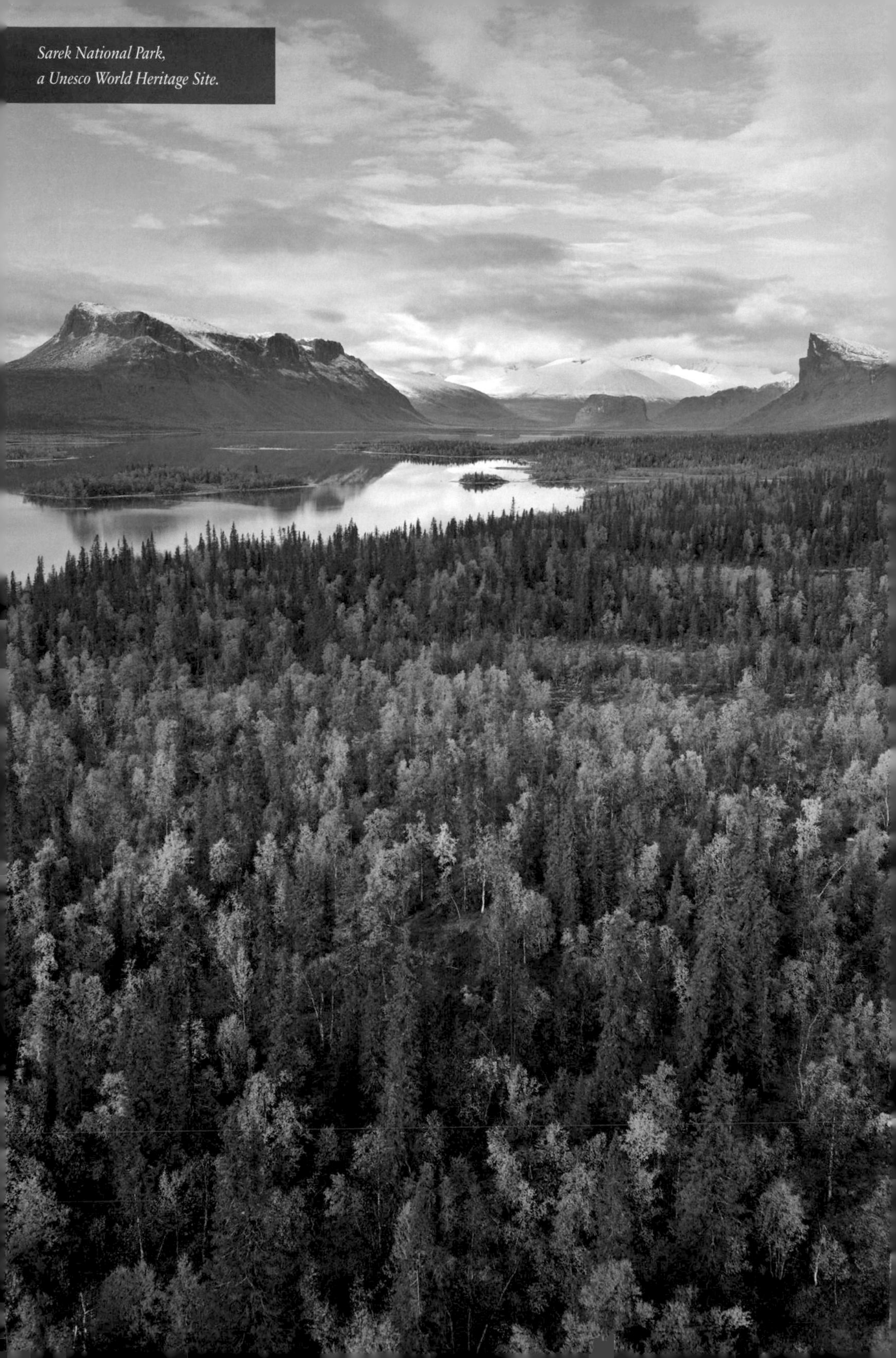

Sarek National Park, a Unesco World Heritage Site.

A WILD LAND

Sweden's countryside is cherished by its green-minded inhabitants, a spiritual retreat full of lush berries and wild animals.

Stretching from mainland Europe to the North Pole's back yard, Sweden's long, thin territory covers all manner of environments. From fertile farmland to bear-filled forests; from glinting lakes and white-sand beaches to high mountain peaks where the snow never melts – there's a Swedish habitat to suit every mood.

Country retreats

Swedes, many only a few generations away from rural life, have a deep-rooted love of nature. With thousands of square miles of pristine countryside, and an enshrined legal freedom to roam through it at will, it's no wonder that they head for the hills at every opportunity. In Sweden, the family *stuga* is not just a holiday cottage, but a place for spiritual rejuvenation.

Berry-picking is a common summer pastime – crowberries, bilberries, lingonberries and precious Arctic cloudberries appear on kitchen tables, supplemented in autumn by earthy mushrooms including highly prized golden chanterelles.

Swedes have always integrated home and landscape, from wood-built cottages to turf-roofed houses. Modern architecture uses glass to bring nature inside, and the simple lines of Swedish design often echo the curves of a lakeshore, or the pale slant of winter sunlight.

Swedish landscapes

Dramatic events – earthquakes volcanoes and glaciers – in Sweden's geological history have shaped its landscapes. Sweden was flattened during the Ice Age. As the earth warmed, the melting ice sheet left behind low rounded hummocks and hills and tens of thousands

Western coast landscape.

of lakes – an angler's delight and perfect for wild swimmers.

Freed from the crushing weight of the ice, the land is still rebounding, creating one of Sweden's most beautiful stretches of coastline, the Höga Kusten on the Gulf of Bothnia. Today it is a Unesco World Heritage site, its high cliffs and scattered islands a boater's delight in summer.

And Sweden hasn't just been shaped by earthly forces. Dazzling Lake Siljan at the heart of the folkloric region of Dalarna is the southwestern edge of the largest-known impact crater in Europe. This epic dent was formed when a 2.5km (1.5-mile) wide meteorite crashed to earth 360 million years ago.

Midnight sun

Like Swedes, the sun in summer shows no inclination to sleep. From within the Arctic Circle, it appears to observers that the 'midnight sun' never sets, but simply travels around the horizon in a circle. The further north you go, the more days of midnight sun there are – in Abisko, one of the most northerly towns in Sweden, the sun sails around the sky for an incredible 56 days without disappearing, from late May to mid July. The phenomenon is caused by the tilt of the earth as it orbits the sun. This lopsided angle ensures that the North Pole always faces sunwards in summer… and sits in darkness all winter long.

Northern Lights

As summer ebbs away, the gloom is relieved by the bewitching greens, purples, pinks and reds of the aurora borealis, or Northern Lights, which flicker and pulse across the winter sky. The Sami believed that the lights were the spirits of the restless dead. Bad luck would come to anyone who was not quiet and respectful beneath the aurora, and

The Northern Lights in Sweden's far north.

SWEDISH WILDLIFE

Sweden contains an exciting array of wildlife, including big beasts like the brown bear (Ursus arctos), the undisputed King of the Forest. Your chances of spotting one of these shy creatures in the wild are slim, but you can always cheat and visit Orsa Rovdjurspark in Dalarna, Europe's biggest bear park.

Grey wolves (Canis lupus) are fighting their way back from extinction across the region. Reindeer herding has kept wolves out of the northern half of the country, so central Sweden has the highest concentration. Even scarcer is the lynx, whose nocturnal habits mean that they are rarely seen by visitors. The wolverine, actually part of the weasel family, is the most secretive of all

Sweden's predators, with around 600 individuals hidden in the remote northern mountains. The sharp-eyed and silent-footed might spot Arctic foxes while walking or skiing along the Norwegian border.

Knobbly-kneed elk can grow to 2 metres (6.5ft) tall, or up to 2.7 meters (9ft) for a bull elk with antlers, and have a dangerous habit of lolloping in front of moving cars. Various elk farms around the country give visitors a chance to get up close. One of Sweden's most charming creatures is the beaver: as it has no predators in the water, it is best observed from a boat, at dawn or dusk; and with around 150,000 of the critters, you have a good chance of seeing one on one of the country's central lakes or rivers.

whistling in their presence would cause the lights themselves to swoop down and carry the whistler away.

The scientific explanation for the phenomenon is no less astonishing. The lights are caused by streams of charged particles – 'solar wind' – that flare into space from our sun. When the wind comes into contact with the earth's magnetic field, it is drawn towards the poles where its electrical charge agitates particles of oxygen and nitrogen in the atmosphere, making them glow. Solar activity follows an 11-year cycle, due to peak again

> The Arctic skies contain other odd light displays besides the aurora borealis. Sundogs, ice pillars, arcs and coronas often appear in high-latitude skies, as ice crystals in the atmosphere cause the sun's light to refract.

in 2022. The light displays during this period will be even more spectacular, and witnessed in areas that don't usually experience these mesmeric manifestations.

Environmental challenges

Sweden is blessed with vast uninhabited landscapes, and a small, environmentally-aware population who recycle, have a passion for bicycles and public transport, and see their countryside as a national asset that must be protected. Their environmental record puts much of the rest of Europe to shame. Stockholm was designated Europe's first Green Capital in 2010, and the country as a whole is determined to be carbon-neutral by 2050.

Swedes have a talent for innovation, and the challenges of excessive energy consumption have led to some creative solutions. Passive houses, heated by energy from sunlight, electrical appliances and the heat from human bodies, have been built in a number of places across the country. Stockholm is expanding, with an entire new suburb being created at Hammarby Sjöstad (due for completion in 2017), where 26,000 people will live. The whole district has been planned along ecological lines, and its environmentally sensitive construction methods are

being held up as a model for the rest of the world.

There are some headaches, however. Nitrogen run-off from Sweden's southern farmland contributes to Baltic Sea pollution (already one of the most polluted seas in the world); the World Wide Fund for Nature (WWF) has criticised the country for irresponsible timber harvesting, with 2,000 forest-dwelling species listed as 'threatened'; and Swedes are reassessing the existence of its 10 nuclear reactors following the failure of Japan's Fukushima nuclear power plant in 2011.

Moose at dawn.

Ripe for exploration

A startling 97 percent of Sweden is uninhabited, giving visitors space to breathe and room to explore. Sweden's south, characterised by mild, fertile farmland and the country's three big cities, soon starts to run out of people as you head up country. Leaving Skåne, the land gives way to vast lakes and heavy woods. In the northwest of Sweden, the land rises higher, Alpine peaks shrug off their tree cover, and huge boulders, glaciers and rushing rivers dominate the scenery. In the far north is Europe's last great wilderness, the traditional reindeer grazing grounds of the Sami, where the vast, empty plains and mountains stretch silent and unspoiled.

DECISIVE DATES

Viking warrior, c. 9th-11th centuries.

The First Swedes

From 10,000 BC
Hunter-gatherer tribes follow the melting ice northwards, establishing settlements and farming communities.

1500 BC
Trade routes are forged through the rivers of Eastern Europe to the Danube.

400 BC–AD 400
Trade extends south to the Roman Empire. Roman historian Tacitus mentions the Sveas (Swedes) who inhabit what is now central Sweden.

AD 500
The Sveas conquer the Goths living in what is now southern Sweden. Lake Mälaren becomes their power base.

The Viking Era

AD 800–1060
Scandinavian Vikings earn a reputation as sea warriors. In 862, Prince Rurik leads the Swedish Vikings east to bring order to the principality of Novgorod. They extend their rule south to Smolensk and Kiev, controlling trade routes to the Black Sea and Byzantium.

The Arrival of Christianity

AD 830
A Benedictine monk, Ansgar (801–65), lands on Björkö and founds a church.

12th century
Christianity finally replaces paganism with the conversion of King Erik Jedvarsson (St Erik, patron saint of Sweden). Sweden colonises Finland.

13th century
Trading ports such as Visby become centres for the powerful Hanseatic League of German merchants. In 1252 the regent, Birger Jarl, builds Stockholm's city walls.

1397
The Kalmar Union unites the kingdoms of Sweden, Norway and Denmark.

1434
Swedes rise up against Eric of Pomerania; nationalism spreads.

1477
University of Uppsala founded.

1520
Christian II of Denmark invades Sweden and massacres the nobility in the "Stockholm Bloodbath". Gustav Vasa drives Christian out of the country. The Kalmar Union is disbanded.

The Vasa Dynasty 1523–1720

1523
Gustav Vasa becomes king of an independent Sweden with Stockholm as his capital. Vasa strengthens central authority, banishes the Hanseatic League and adopts Lutheranism as the state religion. He curbs the power of the nobles and makes the monarchy hereditary.

1560–1611
Vasa is succeeded by his eldest son, Eric XIV, who is imprisoned by his brothers, and Johan III takes the throne. Johan marries the daughter of the king of Poland. His son, Sigismund III of Poland, succeeds him and tries to impose Roman Catholicism. In 1599 he is deposed by Vasa's youngest son, the future King Carl IX.

1611–32
Carl's son, Gustav II Adolf, turns Sweden into a great European power. He takes the Gulf of Finland from Russia and Livonia from Poland. In the Thirty Years War (1618–48) he presses south into Poland. He dies on the battlefield at Lützen, Germany.

1632–54
Six-year-old Queen Kristina succeeds her father. She grows up to preside over a glittering Baroque court and earns a reputation as patron of the arts. In secret, Kristina turns to Catholicism; in 1654 she abdicates and leaves for Rome. The Peace of Westphalia in 1648 ends the Thirty Years War and makes the Swedish monarchs princes of the Holy Roman Empire.

1654–97
Carl X recovers southern Sweden from Denmark. Carl XI sets about reducing the power of the nobles.

1697–1718
The reign of Carl XII, the "warrior king", his defeat by the Russians in 1709 and his death in the Great Northern War (1700–21) trigger Sweden's decline.

The Age of Freedom

1718–71
The parliament becomes more powerful, and two factions, the Hats (nobles) and Caps (urban traders), dominate politics. Mining and manufacturing develop. The Swedish Academy of Science opens (1739).

1771–92
Gustav III restores absolutism. Fine arts flourish. He is assassinated at a masked ball.

1792–1809
Gustav IV Adolf loses Finland to Russia in 1808 and is deposed by his uncle, Carl XIII.

The Bernadottes

1810–44
Jean-Baptiste Bernadotte, French marshal of Napoleon, is elected crown prince and succeeds to the throne as Carl XIV. Sweden is united with Norway.

1844–1907
The reigns of Carl XIV's heirs, Oscar I, Carl XV and Oscar II, witness liberal reforms, industrial development and the building of the railways. Over a million Swedes emigrate to the US. In 1866 the Riksdag is reformed and the monarch's role reduced. The foundations are laid for the Social Democratic Party, which dominates 20th-century politics.

Modern Sweden

1932
The Social Democratic Party is elected to government and establishes a welfare state.

1914–49
Sweden remains neutral in World Wars I and II. It does not join NATO in 1949.

1951–76
Social Democrats hold office. In 1969 Olof Palme becomes prime minister, reducing the Riksdag (parliament) to one chamber (1971) and removing the monarch's constitutional powers.

1973
Carl XVI Gustaf ascends to the throne.

1976–82
For the first time in 40 years, power moves away from the Social Democrats to the Centre Party under Thorbjörn Fälldin.

1986
Social Democrat leader, Olof Palme, assassinated.

1995
Sweden joins the EU.

2000
Öresund Bridge opens, linking Malmö (Sweden) with Copenhagen (Denmark).

2003
Single European currency rejected in referendum, days after Anna Lindh, Swedish foreign minister and pro-Euro campaigner, is fatally stabbed.

2006–2014
Fredrik Reinfeldt's centre-right government in power.

2010
Julian Assange, founder of WikiLeaks, taken into custody in the UK after Sweden requests his extradition. He is then granted political asylum (2012) by the Ecuadorian Embassy in London.

2013
Rising immigration leads to increasing racial tension. The Stockholm Riots break out in a predominantly immigrant suburb after police shoot dead an elderly man.

2014
Social Democrat Stefan Löfvén becomes Swedish Prime Minister, forming a minority coalition. Sweden becomes first EU country to recognise the state of Palestine.

2015
Prince Carl Philip marries Sofia Hellqvist, a former reality television star.

2016
In January, Sweden introduces identity checks for travellers from Denmark in an attempt to reduce the number of migrants arriving in the country. Sweden received more than 150,000 asylum applications in 2015.

The wedding of Prince Carl Philip of Sweden and Princess Sofia.

The Vikings on their way to invade Britain, 1130.

GLACIERS, GRAVES AND VIKINGS

Ten thousand years ago, as the glaciers began
to retreat, Sweden's first inhabitants arrived
to occupy the newly revealed land.

Sweden's history is a patchwork, with periods of economic and political greatness contrasting with longer periods of decline in international importance. One factor has remained constant: the significance of the sea and of the country's inland waterways.

From prehistoric times, the distant ancestors of today's Scandinavians were seafarers who used the sea, lakes and rivers as a means of transport through their densely forested lands. Later, as Vikings, their voyages ranged over every part of the then known world.

Not for Sweden the glories of the early Christian church, when earnest monks chronicled the doings of kings and prelates. Sweden did not become Christian until the 11th and 12th centuries, so the country's written history began late. If there were triumphs, they were remembered only in legend and saga.

The Vikings were Sweden's first conquerors and traders, followed by the monarchs of the Vasa dynasty, who extended this small country's boundaries far into Europe. At that time its leaders looked over their shoulders to Russia in the east, the traditional source of threat. Not until the 19th century did Swedish preoccupations shift towards the west. Abruptly, the government renounced all pretensions to conquest and has since lived within its own boundaries. In the 20th century, its hardest fought campaigns were for peace among nations.

But long years of war had left a legacy of poverty and hardship, and Sweden entered the 20th century as a poor, backward nation. Within a few decades, however, the country had transformed itself into a model of peace, prosperity, neutrality and good living.

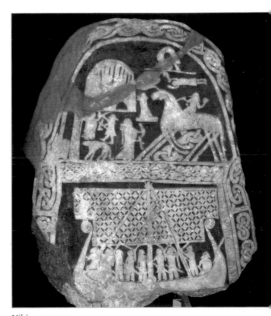

Viking runestone.

In the beginning

Sweden's known history began 10,000 years ago at the end of the last glacial period. As the melting ice retreated northwards, a peninsula of raw new land was revealed on the northern edge of the European Continent. A thousand years later, a single great cataclysm severed what would become Sweden from the land that would become Denmark.

As life became possible, Stone Age hunters followed the melting glaciers north. Modern archaeological finds of implements and camp sites witnessed the slow establishment of settlements and agriculture, as these primitive people began the long evolution from hunters and gatherers to farmers.

Already, these unknown people had established a rapport with the sea and, by 1500 BC, their trade routes extended to the Danube. Bronze began to appear in Scandinavia, thanks to these early traders who almost certainly brought back the raw materials as well as the knowledge of how to manufacture the metal: Sweden's own rich deposits of copper and tin were not discovered for many centuries. It was some 500 years later that the Swedes began to make iron for themselves. One of the earliest chroniclers to mention these northern tribes was the Roman historian Tacitus, who visited northern Europe during the 1st century AD. He

The contemporary Anglo-Saxon *Beowulf* saga, more historical fiction than history, describes with awe the exploits of several Swedish "kings", or tribal chieftains. According to *Beowulf*, they fought in crested boar-helmets, stabbing and slashing at their enemies with spears and longswords with patterned blades. Three impressive burial mounds at Old Uppsala, near the site of Sweden's last heathen temple, are mentioned in the *Ynglingatal*, a 10th-century Norse poem about 6th-century Uppsala. The poem claimed that these grave mounds belonged to three members of the ruling family,

The Battle of the Neva on 15th July 1240 between the armies of Sweden and the Republic of Novgorod.

wrote briefly of a people who appear to be from Scandinavia called *fenni*, but his successor Procopius gave the more evocative description of the people of Thule (Scandinavia) as skiing hunters.

Tales and tombs

The pace of history began to pick up about AD 500, when the fertile valley surrounding Lake Mälaren grew into a centre of power. This was the start of unending minor wars and feuds, a tradition inherited by the later Swedish nobility, as the Svea tribe began the struggle to supremacy over its neighbours. The Svea tribe gave its name to Sweden or *Sverige* (the Realm of the Sveas) and its base was Uppland (then called *Svitiod*), centred on Old Uppsala.

Aun, Egils and Adils. Another member of the same ruling family, Ottar, was killed at Vendel, north of Uppsala, which has a mound known as Ottar's Mound.

More came to light about the society of these times when excavation of the mounds began in the 19th century. Archaeologists unearthed the burned remains of humans and animals, precious objects, and weapons reminiscent of the helmet and weapons described in *Beowulf*, indicating an ordered way of life in Uppsala in the 6th century. What is certain is that, by the beginning of the early Viking era, the militant Sveas had expanded into territory to the west and south, covered by the present-day provinces of Västmanland and Södermanland. They were the power in the land.

The Vikings got around on skis, and even had their own skiing god, Ullr, mentioned in many Old Norse poems and depicted on his skis on the Böksta runestone, southwest of Uppsala.

The marauders

During the next 500 or 600 years, the Scandinavians entered the European theatre in the role of marauders. Their first recorded appearance was in the late-8th century at the rich abbey of Lindisfarne on the northeast coast of England. It was attacked, plundered and burned by "vicious barbarians from Outer Tule. So primitive they are, they spared not the library from the torch nor the timid monks from the sword." By the year 1000 the Norsemen had learned the value of books in barter and destroyed no more libraries.

Such lamenting reports of the destruction of one of European civilisation's major centres of book illumination and learning were not taken seriously by the court of Charlemagne. The idea of unexpected, pillaging savages was preposterous – at first. They soon learned their error for, within a few years, Charlemagne was defending the long coastline of civilisation against the repeated incursions of the Norse.

Overpopulation at home seems to have been the primary reason for the sudden appearance of the Vikings, a name derived from the Nordic word for bay or shallow inlet. At first they were simply summer raiders but, as this became more organised and part of the way of life, superior ship-building technology, superb seamanship, and a lack of respect for the European Continent's moral code were the reasons for their success in ravaging Europe.

Their methods of construction allowed their longships to withstand heavy seas by twisting through surging waves, and the ship's shallow draught made it possible to beach the craft in shallow waters for surprise attacks on unsuspecting settlements. The Viking strategy depended heavily on hit-and-run tactics, but later many Vikings came to trade and settle in the lands they had terrorised.

Sailing east

Swedish Vikings directed their longboats eastwards across the Baltic, first to the Baltic coasts, then deep into present day Russia along the rivers Volga and Dnieper. The rivers, and short portages across flat lands, in slow stages at last brought the Swedes to Constantinople, or as they called

it, Miklagård – the big city. The attraction of the east was tremendous.

The Swedes developed trade with the Byzantine empire and the Arab domains, and set up short-lived principalities in Russia such as Rurik at Novgorod. Many Norsemen remained in Byzantium as an elite imperial guard.

Throughout Sweden, but especially in Skåne, Gotland, Öland and Uppland, these proud travellers raised large flat stones inscribed with serpents, legends and inscriptions which give insights into Viking society. "Commemorating Wulf and Alderik who died fighting out east

An 11th-century statuette of Freyr, the Nordic god of fertility.

in the big City. This stone was raised by their mother, Bodil."

The profitable trade in furs, honey and amber in the east led to the founding of Kiev by Swedes around AD 900. They brought back from the Black Sea and Constantinople gold, silver, luxury cloths, and trinkets such as the small gilt bronze Buddha excavated at the early town of Birka, on Björkö.

This island on Lake Mälaren (the lake where Stockholm now lies) was the site of Sweden's first "city" – a crowded, dirty but rich trading centre, with an interest in luxury items and precious metals. At Birka coins from faraway countries in Arabia have been found, a tribute to the skilled seamanship, ruthlessness and endurance of these Norse trading warriors (see page 30).

SWEDEN'S MARAUDING MERCHANTS

The legacy of the Vikings isn't all murder and mayhem. Excavations on the island of Björkö have revealed evidence of a rich trading culture.

In June 793, the peaceful prosperity of 8th-century Europe was shattered by the arrival of a new menace from the sea. The image of the bloodthirsty Viking plundering all in his path is one that was to haunt medieval Europe for the next 300 years. But archaeological finds have forced us to re-evaluate the image of the rampaging Viking: none more so than the discoveries at Birka – Sweden's first Viking town, on the island of Björkö west of Stockholm.

The finds at Birka illuminate the elaborate trading networks of the Viking Age, pointing to a society of traders, merchants and skilled craftsmen. The coins, silks, beads, pottery, glass and jewellery found in the graves that surrounded the town reveal connections with countries as far afield as the Byzantine Empire and China.

For nearly 200 years Birka flourished as the northernmost mercantile centre in Europe. More than 700 people are thought to have lived in the town, which was a major marketplace for the people around Lake Mälaren. No one knows why Birka was abandoned. The emergence of trading towns such as Sigtuna is one of the possible reasons for its demise. A thousand years on Birka has risen again, this time as part of Sweden's cultural landscape, with its own museum and a place on Unesco's list of World Heritage sites.

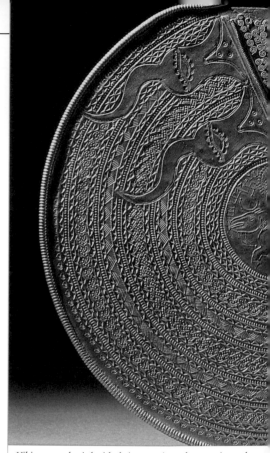

Vikings were buried with their possessions, the quantity and quality of which, such as this pendant, were a reflection of their status in life.

Silver-gilt box excavated in Gotland.

The Vikings opened up new lands for settlement and established trade routes that were to shape history.

Ansgar monument on Birka.

THE APOSTLE OF THE NORTH

Sweden was, by the 9th century, one of the last outposts of paganism in Europe. Missionaries feared the Vikings, while in Birka the people attributed their own success to their pagan gods, and so they saw no reason at all to renounce them.

In AD 830 the Benedictine monk Ansgar arrived from Germany to convert Birka's pagan residents to Christianity. Ansgar was a man of burning faith whose tireless work to bring Christianity to Scandinavia eventually earned him a sainthood. He was welcomed politely in Birka, probably because the people believed it would help to promote trade with the Christian continent, and allowed to build a little church. However, his preaching had a limited impact on the prevailing faith, and Birka was never evangelised. Christianity would not defeat the pagan gods for another 250 years. Its advent brought the Age of the Viking gods to an end, for the new Christian god refused to tolerate rival divinities.

A pair of harness mounts from Gotland, known as Odin's Birds, with exaggerated beak and talons.

Danish, Frankish and Arabic coins have been found on site, but no coins were ever minted by the Birka kings, despite their prosperity.

A bishop's crosier from Ireland is proof of Birka's long-distance trade with southern and western Europe.

noe fnume. ſpa hine nengðho hehr. hynðe þam hal
gan. hæðpon cyninge ongan. oꝼoꝛt lice þ hoꝛ pyꝛcan.
micle mǣhe cꝛꝺ̄e. magum ꝛægꝺe. þpæt hꝛſulic þing.
þðoum toꝼtynð. ꝛeðe pite. hie nepohton þær. ge
ꝛǣh þa ymb pinqua poꝛn. pæn ꝼæꝛt mæoð. ꝼbꝛon
hura mǣꝛt. ꝼæno hluꝛꝺtan. innan ꝺutan. tonðan
lime. ꝼeꝼæꝛtnoꝺ piꝺ ꝼloꝺe. pær noð. þy ꝛeꝼæꝛtan.
þiꝛ ꝛynꝺꝛuꝺ cynn. Symle bꝛꝺ þy hꝛanꝺꝛa. behꝛt hꝛꝺoh
pæchꝛ. ꝛplunꝺꝛ ꝼæ. ꝛꝼnꝺamaꝛ. ꝛpiꝺ on bꝛhꝛuꝺ.

CHRISTIANITY AND THE MIDDLE AGES

By the 14th century Sweden had emerged from the Dark Ages and formed a turbulent alliance with its neighbours.

Once the Vikings had drawn Europe's attention to Scandinavia, the continent could not leave its northern neighbour alone. The first purpose was to spread the Gospel, in the pious hope that Christianity might change the Viking temperament.

In the 9th century, the first notable Christian missionary arrived. He was Ansgar, who landed on Björkö in Mälaren. Here he founded a church and converted some islanders before returning to Germany as Bishop of Hamburg. Sweden's conversion was only skin-deep and in AD 936 another missionary, Bishop Unni of Hamburg, was murdered in Birka. Sweden had to wait until the second half of the 11th century for true conversion.

Pagan rituals

The clerical scholar Adam of Bremen left a picture of Norse paganism when he included Scandinavia in his history of his own bishopric. The temple at Uppsala, Adam wrote, was the very heart of paganism. Here was a structure covered in scales and wreathed with serpents and dragon heads. A heavy golden chain girt the heathen temple to contain the evil of the idols Thor, Odin and Frej. Even more fearsome was the sacred grove alongside the temple, its branches hung with the sacrificial remains, "seven males of every species from man to the lowly cat."

By the middle of the 12th century, paganism was officially out of fashion. King Erik Jedvarsson, later St Erik, the patron saint of Sweden, had been converted and with "sword and word" saw to it that his subjects bowed to the word of the Lord.

While the Christian church struggled for souls, the kingly families of Erik and Sverker struggled for temporal power. From this time,

Christian artefact, 10th-century silver crucifix.

Sweden began to emerge gradually as a country separate from Norway and Denmark and to turn its attention to the idea of conquest. Swedes living on the Baltic had long traded and raided along the Baltic coasts, but now they began a serious colonisation of the eastern lands populated by Finnic tribes. Sweden and Russia squabbled over the territory for much of the next 800 years, before it eventually became an independent country – Finland.

The German centuries

German traders had become a familiar part of life on the small island that became Stockholm at the mouth of Lake Mälaren. But the 13th century brought the turn of the German Hanseatic trading cities, grouped under Lübeck, eager to get a foot into the Swedish door.

The German merchants conquered through commerce and eventually gained almost total control of Swedish foreign trade and its domestic economy and politics. Many new towns grew up to accommodate the lively commercial activity instigated by the Hansa and the German traders lived alongside their Swedish neighbours. They were particularly strong on the Swedish island of Gotland where they left medieval walls and part of their trading city.

During the next few centuries Germany

Up to this point, the important families of the country were known familiarly as "big farmers", and were descendants of the early chiefs. Now, true nobles began to make their appearance. Many of these families still exist, such as the once royal Bondes (meaning farmer), Svinhuvuds (Pigheads), Natt och Dag (Night and Day), and Bjelke (Beam). Feuds were endemic and ballads and chronicles record the bravery and the treachery of these struggling families.

By the 14th century, monasteries and convents were flourishing in Sweden. St Birgitta founded a new religious order, and had a huge impact on

Tapestry illustrating the struggle between Christianity and paganism.

dominated the Swedish world. German manners were *comme il faut*, German architecture was fashionable. Even the Swedish language assimilated many of its present linguistic forms from the Platdeutsch of the Hanseatic traders.

The concentration of interests on Stockholm, the country's political centre, led to the advent of a noble class in Sweden. As early as 1280, King Magnus Ladulås had introduced a form of European feudalism. To some extent, this countered the old Viking democracy, where the chief was but first among equals, but the ordinary farmers held tightly to their ancient rights and privileges. These verbal rights were written down during this period to form one of Europe's oldest bodies of written law.

European thinking with her mystical *Revelations*. Her writings sought to influence the religious and political structure of Europe, advocating the return of the Pope to Rome (he was based in Avignon at the time) and seeking an end to the Hundred Years War. She was canonised in 1391.

A new union

By this time, Sweden and the rest of Scandinavia had acquired enough sophistication to object to the heavy political and economic control of the Hansa and, in 1397, the three countries formed the Union of Kalmar. It involved an undertaking that all Scandinavia should have one and the same monarch, Queen Margareta of Denmark.

> *Sweden's system of rights for the ordinary person was brought to England by the Vikings. It was later adopted in the United States in the form of "bylaws", from the Norse for "village ordinances".*

Margareta's new, loose-knit domain was enormous and not easily ruled. But she maintained the union, especially at times when external threats were serious. Her greatest success was in using the danger of such incursions to strip the Hansa of some of its power.

The Miners' revolt

As the most advanced of the three Scandinavian states, Denmark dominated the Kalmar alliance, but the union was marked by conflict between the monarch on the one hand and the high nobility and intermittently rebellious burghers and peasants on the other.

In 1434, intolerable Danish tax demands coupled with general social anxieties led to a revolt against Margareta's successor, Erik of Pomerania, by Sweden's first great national hero, Engelbrekt Engelbrektsson. A minor noble, he raised the peasants and miners from his native Dalarna, and stormed towards Stockholm. There, it is said, he forced the council to support him by taking one member, a bishop, by his collar and threatening to throw him out of the castle window. Despite his successes, Engelbrekt was murdered by Magnus Bengtsson Natt och Dag, the son of one of his enemies, but his legend lived on. The political might of ordinary people had become evident.

King Erik was deposed but nationalism spread. The struggle continued between powerful families who were for or against the union. The Hanseatic League conspired, more often than not now with the complicity of the Swedes, and the Danes threatened.

Victory over the Danes

Against this background, another national hero emerged. Sten Sture changed Sweden's history, and yet he was not of royal birth. Through his leadership in 1471 at the Battle of Brunkeburg just outside Stockholm, Sture gained a decisive victory over the Danes. Although the Kalmar Union still had nearly 50 years to run, this fierce victory – and later Sten Sture's actions as statesman rather than soldier – saved Sweden

from being reabsorbed completely into the northern union.

First parliament

By this time Sweden had a national assembly (the Riksdag) of four estates – nobles, clergy, burghers and peasants – the first step towards parliamentary government. Swedish nationalism and a renewed alliance with the Hansa, as well as a struggle emerging between church and state power, led to more Danish attacks.

In the early 16th century, the Riksdag voted to burn the fortress of the Archbishop of Sweden, a

George and the Dragon statue built to commemorate the victory of Sten Sture at the Battle of Brunkeberg in 1471.

pro-Dane, Gustav Trolle. In the event, Trolle was merely imprisoned.

In 1520 the Papal Court excommunicated Sten Sture the Younger for this act and Kristian II had his justification for invading again. In the hope of saving their city, the burghers of Stockholm opened the gates, and Kristian retaliated with a feast in the palace where he gathered together Sweden's leading nobles.

On the pretext that the Papal excommunication released him from any promises of safe conduct, Kristian chopped off the heads of 82 of Sweden's finest and of many innocent bystanders, too. This "Stockholm Bloodbath" was the catalyst that raised the nation.

FOUNDER OF A DYNASTY

Gustav Vasa, the first of the Vasa monarchs, ousted
the Danes, introduced the Lutheran Reformation
and gave Sweden its national identity.

Gustav Vasa, founder of the Vasa dynasty.

Olaus Petri's statue in Stockholm.

Young Gustav Eriksson Vasa (1496–1560) was fortunate to escape the Stockholm Bloodbath in which his father, two uncles and a brother-in-law were killed. He was in Denmark at the time, held hostage by King Kristian, who had been trying to force talks between Sweden and Denmark. By the time Kristian was killing his kin, however, this resourceful young man had already escaped from Denmark and slipped into Sweden to rouse the countryside, spurred on by news of what had happened in Stockholm.

After hard fighting, Gustav Vasa subdued Kristian and the Danes, who retreated south, killing and burning as they went. In 1523, a grateful nation invited Gustav to take the Swedish throne.

Though Gustav still had many further struggles against dissident factions in his own country, centred on the Sture family, he set about enhancing the power of the king and reorganising the government, the monetary system, the administration and the army. Nothing escaped his attention. He ran Sweden as though it were his family estates and set the country on the road from the Middle Ages to a national state.

Gustav Vasa's reign merely coincided with the Swedish Reformation, and did not bring it about, but he was quick to make use of it. His struggle against the Danes was also a struggle against the Roman Catholic Archbishop Gustav Trolle, whose accusations of heresy had led to the Bloodbath.

Trolle had fled into exile at Gustav Vasa's victory and the Pope refused to consecrate a successor, but the bishops were still unruly and it suited Gustav to support the Reformation. Though he was not particularly religious Gustav needed money and less interference from Rome.

His success against the Danes cost money, however, as did his internal struggle against rival factions, which continued throughout his reign, and later foreign campaigns. He was also in debt to the Lübeckers, who had continued to involve themselves in Swedish affairs by providing funds to fight Kristian.

Though he curbed some traditional Swedish liberties and ruled firmly, Vasa was more than a straightforward autocrat. He was a great orator, he had charm, he was not uncultured, and he both loved and played music. He was also a successful trader, who became the country's richest man, with treasure hoards in Gripsholm and Stockholm castles. But his greatest strengths were his skills as organiser and manager, and his ability to give Sweden a sense of nationhood. When he died in 1560, Vasa had welded his country together and made it strong. He also had 11 children, thus securing the Vasa rule for more than a century ahead.

Vasa reforming the Swedish nation.

In his great need, the wily young king was not slow to see the rich pickings in the churches and monasteries. He confiscated Roman Catholic property and prepared the ground for a state Lutheran religion.

An enlightened ruler

Gustav's achievements were remarkable and far-reaching. He not only succeeded in bringing about the supremacy of state over church in order to curb the power of the nobles, he also strengthened the monarchy by making it hereditary. When he recalled the Riksdag in 1544, it was to reform it, and to plan what became a form of national military service, to make Sweden the first European country to have a standing peacetime army.

OLAUS PETRI

Olaus Petri was one of Gustav Vasa's closest advisors. A man of humble birth, he was known as the Father of the Reformation in Sweden, and the country's first "modern" writer. He translated the New Testament into Swedish and was a fearless preacher of Lutheran doctrines. He was chancellor to Gustav for two years. Inevitably, the two strong characters quarrelled, and in 1540 Petri was sentenced to death for alleged complicity in a plot against his master. In fact, his only crime was in refusing to divulge a secret of the confessional. Gustav reprieved his old counsellor, who then produced his most famous work, *A Swedish Chronicle*, a history of Sweden up to 1520.

Gustav II Adolf leading his country to victory at the Battle of Breitenfeld.

A GREAT EUROPEAN POWER

The 16th and 17th centuries were dominated by two military geniuses, Gustav II Adolf and Carl XII, whose conquests shaped the nation.

After the death of Gustav Vasa, his eldest son Erik (XIV) succeeded him according to the decision by the Riksdag in 1544. Erik's brothers, Johan and Carl, supported him in the beginning. But, after he had married a simple guard's daughter and even murdered two noblemen in a burst of insanity, they turned against him and a civil war broke out. Erik was imprisoned and Johan III succeeded him.

Under the Vasa prosperity, Sweden grew in ways other than conquest. The University of Uppsala, which had been founded in 1477, flourished. The Vasas encouraged immigration by Belgian Walloons, Scots and Germans, who were knowledgeable in the working of iron into swords and cannons. Sweden, fortunately, was abundantly endowed with deposits of pure iron and copper.

With weapons and a standing army, Sweden had become a military power. The Vasa sons now looked for expansion in trade and territory in what became the Seven Years' War of the North, after which Denmark accepted the *status quo* and renounced claims to the independent state of Sweden.

Family infighting

Johan had married the daughter of King Sigismund I of Poland and, on Stefan Bathory's death in 1586, Johan's son, Sigismund, was elected King of Poland. When Johan died in 1592, Sigismund tried to turn Sweden into a Roman Catholic country. His uncle, Carl, Gustav Vasa's youngest son, opposed this strongly and, at a meeting in Uppsala in 1593, it was decided that only if Sigismund accepted the Lutheran state religion would he remain as King of Sweden.

But Carl's ambitions aimed higher than being a duke and a subject of his nephew

Naval battle between the Russians and the Swedes.

Sigismund. Once again, Sweden was involved in a bitter civil war. Sigismund left for Poland, but he never renounced his claims to the Swedish throne – an attitude which was to affect Sweden's relations with Poland and be the cause of a war that would last long into the 1600s. The tests of strength continued, but Carl asserted his authority with cruel force and curbed the nobles' power by executions and banishments.

Military leader

With the accession to the throne in 1611 of Carl's son, Gustav II Adolf, Sweden acquired a military genius. Gustav Adolf was intelligent, his education was thorough and, having a German mother, he spoke both German and Swedish. He had all the strength, determination and enthusiasm of his celebrated grandfather, Gustav Vasa. One difference was Gustav Adolf's belief in the Lutheran faith. His piety induced him to hold regular prayers for his army in the field.

Gustav Adolf was backed by an equally robust chancellor, Axel Oxenstierna. The two believed that Sweden was circled by enemies who thought themselves stronger and that its friends didn't understand Sweden's problems.

In the War of Kalmar, which Gustav Adolf fought at the beginning of his reign, the Danes captured the only port to the west, Älvsborg.

Skansen Kronan, Gustav II's fort at Göteborg.

To regain this vital port, Sweden had to pay the enormous ransom of 1 million Riksdaler. Even the king himself contributed by melting down some of his plate.

Gustav Adolf was luckier, however, in the war against Russia, and in the Peace of Stolbova, reached in 1617, Sweden was left in sole control of the Gulf of Finland.

Wider conflict

The start of the Thirty Years' War in 1618 involved Sweden in the wider conflict. Over the next years, Gustav Adolf's army drove far into Europe and south to the rich trading area of the Vistula. After the defeat of Sigismund at Mewe, it marched into Poland, where Gustav Adolf defeated the Polish cavalry at Dirschau, to give Sweden a strong presence in Europe.

After these successes, Gustav Adolf spent several less satisfying years of intense diplomacy with Denmark. He also tried to bring together the Scandinavian countries and the participants in the Thirty Years' War.

In 1630, the king sailed again to Pomerania on what was to be his last campaign. Gustav Adolf had the satisfaction of knowing that he had brought low the power and prestige of his Danish rival, Christian IV, and had the support of his Riksdag and people. Yet the sense of foreboding was strong in his last speech to the Riksdag, almost as though he knew his fate.

The Swedes marched firmly across Europe and crossed the Elbe. The decisive battle of this year was Breitenfeld, which lasted five hours, with the Imperial cavalry charging and charging again. By sunset, it was a clear victory for Gustav Adolf and his veterans, thanks to the new military tactics he had perfected with his well-trained army.

Gustav Adolf's aim was to unite all the Protestant countries and his diplomacy-on-the-march continued until just before the final battle, at Lützen, near Leipzig. The November day was misty as Gustav Adolf's Swedish and Finnish troops fought the Catholic Imperialist army. Few saw Gustav Adolf's death because the mist had again swirled low. He was shot three times and died immediately. As rumours of his death whispered along the lines, the Småland companies almost wavered until Gustav Adolf's chaplain, Fabricus, began to sing the hymn "Sustain Us By Thy Mighty Word". Inspired to vengeance, the Swedes won a battle so fierce that one-third of the army fell alongside its king.

Gustav II Adolf was Sweden's most successful military leader. He made Sweden a great power, captured huge territories in the Baltic, the east, and south as far as Poland. He also made his country for the first time more powerful than Denmark. His military innovations, advanced techniques and trained army won battle after battle but they did not stop the fatal bullet at Lützen in 1632.

Infant heiress

When Gustav Adolf fell, his daughter Kristina, whose name figures in many Swedish towns and institutions, was only six years old. But she had the advantage of her father's chancellor, Axel Oxenstierna, who became Regent during

Gustav II Adolf, the "Lion of the North", sent back treasures from Europe that are now to be found generously spread throughout Sweden's palaces.

her minority. Oxenstierna continued the king's policies at home and overseas. The formidable army in Europe subdued more German and Slavic domains and, by 1645, Denmark had ceded territory, including the islands of Gotland and Ösel, to Sweden.

Europe and shocked her former subjects when in Rome she announced her conversion. And so the daughter of one of the great champions of the Protestant faith renounced it. As a final irony, she took with her to Rome many of the same treasures her father had plundered from the Catholic rulers of Europe.

Continued greatness

Although Kristina had gone, Sweden's power continued to grow. In 1658, Sweden astounded Denmark by a surprise attack, partly due to Carl X Gustav's luck. The winter of 1657–58 was one

The Battle of Lützen (1632), at which the great military leader Gustav II Adolf was fatally wounded.

Oxenstierna and the foremost nobility soared high in the see-saw of power between throne and council by introducing a new constitution that placed effective power in the hands of the nobles.

When she came of age, Queen Kristina presided over a shining Baroque court filled with massive silver furnishings and dark intrigues. She had been well educated and gathered around her the brilliant young minds of the age. But, by now, the relationship between Kristina and her elderly chancellor was not sympathetic and the country stagnated.

In one of history's unexplained decisions, she decided to abdicate, probably because she was drawn to the Roman Catholic faith. After she stepped down in 1654, she travelled through

of the coldest in a century and froze the sea between Sweden and Denmark, and between Denmark's first and second main islands. Though two squadrons of horses and riders fell through the ice, an army of 1,500 cavalry and 3,500 foot soldiers came safely across and overran the island of Fyn almost before the Danes knew what was happening. The Treaty of Roskilde gave Sweden all the provinces in the south Swedish mainland that Denmark had traditionally ruled – Skåne, Blekinge, Bohuslän and Halland.

The last decades of the 17th century saw the tentative start of an Age of Enlightenment. This came to maturity in the 18th century, as it did in many parts of Europe, as a time of scientific discovery, a flowering of artistic talent, and of freedom of thought and expression. One of its first exponents was Olof Rudbeck. From Uppsala, he became Sweden's first internationally recognised genius, contributing significantly to medical and scientific advancement, with discoveries such as the human lymphatic system.

But, as the 17th century ended, with the country still at the height of its political rather than intellectual powers, Sweden produced its greatest romantic warrior king, Carl XII. Every European country has its royal figure of romance and how much Carl's reputation derived from the fact that, of his 21 years as monarch, he spent

Queen Kristina presided over a glittering court before abdicating.

Swedes still argue about whether it was a Norwegian bullet or one from the gun of a disaffected Swedish soldier that killed the romantic warrior king, Carl XII, in 1718.

18 away at the wars is not clear. To many, he is Sweden's greatest king – certainly to those of a romantic and nationalist temperament.

The warrior king

All Carl XII's successes and failures were inextricably mixed with European issues, the struggle between Protestant and Catholic, and the race for trade and sea routes. His strong personality brooked little opposition and, three years after he came to the throne as a minor, he first showed his military skills by landing on the nearest main Danish island of Zealand. This led to an early peace treaty and left Carl free to turn to the east. Meanwhile, Tsar Peter of Russia had declared war on Sweden and Carl hurried through Estonia to relieve Narva. Soon Poland was involved in the war, and Carl's victorious army swept through Poland, taking Warsaw and Krakow, as well as Danzig. By 1705 Poland had signed an alliance with Sweden against the Russians.

In his mission to save Europe from the Russian bear, over the next few years Carl rampaged over Germany and Russia. However, in 1709, at one of the most important battles of the 18th century, the Swedes met their match. Everything conspired against the Swedish army. Carl had already been wounded in the foot and had to command from a litter. At the end of a day of victory and defeat, the Swedes retreated to Perevolotjna, where the king was at last persuaded to cross into Turkey.

From his distant "court" in Turkey, the frustrated Carl attempted to guide his realm and, at times, almost persuaded the Turks to go to war against Russia. By 1714, Carl realised that he must return to Sweden, and he made a journey of more than 1,300 miles by horseback across Europe to Stralsund in Germany. That he did the journey in 15 days with just two companions says much for the king's determination and endurance.

Only Stralsund and Wismar remained of the vast Swedish European Empire. At Stralsund, Carl was still not safe from the alliance that had formed against him, and eventually he fled secretly to Sweden. Fifteen years after his first triumphs, Carl devised plan after plan to defeat his traditional enemies, the Danes. In 1718, he invaded southern Norway to besiege the border fortress of Fredriksten. On 30 November, he went out to inspect his troops, when a bullet struck his skull and he died instantly.

Next to Gustav II Adolf, Carl was undoubtedly Sweden's greatest military genius. But while the former left Sweden powerful, Carl left the country divested of all its conquests except Finland. From the moment the fatal bullet found its target, Sweden ceased to be a great fighting power.

Bringing home the body of King Carl XII, Sweden's most romantic warrior king.

The botanist Carl von Linné (Linnaeus) in Sami dresss after his expedition to Lapland in 1732.

THE AGE OF FREEDOM

Great advancements in science and the fine arts,
under the patronage of enlightened monarchs,
characterised life in the 18th century.

The death of Carl XII in 1718 and the end of his long exhausting wars left Sweden shrunk in size, weak, and forced to negotiate from an inferior position. The council and Riksdag were tired of absolute monarchs and warfare. The lack of an obvious heir provided their opportunity to begin a new "Age of Freedom".

At first the crown went to Ulrika Eleonora, the dead king's sister. In return for the Rikdag's support of her succession to the throne – her nephew was also a contender – Ulrika agreed to a major constitutional change. In 1719 the Riksdag abolished absolute monarchy and the right to inherit the throne. The queen intended her politically ambitious husband, Fredrik of Hesse, to reign as co-monarch, but the proposal was denied by parliament. After a tense year, Ulrika stepped aside in 1720 to allow her husband to succeed her as Fredrik I.

He, too, was threatened by rival claimants to the throne and, over the years, Sweden's cautious path was plotted by the Finnish politician Arvid Horn, who trod a delicate diplomatic road to compensate for Sweden's weakness. When Fredrik died in 1751, the Swedes had the satisfaction of knowing that the successful claimant, Adolf Fredrik, had at least a few drops of Vasa blood.

As democracy began to gain a foothold, the estates of the Riksdag took on the job of nominating the members of the council and, though its own proceedings were still a well-guarded secret, the Riksdag passed a Freedom of the Press Act in 1766, the world's first attempt at press freedom which is still in force today.

In political terms, this era was dominated by two factions, the Hats (mercantile nobles or Whigs) and the Caps (liberal commoners and urban traders similar to Tories). In diplomatic terms, Sweden was lucky in having a leader

King Gustav III, patron of drama and fine arts.

whose cautious temperament suited the age. During the 1720s and 1730s, Arvid Horn continued to steer Sweden through dangerous foreign shoals. Despite minor alarms and Russian inroads and the swings in the allegiances of the Caps and Hats to foreign powers, he contrived to keep an insecure peace with the old enemy, Denmark, as well as Russia and Prussia.

Trading opportunities

In 1718 the wars of Carl XII had killed not only the king but also many of the strongest young men in Sweden and Finland. Bad harvests added to the economic problems. Although Sweden remained primarily an agricultural country until late in the 19th century, the Age of Freedom saw

In 1742 Anders Celsius invented the Celsius scale of temperature and the 100-degree thermometer. He set up Sweden's astronomical observatory at Uppsala.

the start of a transformation into a trading nation.

The government encouraged mining of iron in the many small works, and copper from the great mine at Falun. Hand manufacturing of many kinds also began. Swedish ships carried Swedish goods all over Europe and further,

and a pioneer of inoculation against diseases.

Carl von Linné (Linnaeus), a student of the first great scientist, Olof Rudbeck, developed his theories that plants, like animals, reproduced sexually. It became the basis for his great work *Species Plantarum*, which classified almost 6,000 plants. Sweden also produced good chemists: Tobern Bergman, the founder of chemical analysis, Johan Wallerius and Axel Cronstedt and, most famous of all, C.W. Scheele, the first person to analyse air as oxygen and nitrogen.

This outpouring of science and scientists, many of whom worked closely together, led to formal

Gustav III visits the Royal Academy of Arts.

through companies such as the new Swedish East India Company, which lasted into the next century. The ships carried iron and returned with luxury items such as silk and provided young Swedes with an adventurous challenge.

Scientific pioneers

Away from these affairs of politics, diplomacy and trade, the Age of Freedom was also an Age of Science which produced a royal flush of original thinkers. High among them was Emanuel Swedenborg, a scientist who edited the first Swedish scientific journal but is also known for his studies on the human brain and his religious writing. Nils Rosén was one of the earliest to study and practise paediatrics. He was also an anatomist

co-operation in 1739 when the Swedish Academy of Science was opened in Stockholm, with Linnaeus as one of its founders. Sweden began to gain prestige abroad, and many botanical pilgrims came to Linnaeus's garden in Uppsala.

At home, scientists used their talents to advise the new industrialists and the farmers – practical scientific work that laid a foundation for prosperity and future study. Although it continued into the reign of Gustav III, it was inevitable that such a flood could not continue at the same volume indefinitely. In any case, Gustav III did not encourage freedom but another form of enlightenment. His sphere of interest was the arts and the encouragement of a national Swedish culture.

Autocracy returns

During Gustav III's reign, the Age of Freedom gradually faded, though study of science and economics continued. He was influenced by his mother, Louisa Ulrika, sister of Frederick the Great of Prussia, a strong-minded woman who had spent her life in political schemes and in grooming her son for the monarchy. At the age of 25, Gustav III started out as a golden figure. He was proud of being the first Swedish-born king since Carl XII, and was well educated for his role. He loved France and the theatre, where he both wrote and acted, and his sense of drama loomed large throughout his 21-year reign.

In the Riksdag, the Caps were supreme, moved by common cause against the Hats, who represented the nobility. Gustav III was beset by threats from Russia and Prussia; in the countryside, two bad harvests had raised political discontent. In 1772, the king organised a bloodless *coup d'état* that condemned the aristocracy and demanded a return to the ancient constitution, but, essentially, gave him absolute power.

War and peace

Like his predecessors, Gustav did not escape conflict with Russia. In 1788, he declared war, partly in the hope that external strife would allay the unrest caused by his growing despotism, partly to make the most of Russia's preoccupation with a Turkish war. At first, Gustav succeeded in pushing far into Finland but the support of his Finnish officers could not be guaranteed and a group of more than 100, the Anjala Confederation, made contact with the Empress Catherine in an attempt to restore the Finnish boundaries of 1721. When a Danish-Norwegian force invaded near Göteborg, Gustav returned to Sweden and a surprising naval victory at Svensksund, when the Swedish fleet sank 50 Russian ships, which led to peace and, against all the odds, left Sweden with its reduced territory intact.

A king of many talents

This unlikely victory did not make Gustav III a notable warrior, and his fame lies not in his political or military skill. He is remembered for the upsurge he encouraged in all the fine arts. Though the king loved France, he was a patriot who founded Swedish drama when he built Stockholm's Royal Dramatic Theatre, replaced the French actors in his mother's theatre at Drottningholm, and hired Swedish actors and writers to develop a native theatre.

The most important of the arts in the Golden Age was opera and, in 1782, Gustav opened the magnificent Royal Opera House alongside Strömmen, where Lake Mälaren pours into the beginnings of the sea. Gustav commissioned the first opera in Swedish at the Dramatic Theatre, followed three years later by *Thetis and Peleus*, which he planned, and staged six major tragedies and other plays, in four of which the king himself took part.

Gustav's old tutor Olof Dalin was one of the earliest of this age of writers with his popular

Conversation at Drottningholm Castle, 1779.

LINNAEUS, THE PLANTS MAN

Carl von Linné (Linnaeus), the acclaimed Swedish naturalist, devised the modern classification system for plants and animals in the 18th century. Born in 1707, Linnaeus studied medicine at the University of Lund and botany at Uppsala. He travelled widely in Sweden and abroad and was a leading figure in the founding of the Swedish Academy of Science. As chair of botany, dietetics and *materia medica* at Uppsala he pursued his research into nomenclature. His most important publications included *Systema Naturae* (1735) and *Philosophia Botanica* (1751). Linnaeus died in 1778. His house and botanical garden can be visited at Uppsala.

critical essays in *Then Swänska Argus* (The Swedish Argus). Most unusual of the early writers was Carl Bellman, a troubadour who wrote poetry about the ordinary people of Stockholm's tav-

Troubadour Carl Bellman.

erns and markets. Another in the same mould was Jakob Wallenberg, whose robust words were Bellman's prose equivalent, Carl Cristoffer Gjörwell described nature, and another distinguished poet, Johan Kellgren, helped Gustav to translate his plays into Swedish – the king knew French so well that he always wrote that language better than Swedish.

Many more poets and prose writers clustered round Gustav when he founded the Swedish Academy of Literature in 1786. Gustav also founded the Musical Academy in 1771, the Literary, Historical and Antiquities Academy, and the Academy of Art.

Gustavian life was rich in culture and the court went to the theatre and opera in silks and brocades. The middle classes also prospered in the atmosphere of expanding commercial contacts abroad. Only the old noble families felt neglected. Gustav III had manoeuvred them out of their traditional roles and political power and replaced them with more pliable commoners and the newly-great *parvenus*.

So much of Gustav's energies had been centred on his artistic protégés that he may have been lulled into a false sense of political security. As with so many Swedish monarchs, he had become more autocratic, and this was the era of the French Revolution.

The curtain on Gustav's drama came thundering down at an opera masquerade in 1792. A group of conspirators formed the plot and a disgruntled minor nobleman, Jakob Anckarström, shot Gustav III. The king died from an infection two weeks later. The Golden Age was at an end.

Afterthoughts

The Gustavian era trailed on for another 17 years under the young king, Gustav IV Adolf. His one real achievement was land reform which resulted in larger farming units. Earlier, the land had been split up in smaller units after every division of inheritance, thus leaving farmers with small and widely dispersed fields.

There was also one last gasp of territorialism. The Swedes had already fought an unsuccessful war over Pomerania, but this was the time of the Reign of Terror in France. Gustav IV Adolf embarked on a campaign against France which eventually found him in opposition to Russia. Russia immediately abrogated the Treaty of Armed Neutrality between the two that had left Finland as part of Sweden. In 1808, Tsar Alexander invaded Finland. For the Swedes, the campaign was disastrous. The Finns were disillusioned, and the Swedes forced to retreat to the Gulf of Bothnia.

Under the Treaty of Fredrikshamn, 1809, Sweden lost Finland for the last time. Gustav IV Adolf had already abdicated in April and, by 1810, Sweden had made peace with all its enemies. Old Duke Carl (who had once been regent to his nephew Gustav IV Adolf) resumed the role under a new constitution as Carl XIII. This allowed power to move gradually from king to Riksdag, signalling the end of autocracy and the start of Sweden's democratic monarchy.

The assassination of King Gustav III.

The former French Marshal Jean-Baptiste Bernadotte became King Carl XIV Johan in 1818.

A CENTURY OF CHANGE

Agricultural and political reform, and growing industrialisation, were not enough to deter 19th-century Swedes from emigrating in large numbers.

Once the last faint link to the great Vasa dynasty was gone, Sweden elected the French Marshal Jean-Baptiste Bernadotte as Crown Prince. By 1810, the new prince had converted to Lutheranism on his way north to Sweden, taking the name Carl Johan.

The election of a Frenchman as heir to the throne and the loss of Finland to Russia the year before turned Swedish eyes away from the east. As Sweden's interests and identity became more and more involved in Western Europe, foreign policy lost much of its preoccupation with its great eastern neighbour, though that did not preclude treaties with Russia.

At the time, many believed that a French marshal was bound to be no more than an emissary of Napoleon, but Carl Johan soon proved them wrong. A few weeks after his arrival, he took over state affairs when the elderly Carl XIII had a stroke, and later became the legal regent. The Swedish aristocracy remained hostile, but Carl Johan steered a quiet course through the tangle of European diplomacy. By 1812, Sweden had broken its long-held treaty of alliance with France and in 1813, after campaigning in Europe, Carl Johan allied Sweden with Russia and Prussia against his former leader, Napoleon. In return, Carl Johan was allowed to prise Norway from Denmark and unite it with Sweden.

An uneasy union

Although Denmark agreed in the Peace of Kiel (1814) to the transfer of Norway, and received in exchange Swedish Pomerania (which was later "sold" to Prussia), the Norwegians were less than delighted at being handed over like a parcel and wrung many concessions from the Swedes before agreeing

King Gustav IV Adolf, the agricultural reformer.

to a loose-knit union under the Swedish king. The new union struggled on for almost a century but had the effect of arousing Norwegian nationalism still further until, in 1905, Norway's separation into a sovereign state became inevitable.

Curbing the monarchy

In 1818, the former French marshal became King Carl XIV Johan under the 1809 constitution drawn up during the *coup d'état*, which separated and rebalanced the powers of government and monarch. Though Carl XIV Johan was himself a conservative, a liberal opposition began to form during this period and expanded during the reigns of his son,

Exodus to America

At the end of the 19th century and the start of the 20th, more than 1 million Swedes – that is, one fifth of the population – left the country.

So many Swedish emigrants came from the poor agricultural areas of Småland, Bohuslän and Värmland that some found themselves exchanging a Swedish village at home for a small American

The Emigrants' Statue at Karlshamn, Blekinge.

community in Minnesota or Wisconsin whose population also spoke only Swedish. Their story is best summed up in the emigration trilogy of the 20th-century writer Vilhelm Moberg, *The Emigrants*, *Unto a New Land* and *The Last Letter Home*. Moberg was a Smålander and he wrote about his own people who left the county's stony ground for a better future.

The motives of the Swedish emigrants were not simple. Unlike the Highland Scots, forced out in the Clearances by their own chiefs, who found sheep more profitable than people, the Swedes were not obliged to leave. But changes in agriculture from communal crofting villages to individual farms had split the old communities. Some moved first to the city, and then to America; others went

direct to build a new life for themselves, encouraged particularly by the United States Homestead Act of 1862, which promised land almost free to settlers who dared to travel west. To the United States, the Swedes took their virtues of hard work, thrift and honesty and, given the wide open opportunities of the New World, many made their fortunes. The new settlers sent back glowing accounts of their lives in America, and a great deal of money to support those left behind. These signs of prosperity encouraged others.

The movement became highly business-like. Shipping companies used agents to recruit new settlers and so provide passengers for their ships, and introduced a system of pre-paid tickets for emigrants to send home for a younger sibling. Some agents were rogues who preyed on the would-be settlers and disappeared with their money. But most emigrants prospered and added to the success of their adopted country.

In Sweden, this mass movement of people coincided with the start of the country's Industrial Revolution, just when the new mills were beginning to attract workers to towns and cities. Gradually, the administration realised that Sweden was in danger of losing too many of its youngest and most able citizens. In the early years of the 20th century, the Riksdag began to encourage people both to stay and to return, and compiled a survey of what had brought about the exodus. It revealed a sorry tale of oppression, poverty and discontent with life in Sweden.

Around one fifth of all those who had emigrated came back to Sweden, many of them bringing their new riches to put money into the poorer areas. Swedes have always had a great love of their country and the opportunity to better themselves was the real lure of America. When they had done that, they could sometimes afford to come home.

In 1968, a group which included Vilhelm Moberg founded the Emigrant Institute – the House of the Emigrants – in Växjö in the centre of Småland. The largest European archive on emigration, it has 2,000 Swedish-American church and club record books and a library of 25,000 volumes.

More than anything, the emigrants helped those who remained behind through the realities revealed in the 1908 survey. These alerted the powerful to the ills and indignities of a system that was still far from egalitarian. Many of the sweeping democratic reforms of the 20th century owed much to the insights provided by those 19th-century Swedes who left for a better life.

Oscar I, and his grandson, Carl XV.

By 1862, Sweden had local self-government and four years later the reform of Parliament abolished the four estates that had formed the Riksdag for over 400 years and reduced it to two chambers.

From this time until 1974, the monarch's power was only marginally greater than it is today and history has become a chronicle of Riksdag and people. In 1971, the Riksdag became a single chamber and a new constitution in 1974 gave the present king, Carl XVI Gustaf, purely ceremonial functions.

of Skåne, Rutger Maclean. Some 20 years before Gustav IV Adolf introduced his land enclosure laws of 1803 and 1807, which prevented the subdivision of land into ever smaller, uneconomic portions, Maclean had already reformed his own estate into manageable lots and abolished some of the near-feudal duties of his peasants.

At first, this reform met with bitter hostility: if an independent farmer failed, he was usually reduced to the status of landless labourer. Maclean persisted and, when he died in 1816, most of his tenants were able to buy their farms. Maclean's example took a long time to filter

The opening of the Göta Canal on 26th September, 1832.

Population doubles

The Napoleonic wars and the loss of Finland left Sweden low in morale and poorer than it had been for a century. The earlier growth in agriculture and trade stagnated and meant poverty and even starvation for the large numbers who earned a living from the land.

The greatest potential for disaster was the population explosion, which took numbers in Sweden from less than 2.5 million in 1800 to more than 5 million by 1900, due in part to a much reduced death rate.

Land reform

The real father of the Swedish agricultural revolution was an estate owner in the southern province

through, but the greater productivity it brought did something to put food in the growing number of stomachs.

Transport revolution

By the second half of the century, Swedish transport, which had changed little since the days of Gustav Vasa, began to improve. Water had always provided trading and travelling routes and Baltzar von Platen's Göta Kanal, which opened in 1832, made full use of Lakes Vänern and Vättern to link east to west.

In 1853, the engineer Nils Ericsson took charge of railway building and began the construction of a part-state, part-private network. Rail transport encouraged the new forest industries to make use of Sweden's endless wooded acres for sawmilling and later wood-pulping, and, by the last decades of the 19th century, the first glow of the Swedish inventive genius had begun to show in men like Gustav Pasch, who invented

> The first Swedish union, started in 1874 for tobacco workers in Malmö, was founded by Danes, afraid that the unorganised Swedes might move into Denmark and bring down wages there.

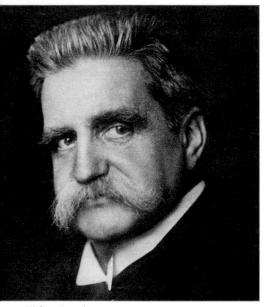

Hjalmar Branting.

the safety match; Lars Magnus Ericsson, whose invention of the table telephone led to the start of the company which bears his name today; and Alfred Nobel, the inventor of dynamite. The economic stage was set for the country's swift industrial development in the next century.

The Riksdag introduced compulsory elementary education in 1842 – almost 30 years before Britain. Better education played its part in the growth of Swedish democracy and the rise of popular movements. Frederika Bremer was one of the founders of the women's movement, and wrote many books, from her early *Sketches of Everyday Life* to her polemical novel *Hertha*, which put forward the women's cause. Late in the century another writer, Ellen Key, shocked polite society with her support for free love. In the country, where sex was considered natural and marriage after the conception or birth of a child was customary, these ideas were less startling.

Workers' rights

Growing industrialisation created a new social class of workers, and the abolition of the medieval guilds of craftsmen in 1846 led to new associations that were the beginning of trade unions. The first notable workers' confrontation happened in 1879 in Sundsvall where the sawmill owners proposed a 15 to 20 percent reduction on already minimal wages. Oscar II sent his troops to face several thousand strikers and, though no violence occurred, many were alarmed at the official high-handedness. Workers began to realise that they must organise to win and militant socialist trade unionists were soon taking over these "liberal" unions.

Birth of the Social Democrats

Other popular movements included the formation of free churches and a crusading temperance league. The co-operative movement was very strong in 19th-century Sweden. Most far-reaching of all were the beginnings of what later became the Social Democratic Party. Its progenitor, August Palm, converted to socialism in Denmark; a radical and eccentric troublemaker, he was expelled from Germany and imprisoned when he returned home. He started a radical newspaper and, from prison, launched the congress that founded the party.

But Palm was a wayward founder and a steadier guiding hand for the new party came from Hjalmar Branting. He had been an early associate of Palm but realised that the latter's disruptive influence would kill the party in its infancy.

In 1892, Branting succeeded in having Palm declared unfit to lead the party and took over himself. For a long time, he was the only party-affiliated Social Democrat in the Riksdag, but between 1895 and 1905 party membership multiplied and returned 13 to the Riksdag.

This new Social Democratic Party expressed the hopes and aspirations of an industrial population that exploded in size before and during the Industrial Revolution.

With the workers behind it, the party could scarcely fail and, more than anywhere else in Europe, the 20th century was to belong to the Swedish Social Democrats.

Stockholm Olympic Games poster, 1912.

OLYMPIC GAMES
STOCKHOLM 1912
JUNE 29 th — JULY 22 nd.

Volvo production line at Torslanda.

THE INDUSTRIAL MIRACLE

Sweden's transformation from an impoverished
rural economy to a leading industrial nation was
its most striking feature in the 20th century.

Few nations have experienced such a rapid development as that of Sweden from 1900 onwards. Just a century ago Sweden was one of Europe's poorer countries, with an economy entirely based on agriculture. Today it is a highly industrialised nation, which for many years topped the European gross domestic product league.

It was Sweden's natural resources, such as timber and iron ore, that formed the basis of its new-found wealth. Industries including paper and pulp, steel and engineering all relied on these resources, and as demand grew for their products following the two world wars, so exports increased. Sweden was also able to draw on skilled workers and an entrepreneurial spirit. New companies were born, and Sweden's industrial output diversified.

Rapid expansion

At the beginning of the 20th century, Sweden experienced a mass emigration to the United States. There was not enough work to go around, and farming could not feed a growing population. Those that remained turned to the cities for work. New companies such as the telecommunications firm LM Ericsson, the bearings company SKF and the electrical experts ASEA were expanding as export orders grew and provided sought-after employment.

At the outbreak of World War I, Sweden had achieved the same per capita income as Great Britain. Although the country remained neutral during the war, it nevertheless experienced the post-war depression of the late 1920s and early 1930s. Industrial empires – including that of the famous match-king Krueger – crashed and brought unexpected poverty to the new middle classes. Bankruptcies were

Wood pulp mill.

followed by political unrest and strikes.

The election of the Social Democratic Party in 1932 eased the unrest and marked the beginning of an electoral love affair that would not end until 1976.

After World War II – during which Sweden again remained neutral – there was a change in emphasis. Employment in traditional industries such as mining and manufacturing peaked around 1960, and Sweden, like many other Western countries, veered towards a service-based economy. The public sector expanded rapidly on the back of the welfare society. Between 1960 and 1995 the numbers employed in the public sector rose by 800,000, while the increase in the private sector was only 250,000.

Industry and innovation

The 1990s saw a shift in Sweden from manufacturing based on domestic raw materials to a wider variety of goods. Engineering expanded rapidly and accounted for almost half of manufacturing output. Sweden also put money into the telecommunications field, today dominated by major players TeliaSonera and Ericsson. Sweden has always invested in industrial research and development, and that situation has not changed. In 2014, businesses were given tax incentives to invest in research and development.

Partnership for industry

Swedish Social Democracy is a pragmatic affair that recognises that strong markets create the resources necessary to construct a strong welfare system. Sweden's welfare state has been built with the aid of industry, and industry has been allowed to prosper with the blessing of all the post-war governments. The door of each post-war prime minister has always been open to the representatives of the leading industrial families.

Former prime minister Göran Persson nurtured an open relationship with Sweden's industrial barons, and some Social Democrats

Forsmark Nuclear Power Station, Uppland.

SWEDEN'S NUCLEAR DILEMMA

Nuclear power is a hot topic in Sweden. Swedes have generally supported nuclear power, but the tide turned after the 2011 Fukushima disaster in Japan: a poll revealed that 64 percent now oppose the building of new reactors.

In contrast to prevailing public opinion, the major political parties have never been gung-ho nuclear enthusiasts. Sweden's reactors were built in the 1970s and 1980s, and were intended to last for 40 years, but two were closed as early as 1999 and 2005, with the government of the day resolving to shut the rest by 2010. That plan has since been reversed, a policy supported by current prime minister Stefan Löfven, who acknowledges their necessity – the country's 10 reactors provide 41 percent of its electricity.

However, Sweden's nuclear power plants are becoming unreliable with age. In 2005, radioactive water leaked from a nuclear waste store at Forsmark; and in 2006 two emergency power generators at the same plant failed. Plans are underway to decommission the Oskarshamn 1 reactor, which has been in service for 50 years; two reactors at the Ringhals plant will shut by 2018 and 2020; and in 2015, it was announced that Oskarshamn 2 in southeastern Sweden would close by 2020 because it has become unprofitable.

The question of what will replace them – new reactors, or alternative forms of energy production – remains to be seen.

of the old order accused him of being too cosy with the establishment. His predecessor, Ingvar Carlsson, was more detached in his dealings with industry, as was Olof Palme in the 1970s and 1980s. During the post-war periods when the Social Democrats were not in power, there was little difference in the constructive co-operation between the state and industry.

Swedish democracy is based on equality. It has been so ever since the two chambers of parliament were introduced in 1866 to replace the four estates (assemblies) to which the aristocracy and clergy were automatically invited.

Federation was the common way to solve disputes until the early 1980s.

One reason for relative peace in the labour market was low unemployment. This changed in the late 1980s. Swedish manufacturing exports lost more than 25 percent of their global market share between 1970 and 1992, and the government was forced to devalue the currency several times to increase Swedish competitiveness.

The economy bounced back to rosy-cheeked good health between 1995 and 2006, but was hit again by the 2008 financial crisis. Sweden got off lightly compared to some countries,

Fish is a valuable food resource in Sweden.

Women were given the vote in 1921 but, although today almost half the members of parliament are women, not one has yet made it to prime minister.

The openness between state and industry has also coloured the relationship between employers and employees, allowing Sweden to experience generally peaceful labour relations during the post-war era.

Pay bargaining

The Swedish labour market is characterised by a very high degree of unionisation; some 70 percent of employees belong to a trade union. Centralised bargaining between the Swedish Trades Union Council and the Employers'

thanks to a cautious banking sector, Sweden's decision to stay out of the Eurozone, and a bit of blind luck; but austerity measures taken across Europe since the crisis have affected the country, which relies heavily on its exports. Unemployment soared to 9.3 percent in 2010, from where it has slowly fallen to 7.8 percent in April 2015. The country's economy is sluggish, with GDP growth expected to be just over 2 per cent per annum in the next few years.

Industrial exodus

Following the recession of the late 1980s and early 1990s, increased global competition and rampant merger-mania led to some startling changes in Sweden. National icons such as

Engineering products, including aircraft, motor vehicles, electrical and electronic equipment, and specialised machinery, make up 80 percent of Swedish exports.

Volvo and Saab fell into foreign hands in 1999 and 2000 respectively. Hasselblad, most famous for producing the cameras used in the Moon landing, was sold to a Swiss firm in 1996. Swedes found these sales difficult, with each loss followed by much hand-wringing. Equally

and the equally prosperous fashion chain H&M, moved abroad.

As more Swedish companies end up in foreign hands, there is a growing concern that jobs will be lost. This has not happened yet: new companies in technology and services have entered the market, and the Internet explosion has delivered several fast-growing enterprises. Which of these will be tomorrow's Ericsson is too early to forecast.

Inventors mean business

One Swede who is famous worldwide and whose memory is celebrated each year on 10 Decem-

Farmer ploughing his field.

disturbing was the flight of companies moving abroad. Ericsson was hit badly when the telecom market crashed. After a round of lay-offs and outsourcing, it turned to Sony of Japan as a new production partner for its mobile handsets.

During 1998, mergers swept through Swedish industrial corridors at a rate greater than that of Germany, where the economy was 10 times larger. Much of the merger rush was due to restructuring within the Wallenberg empire, Sweden's leading industrial family. Many analysts saw the shake-up as just an appetiser.

The industrial exodus put pressure on Sweden's government. With tax rates touching the ceiling, entrepreneurs, including the founders of the successful IKEA home-furnishing empire

ber is Alfred Nobel (see page 68). He invented smokeless gunpowder and dynamite and made his fortune. Most of today's industrial conglomerates have their roots in a simple invention.

In 1876 – the same year that Alexander Graham Bell invented the telephone – Lars Magnus Ericsson set up a workshop for repairing telegraph equipment. A few years later he started the production of an improved telephone and, in 1882, he introduced the world's first table-top model. Ericsson was quick to see the importance of exports and he set up a UK subsidiary in 1898.

AGA was built on Gustaf Dalén's invention of the sun valve, which switches lighthouse beacons on and off. The company now mostly produces industrial gases. Its famous AGA cookers were sold to a British firm many years ago.

SKF is the world's largest manufacturer of industrial ball-bearings, another Swedish invention – it might not sound like much, but industrial equipment, trains, cars and aeroplanes the world over would literally grind to a halt without them. Electrolux refined the vacuum cleaner and is now a world leader in electrical appliances.

TetraPak is the world's largest food processing and packaging company. It was based on tetrahedron-shaped paper packaging, an invention by Ruben Rausing. Alfa-Laval is built on

the invention of the separator, in which cream can be quickly separated from milk through centrifugal force. It is now part of the TetraPak Group, but still a world leader in its field.

Not all of Sweden's inventive successes are tangible objects: Skype, which was sold first to eBay and then in 2011 to Microsoft for US$8500m, was invented by Swedish and Danish entrepreneurs; and the most infamous of all torrent sites, The Pirate Bay, was cofounded by Swedes Fredrik Neij and Gottfrid Svartholm. Both were convicted in 2009 of promoting other people's infringements of copyright laws, and the .se

IKEA, a Swedish success story.

WHO'S WHO IN PARTY POLITICS

Anyone can establish a political party in Sweden. Political donations are illegal, and the state contributes an estimated 150 kronor per head of population per year to support the political parties. The country has a system of proportional representation, with eight parties represented in the Riksdag (parliament). This proliferation of parties has led to a succession of coalition governments.

Social Democratic Party Aims to make all citizens equal partners in administering society's productive resources; similar to New Labour in Britain.

Moderate Party (formerly known as the Conservative Party) Believes in a market economy, control of public sector expansion, and a public authority to guarantee

social security.

Sweden Democrats Have achieved sudden success on a nationalist, anti-immigration platform.

Green Party Aspires to a society in ecological balance with the environment.

Centre Party (formerly Agrarian Party) Based on free enterprise, individual and co-operative ownership.

Left Party (formerly Communist Party) Strong believer in public ownership.

Liberal Party Manifesto built on a socially orientated market economy.

Christian Democratic Party Promotes pro-family values and environmental responsibility; Conservative.

domain itself was seized following a court ruling, but The Pirate Bay continues to thrive.

Celebrating success

Corporate centennial celebrations have become run-of-the-mill, but no company in the world can beat the paper and timber company Stora, which celebrated 700 years in the mid-1980s. In 1998, Stora merged with its Finnish competitor, Enso, and moved its corporate headquarters to Helsinki.

IKEA has almost single-handedly changed the face of furniture retailing. The founder, Ingvar Kamprad, started out by selling pens by mail order at the age of 17, moved into kitchen chairs in the 1950s, and today controls a vast enterprise with outlets worldwide.

The car-manufacturing sector is also strong. Volvo has been at the forefront of automotive safety standards, and Sweden is the world's largest exporter of trucks – a remarkable achievement for such a small nation. Volvo might now be in the hands of Chinese company Zhejiang Geely, but the strength of its brand name is still its Swedishness, synonymous with safety.

Eco-village Understenshöjden.

ENVIRONMENTAL AWARENESS

The Swedes are strongly committed to environmental causes. Sweden is one of the EU's top recyclers of drinks cans, bottles and paper, and gets the highest share of its energy from renewable sources. The country is also the EU's top consumer of organic food. Swedish industry takes seriously its environmental responsibility to reduce potentially hazardous emissions and has invested heavily in environmental protection measures. The government is keen to do its share too, allocating around 400 million kronor per year for research into environmental technology.

The defence industry is healthy, which is a curious situation in a country that has not experienced war since the early 1800s and which has a world-wide reputation for its peacemakers. But Sweden's two biggest exports are refined petroleum, accounting for 6.75 percent of its total exports in 2013, followed by packaged medicaments, which accounted for 4.24 percent. This last figure is a vindication of the government's high level of investment in research and development in the pharmaceutical sector, which goes back to the 1950s, when the first pacemaker was fitted at the Karolinska Institute. Today British-Swedish company AstraZeneca is one of the world's biggest biopharmaceutical players.

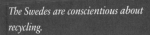

THE PEACEMAKERS

Swedish negotiators have increasingly been
called in to help resolve international conflicts.
What makes their skills so special?

It may be Sweden's long-held traditions of neutrality and its position as a buffer between the power blocs, but from a population of only 9.8 million it has produced a remarkable number of dedicated peacemakers of international repute. World War II, in which Sweden was relatively untouched, saw the start of this trend, when in 1939–40 (during the bleak Finnish Winter War against the Soviet Union), many Swedes opened their homes to Finnish children.

After the German attack on Denmark and Norway, a stream of refugees crossed the long border between Sweden and Norway and many Danish Jews were also able to find asylum in the neutral country.

Release of prisoners

From this period, the names of two humanitarians stand out: Count Folke Bernadotte and Raoul Wallenberg. The first of these had high connections and a royal name. He was the nephew of King Gustav V, and an army officer as well as chairman of the Red Cross. His talent was for negotiation and he was one of the first to recognise that, whatever a country might think of the Nazi regime, it was better to engage in a dialogue with it than to allow its victims to die. Bernadotte's first success was to secure the release of thousands of Scandinavian prisoners, and later prisoners of other nationalities, from the concentration camps.

In 1947, Bernadotte's already proven skills recommended him to the United Nations Security Council, which was seeking someone to mediate in the delicate situation between the Jews and Arabs in Palestine.

Bernadotte moved to Palestine but, although he successfully negotiated a ceasefire, both sides rejected his terms of settlement of the war. He

Raoul Wallenberg, saviour of Jews.

was also faced with many who had a vested interest in making sure that he didn't succeed and were prepared to go to any lengths to continue the struggle.

After a number of threats against his life, his car was ambushed in September 1948 and he was shot down by Jewish extremists.

Escape route

Raoul Wallenberg's aim was also to help the Jews. When in 1944 the United States established the War Refugee Board to save Jews from Nazi persecution, the Board's Stockholm representative called together a group of Swedish Jews to suggest candidates suitable, brave enough, and willing to go on a rescue operation to Budapest.

At this point, the lives of Folke Bernadotte and Raoul Wallenberg came together because Bernadotte was the first choice. When the Hungarian Government would not accept him, Wallenberg was appointed.

The 32-year-old member of the great industrial and banking family became First Secretary of the Swedish Legation in Budapest and began his dangerous mission. His best protection was his authority to deal with anyone he chose and to use diplomatic couriers outside the normal channels. By the time Wallenberg arrived in Budapest, he was too late to save two-thirds of the Jewish population. Already, 400,000 Jews had been transported to the camps, but there were still around 200,000 left in the capital.

Wallenberg's first step was to start to issue protective passports and to open "Swedish Houses" all over the city, where Budapest Jews could take refuge. He used everything from bribery to threats and blackmail, and it is said that as many as 100,000 Jews owe their survival to Raoul Wallenberg.

The saviour could not save himself and his own fate is veiled in mystery. Towards the end of the war, Wallenberg fell into the hands of the Russians, who seem to have believed that he was a spy. They later declared that Wallenberg had died in captivity and have since refused to re-open the question, though eye-witnesses claim that he was alive and still imprisoned as late as the 1980s. Many in Sweden are reluctant to believe that this brave man died as early as 1947, and his family and voluntary associations are still tireless in their efforts to find out what happened to Raoul Wallenberg.

Dag Hammarskjöld, United Nations leader.

The Swedish peacemaker Dag Hammarskjöld, second secretary general of the United Nations (1953–61), was instrumental in improving the reputation and effectiveness of the UN.

Keeping the peace

When the United Nations was established after World War II, its first secretary general was a Norwegian, Trygve Lie. He was succeeded in 1953 by another Swedish peacemaker, Dag Hammarskjöld, who became the founder of the UN Peacekeeping Force. Hammarskjöld was an economist and had been a civil servant and son of a former prime minister of Sweden.

Apart from the establishment of the Peacekeeping Force, Hammarskjöld's other main achievements were to arrange the release of captured American pilots from China. He was also the champion of the small states of the UN, and the guardian particularly of the interests of the Third World against the major powers.

Congo mission

Hammarskjöld's stewardship ended when he decided to send UN troops to the Congo after civil war broke out there in 1959. As the political repercussions of Hammarskjöld's actions spread, Russia demanded his resignation, but he remained. It was in the Congo that this independently-minded man met his death in mysterious circumstances, as so often has been the fate of the peacemaker.

Olof Palme campaigned internationally for arms reduction.

In 1961, when Hammarskjöld was on a peace mission to that war-torn country, his plane crashed, killing all on board. The reasons have never been explained and even today many speculate that this, too, was an assassination.

Demands for disarmament

Sweden's principal woman peacemaker, Alva Myrdal, was also closely connected with the UN and was the first woman to achieve a position as a top-ranking director within that organisation, when she became head of the Department of Social Affairs.

Myrdal's main contribution was her tireless effort to promote disarmament and peace during the 1960s when she was involved in the Geneva

disarmament talks. Through what must have been a series of dispiriting meetings over a number of years, she held on to her belief that in the end common sense would prevail. In 1964, she was one of the founders of Stockholm's International Peace Research Institute and its first chair. She published a number of books and articles. In 1980 she was the first to be awarded the Albert Einstein Peace Prize, and in 1982 the Nobel Peace Prize. She died in 1986 at the age of 84.

That same year, the Swedish peacemaker Olof Palme was gunned down in a Stockholm street as he strolled home from a visit to the cinema with his wife.

Champion of the oppressed

Even before Palme became prime minister in 1969 at the age of 42, he had already begun to acquire an international reputation, mainly in connection with the Vietnam War. For several years, his robust condemnation of American policy in Vietnam led to acrimonious exchanges with the United States administration in Washington and also occasionally with the US Embassy in Stockholm.

In domestic politics Palme's priorities were to combat unemployment and to promote social reforms, building on the work of his predecessors. In foreign policy, however, he broke new ground. He argued constantly against colonialism and the arms race and, during the 1970s and 1980s, he became one of the world's foremost champions of oppressed peoples.

As a member of the Brandt Commission, he helped to formulate proposals for narrowing the gap between North and South, and his own "Palme Commission" presented a concrete plan for reducing armaments and increasing global security. He, too, was involved in the work of the United Nations when he acted as mediator in the Iran-Iraq war at the request of the secretary general.

Swedes had concentrated more on Palme's domestic policies than on his international achievements, but his shocking assassination, and the world's reaction to it, opened their eyes to his international reputation as a peacemaker and statesman. In the 1990s the peacemaking banner was taken up by the conservative politician, Carl Bildt (Prime Minister 1991–4), in efforts to bring an end to the war in Bosnia. In a vain attempt to avoid war, Hans Blix led a team of UN weapons inspectors in Iraq prior to being withdrawn in 2003 to make way for coalition bombing of the country.

The Non-Aligned Nation

Sweden has remained neutral during two world wars, but retains its own forces for security.

Sweden's King Carl XIV Johan was the first to lay down his country's long-lasting belief in neutrality. In the 1830s he assured both the Russian and British governments that Sweden had abandoned all thoughts of regaining the provinces on the eastern and southern shores of the Baltic lost as a result of the Napoleonic wars. Sweden, he insisted, would not want to do anything that might endanger its existence as a state.

That was the official position – but there were forces within the country which challenged it. The loss of Finland in 1809 to Russia was a blow to Swedish national pride. The aristocracy in both countries had close connections, and Swedish was the official language of Finland. The union with Norway entered into in 1814 could not make up for the loss of Finland. Only a policy of greatest constraint could keep the two countries united and the union was finally dissolved in 1905.

During the years before World War I Sweden, feeling under threat of attack from Russia, moved closer to Germany. It became clear that the Germans were only interested in using a friendship with Sweden as a threat to Russia. A few days after war was declared, Sweden issued an official declaration of neutrality.

Towards the end of that war, neutrality was under strain as civil war broke out in Finland between the Russian-backed Reds and the Whites. Victory for the Reds was a threat to Swedish security, but it was felt that military intervention would entail an even higher risk.

By 1920 Sweden was more favourably placed than ever before. Germany and Russia had lost the war, an independent Finland emerged, German influence over Denmark had disappeared, and none of the other Nordic states were under obligation to a great power. Sweden now concentrated its efforts on limiting the growth of power in other countries through the League of Nations. It adopted unilateral disarmament in 1925.

Sweden stayed out of World War II officially but a number of volunteers from the Swedish forces joined the White Army to fight with the Finns against Russia. At the same time, Sweden recognised the urgent need to rearm. Denmark and Norway were both occupied by the Germans in 1940 and Sweden was under threat of invasion. Public opinion in Sweden put pressure on the government to take sides.

The coalition government decided to keep Sweden out of the war at almost any cost and reluctantly conceded to German demands to transport troops on leave from Norway through Sweden. This was seen by many as immoral. Others felt that because Sweden stayed out of the war, it was able to make a humanitarian contribution which outweighed any military contribution. After the war,

A EUFOR Swedish soldier.

recognising the need for protection, Norway and Denmark joined NATO, Finland signed a treaty of friendship with the Soviet Union in 1948, but Sweden resolved to maintain its non-alliance in peacetime, leading to neutrality in war time. It has since been very active in the United Nations, promoting peace and disarmament.

Armed neutrality puts Sweden in something of a cleft stick. In order to maintain an up-to-date defence, Sweden has to have an armaments industry. An armament industry supplying only Swedish needs would be an intolerable drain on the nation's resources and manufacturers have had to look for customers elsewhere. The peace-loving Swedes are now the third largest arms exporter per capita after Israel and Russia.

ALFRED NOBEL

He made a fortune from weapons of war.
Then he gave his name to an international
award for peacemakers. Why?

Some of the most fascinating contradictions of the human character came together inside Alfred Nobel. How, for instance, could one man both found the renowned Nobel Peace Prize, awarded each year to those who have made the greatest contributions to world peace, and at the same time be the father of Sweden's vigorous armaments industry, which today provides a substantial amount of the weapons held by one half of that same world against the other?

The young inventor

Alfred Nobel was born in 1833 in Sweden, one of three brothers. He clearly inherited his talents as a chemist and inventor from his father, who went bankrupt during Alfred's early childhood. Despite the bankruptcy, Nobel Senior moved the family to Russia where he became a very successful industrialist.

Life in St Petersburg gave Alfred the chance of an international education. He was particularly well tutored in chemistry and, in addition to Swedish, spoke French, Russian, English and German. Nor was he confined to Russia. As a young man he took educational trips all over Europe and to the United States, before joining his father in St Petersburg as a chemist. In 1853, the Nobel family moved back to Sweden, leaving Alfred's two brothers, Robert and Ludwig, to look after their father's business.

An early interest in explosives was also stimulated by Alfred Nobel's father, who in Russia had invented new and efficient land and sea mines which the Russian armed forces used in the Crimean War. Alfred went further and patented many of his own inventions, of which his most famous was dynamite. This revolutionised mining, road building and tunnel blasting because it gave engineers a manageable form of the highly

Alfred Nobel (1833–96), chemist and inventor.

sensitive explosive, nitroglycerine. He also turned his fertile mind to synthetic materials, telecommunications and alarm systems and in his lifetime clocked up the ownership of 355 patents.

International industrialist

Alfred Nobel was more than an inventor. He was a pioneer in the swift industrial exploitation of his discoveries and the founding of multinational companies. His ultimate total was 90 factories and companies in 20 countries, on five continents around the world. At the same time, he did not neglect his Russian interests and entered into partnership with his brothers, who by this time were successfully exploiting the Baku oilfields and became known as the Russian Rockefellers.

> One of Alfred Nobel's biographers described him in early life as "a prematurely developed, unusually intelligent, but a sickly, dreamy and introspective youth."

The Nobels also had a reputation as benevolent employers who provided social care and welfare benefits for their employees, a foretaste perhaps of the Swedish style of today.

To the world outside, Alfred Nobel was a man with a penetrating mind, shrewd in business and with a sceptical idealism. He was also melancholic, slightly self-deprecating, yet with a good sense of humour. Despite his success, he was not a happy man and wrote of his life as "a miserable half-life, which ought to have been choked to death by a philanthropic physician as, with a howl, it entered life". Although he had homes in six different countries, his life was that of a vagabond. Paris was close to his heart and so was Bofors in Sweden, where he spent his last years. Today, it is the stronghold of the armaments industry he founded.

Nobel in love

A lonely man, Nobel never married but in later life developed a strong friendship with Bertha von Suttner, an Austrian baroness. Theirs was a close but platonic relationship, as the baroness was not free to marry. Bertha von Suttner was a pioneer in the peace movement and her friendship may well have influenced Nobel's thinking about peace. In any event, she was awarded the Nobel Peace Prize in 1905.

The real love affair of his life was with an Austrian girl, who was 23 years his junior. But even here, his complex mind seemed unable to forget her social and educational inferiority. Despite that, the liaison lasted for 18 years.

He tried his hand at both poetry and prose and, in his youth, was so strongly influenced by Shelley's pacifist views as to call war "the horror of horrors and the greatest of all crimes". Despite that, Nobel apparently saw no wrong in profiting from the weapons of war and during his lifetime he amassed a huge fortune.

He was not the sort of rich man who prided himself on his frugality, nor did he wait until he was dead to become a philanthropist. His philosophy was always to prefer "to take care of the stomachs of the living rather than the glory of the departed in the form of monuments".

Prize fund

A year before his death in San Remo in Italy, Nobel signed the will which, in less than 300 words, stipulated how to convert his estate into an investment fund. The proceeds were to be used for annual prizes to be awarded to individuals who "shall have conferred the greatest benefit on mankind". There were to be five categories: physics, chemistry, physiology or medicine, literature and the well-known Nobel Prize for Peace for "the best work for fraternity between nations, for the abolition or reduction of standing armies and for the holding and promotion of peace congresses".

Nobel Prize-winning ceremony at the Stockholm Concert Hall, attended by the Swedish royal family.

The first four were to be awarded by Swedish institutions. For the Peace Prize, Nobel went outside Sweden and named a committee appointed by the Norwegian Parliament to make the award. In 1968, the Central Bank of Sweden added a prize in Economic Sciences to the original categories, in memory of Nobel.

Today, the contradictions of Nobel's complex personality have left a second legacy, quite apart from the Nobel Prizes. Sweden's vigorous armaments industry provides a substantial part of Swedish exports each year. It is as though that strange marriage between peace and war that existed in Alfred Nobel's mind continues in his own country today.

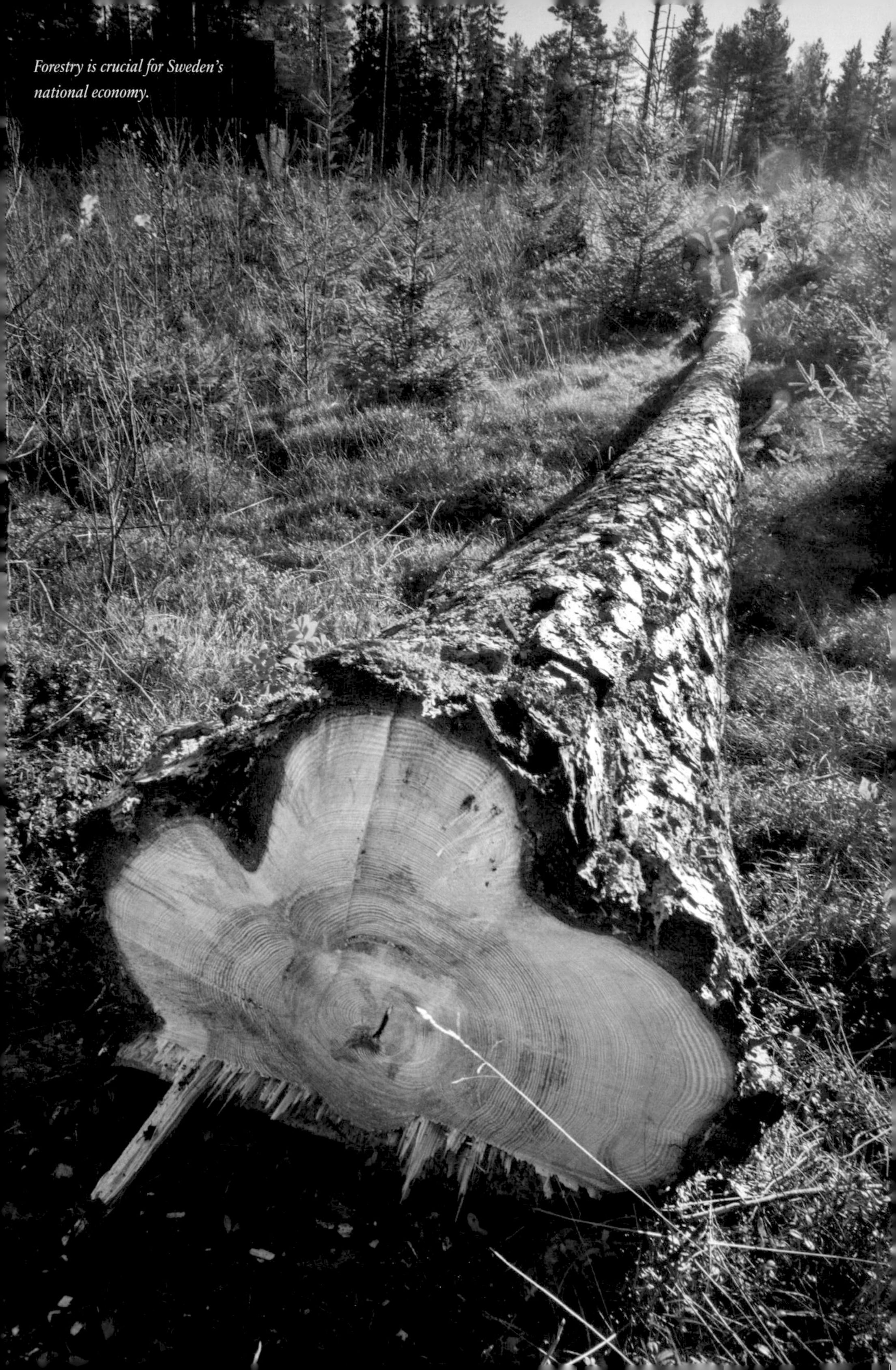

Forestry is crucial for Sweden's national economy.

THE SWEDISH MODEL

Close collaboration between employers, employees, the state and trade unions has created a working relationship that's the envy of many nations.

Politicians worldwide have for decades pointed to the Swedish Model, in which socialism and capitalism work hand in hand, as the right way forward. The Americans first latched onto it in the late 1930s with the publication of the book *The Middle Way* by Marquis W. Childs, which outlined the route taken by the Swedish government to combat unemployment and declining competitiveness. However, it was during the 1950s, 1960s and 1970s, when the economy was strong and expanding, that the Social Democratic Party had the money and the mandate to build the modern Swedish welfare state.

US politicians held up Sweden as an example at a time when the Americans were experiencing rising unemployment and labour strife. The British Labour Party also flirted with the Swedish Model during the 1960s and 70s, and again under the leadership of Ed Miliband – his defeat in the 2015 general election was a disappointment to the Social Democratic Party, who had hoped for closer ties. In the 1980s, Soviet officials looked to their Swedish neighbours across the Baltic to provide the safest method of merging old-fashioned socialism with entrepreneurial capitalism.

However, the Swedish Model has faltered over the last few decades. In 1999, the British magazine *The Economist* suggested that the Middle Way had become a cul-de-sac. More recently, high unemployment and Sweden's fast-growing immigrant population have caused social unrest in Sweden, starkly witnessed in the sudden rise to power of the far right party the Sweden Democrats, who won 12.9 percent of vote in the 2014 election. With politics in upheaval and the Social Democratic Party in crisis, the Swedish Model has certainly lost its lustre;

Industrious Swede.

but then, times have changed since it was first mooted as a panacea for all social ills.

Rich and poor

The Swedish Model certainly achieved the unachievable. Thanks to close collaboration between business, labour and government, Sweden was transformed from one of Europe's poorer nations into one of its richest. It also helped to create a society that enjoyed a narrowing gap between rich and poor, and where the social welfare system provided security for everyone from cradle to grave.

From 1932 onwards, with only a few lost elections, the Social Democratic Party has ruled and shaped Sweden. The term socialism is misleading, unless we think of socialism as envisaged by former British prime minister Tony Blair. Some call it "socialism with a prosperous face", others see it as pure pragmatism. In order to create the wealth that was needed to pay for Sweden's welfare system, the labour force and business were encouraged to collaborate and given full support by the government.

The Swedish Social Democratic Party saw co-operation as the only way forward and worked closely with the captains of industry from the day it came to power. Co-operation was made easier by the fact that more than half of Swe-

the cost of these strikes, both to the economy and to society as a whole, and threatened to intervene by introducing strict labour laws.

The Employers' Federation and the trades union association Landsorganisationen (LO) agreed to resolve the issue between themselves. In 1938, at a historic meeting at the Saltsjöbaden Grand Hotel, near Stockholm, the two parties finally agreed on rules for collective bargaining and how to solve industrial disputes. "The Saltsjöbaden Spirit" became synonymous with a new pragmatism, where the benefit for society was more important than that for individual groups.

A happy workplace.

den's industry was controlled by a handful of families. The most important was the Wallenberg family, still the powerhouse of Swedish industry, controlling businesses worth around €250 billion in 2015. The Wallenbergs were clever enough to see that close links with the political rulers would benefit them, too.

By working with business, the Social Democratic Party set an example for the strong trade unions, and co-operation between the Employers' Federation and the trade unions followed the same pattern.

Through the early part of the 1900s, trade unions and management had been locked in bitter combat, and strikes were common. The new Social Democratic government recognised

Peace pact

Under this peace pact, unions were required to give advance notice of any planned industrial action, which meant a cooling-off period for talks and further negotiations. Wage levels would be agreed upon for the whole labour market by the two confederations representing trade unions and management. The ensuing order and calm of the Swedish labour market became the envy of most industrialised nations. It guaranteed the Swedish industrialists peace to build up their factories and invest in the knowledge that they would not suffer costly strikes. The Swedish Model, the Middle Way, was in place. Then World War II intervened.

Generous benefits

The post-war era was one of industrial growth, no doubt helped by the fact that Sweden had remained neutral during the war. With a strong economy, rising exports and no unemployment, the government introduced an ambitious programme of social reforms. Ministers realised that a profitable private sector would secure jobs and help to expand the economy, and, with this in mind, corporate taxes were set at a minimum. Corporate tax levels are still among the lowest in Europe at about 28 percent.

half-day. It is a miracle that any work gets done, but it does, and efficiently, too.

Many attribute this miracle to the placid nature of the Swedes. Consensus is important, and political strife on the factory floor or in the boardroom is a rare occurrence. However, during the 1980s, peace in the workplace took a hammering. Corporate mergers changed the temperature, and powerful investors became more interested in the bottom line than industrial harmony. The beneficial influence of the industrial dynasties waned as their ownership was watered down.

Parental leave is shared.

The Social Democrats found other ways to raise money – social security contributions paid by companies for each employee are among the highest in Europe. Staffing has become very expensive, and laying off staff even more so. This could be one reason why unemployment has risen: employers dare not commit themselves to taking on permanent staff.

The benefits that Swedish employees now have the right to insist upon are numerous. Each employee has the statutory right of five weeks' paid holiday a year; most have six by contract. Add to that 13 public holidays and the choice of taking double time off in lieu of overtime. The Swedes also have a system whereby the day before a public holiday counts as a

TRADE UNION PARTICIPATION

About 70 percent of all employees are members of a trade union, affiliated to the Trade Union Confederation (LO) for manual workers, the Confederation of Salaried Employees (TCO) for white-collar employees, and the Confederation of Professional Associations (SACO) for graduate-level employees. Employers are represented by the Swedish Employers' Confederation (SAF). About 63 percent of the population are in the labour force. More than 76 percent of all women between 16 and 64 years are in employment. About 25 percent of the labour force work part-time. A further 3 to 4 percent are on assisted training schemes.

Adding up the costs

Sweden's public social expenditure for 2012–13 was the fifth highest in Europe, accounting for 28 percent of its GDP, according to the OECD (Organisation for Economic Co-operation and Development).Swedes enjoy excellent health and social services and top-quality subsidised child care. The streets are clean, and the crime rate lower than in most European countries. Pensioners have a decent standard of living, and the school system churns out well-educated youngsters.

However, whether this state of affairs will continue remains to be seen. In 2007, finance minister Anders Borg cut tax rates to boost the economy, and made cuts to the welfare system to pay for it. By 2012, Sweden had seen one of the biggest increases in disposable income inequality in Europe, and today poverty in the country has grown to a level that places Sweden close to the EU average. The country also has an aging population – there is one person over the age of 65 for every three workers in Sweden.

The Social Democrats, creators and propagators of the Swedish Model, did poorly in the 1998 election; lost in 2006 to a centre-right alliance; and lost again in 2010 where they

A free-newspaper vendor.

SOCIAL WELFARE – FROM CRADLE TO GRAVE

Health Swedes are covered by national health insurance. The patient is charged a fee for medical consultations and any drugs prescribed up to a specified limit. Thereafter, costs are paid by national insurance. If a person is ill or needs to care for a sick child, he or she will receive a taxable daily allowance of 80 percent of lost income.

Parental leave Parents are entitled to 480 days of paid leave when a baby is born (although this looks set to decrease in 2017). This leave can be shared between the father and the mother to suit them and can be used at any time before the child's eighth birthday.

Housing Low-income families and pensioners are eligible for housing allowances.

Unemployment benefit Unemployment insurance is provided through trade unions. Those who do not belong to a trade union rely on state benefits. There are many state-funded schemes to help the unemployed to find new work.

Pensions A basic old-age pension, financed by both employees and employers, is paid to everyone at the age of 65. The state also pays an income-related supplementary pension financed from employer payroll fees, and together these two pensions should reach the level of two-thirds of the pensioner's previous earnings. As in other European countries, the government is looking into self-funded pension schemes to reduce the burden on the state.

There are high levels of civic participation in Sweden. Voter turnout for the 2014 election was 86 percent – impressive compared to the US presidential election (57.5 percent in 2012), the UK general election (66 percent in 2015) and the OECD average (68 percent).

stood as part of a coalition with the Left Party and the Greens. In September 2014, the Social Democrats were back in government as part of a minority centre-left coalition. By December, the

name for the social welfare system that shelters them from cradle to grave, and are willing to pay for it.

The Swedish workplace

The Swedish style of management is admired throughout the industrial world. Organisations are flat rather than hierarchical. Top executives have simple offices and often answer their own telephones. Pinstriped suits are only for bankers, and instead, casual clothing is common – the management team of the furniture retailer IKEA, for instance, has never worn ties. The Brit-

The Swedish workplace is laid-back but efficient.

centre-right opposition parties had joined forces with the Sweden Democrats to block the new government's budget.

After a tense stand-off, it was agreed that the government would implement their opponents' tax and spending plans for four months, after which they could continue with their own economic plans. In April, the government announced several expensive new welfare reforms, including increasing the number of workers in the elderly care sector, and upping unemployment benefit and child support payments.

The obituary for the Swedish Model does not have to be written yet. Although Swedish society is changing, most Swedes are still very attached to *Folkhemmet* (The People's Home), the poetic

ish entrepreneur Richard Branson would feel at home in a Swedish boardroom.

Power sharing has become just as important as money. During the mid-1970s, the unions insisted on placing employee representatives on the boards of each company with more than 25 staff. Companies complained bitterly at this decision, but they have found that a staff which is involved and informed is less likely to take action.

Employees do not suffer from the divisive "them-and-us syndrome". Swedish management wants to be close to its colleagues, and endless conferences and team-building exercises are part of strategic planning. Since individuals are highly taxed, conferences and training seminars in exotic locations have become a way of rewarding employees more tax-efficiently.

The trade unions have changed, and collective wage-bargaining has been abolished, to the delight of both sides. Certain industrial sectors see it as an advantage to be able to negotiate lower pay rises during cyclical downturns, and the stronger unions can flex their muscles.

At work and play

Swedes have recently learnt the noble art of relaxing. The work ethic was deeply ingrained, but now, bolstered by the state, Swedes spend more time with friends and family, and on self-improvement.

Universities are free.

Taking a sabbatical is no longer seen as a cop-out, but a healthy break. A curious phenomenon in Sweden are study circles, born in the early 20th century from the workers' movement, where groups of people get together to discuss the issues that matter to them, from politics to religion to woodworking. Their popularity reached a peak at the end of the 1970s, but the number of participants is still very high – around 275,000 study circles exist, with around 1.9 million participants. Others have hobbies ranging from choral singing to weaving. Young men on the middle rung of their career ladders take time off for paternity leave, and it is not seen as odd when high-flyers rush off at 5pm to collect their young children from kindergarten. With so many women working, sharing child care and domestic chores is a necessity.

Curbing absenteeism

Absenteeism used to be a common problem among employees. Volvo once complained that only 75 percent of its staff turned up on Mondays and that employees took a staggering 27 days sick leave a year. When the government introduced a rule that the first day of sickness had to be unpaid sick leave, absenteeism plummeted. Rising unemployment has also had a salutary effect on absenteeism.

The effect of stress still shows itself in high levels of alcoholism and other stress-related illnesses. Industry has done its utmost to make offices and factories into stress-free zones. Swedish design is at its best in the workplace. Staff have access to facilities for gym and sports, and most canteens would be classified as luxury restaurants in other countries. Larger companies provide crèches for the young children of staff. Training and personal development are also high on the agenda – bigger organisations must by law set aside a percentage of profits for training.

Much of the stress and melancholy can be blamed on dark and interminable winters. As one British diplomat said after serving three years in Stockholm, "There are the Winter Swedes and the Summer Swedes, and in no way are they related." The gloomy Winter Swedes turn into fun-loving extroverts as soon as the first pale rays of sunshine are seen, and cafés move their tables out onto the narrow pavements when spring arrives. When the sun shines, most Swedes will admit that Sweden is pretty close to Utopia.

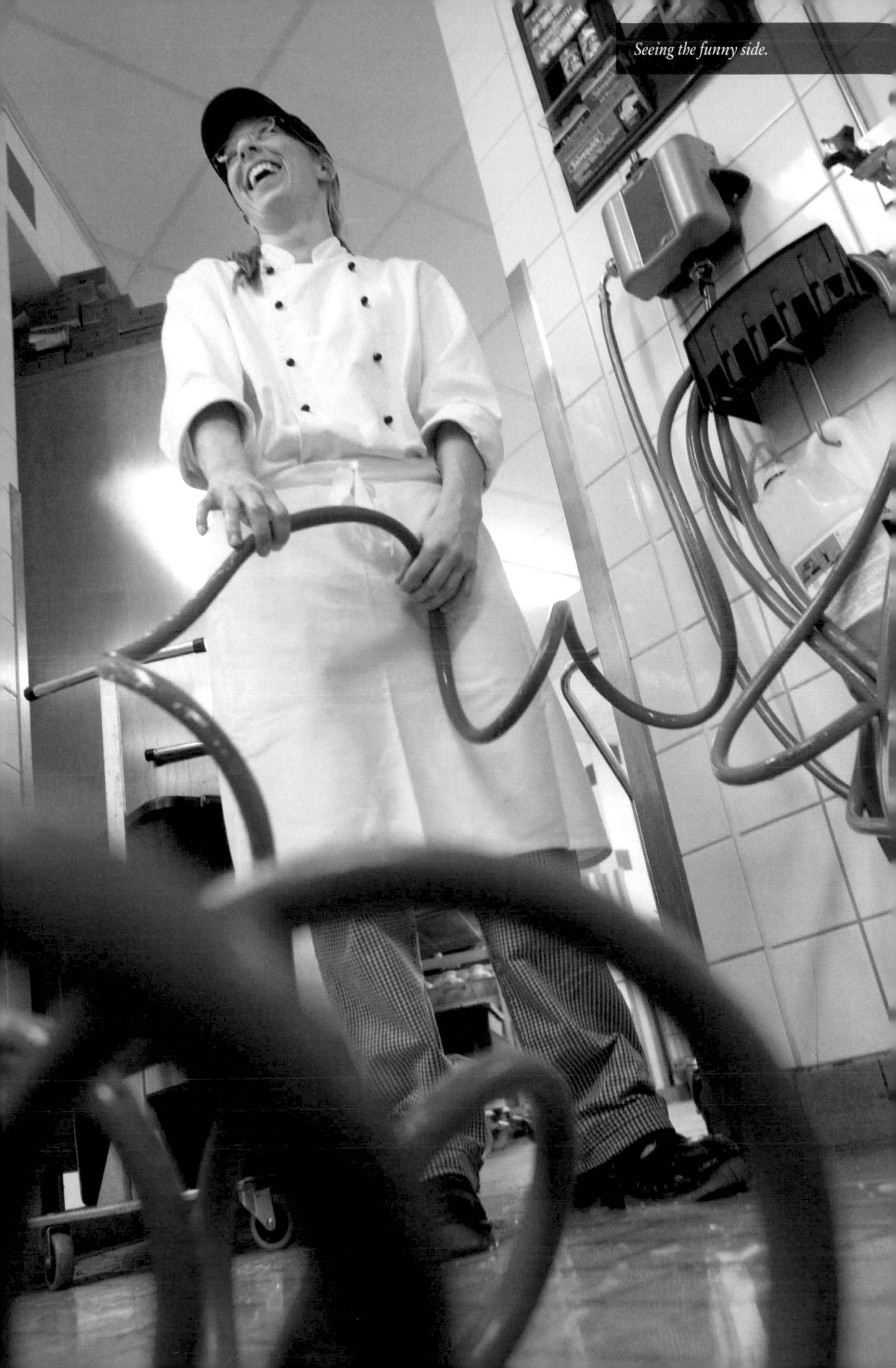

Seeing the funny side.

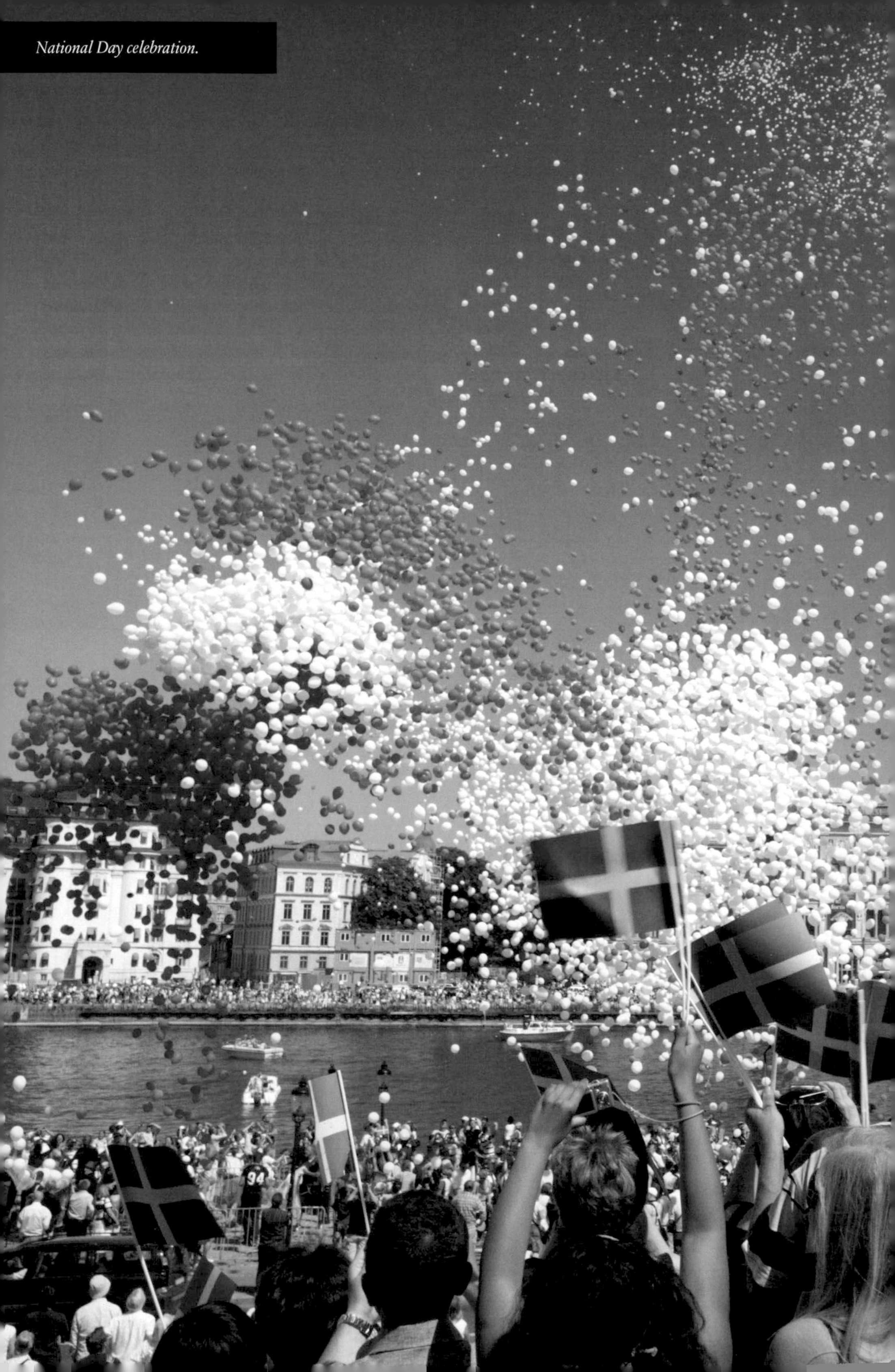

National Day celebration.

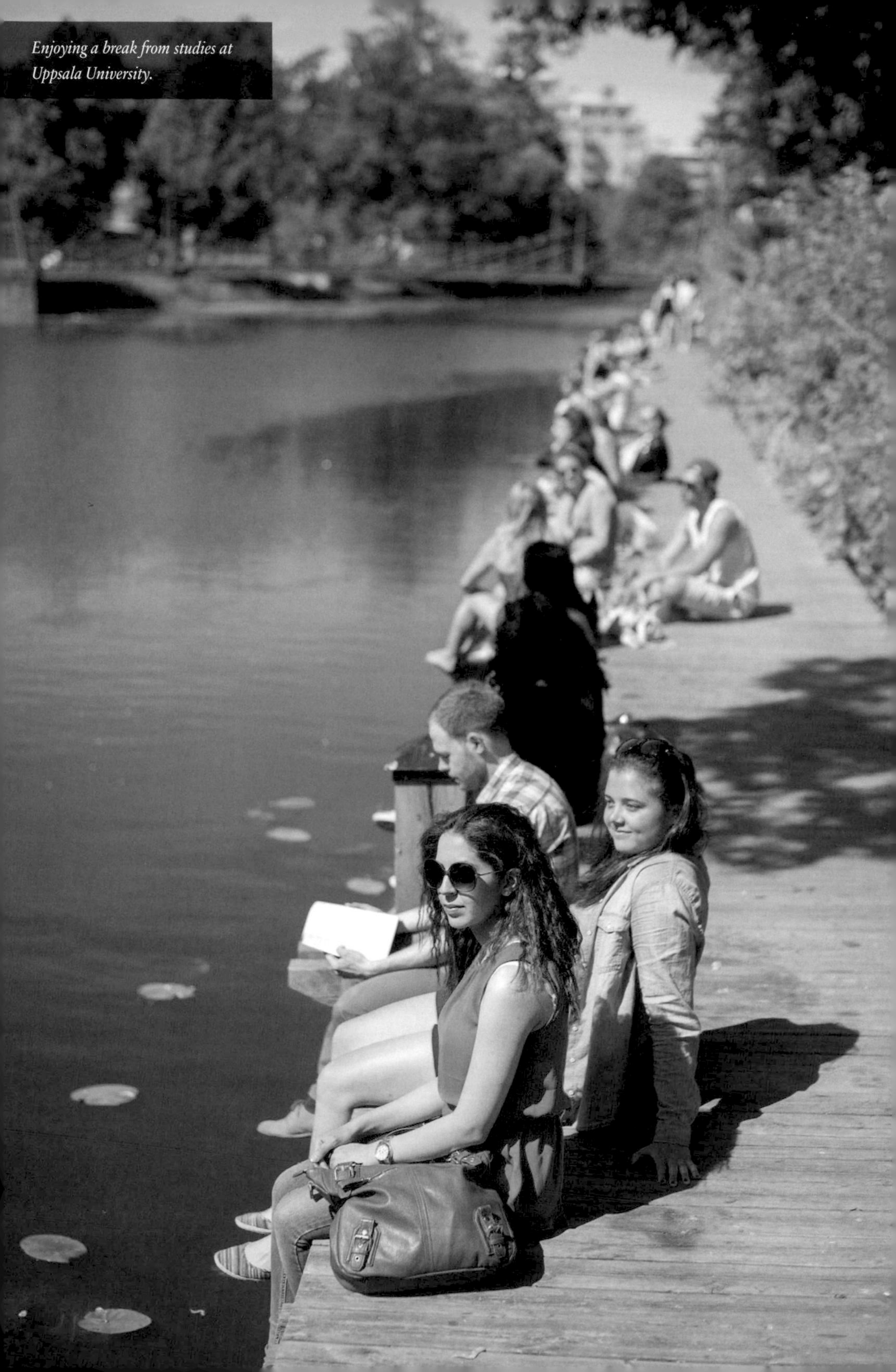

Enjoying a break from studies at Uppsala University.

THE SWEDES TODAY

Beneath the cool, reserved exterior, Swedes
harbour deep commitments to their country,
to nature... and to schnapps.

Most visitors know all about the stereotypical images of Sweden before they have even set foot in the country: blonde blue-eyed beauties, Arctic winters, pop sensation ABBA, reliable cars and flat-pack furniture. And while all of these images ring true, Sweden today is a country of growing cultural and social diversity; a country in which the traditional mingles with the ultra-modern and in which the political arena has been shaped by a strong democratic tradition that has helped to form the foundation of modern Swedish society.

At first glance, today's Swede may appear something of a paradox: as equally at home in the concrete jungle as on the grassy plains of Skåne, Swedes are a confusing blend of the urban and the provincial. They are sophisticated city-dwellers, yet are never happier than when they can kick off their shoes and go barefoot, swim naked and bond with nature.

A Midsummer kiss.

Breaking the ice

Swedes may often seem a little cool at first, reserved, even formal. But don't let this fool you. Underneath that composed exterior, beneath that unmistakable aura of self-satisfaction with all things Swedish, and below that tacit conviction that Swedes know best, they are essentially a warm and friendly people – particularly after one or two schnapps.

Indeed, there's nothing like schnapps for breaking the ice. Like vodka to the Russians or wine to the French, schnapps is part of the Swedish cultural tradition. Delicately flavoured with fruits or spices, a bottle of this perennial tipple is as likely to be found on the table at Midsummer as it is at Christmas. Every Swede can name his or her personal favourite.

Strangely, for a nation whose capital was home to some 700 inns by the 18th century (that's one for every 100 inhabitants at the time), Swedes have a rather uncomfortable relationship with alcohol.

The open and liberal approach to life, which once made them the envy of more conservative societies, makes the prevailing attitude towards drinking (surrounded as it is by taboos and much moral pontificating) all the more perplexing. Alcohol remains a contentious issue for modern-day Swedes. High prices and a state monopoly on retail sales conspire to create a sense of deprivation and prohibition – although prices have fallen considerably since Sweden joined the EU, standing 30 to 40 percent lower than in Norway.

It's not so strange, then, that when the chance to indulge presents itself, Swedes throw themselves into the fray wholeheartedly.

Strict etiquette

The drinking habits of the Swedes may appear excessive to some and perhaps even raise eyebrows, but when it comes to dining, their conduct is beyond reproach. Be it state banquets or family get-togethers, Swedes are sticklers for etiquette. From arriving punctually to the smallest of glances exchanged with other dinner guests – both before and after a toast is made – the formalities are upheld to the last drop of schnapps (see page 140). Yet Swedes will happily tuck into a crayfish feast, ripping off claws with their hands, clashing beer glasses in a toast, in a fashion oddly reminiscent of their Viking forebears.

National pride

As it did with their ancestors, the travel lust runs deep in the veins of 21st-century Swedes. Although they no longer plunder their southern neighbours, they remain very vocal when abroad. Swedes, like Americans, become intensely patriotic when they are away from the motherland.

School's out – graduation day.

SWEDISH CHARACTERISTICS

The big debate Though naturally inclined to avoid confrontation, nothing gets the ordinarily even-tempered Swede up in arms like a good debate. There is a popular television debating programme for every night of the week in which topical issues are addressed and opposing factions can air their differences in an open forum.

Thirst for coffee There is something that is even more Swedish than debating, and that is drinking coffee. Coffee-drinking is an intrinsic part of daily life and is, to all intents and purposes, a national pastime. The Swedes even have their own verb for it: *fika*. After the Netherlands and Finland, Sweden has the biggest group of coffee-drinkers in the world, with a per capita consumption rate of 1.4 cups of coffee a day. Meeting for coffee, or *fika*, is a popular way to socialise or celebrate, and rounding off a good meal, either at home or at a restaurant, would not be complete without it. A snug place in which to drink *fika* is crucial, as is a piece of cake, usually a cinnamon bun (*kanelbullar*).

All in line The Swedes' penchant for queuing is a reflex akin to the herding instinct; they form orderly queues everywhere from the bank to the water fountain.

Flags are a common sight. Indeed, on national holidays and during the summer it can certainly seem as though there are more Swedish flags flying than there are Swedish people. And the Swedes do not join in the cynical British and American habits of turning their national emblem into boxer shorts or carrier bags. Everywhere the gold cross on the blue background stands out against the sky: on buses, on buildings, and on the shoals of steamers and boats that crowd the country's lakes and waterways in high summer. But nowhere do you see the national flag more often than fluttering like

Why this hankering for the great outdoors? It's simple really. Little more than a century ago, Sweden was predominantly an agrarian society. Today this affinity for the land lives on, buried deep inside the Swedish soul. You can take the Swede out of the countryside, but you can't take

Lagom is a Swedish word that continues to defy translation but has come to stand for what is essentially the Swedish attitude to life – all things in moderation.

Swedes are at one with nature.

streamers on the long flagpoles outside the Swedish *stugor* – the small wooden cottages that are dotted all over the countryside.

The little red cottage is perhaps Sweden's most enduring image, and there's almost nothing that Swedes of all ages like better than to take off to their country hideaway for a weekend or for a longer spell during the summer months.

Affinity with nature

Swedes long for the often short summer months when they can cast their cares aside and get back to nature – an interest which is clearly in the genes, for every Swede can name at least 20 of the most common types of trees and berries with uncanny accuracy.

the countryside out of the Swede.

Ensconced once again in their natural habitat, at the least excuse Swedes will happily dress up in their national costume, weave wild flowers into their hair, and sing and dance to the old tunes. They have even developed their own particular style of Country and Western music known as *dansband musik*.

Music-making

Although most urbanites cringe at the very idea, *dansband musik* is still very popular among the rural population. When it comes to more mainstream music the Swedes have more than punched their weight on the international music stage. ABBA took the world by storm in the 1970s, followed by Roxette, Neneh Cherry, The Cardigans, The Hives and Ace of Base. More recently, music lovers have delighted in the electronica of The Knife, Fever Ray and Lykke Li, to the dance music of Swedish House Mafia and DJ Avicii. It's a pretty impressive record for a country with a population of just under 10 million.

Winter activities

Winters in Sweden are famous for their longevity, Arctic temperatures and the sun's prolonged absence. Swedes eagerly await the spring and the return of sunlight with all the excited antic-

Midsummer music.

ipation of children at Christmas. Like hibernating animals re-emerging after the long, dark winter, sun-starved Swedes are wont to stand on street corners, at crossings, at traffic lights, and any other spot they can find with a south-facing aspect, soaking up the first warming rays of spring.

But do not think that winter is entirely abhorrent to the Swedes. For many, the lengthy winter is a time for robust, outdoor activity. The Swedish people have learnt how to make the most of their winter, and winter sports are popular with Swedes of all ages: from long walks in the country to skiing in the mountains of Dalarna, from ice fishing in Jämtland to long-distance ice skating on Lake Vänern.

> *Arctic winters have yet to break the hardy Swedish resolve or bring the country to its knees. Streets are quickly snowploughed, roads salted, and life goes on.*

Sport

Unsurprisingly, considering its long winters, Sweden occupies a covetable position at major winter sports events. In the 1970s, slalom champion Ingemar Stenmark became a hero as big as Björn Borg in Sweden. Anja Pärson also brought glory to her country, with an Olympic gold medal, seven World Championship gold medals, and 42 World Cup wins. The Swedish national ice hockey team, its most successful export on the international sports scene, has won the World Championships nine times – most recently in 2013 as host nation, when it thrashed Switzerland in the final 5–1.

Present-day challenges

The 1990s were a time of change in which Sweden was forced to redefine itself and re-evaluate its global position in the face of new economic challenges and growing questions of social inequality. The high standard of living enjoyed by Swedes and their enviable cradle-to-the-grave social welfare system came under increasing pressure during the economic slump of the early 1990s. The complex question of how to maintain the social welfare system continues, with an ageing population with an increasing life expectancy expected to add further stress to the system in the future.

Immigration continues to influence the country's social, cultural and political landscape. The most recent challenge to Sweden has been the Syrian refugee crisis. Sweden takes in the second largest number of asylum seekers in the EU, with 74,000 asylum applications expected by the end of 2015.

While many Swedes flock to help the refugees, a significant number are discontented with, and increasingly vocal about, Sweden's open borders, with the anti-immigration Sweden Democrat party seeing an increase in support throughout 2015. Many newcomers to Sweden live in poverty, are socially excluded, and have difficulty finding work – the problem of social inclusion is one that Sweden has not yet solved.

FAMILY LIFE

Divorce rates are high and separation is
commonplace, yet the family remains
the backbone of Swedish society.

When it comes to gender equality, Sweden is among the most equal places in the world. Scattered along the benches in one of Stockholm's leafy green parks, you'll often see young dads quietly scanning the latest hockey results, while gently rocking a child's pushchair in which a toddler is sleeping peacefully.

It's true that men's attitudes in this country certainly seem to have changed a lot faster than they have elsewhere. The Swedish father can often be seen pushing a baby round the supermarket in a trolley and is no slacker when it comes to changing nappies either. But this was not always the case: and the modern approach to family life perhaps owes more to statutory intervention than genuine male enlightenment.

The new-look family

Family life in Sweden has undergone a dramatic change in the past 100 years. Large families were common in the agricultural society of 19th-century Sweden. Male and female roles were, as in many other countries, then and now, more clearly defined. Men were breadwinners and women wives, cooks and homemakers.

The Lutheran Church was a dominant influence on family life, and the institution of marriage was sacrosanct. It was a time when children born out of wedlock were a shame and disgrace to the mother, and a husband was perfectly within his rights to beat his wife, his children and his servants if he so wished. As late as the 1970s, single mothers were forcibly sterilised.

Of course, nowadays Swedes regard such social mores as prehistoric: now more than half of all children born in Sweden are born outside wedlock; many couples choose to remain unmarried, and divorce rates in Sweden are among the highest in the world. But this does

A summer evening swim.

not mean the end of the family unit. Quite the contrary, in fact.

Separation and divorce

Today the nuclear family takes many forms. Mr and Mrs Svensson with their 2.1 children are a thing of the past – now 20 percent of families are headed by a single parent. One child in every seven in Sweden currently lives in "mixed" families, in other words, families in which the parent granted custody is living with a new partner.

Couples who live together are known as *sambors*, an informal term derived from the word *samboende*, which means "living together". Cohabitation is something of a social institution and so widespread that it prompted the government to pass the Unmarried Couples Act in 1988. Although such couples are recognised by the law and their rights to property and inheritance are similar to those of married couples, there are still major legal differences that favour married couples; for example, only married couples can adopt children.

Divorce rates are high in Sweden: some 47 percent of marriages end in divorce nowadays. In 2013 there were 25,100 divorces in Sweden, the highest figure since 1975 (when the law changed to make divorce faster). Joint custody of children after divorce is automatic unless

Birth rates have fluctuated since the 1950s, but according to recent statistics the Swedish woman gives birth, on average, to 1.9 children, while the Swedish man fathers 1.7 children!

Studies show that the vast majority of all Swedish women continue to work until the child is born and that an increasing number of them return to work within a year of the birth.

Role reversal

Swedish family policy has been increasingly aimed at enabling both mothers and fathers to combine employment with parenthood. For

Twenty percent of Swedish families have a summer house.

opposed by one of the parents, providing a framework in which families can continue to function despite the breakdown of the marriage.

This can call for so much contact and co-operation between the former couple, that one wonders why they simply didn't stay together in the first place. Perhaps in recognition of this, the government introduced new financial initiatives in 2009 designed to help separated parents co-operate in caring for their children. Around 50 percent of children with recently divorced parents now alternate between both parents' homes.

Parenthood is nonetheless an important part of life in Sweden. Despite the fact that 77 percent of Swedish women are in the labour force, birth rates are among the highest in Western Europe.

women the real breakthrough came during the 1960s at the height of the women's movement. With the labour market in short supply, more women sought employment outside the home, which pushed the government to initiate extensive plans for public child care.

Then a series of laws affecting parental leave, which were passed in the early 1970s, began a process in which the concept of the mother being the natural choice to stay at home with the children became increasingly antiquated. Such steps have been part of a national plan to increase men's participation in the care of children at home and encourage them to take a greater share of parental leave. In 1985 women took 94 percent of the days that were allowed to them for their parental allowance, while men took just 6 percent. Today those figures have changed to 75 percent and 25 percent.

Day-care centres

Along with parental insurance and child allowances, good child-care amenities are a major cornerstone of Swedish family policy. Local authorities must guarantee a place at a day-care centre for all children between the ages of one and six. For many families these day-care centres, or *dagis* as they are known, have become a natural extension of everyday life, and they are

Gay couples have had legal "partnership rights" since the mid-1990s. In 2009, the law was changed to give same-sex couples the right to marry, in either a civil or religious ceremony.

dryers for the tenants' use, and in the courtyard a line of bicycles of all shapes and sizes, many with a child's seat attached to the back. Bicycles are a popular mode of transport for families with young children, particularly in the city, for the daily trip to and from *dagis*.

Swedes are outside whenever they can.

indispensable for working parents or parents who are both studying. Some parents have even got together to found their own *dagis*: in all such cases the standards are high, the equipment is good and the children are well looked after.

House and home

Just under half of Sweden's population lives in flats. In towns and cities flats are usually rented from local authorities or from housing associations. But living in a flat does not automatically mean poor housing. In fact, many flats have large, comfortable rooms in buildings that are often surrounded by gardens and play areas. Down in the basement you'll find an immaculate laundry room, with washing machines and

Around a third of Swedes live in rented accommodation, but the dream of home ownership is very strong, and most couples, once they start a family, want to buy their own home. Buying a house in Sweden, as in other parts of Europe, is an expensive business, and the country is currently experiencing an acute housing shortage. Over half of Sweden's local authorities say they do not have enough homes, and there is a 20-year queue for property in some areas of Stockholm, for example, the desirable Norrmalm area. The government plans to relieve the shortage by building 250,000 homes by 2020, with a focus on sustainable housing for people on moderate incomes.

Most Swedish houses are on the outskirts of towns and cities, with gardens and plots that back onto woods and meadows beyond. They thus fulfil two fundamental needs of Swedish people: the need for space and the need to be close to nature.

Caring for the elderly

"Mitt hem är mitt borg." Loosely translated, this means "My home is my castle", a sentiment that most people (regardless of their nationality) recognise and understand only too well.

The Swedish family home is a place where friends and family are entertained. Swedes love to get together to celebrate the big holidays, such as Christmas, Easter and Midsummer. But unlike

Making the most of a glorious winter's day.

many Southern European families, for example, one thing you won't find in the average Swedish home is more than two generations living together.

Despite fluctuations in birth rates, the number of elderly people in Sweden has continued to rise steadily, as it has in other countries in Europe. Around 18 percent of the total Swedish population is now more than 65 years old. As in the case of child care, care of the elderly was made the responsibility of the state under Swedish law.

The country's housing policy is aimed at helping pensioners to live in their own homes for as long as possible, and there are a number of care and housing options that are available to them when this is no longer feasible. Consequently, it is rare to find elderly people living with their families.

However, growing pressure on Sweden's social welfare system means that families are likely to come under increasing pressure to care for their elderly family members in the future.

Children are central

As with most families, whatever the country, family life in Sweden is centred on the children, their needs, daily routines and activities.

The day starts early, with the parents of small children taking them to the day-care centre on the way to work. Children of school age are encouraged to take part in extra-curricular activities, from sports to more cultural pursuits. A recent study showed that 29 percent of girls and 26 percent of boys aged 13 to 15 play a musical instrument. Parents, it seems, are constantly on their way to either *hämta* (pick up) or *lämna* (drop off) their offspring. *Hämta-lämna* is almost an activity in its own right and is certainly a way of life for busy Swedish families today.

Children and young people under 18 account for one-fifth of the Swedish population. Swedish children enjoy a good standard of living and most want for nothing. Brought up on a diet of literary free spirits like Pippi Longstocking, Swedish children are encouraged to think for themselves and question societal norms. In 1979, Sweden became the first country in the world to pass a law making beating or spanking children a criminal offence. This law is Sweden's expression of a very fundamental principle: respect for children.

Off to the country

On any Saturday morning in summer you are likely to spot a Swedish family setting out for the day, a small boat atop the Volvo or Saab, with a picnic basket filled with goodies in the back. Or perhaps they are off to spend a weekend out in the country at their cottage. More than 1.8 million Swedish families own a summer home.

When the Swedish family comes together to celebrate Midsummer, for example, despite that stiff wind and the growing threat of rain, they remain united in their collective obstinacy to sit out and dine alfresco. It matters not one iota that they are all forced to rush indoors, taking feast and table with them when the heavens finally open, or that they insist on going out again the minute it stops. All that matters is that they are together.

The Swedish family may take many forms in the 21st century, but it remains the backbone of modern Swedish society.

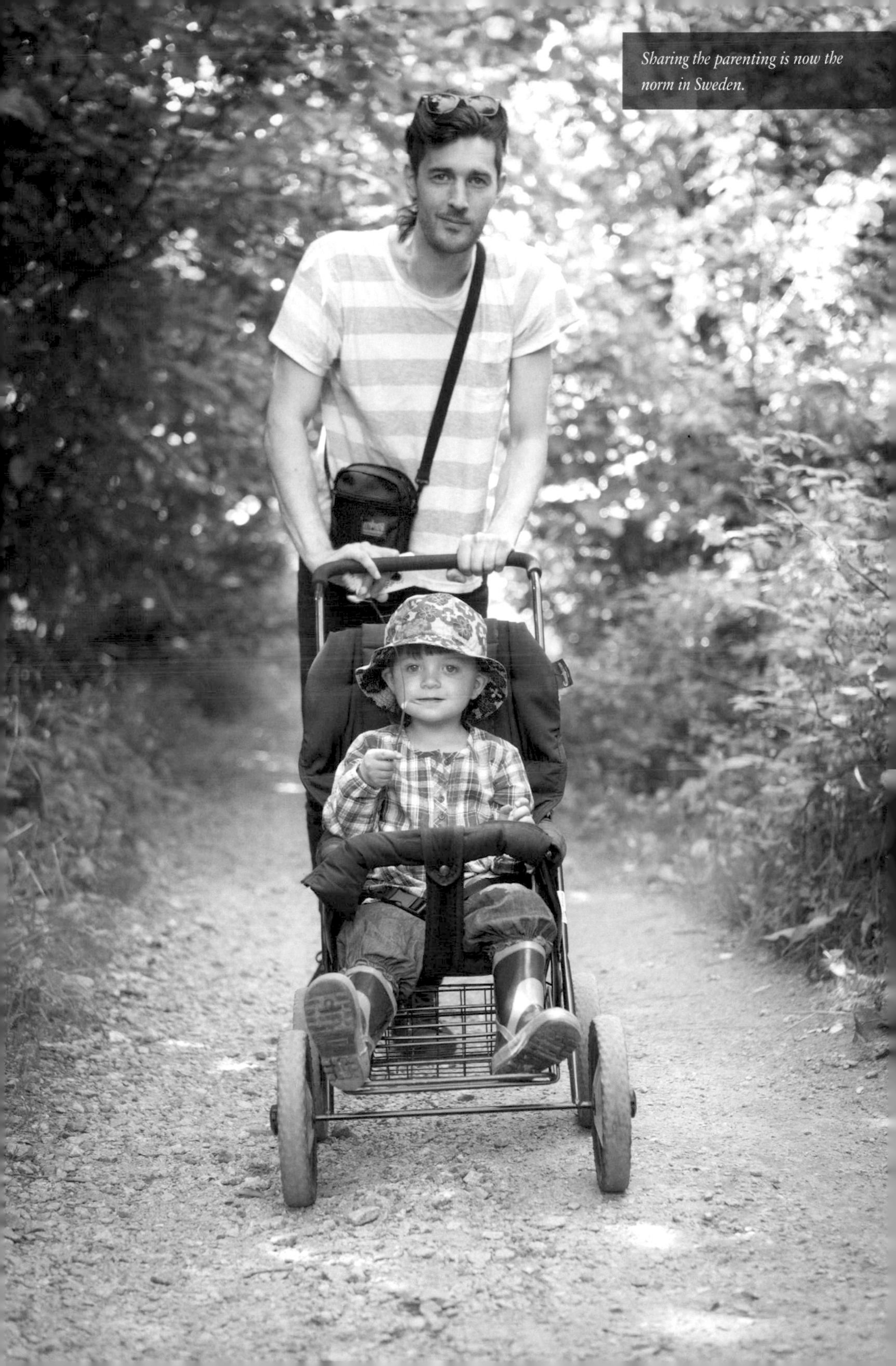

Sharing the parenting is now the norm in Sweden.

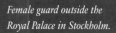
*Female guard outside the
Royal Palace in Stockholm.*

THE QUEST FOR EQUALITY

Class distinctions barely exist and egalitarian
policies affect all areas of life, but the struggle
for equality is far from finished.

A century ago, Sweden was divided by a
rigid class system. "Poverty, overcrowding,
starvation and sickness were common,"
wrote the historian Åke Elmér. "In contrast,
there was an upper class, which in magnificence
and wealth stood far above the great mass of
people." A small intermediate group of proper-
tied farmers, middle-class merchants and white-
collar workers "were objects of contempt to the
upper class and envy to the working class".

The elite of nobles, senior bureaucrats, military officers and professors were addressed with
the respectful *Ni* (you) and a tip of the cap by
common folk and they would respond with the
more familiar *du*. Railway carriages had three
different classes and boats four. Industrial workers normally toiled 12 hours a day, and office
workers a leisurely four or five.

Today, foreigners seeing the well-dressed
crowds and comfortable homes have difficulty
noting any class distinction. Swedes are near
the top of the international league of such indi-
cators of living standards as ownership of the
latest mobile phones, iPads and cars. Slums are
rare, and cases of individual hardship are widely
reported in the newspapers.

Swedes themselves have trouble identifying
the class origins of their fellow citizens. Many
of the signposts that denote class in Britain, for
instance regional or class accents in speech, as
well as the use of *Ni*, have largely disappeared.
The uniform high standard of the Swedish
press removes the distinction between the
readers of quality newspapers and tabloids that
exist elsewhere in Europe. Attending university at Uppsala and Lund, Sweden's two oldest
learning establishments, does not carry quite
the same cachet as being a graduate of Oxford
or Cambridge.

On the production line.

Only 25 years ago, most Swedes still identified with the working class; almost everyone now labels themselves middle-class. One
indication of this trend is the rapid change in
surnames. People are abandoning rural family
names – those ending in -son (Ericsson or Carlsson) – and adopting the Latinised surnames
(such as Beckérus or Glanzelius) of the 18th-
century learned classes, to create the impression that one's forbears enjoyed a higher social
status. Meanwhile, the Swedish nobility prefer
to hide their titles rather than flout them. And,
although any Stockholmer will tell you that the
Östermalm district is upper-class, Norrmalm is
middle-class and Söder is working-class, the differences have become increasingly blurred.

Narrowing the gaps

There are two main reasons why Sweden has so few class differences. One is the country's spurt of economic growth – the second fastest in the industrial world in the past century after Japan. And though it is relatively easy to spread the national wealth among a small population of 9.8 million, this has been aided by the policies of the long-ruling Social Democrats.

When the Social Democrats came to power in 1932, they eschewed the traditional socialist doctrine of nationalising industry. Instead, they concentrated on ensuring the even distribution through the 2000s, a pattern repeated across the Nordic countries.

Taxing for equality

Taxes in Sweden are used not only as a levelling device: they also pay for the country's extensive social welfare system, which guarantees that those such as the elderly, the sick and the disabled will not suffer a fall in living standards. Even the tax system itself is subject to egalitarian principles. Local taxes, which pay for the bulk of social services, do not vary greatly between regions.

Housing and education have also received gov-

In the mine.

of what is produced in the private sector and promoting equality of opportunity. In the long run the approach seems to have worked: a 1993 UN Development Programme report declared Sweden the world's most equal country.

Class differences also lessened as gaps in income narrowed, partly due to the equal pay for equal work policy championed by the trade unions. In the 1960s, skilled workers were paid 54 percent more than unskilled labourers. By the mid-1980s, this had narrowed to 25 percent. Differences in income are further reduced by steeply progressive tax rates. However, it appears that the trend towards financial equality may now be reversing: a 2011 OECD report found that the gap between rich and poor had increased

ernment attention in its push for egalitarian living standards. Before World War II, half of all Swedish urban households lived in tiny quarters with one room and a kitchen. The government embarked on a major construction programme that included rent subsidies to allow low-income families to live in more spacious dwellings. Unfortunately, housing construction has never kept pace with population movements to the cities. Paradoxically, central Stockholm's cramped flats, built a century ago to house the working class, have become highly desirable: Gamla Stan, a working-class slum 60 years ago, is today one of the city's most chic addresses.

The Social Democrats also felt that the education system they inherited maintained class barriers since it streamed pupils into "ability" groups.

An American-style comprehensive school system was gradually introduced, making it easier for the children of working-class families to gain admission to university. Sweden now has the highest proportion of working-class youth in Western Europe at university.

By the late 1960s, with progress made in achieving economic equality, the government turned its attention to promoting gender equality. A change in the tax rules, to require husbands and wives to file separate tax returns, encouraged the entry of women into the workforce since it penalised one-income households. Today, some 77 percent

> The principles of gender equality in Sweden are enshrined in the Swedish Constitution and upheld by the catchily-named Diskrimineringsombudsmannen (Equality Ombudsman).

women's rights to equal pay for the same jobs undertaken by men. Women's position in the workforce has been helped by government training programmes and projects to support women starting their own businesses. However, women, on average, still earn less than men, and the

In the lab.

of Swedish women are in the workforce, and of these 47 percent are in full-time work.

Not there yet

The political arena leads the way in promoting gender equality in Sweden. The Swedish government has a Minister for Children, the Elderly and Gender Equality. The 2015 Swedish parliament and cabinet consist of an equal number of men and women, making it the world's most equal parliament.

The good news doesn't end there. Pay differences between the sexes are much smaller in Sweden than in many other countries. By law, Swedish women have the right to employment in all areas, including the armed forces. Collective agreements on gender equality have protected

majority do relatively low-paid "women's" jobs, such as nursing and secretarial work.

The problem women face in securing influential positions underlines the fact that Sweden has by no means achieved the perfect egalitarian society. The country's sizeable immigrant population also has difficulties in achieving the same standards of living as native Swedes despite government attempts to assimilate them into society. And while income distribution is relatively even, the distribution of wealth is not, with Swedish industry controlled by an oligarchy of family dynasties.

As the distinction between male and female roles becomes fuzzier, one thing is clear: that even in a country as progressive as Sweden, the struggle for equality is not over.

Greeting ceremony for immigrants on National Day in Stockholm's City Hall.

THE IMMIGRATION DILEMMA

Sweden is no stranger to immigration, but growing cultural diversity and new economic realities raise the spectre of racism.

Immigration – and its natural counterpart, emigration – has been a vital part of Swedish history for centuries. Not only have people from a host of nations made Sweden their temporary or permanent home over the ages, but hordes of Swedes left their homeland during the second half of the 19th century and the early 20th century, choosing to start over, most often in America. Virtually every Swede has at least one distant relative who emigrated to the New World.

During the 1990s ex-ABBA members Benny Andersson and Björn Ulvaeus wrote *Kristina från Duvemåla*, a new musical based on a Swedish novel-series, *Utvandrarna (The Emigrants)*. The story behind this internationally acclaimed musical is well known to most Swedes: the trials and tribulations of Kristina and her family as they emigrated from southern Sweden to Minnesota in the United States. It is interesting that this beloved Swedish tale was revived for the stage at a time when the subject of immigration began to provoke very mixed emotions within political and social arenas. From being a topic of historical and genealogical interest, immigration has become a hot issue linked with unemployment, crime and urban problems.

Social housing in Stockholm.

Historical upheavals

Although there were colonies of German merchants and craftsmen in Sweden as early as the 13th and 14th centuries, major immigration started from neighbouring Finland in the 16th century. The first non-Nordic wave of foreign immigration can be traced to the arrival of Dutch merchants and Walloon smiths during the 17th and 18th centuries. Their numbers were few by present standards, but even today there are villages, settled by Walloons, where the colouring is darker than average, though their descendants have long since been integrated into the ethnically homogenous Swedish society that existed until recently.

The first wave of modern immigration during the 1930s didn't affect Sweden's homogenous nature as they were mostly ethnic Swedes who returned to escape the Depression in the United States. Also during the 1930s, immigrants outnumbered emigrants for the first time. In only two years since then, 1972 and 1973, has the outflow been larger than the inflow.

During and immediately after World War II, a different type of immigrant arrived, refugees

The Finn Connection

No two nations are more inextricably linked in past and present than Sweden and Finland.

At any given time, there are probably more Finnish immigrants in Sweden than there are ethnic Swedish-speaking Finns living in Finland. The Finns have been emigrating to (and emigrating from) Sweden since the 16th century. Today Finns make

Friendly rivalry at the Finland–Sweden Athletics Meet (Finnkampen).

up the largest group of foreign-born people in Sweden – there are around 158,000 of them – and Finnish is an official minority language.

Their lifeline is the ferry traffic dominated by the Viking and Silja Lines with the main routes operating from Stockholm to Helsinki and Turku in Finland. These ferries across the Baltic carry around eight million passengers a year between the two countries, often Finns on visits to relatives and friends in Sweden or Finland. Recent traffic growth has turned the ferry into a floating luxury hotel, with berths in cabins for 2,500-plus passengers, and a choice of restaurants, nightclubs and bars to idle away the time.

Finnish domination among Sweden's immigrant population can be traced back to the historical relations between the two nations and, more recently, to the common labour market that allow citizens of the Nordic countries to cross borders without the need of a passport or work permit. But the ratio between immigration and emigration for Finns in Sweden is now almost even, with as many people returning each year as arriving; this is because Finland's economy is at least as strong as Sweden's.

For more than 500 years, Finland was a part of Sweden, and the Finns were more often than not the footsoldiers for Swedish generals. The 16th and 17th century immigrants were usually retired soldiers who helped to settle wilderness areas in central and northern Sweden. Succeeding waves of Finnish immigrants worked in Sweden's mines and forests, then in its factories and hospitals.

Although the two nations have a distinctly inter-related history, their differences are quite significant. This is evident from the three Finnish groups that live in Sweden: Finns with Finnish as a mother tongue (Finnish Finns); Finns with Swedish as a mother tongue (Finnish Swedes); and Swedes with Finnish as a mother tongue (Sweden Finns).

Finnish Finns, the largest immigrant group, are the ones most likely to return to Finland after a while. They usually cross the Baltic Sea to work in Sweden, but even if they establish roots there, they never forget that Finland is at most a 10- to 12-hour boat ride away.

Finnish Swedes, on the other hand, are likely to stay for a long time. Their Swedish mother tongue is often a hangover from the time when Swedish was the official language in Finland and used for all bureaucratic purposes. Today, they are a minority in their own country, accounting for around 3.8 percent of Finland's total population, and they often have family ties to Sweden.

The Sweden Finns – the smallest group – usually live along the northern border between the two countries and strictly speaking cannot be counted as immigrants.

Despite these differences, all Finns living in Sweden unite in common cause at least once every year. They all shout for Finland during the two-day annual track and field meet, held alternately in Stockholm or Helsinki, that pits a Swedish national team against a Finnish national team. More often than not, the Finnish teams, both men and women, come out on top – which is no small achievement since Sweden has almost twice the population of Finland. It is a sweet victory for all Finns, who have had to put up with a "poor cousin" relationship with the Swedes for centuries.

from the war and suppression in the Baltic states and central Europe. They included 122,000 refugees from the other Nordic countries, including 60,000 Finnish children. Many Finns returned to Finland in the 1970s when the economy began to boom; those who stayed in Sweden have mostly become Swedish citizens.

In 1950, foreign nationals in Sweden totalled only 1.8 percent of the population, which was then a little over 6.9 million. A wave of newcomers arrived in the 1950s and 1960s, mainly "guest workers" who were invited by Sweden to work in its factories and help expand industrialisation. They came principally from Italy, the United Kingdom and West Germany. The 1950s and 1960s also brought immigrants from Hungary, Czechoslovakia, Greece, Poland, Turkey and Yugoslavia. Many other Nordic country nationals, especially Finns, also moved to Sweden in the late 1960s – a trend facilitated by the common Nordic labour market, which does not require work permits.

With changing economic conditions in the 1970s, Sweden sought to stem the tide of economic immigrants, but still took in humanitarian immigration and political refugees – including Chileans, other Latin Americans and Kurds. By 1975, the number of foreign settlers jumped to 5 percent of the population, which had increased to nearly 7.8 million. In 1979, a large wave came from Iran, including many Kurds. In the 1980s and 1990s came Palestinian refugees from war or terror in Lebanon, Iraqis, Africans from Somalia, Ethiopia and Kenya, and refugees from war in the Balkans. The Iraq War (2003–11) saw more dispossessed people arriving in Sweden.

Refugees from active war zones form a significant proportion of the incomers to Sweden today. Syria's brutal civil war began in March 2011, after which Sweden saw a large influx of Syrian refugees trying to escape the violence in their war-torn country. The number of refugees coming to Sweden nearly tripled between 2010 (12,130) and 2014 (35,642), with around 9 percent of them being unaccompanied children.

Immigration figures for 2014 showed that 1.6 million people out of a total population of 9.6 million were foreign-born, around 739,000 of whom have become Swedish citizens. Immigration's record year was 2014, when arrivals peaked at 127,000.

Racism rears its head

The later arrivals from the Middle East are not as welcome as the earlier immigrants. To some Swedes, they appear both too different, too many, and too unable to assimilate into Swedish society. Liberal Sweden, long the conscience of the world, now has its share of skinheads and other racists. Over the last 10 years, the far-right anti-immigration party the Sweden Democrats has risen from nowhere to achieve the support of around 18 percent of the country in 2015. Founded in 1988, the party first hit the headlines in the 2006 elec-

Friends enjoying fika-time.

tion when they won around 13 percent of the vote in some southern municipalities. In 2010, they crossed the threshold necessary to achieve parliamentary representation, winning 20 parliamentary seats, which increased to 49 seats in the 2014 election.

The problem of racism – and its by-product, discrimination – has surely been compounded by social and economic problems unknown to post-war Swedes until the late 1980s. Earlier in the 20th century, unemployment was virtually zero and immigration was essential because there were not enough Swedes to do all the work. By the mid-1990s, unemployment was over 10 percent, with immigrants making up a large number of those out of work. This problem was both caused and exacerbated by the global downturn in the economy and the critical situation of the Swedish national debt. Cutbacks were increasingly widespread as a result of both. The amount of money spent on social relief programmes regularly came under attack. A similar situation following the 2008 global downturn has seen Sweden facing a mix of economic troubles, increasing populations of immigrants, and the need to curb cradle-to-grave social welfare – central issues to problems of racism in Sweden.

Being looked after at a healthcare centre.

Unemployment – the number one problem facing immigrants – and discrimination are clearly interconnected. Language is the primary obstacle for most newcomers. And in a country where foreign names are easily detected, getting shortlisted for a job is difficult. The government has tried a variety of remedies, including temporary job projects *(praktik)* aimed at helping to introduce immigrants into the working community and to get the obligatory *betyg* (certificate or reference issued in recognition of all educational and employment endeavours).

Along with unemployment, poverty, social isolation and racism have led to increasing frustration for the newcomers. In May 2013,

> Since 2012, an increasing number of Roma people have been making their way from Romania to Stockholm, Gothenburg and Malmö. The government has promised to invest 52 million kronor to help integrate them into Swedish society.

racial tensions exploded into six nights of arson and violence during the Stockholm Riots. The riots began in the suburb of Husby, a predominantly immigrant suburb, apparently sparked by the police shooting of a 69-year old resident earlier in the month. Rioting then spread to other suburbs in the city, and to other Swedish towns.

Integrating new arrivals

Today's Sweden has some suburban housing projects where the population of migrants far outnumbers the ethnic Swedes. There are also schools with students from up to 100 different nations and day-care centres with almost as many nationalities as there are children.

Creating ghettos is not the intention, and Swedish authorities have made many successful attempts to integrate the new arrivals, including free Swedish lessons which may be taken with full pay during working hours. Many municipalities are concerned about isolated immigrant communities and are creating programmes to encourage integration and reduce unemployment. However, a survey held in March 2015 found that although six in ten Swedes think immigration is mainly beneficial to the country, the same number also feel that integration is not working well.

Even if they are not naturalised, incomers have some say in how their lives are run, with a right to vote in municipal and county council elections but not in national elections, provided they have been residents for three consecutive years. The percentage exercising this right, however, is far below the national average. This may be because some newcomers have never before participated in a democratic process, they do not understand the differences between the numerous political parties, they do not feel that the political parties are addressing their interests, or perhaps they hope that their stay in Sweden will not be permanent.

Mother and child in Husby, a district in Stockolm where the majority of the population are immigrants from the Middle East and Africa.

THE SAMI

For as long as anyone knows, the Sami have
lived in the wilderness of Lapland, dependent
on the seasons and their reindeer.

They call themselves "the people of the
eight seasons". They are the indigenous
Sami (once known as the Lapps), whose
homeland – Sápmi – stretches across the far
north of Norway, Sweden, Finland and the Kola
Peninsula in Russia. Altogether, the Sami total
around 80,000 people, with 20,000 living in
Sweden's most northerly province of Lapland –
a vast wilderness where nature and the reindeer
set the course of the year.

In the eighth century a Lombardian monk,
Paulus Diaconus, described the reindeer as a
strong and hardy little animal that was "not
unlike a stag". But that was not the first written
reference to the Sami and their country. Both
the Roman historian Tacitus and the later Procopius had already mentioned Scandinavia. It
is unlikely that Tacitus or Procopius visited the
far north, but perhaps Paulus Diaconus found
his way there: he describes the snow-covered
mountains, the dress of the Sami and the skill
with which they managed to move along. His
writings were also the first to mention the Midnight Sun and the winter solstice.

Traditional Sami knives.

Hard times

The eight seasons of Lapland start with spring-
winter in April, when there is still heavy snow
cover over the plains. The reindeer must dig
deep through the snow to find their most
important food, the lichens – reindeer lichen,
beard lichen which hangs heavily from the
branches of the trees, and the tangled horsehair
lichen, with its comic name of "nervous wreck".
Life is bleak for the reindeer. It is also a hard-
working time for the Sami who breed the reindeer and keep the herds in order.

But spring is in the air and soon they will
be trekking up the high mountains. The stags
have sloughed off their horns and the does are
carrying their young in their swollen bodies.
The sun arrives at the beginning of May. It is
the second season and the doe is ready to calve.

Before long the spring-summer is here. The
mountains blossom with Sami heather, globe
flowers, cloudberries and countless other species, offering a feast for the eye. The region is
botanically rich, and the life of its people provides a rare insight into a unique culture.

Modern methods

The reindeer keeper of today is very different
from his ancestors. In the past, even up until
the early decades of the 20th century, the whole
family accompanied the reindeer up into the

mountains, the draught-reindeer loaded with all the paraphernalia required for the summer, not least the *kåta* or cone-shaped hut to provide shelter. There the family would live out the summer, making the most of the endless daylight, storing up for the long nights of winter.

Today, only about 10 percent of the Sami are involved in reindeer herding. The herder families live in towns and villages and only the men care for the animals and follow the herd. To assist them, they have helicopters and scooters, mobile phones and all the modern-day equipment that makes communication easy. But,

Sami children in traditional costume.

SAMI GRIEVANCES

Historically, the Sami suffered discrimination from the Norwegians, Swedes, Finns and Russians, the repercussions of which are still being felt today. In 1998, Sweden formally apologised for wrongs committed against the Sami. But there is still conflict between the two over land use in the far north, with logging and drilling for minerals and oil clashing with the reindeer herders' way of life. In 2015, the Sami Parliament in Sweden appealed to the UN calling for an end to Sami discrimination, the repatriation of cultural artefacts, a halt to extractive industries in traditional Sami territory, and the granting of decision-making powers and self-determination to the Sami parliament.

despite modern life, the reindeer must stay up on the high mountains where the pasture is rich and a fresh wind blows, in contrast to the birch woods below where the heat is too oppressive for the animals and the insects sting ferociously.

After the spring-summer comes the summer proper, to bring the grazing land that the Sami dream about during the winter. Fresh and clean, the small streams babble and the lakes are rich in trout, Arctic char, and whitefish. Up here, there is not a single tree or bush to be seen.

Reindeer herding is not easy. The men must mark all the new-born calves with their own distinctive criss-cross sign and herd the deer, throwing their lassoes with a skill and accuracy that they learned in childhood games. Today, the lasso is made of nylon and, once the calf is caught, the men make a small incision in its ear with a sharp knife and thread the small pieces of flesh cut out on to a string or sinew. That way, all the men know how many calves are in the herd and which belong to each man.

All too soon the summer is gone and the men must drive their reindeer herds back down the mountains into the folds where they will be separated from each other before slaughter.

In the autumn-summer, the reindeer are fat from the fine pastures. The flies and mosquitoes are gone but heavy storms rage over the mountains and the plains. The knotty dwarf birch will soon shed its leaves but first it goes through a kaleidoscope of yellow, orange, red and brown, turning the mountains into a stunning sight.

Ritual slaughter

The slaughter begins and the ancient scene is like a feast from some primeval rite, full of the strong odours of sweat, blood and dung. The meat that the men do not sell fresh is frozen to become a delicacy – such as thin slices of reindeer fried with onions, mushrooms and cream.

Now it is autumn-winter, the Northern Lights are blazing and the aurora carries frost in its colours. The days grow perceptibly shorter and, when mist and storms cover the stars, the nights are black. On the moors, the reindeer huddle together to keep warm along the edges of the birchwoods where the snow is loose and the lichens are still moist and full of nourishment.

Today, beasts of prey are little danger to the Sami. The wolf is almost extinct in Sweden, the bears hibernate, and the wolverines no longer lie in wait to lap the reindeers' fresh blood.

Traditional market fairs

In every way, the life of the Sami has changed in modern times. It is only for festivals and ceremonial occasions that they put on the knee-length costume, trimmed with handwoven ribbons in red and yellow. But the tradition of handicrafts continues strongly and the best place to see it is at one of the big market fairs at Jokkmokk. The Sami make use of any natural materials from tree bark to reindeer horn.

Visitors come not just from Sweden but from all parts of the world to meet the Sami at this traditional fair. The Jokkmokk fair is unique in that

The kolt, the traditional Sami outer garment, comes in bright shades of red, yellow, blue and green. Those in the know can tell which region a person comes from by their kolt, as decoration differs from area to area and family to family.

In 1732, the botanist Carl von Linné (Linnaeus) made an expedition to Lapland, and some years later a copper engraving was made of him in Sami dress, with the frock, bottle-nosed boots, and the typical Sami accessories. In his hand he

Souvas is the Sami word for "smoked" and it is traditionally reindeer meat.

it has only genuine Sami handicrafts such as the beautifully designed knives, the bowls and baskets plaited from the thinnest root fibres, pieces of carved wood, and ribbons and woven fabrics (see page 282).

Reindeer delicacies

In Jokkmokk, you can also taste all the delicacies associated with the reindeer – the pure Lapland *renkok*, made of marrow bones and shredded liver and served with broth and blood dumplings; or *renklämma*, a thin slice of unleavened bread shaped into a cone and filled with slices of smoked reindeer. The fairs are in August and February, but all over Lapland there are delicacies to taste and Sami handicrafts to buy and to view in museums.

holds a drum with mythological signs, now considered one of the most precious possessions for any Sami. But the mythological signs are another story – a tale from ancient times, from the special religion that belongs to the Sami.

Finding a stronger voice

Independence has always been important for the Sami, and since 1986 they have had their own national anthem and national flag. In 1993, they also acquired their own democratically elected parliament which meets three times a year in Kiruna, with 31 members elected from six parties. Its influence is limited and it acts as an administrative authority under the control of the Swedish government.

ART IN SWEDEN

From medieval times Sweden has embraced artistic
and architectural styles from the Continent – and
made them distinctly its own.

The rich and varied history of Swedish art is highly indebted to the royal and aristo-cratic patronage that fostered many of the most significant developments. Artistic styles brought from the Continent were adapted to Swedish taste and climate, giving them a distinct Swedish quality.

Picture stones

Artistic production in Sweden reaches back to the magnificent rock carvings of the Bronze Age (1500 BC–500 BC). These carvings, known as *hällristningar*, are to be found throughout the southern coastal areas of Sweden, but the richest concentration can be seen in the province of Bohuslän, on the west coast. Featuring images of ships, battles, hunting, fishing and farming scenes, and mating couples, these simple, curvilinear carvings convey a wealth of information about daily living as well as religious beliefs.

Picture stones, images carved with a figural and circular-ornament style on to raised stones (as opposed to the rocky coastlines where the *hällristningar* are found), are the most prominent artefacts remaining from the Iron Age. The majority of surviving picture stones (nearly 400) are on the island of Gotland.

By the 5th century, Scandinavian art is principally defined by the animal-ornament style, a flowing, interlacing abstract design featuring fantastic animal heads and other body parts. Examples are found on ship carvings and portable metal objects, such as brooches and other pieces of jewellery, which constitute most of the art objects remaining from this period.

Ecclesiastical architecture

After the baptism of King Olof Skötkonung, *c.* AD 1000, Christianity became widespread

Runic stone with carved inscription, Uppsala.

CARVED IN STONE

Sweden has around 2,500 of Scandinavia's 3,000 rune stones. Most were raised as memorials to dead kinsmen, around 10 percent of whom died *i wikingu* – on a Viking raid. Others boast of achievements such as the building of a bridge or causeway, or simply state that the raiser was clever, skilful or just plain powerful. Most are from the 11th and 12th centuries, when Sweden was being converted to Christianity. They are a blend of the pagan animal-ornament style combined with the cross. Inscriptions run around the contours of the stone identifying those who erected it, their relatives, and the names of the carvers.

Portrait painter Alexander Roslin (1718–93), admired for his skilled rendition of textiles as well as facial expressions, is one of Sweden's most celebrated artists.

in Sweden. This date also marks the start of the medieval period in Sweden (1000–1520), a time in which, not surprisingly, ecclesiastical art dominated – from the church buildings themselves, to the carvings on them and the sculptural items common to most churches (such

Sweden's prevailing weather. Another unusual feature, again compared with France, is the conspicuous use of brick for building churches.

Court patronage

Beginning with the court of Gustav Vasa (1523–60), the first king to consolidate the Swedish monarchy, art in Sweden experienced a period of dynamic development. The increased power within the Swedish court coincided with the Renaissance, a time when throughout Europe secular art began to supplant religious art. In Sweden, the most notable artistic production

Drottningholm Palace, a baroque masterpiece.

as fonts and triumphal crucifixes). Stylistically, most of the art and architecture of this period is an adaptation of styles imported from England, France and Germany. Many fine examples of works, especially church murals, remain from this period, thanks to the lack of iconoclasts within the Lutheran Reformation.

The first cathedral in Sweden was built in 1103 in Lund, Skåne (which was in Danish hands until 1658). It was replaced in 1145 by the current building, a Romanesque structure clearly influenced by German and Lombardic architecture.

Swedish Gothic architecture, as seen in the cathedrals in Uppsala and on Gotland, is not as flamboyant and ornate as that found in France. This is partly due to problems inherent with

consisted of building castles (Gripsholm, Vadstena, Kalmar) and decorating them. Royal portraiture, often produced by foreign artists, dominated Swedish painting from the 16th to the 18th centuries, with many of the finest examples kept at the National Portrait Gallery, in Gripsholms Slott (castle).

Swedish baroque

During the Thirty Years' War (1618–48) Sweden experienced a lengthy period of prosperity. Queen Kristina (1644–54), a tremendous patron of the arts, commissioned numerous building projects and imported several artists from abroad. It was during Kristina's reign, for example, that work began on Riddarhuset (House of

Nobility), in central Stockholm, which is one of the finest structures in the city.

Tessin the Elder and the Younger, a father-and-son team, were two of the most gifted architects of the 17th and 18th centuries, and Drottningholm Palace was one of their most important undertakings. The structure as a whole remains the finest example of Swedish baroque art.

French influences

King Gustav III (1771–92) was an avid Francophile and a devoted supporter of the arts. Not surprisingly, French culture and style heavily

where they practised *plein air* painting. While few Swedish artists really took up Impressionism per se, some of the techniques of the genres – such as using a looser brushstroke, asymmetrical composition and a brighter palette – found their way into a number of the artists' works.

A touch of romanticism

Upon returning to Sweden in the last decade of the 19th century, many artists embraced Swedish themes. This period is usually defined as National Romanticism. Back in Sweden, Carl Larsson's style changed in favour of much more

Self-Portrait (In the New Studio), by Carl Larsson (1912).

influenced Sweden in the 1700s. Nonetheless, even the most elaborate Rococo-inspired Swedish art is tempered in comparison with its French and Italian counterparts. The lack of exuberance is undoubtedly due, in part, to the Lutheran background, which contributed to a starker aesthetic than that of the Catholic southern countries of Europe. The somewhat austere aesthetics of Protestant Germany and Holland also had a restraining influence.

French art continued to inspire Swedish painters during the 19th century. In the early 1880s, several Scandinavian artists – including Carl Larsson, Karl Nordström and Richard Bergh – travelled to France, spending their summers at Grèz-sur-Loing, not far from Fontainebleau,

AT HOME WITH THE ARTISTS

The homes of Carl and Karin Larsson at Sundborn, and Anders Zorn in Mora, both in Dalarna, are open to the public. The picturesque house at Sundborn is a showcase of the talents of Larsson and his wife Karin. She inherited the house in 1888, and together they created the simply furnished family home that inspired so much of 20th-century Swedish design. The preserved rooms, featuring Carl's artwork and Karin's textiles, are easily recognisable from his paintings. Zorn's 19th-century home is very different – larger and more richly decorated. It houses his collection of art and applied art, and there is a museum of his own work in the grounds.

defined and curvilinear lines and strong, dark contours. Anders Zorn arrived later in Paris and became one of the leading portrait painters for the wealthy in France, Britain and the United States for a time. When not painting portraits, he often painted scenes from his native Dalarna and female nudes in landscapes.

Colourists of the 20th century

In the 20th century, many Swedish artists were proponents of the various "isms" imported from the Continent. They included Isaac Grunewald and Sigrid Hjertén (Fauvism), Otto Sköld (Cub-

Glassblowing is an art at Kosta Boda.

ism), and the Halmstad Group (Surrealism). During the 1930s, several artists based on the west coast painted with brilliant colours inspired by Fauvism and Expressionism; and although they were never a real school, they became known as the Göteborgkolorister (Göteborg Colourists).

Following World War II, Olle Bonniér and Olle Bærtling were among the adherents of Geometric Abstraction. Oyvind Fahlström, influenced and stimulated by European and American Neo-Realism of the 1950s and 1960s, developed a highly unique style, and his art has gained new interest in Sweden.

Though Sweden was not a spawning ground for any very influential art movements of the 20th century, Stockholm became an important

player in the international art scene following the opening of the Moderna Muséet in 1958.

The contemporary art scene in Sweden has plenty of participants (if not many venues for presentation), and the work of women artists, including Charlotte Gyllenhammar, Annika von Hausswolff and Lena Mattsson, is becoming increasingly prominent. Journals and websites follow and analyse the latest trends.

Touring the museums

Nationalmuseum: The National Museum of Fine Arts, Sweden's largest art museum, is closed for extensive renovation until 2017. The original building is beautifully situated on the water in Stockholm in a building modelled on Florentine and Venetian architectural design.

The museum grew from private royal collections, starting with the works gathered by King Gustav Vasa at Gripsholm Castle in the 16th century. Today, the collection includes paintings, sculpture, decorative arts, drawings and prints from the Middle Ages to the 21st century, including works by artists such as Rembrandt, Goya, Degas and Gauguin. In addition to the strong holdings of Swedish 18th- and 19th-century painting, there are fine examples of Dutch 17th-century art and French 18th-century art. Objects from the decorative arts departments, including Scandinavia's largest collection of china, glass, Swedish silver and furniture, span five centuries.

At the time of writing, the museum had opened two temporary venues, at The Royal Academy of Fine Arts and Kulturhuset Stadsteatern. These were showing small, selective exhibitions based on some of the museum's holdings.

ART AND CRAFT TRADITIONS

Swedish glass-making is world-renowned. The centre of this 250-year-old tradition is the Växjö area in southern Sweden, where artists continue to produce glass of the very finest quality. When travelling outside the major cities, the art most often encountered – in craft shows and *hemslöjd* (craft) shops – is handicrafts ranging from wooden cheeseboards, butter knives and serving trays, to handwoven textiles, straw decorations, hand-smithed candlesticks and the distinctive *Dalahäst* (Dala horse). In many of the crafts, simplicity of design is combined with high-quality materials. The same aesthetic principles inspire most of the contemporary furniture production.

The museum's finer works (Rembrandt's *The Conspiracy of the Batavians under Claudius Civilis* (1661–2), and Swedish works including Alexander Roslin's *The Lady with the Veil* (1768), Anders Zorn's *Midsummer Dance* (1897), and Carl Larsson's famous frescoes were in storage, and will be back on display when the original building is reopened.

Moderna Muséet (Stockholm): The Modern Museum opened in 1958 and, under director Pontus Hultén, soon became an important site for exhibitions and artistic exchange. A new building designed by Rafael Moneo opened in 1998, giving the museum the opportunity to

in 2009 in Malmö in a former electricity plant building, whose soaring turbine hall houses changing exhibitions. The museum displays its own contemporary classics, supplemented by selections from the Stockholm museum's rich 20th- and 21st-century collections.

Magasin III (Konsthall, Stockholm): This slightly out-of-the-way, privately funded exhibition space opened in 1987 in an old warehouse in Stockholm's Frihamn (Free Port). Exhibitions feature contemporary art, and the art centre has its own permanent collection of more than 600 works, many of which were made especially for the gallery.

Stockholm's metro is the longest art gallery in the world.

1998, giving the museum the opportunity to expand, both physically and functionally, and become, once again, a major force on the art scene. The building on Skeppsholmen reopened after major renovation work, and now houses the Museum of Architecture and Design.

Moderna's collection is strong in American 1960s art, and includes many pieces of early modern art. Acquisitions of more recent works have a more marked Scandinavian accent. Works of particular note include Rauschenberg's *Monogram* (1955–9) and *Mud Muse* (1971), as well as Picasso's *La Source* (1921) and Ulf Rollof's *Kylrock* (*Cold Mantle*, 1989; see page 170).

Moderna Muséet : Following the success of the Stockholm museum, a branch was opened

Waldemarsudde: On the island of Djurgården in central Stockholm, the former home and studio of Prince Eugen is now a museum featuring art that he both created and collected, mostly from the latter half of the 19th century. The waterside setting and gardens are attractive and inviting. (see page 175).

Konstmuseum (Göteborg): The collection at Göteborg Museum of Art (founded 1861) owes its existence entirely to the donations of private citizens rather than to royal patronage. Some of the most important works in the collection are of Scandinavian art from the end of the 19th century and were donated by Pontus and Göthilda Furstenberg. The Hasselblad Centre for photography forms part of the museum.

TRADITIONAL SWEDISH INTERIORS

Recent years have seen a revival of interest in traditional Swedish style, with its emphasis on simplicity, light and natural materials.

The very restraint of Swedish interior design which makes it so appealing to modern tastes was born from the restrictions imposed by the country's climate and economy. Since sunshine is scarce during the winter, the Swedes have generally sought to maximise light in their rooms, for example by choosing pale colours for the walls.

Since so much of the country is forested, wood prevails in Swedish interiors rather than marble and stone. Similarly, the rich tradition of painted decoration has traditionally provided a cheap substitute in poorer homes for costly wallpapers and multi-coloured, patterned fabrics.

Swedish interiors have been subject to fluctuations of fashion and the income of their owners, but there seem to be certain constant features of Swedish style – a lack of clutter and a love of symmetry and clean lines. Perhaps the purest embodiment of these principles can be seen in the interiors dating from the short reign of Gustav III (1771–92). Gustavian style was really a pared-down form of Neoclassicism, in which gilt was replaced by a more restricted palette dominated by greys, blues, creams and yellows. The simple elegance of that period continues to inspire decorators today, particularly those many people who are buying and restoring traditional country cottages.

Several firms make excellent reproduction antique furniture. This chest of drawers by IKEA displays the clean lines of more traditional pieces.

Many people are painstakingly restoring old homes: the bedrooms in this 17th-century hunting lodge have walls hung with the original handpainted wallpaper.

The woodwork in this country kitchen has been painted in the fresh colours traditional in rural cottages in Sweden.

It is Evening, Good Night, by Larsson (now at Sundborn).

CARL LARSSON AT HOME

The artist Carl Larsson (1853–1919) and his wife **Karin** were instrumental in reviving interest in traditional Swedish decoration and crafts at the turn of the 20th century. They and their eight children lived in a wooden farmhouse in the province of Dalarna, where they created the series of exceptional interiors that Carl recorded in his watercolours.

His illustrated books *Ett Hem* (*At Home*, 1899) and *At Solsiden* (*On the Sunny Side*, 1910), which were hugely popular in Sweden and elsewhere, promoted a traditional style that was given a modern, idiosyncratic twist by the Larssons' absorption of the ideas of the English Arts and Crafts movement and of country crafts. While the emphasis was placed on simplicity, embellishment was added in the form of embroidery, folklore-inspired textiles and hand-painted friezes or panels. Some of the fine 18th-century furniture the Larssons had inherited was painted in bright colours inspired by rural houses rather than using the original, more muted palette.

The Larssons' home at Sundborn is now a museum (see page 257).

At Sundborn, Carl and Karin Larsson combined the old and the new. In the studio, for example, Gustavian chairs were painted bright red.

Stencilling has been a popular method of decoration since the Middle Ages. This pattern was stencilled directly onto a wooden wall.

An essential feature of the traditional Swedish room, the tall tiled stove, kept occupants warm during the bitter winter months.

WORDS, MUSIC AND CELLULOID

Strindberg, Bergman, Garbo... Sweden occupies
a central place in Europe's cultural life, and
continues to champion press freedom.

For a sparsely populated country on the northern edge of Europe, Sweden has given the world an impressive legacy in literature, film, theatre, music and the media. From Sweden emerged the imposing literary figures of Selma Lagerlöf and August Strindberg; beloved children's author Astrid Lindgren; world-famous film director Ingmar Bergman; luminous female movie stars like Greta Garbo and Ingrid Bergman; and the celebrated pop group ABBA.

Less well known is that Sweden, in 1766, was the first country to establish freedom of the press, and the nation has continued zealously to protect the public's right to information and the role of journalist as watchdog. This is particularly appreciated by Swedes, who are among the world's most avid newspaper buyers.

The government generously subsidises the arts, so ticket prices are reasonable. The Royal Opera, the Royal Dramatic Theatre, the Swedish National Touring Theatre and the Royal Philharmonic Orchestra are entirely publicly funded; private sponsorship of the arts is rare.

Traditional Swedish folk dance.

The legacy of the Theatre King

King Gustav III, the "Theatre King", set up the Swedish national theatres in Stockholm in the late 18th century to provide venues for the performance of dramatic arts in Swedish. Until then, opera and drama were performed at the court theatre in their original languages, Italian and French. Kungliga Teatern (The Royal Theatre, now known as the Kungliga Operan, or The Royal Opera) was founded in 1773. In 1788, Kungliga Dramatiska Teatern (the Royal Dramatic Theatre or Dramaten), opened its doors.

The late Ingmar Bergman directed productions of Strindberg and other classics at Dramaten. Lars Norén has since taken over Bergman's former position as Sweden's national dramatist. A poet and prose writer in the 1960s, Norén cemented his reputation as director with the 1980 trilogy *Modet att Döda (The Courage to Kill)*, a claustrophobic middle-class drama reminiscent of Chekhov.

In 1842 the crown's theatre monopoly in Stockholm was abolished, and new theatres raised their curtains. Several municipal theatres opened in the 1920s and 1930s, followed by the advent of regional theatres in the 1960s and 1970s. Today, there are three national and more than 20 regional/municipal theatres in the country. With economic cutbacks, growing commercialism, and competition from electronic media and other leisure activities, theatre in Sweden is less prominent than it has been, but still vibrant.

Performances, however, are nearly always in Swedish. For a taste of the Swedish dramatic scene, try the internationally respected Folk Operan (Swedish Folk Opera) or the Drottningholm Theatre productions of late Baroque plays and ballet. The theatre is part of the royal family's permanent residence, on an island in Lake Mälaren, which itself is well worth a visit.

In 1994, Göteborg Opera opened in its new home by the harbour, giving Sweden another major house for classical productions, includ-

Ingmar Bergman, playwright and film producer.

ing many by Swedish composers, such as Wilhelm Peterson-Berger's *Arnljot* and Ingvar Lidholm's *A Dream Play*, first presented in 1992.

Musical heritage

As with the visual arts, royal patronage and generous appropriation from the Continent were crucial to the history of music in Sweden. The country's best-loved poet, composer and musician is probably Carl Michael Bellman, whose witty lyrics immortalised 18th-century life in Stockholm. Like so many successful Swedish artists, he found his greatest patron in Gustav III. His songs are still very much alive today.

National holidays and folk festivals provide opportunities to enjoy Swedish folk dancing and music. The violin is the most common folk instrument, with fiddlers providing the rhythm for the polka, waltz, *schottishe* or *polkette*.

Following in ABBA's footsteps, other successful musical exports have included Roxette, Ace of Base, Neneh Cherry, The Cardigans, The Hives and José González. More recently, Swedish House Mafia and Avicii have had huge international success. Singer/model Lykke Li won acclaim for her second album *Wounded Rhymes*, while grunge-influenced singer-songwriter Tove Lo reached a huge online fan base, with her song *Habits (Stay High)* being viewed 150,000,000 times in two years. Fever Ray provided the dark theme tune for the popular TV series *Vikings* (2013–).

Sweden hosts several music festivals. At Musik vid Siljan (Music by Lake Siljan), held in the first week of July, ranges from organ concerts to jazz. The biggest jazz festivals, in Ystad (August), Stockholm and Umeå (both October), draw international names. In 2015 Florence & The Machine headlined the massive Way Out West festival, which draws crowds of around 20,000 to Gothenburg in August. Even bigger is Bråvalla, based in Norrköping, which sells around 50,000 tickets every summer. The newer "Summerburst" festival takes place in May/June, rocking Göteborg and Stockholm with house, electronica and explosive firework displays.

Great film-makers

In around 1920, during the silent-film era, Sweden was among the leading cinematic nations of the world. Directors Victor Sjöström and Mauritz Stiller made several films which were regarded as masterpieces at the time and are now considered classics. Some are based on books by Selma Lagerlöf, such as *Körkarlen (The Phantom Carriage)* and *Herr Arnes Pengar (Sir Arne's Treasure)*.

This age of greatness was brief. Sjöström and Stiller went to Hollywood and took with them a rising star named Greta Garbo. When talking pictures arrived in the 1930s, Swedish films took a rather provincial turn. During World War II, directors such as Alf Sjöberg and Hasse Ekman created more serious, artistic work. Following the war, the modern festival system heightened demand for artistic and prestigious theatre. Documentary film-maker Arne Sucksdorff won international praise; Sjöberg won a 1951 prize at Cannes for his production of Strindberg's classic, *Fröken Julie (Miss Julie)*.

Sweden became the subject of global cinematic interest again with the rise of Ingmar Bergman (1918–2007), director of over 60 films and documentaries, including masterpieces such as *The Seventh Seal* and *Wild Strawberries*, and his three Oscar-winning films *The Virgin Spring*, *Through a Glass Darkly* and *Fanny and Alexander*.

For such a small country, Swedish cinema punches above its weight internationally. Lasse Hallström's touching film *My Life as a Dog* was nominated for two Academy Awards in 1988. One in ten Swedes saw Lukas Moodysson's *Show Me Love (Fucking Åmål)* at the cinema. His next films *Together (Tillsammans)* and *Lilya 4-ever* were also big hits at home, as well as gaining critical acclaim on the international film-festival circuit. Tomas Alfredson directed eerie vampire drama *Let the Right One In (Låt den rätte komma in)* in 2008, remade in America as the less compelling *Let Me In*. The most recent Swedish Oscar winner is Malik Bendjelloul, who won Best Documentary in 2013 with *Searching for Sugar Man*.

Cinema audience in Göteborg.

INGMAR BERGMAN (1918–2007)

Born in 1918, the son of a clergyman, Ingmar Bergman was associated throughout his career with the Swedish film industry. He first came to public attention with the script he wrote for *Torment* (1944). His own productions, made with a small company of devoted actors, including Liv Ullman, Bibi Andersson and Eva Fröhling, are often concerned with questions of faith and belief. They include *Smiles of a Summer Night* (1955); *Seventh Seal* (1956); *Wild Strawberries* (1957); *Persona* (1966); *Shame* (1968); *Cries and Whispers* (1971); *Scenes from a Marriage* (1973); *Face to Face* (1976); *Autumn Sonata* (1978); and *Fanny and Alexander* (1981), his last feature-length motion picture. Bergman remained active, writing film scripts and directing productions at Stockholm's Royal Dramatic Theatre. He wrote an autobiography, *The Magic Lantern*, followed by *My Life in Film*, and *Good Intentions*, a depiction of his parents' love affair, marriage, and life together until Bergman's birth. The film version, directed by Bille August, won the 1992 Golden Palm award in Cannes. A year later, Bergman's son Daniel directed *Sunday's Child*, a film that portrays "young Ingmar's" relationship to his father, taking up the theme of childhood and family where *Good Intentions* left off. Bergman's work offers a very personal perspective on what is Swedish, and yet universal.

Three major film production studios are based in Luleå, Ystad and Trollhättan (affectionately known as "Trollywood"), and the Svenska Filminstitutet (Swedish Film Institute), which preserves Sweden's filmic past and promotes new works, is well funded by the state and by a ten percent levy from box-office sales. As in other countries, though, TV, DVDs, Blu-ray and online viewing have encroached on the popularity of the cinema. Since the mid-1950s, the number of cinema visits has dropped from 80 million to 16.3 million a year in 2014.

Selma Lagerlöf, great Swedish writer.

The star quotient

Sweden's female movie glamour queens are perhaps most associated with the country's cinematic history. The greatest was Greta Garbo, who made silent films in Sweden before going to Hollywood. The "divine" Miss Garbo came to exemplify the idea of the movie star for decades, with such films as *Anna Karenina* (1927 and 1935), *A Woman of Affair* (1929), *Queen Christina* (1934) and *Camille* (1937). Another Swedish-born movie goddess was Ingrid Bergman. She went to Hollywood in 1939 to play opposite Leslie Howard in an American version of the Swedish film *Intermezzo*, which made her a star. In Hollywood she shared top billing with Humphrey Bogart in *Casablanca*, Gary Cooper in *For Whom the Bell Tolls* and Gregory Peck in *Spellbound*.

Other Swedish film stars who have come and gone over the years include Lena Olin, Max von Sydow and Stellan Skarsgård. Four of Stellan's eight children are also actors – most famously Alexander, who played Eric Northman in the HBO series *True Blood*; and Gustaf, who appears as Floki in History's *Vikings*.

The literary century

The 20th century was the defining period of Swedish literature, with the transition from poor, agrarian society to industrialised country. Literature through these tumultuous decades varied with the public, political and private moods of the day, from folk romanticism and expressionism to social criticism and surrealistic poetry. Prevailing themes in

AUGUST STRINDBERG (1849–1912)

The son of a serving woman and a bankrupted ex-gentleman, Strindberg knew poverty and misery from childhood. Later, he was variously employed as a journalist, a tutor, and an assistant at the Royal Library. His first significant play was *Master Olaf* (1874). It was followed by *Lucky Per's Travels* (1880), reminiscent of Ibsen's *Peer Gynt*, and *Sir Bengt's Wife* (1882), an answer to Ibsen's *A Doll's House*, which Strindberg hated. His satirical novel *The Red Room* (1879) is considered the first example of modern Swedish realism. For the satirical, bitter stories in *Married* (1884–6), he was prosecuted for blasphemy. Strindberg's life was characterised by periods of mental crisis and marital

breakdowns. The work of his realistic-naturalistic period centres on the duel between the sexes. In *Miss Julie* (1888), he depicts both sexual antagonism and class conflict in the figure of the aristocratic girl who seduces her father's footman. After Strindberg's brush with madness in 1896 he wrote the haunting, surrealistic "dream plays" that became the forerunners of modern expressionism. Strindberg's collected writings – plays, fairy tales, poems, short stories, prose sketches, essays, autobiographical writings, novels – fill 55 volumes. His autobiographical works include *The Son of a Servant* (1886), *A Fool's Defence* (1893) and *Alone* (1903).

society, from the collapse of the welfare state to the fragility of the individual, have been expressed in a variety of voices.

Two great figures dominated Swedish literature at the turn of the 20th century: Selma Lagerlöf (1858–1940) and August Strindberg (1849–1912). Their influence on literature and drama has been felt ever since. Strindberg's *Röda Rummet (The Red Room)*, 1879, and Lagerlöf's *Gösta Berlings Saga*, 1891, are considered to be the first modern Swedish novels.

In the first decade of the 20th century, writers often turned to social issues. Hjalmar

> *Swedish Nobel Laureates in Literature: Selma Lagerlöf (1909), Verner von Heidenstam (1916), Erik Axel Karlfeldt (1931), Pär Lagerkvist (1951), Eyvind Johnson/Harry Martinsson (1974) and Tomas Tranströmer (2011).*

Bergman (1883–1931) was one of the best storytellers of Swedish literature, with his 1919 novel about small-town life, *Markurells i Wadköping (God's Orchid)*. Modernist poets like Pär Lagerkvist and Birger Sjöberg emerged in the 1920s and 1930s, along with writers with working-class roots, such as Vilhelm Moberg, whose four novels about 19th-century Swedish emigration to America, *Utvandrarna (The Emigrants)* became a film as well as a literary classic.

In the 1970s, the broad epic novel became prominent. *Jack*, the best-selling novel by Ulf Lundell, became associated with "the young Seventies". In the spirit of the Beat generation, Lundell wrote novels that portray contemporary life and are self-reflective. Kerstin Ekman is a writer who celebrates, among other themes, the strength and endurance of women, most comprehensively in *The Women and the Town (Kvinnorna och staden)* quartet. However, her most famous book outside Sweden is probably *Blackwater*, a tense investigation of a double murder.

Modern best-sellers

Sweden is riding the wave of Nordic Noir. Camilla Läckberg and Jan Arnald (who writes under the pen name Arne Dahl) are big names, but the most famous crime fiction

writer is undoubtedly Henning Mankell. His ten novels about brusque police inspector Kurt Wallander have been translated into more than 40 languages and made into several films and a successful BBC series.

An even more astonishing phenomenon was Stieg Larsson's Millennium trilogy, published posthumously. *The Girl With the Dragon Tattoo* and its two sequels, *The Girl Who Played With Fire* and *The Girl Who Kicked the Hornet's Nest*, have sold 80 million copies worldwide to date.

Another recent best-seller was Jonas Jonas-

Enjoying a Pippi Longstocking story.

son's *The 100-Year-Old Man Who Climbed Out of the Window and Disappeared (Hundraåringen som klev ut genom fönstret och försvann)*, which was turned into the most popular home-grown film of 2014, attracting 1.57 million Swedish cinema-goers.

Children's books

Sweden is forever identified with pioneering children's literature, thanks to Astrid Lindgren (1907–2002). As of 2015, her 74 original works have been translated into 97 languages and sold around 150 million copies. *Pippi Longstocking* (written in 1945) is the most famous of her independent and unconventional characters, accounting for almost a quarter of those book sales. The country voted it one of the top 20 most important Swedish books of the last 100 years, along with two other Lindgren works, *The Brothers Lionheart* and *Emil of Lönneberga*. Lindgren defended the right of children to be treated like human beings without being oppressed: if children are given love, good behaviour will look after itself, she wrote. Lindgren is a heroine to Swedes: around 100,000 people lined the streets of Stockholm for her funeral procession, and in 2015 her portrait replaced Selma Lagerlöf's on the new 20 kronor banknote.

Dagens Nyheter, the national newspaper.

SELMA LAGERLÖF (1858–1940)

Nobel laureate Selma Lagerlöf, novelist and short-story writer, is a major figure in 20th-century Swedish literature. Uncomfortable with the literary realism current in her day, Selma Lagerlöf returned to the past for her stories and wrote in a romantic, imaginative manner. Her best-known works are the novels *Gösta Berlings Saga* and *Jerusalem*. *The Wonderful Adventures of Nils* (1906–7), a much-loved children's book which serves as a playful introduction to Sweden's geography, tells the story of a young boy's adventures when he travels all over the country on the back of a wild goose. This was followed by *Further Adventures of Nils* (1911).

The media scene

About 90 newspapers are published daily in Sweden. People still read them keenly, although print circulation figures have dropped by about 50 percent over the last five years as more people turn to online editions.

Traditionally, newspapers have tended to sympathise with and even actively advocate political party programmes and ideologies. Most newspapers are backed by large media houses like Bonnier and Schibsted of Norway, although the publishers' political preferences have rarely reflected voters' preferences.

The press is also extensively subsidised by the government. Concerned that newspaper closures would weaken the democratic system, the government instituted subsidies in 1969. While this practice may seem to the outsider to support an artificial democracy, the majority of Swedes defend it vigorously.

The free newspaper *Metro*, distributed Monday to Friday on the Stockholm underground, was launched in 1995 and today has the highest circulation (around 580,000 in 2015) of all Sweden's newspapers. The business model was exported to dozens of other cities around the world. Of the paid-for press, the national newspaper *Dagens Nyheter* has the largest print circulation (282,800 in 2013), followed by the regional *Göteborgs-Posten*, the Stockholm *Svenska Dagbladet*, the national tabloids *Aftonbladet* and *Expressen*, and then the Malmö-focused *Sydsvenska Dagbladet*.

Television and radio

Satellite-borne television in the mid-1980s paved the way for increasing commercialism of Swedish television and radio. In 1991, TV4, Sweden's first commercially financed television broadcasting company, was launched. Two years later, commercial radio was introduced. Yet many Swedes remain loyal to public radio and television, despite the choice offered by cable and satellite programming.

With the legacy of its literature, film and theatre, and the values of democracy consistently voiced by the press through the decades, Sweden maintains a strong cultural life. One need only look at the emergence of Greta Garbo from the poor Söder quarter of Stockholm to become the world's most celebrated film star to realise that this cultural life is synonymous with the creative and the unexpected.

THE GREAT OUTDOORS

With its richly varied landscapes and its wealth
of sporting activities, Sweden offers something
for everyone who loves the open air.

S weden is one of the world's most sporting
nations, with nearly half the population
engaged in some form of sport or outdoor recreation. On any given day, you can find
them walking, hiking, cycling, sailing, rafting,
skiing, skating, golfing, rock climbing, balloon-
ing, hang gliding, and even dog-sledding. All of
these activities beckon to the visitor as well, in a
splendid variety of landscapes, from deep forest
and high mountains to gentle meadows and the
vast archipelago.

One of the least densely populated countries
in Europe, Sweden has room to breathe, and
when they get the chance many Swedes love
to step outside their front doors, draw a deep
breath of fresh air and wander off into the great
outdoors. Not surprisingly, walking is a popular
pastime, but a day's walk is rarely sufficient to
satisfy anyone's desire to commune with nature,
and there is always an urge to take part in much
longer treks.

Kayaking off the Bohuslän coast.

Nature trails

Throughout the country, there's an excellent network of waymarked footpaths. Close
to Stockholm is Sörmlandsleden (Sörmland
Route), a lowland hiking trail that comes in at
around 1,000km (620 miles) long, and starts at
the Björkhagen underground station. Carefully
laid out, the trail offers hikers constantly changing vistas of deep forest, historic sites, lookout
points and lakes. It passes several camps where
you can eat, rest and buy supplies, with shelters at regular intervals. Sörmlandsleden is an
easy hike, but it offers plenty of excitement. You
rarely meet another soul, particularly in spring,
autumn and winter, but you will spot deer, elk
(moose), capercaillie, hawks and grouse. The
area is full of mushrooms and berries to pick.

For the most exotic views, however, head for
the moors and mountains of northern Sweden. The country's most famous long-distance
hiking route is Kungsleden (The King's Trail),
which runs for 450 km (280 miles) between
Abisko and Hemavan. Waymarked footpaths
are found in the more scenically outstanding areas like the national parks. These areas
are often well away from towns and villages,
and as a result many of them have a chain
of mountain stations set a comfortable day's
walk from one another along the footpaths,
providing shelter for walkers. Most of the
mountain stations are equipped with cooking
facilities, a shop and comfortable beds. Some
even have a self-service restaurant and a sauna.

They are not hotels but simple accommodation designed to provide a haven at the end of the day for tired walkers.

Camping out

Not all areas, though, are so well off for comfort and a tent becomes a necessity. With a sleeping bag, cooker and food, it can mean a walker has to carry 18 kg (40 lb) of gear, or more. There are no camp sites in the Swedish wilderness, but camping out is never a problem, thanks first of all to a plentiful supply of fresh water from the many lakes and streams,

and secondly to *Allemansrätten* or Everyman's Right. This is an old custom that permits you to camp anywhere for a night, or to walk, ski or paddle a canoe anywhere, as long as the area is not fenced in or too close to a private home, and as long as you leave it just as you found it – undisturbed.

While the forests, particularly in northern Sweden, are home to bears, wolves, lynx and elk, it is rare that hikers would glimpse these shy animals, aside from the occasional elk. However, there is one beast that walkers fears, a beast that will attack the ill-prepared walker in

Enjoying a campfire after a hard day's conoeing in Långeskär, Bohuslän.

A BIRDWATCHER'S PARADISE

In Sweden, with its many lakes, wetlands and forests, birdwatchers can spot species that they would not see in Continental Europe, such as the great grey owl, the great black woodpecker and the three-toed woodpecker. Several wetland species are also special to Sweden: the ruff, the godwit, the curlew and the whimbrel, for example. Sweden has some 50,000 birdwatchers and some 20 bird stations. The tradition of birdwatching dates back to Carl von Linné, or Linnaeus (see page 46), the father of modern botany and Sweden's first avid birder. He named most of Europe's bird species.

The best places in Sweden to birdwatch are the Ottenby bird station in southern Öland, with its nature

and science centre; Falsterbo and Skanörs Ljung in Skåne, and Lake Hornborgasjön in Västergötland. The lake is famous for the thousands of cranes which rest there for a while during their migration to nesting grounds in the north of Sweden. They perform a sort of slow-motion ballet in their mating rituals, and thousands of birdwatchers from all over Europe make the pilgrimage to Hornborgasjön each March and April to watch this spectacle. Finally, Tysslingen Lake near Örebro, where 7,000 whooper swans migrate each April, and Getterön near Varberg are also worth a visit.

For more information, visit the Swedish Ornithological Society's website www.sofnet.org.

large numbers and leave him or her a quivering wreck: the mosquito. The forests are full of mosquitoes in the summer, and all that walkers can do to combat them is plaster themselves with liberal quantities of insect repellent.

On your bike

Cycling and mountain biking are popular outdoor sports for Swedes, and there are many well-designed and well-lit cycle routes all over the country. You could spend a week touring the island of Gotland on a bike. Keen cyclists also head for Östergötland, particularly along

season. Around Lake Vänern, there are boat excursions for golfers to try different waterfront courses. Most courses in Sweden are a combination of rolling parkland and forested hills, although there are some links courses along the south coast.

Skis and skates

When the snows come – and in the north that means October – walking becomes more difficult and much less of a pleasure. Away go the walking boots and out come the skis and the skates.

Mountain biking in the woods.

the banks of the Göta Kanal where the towpaths make ideal cycling tracks. You can hire bikes at several places, and the most popular route for cyclists is between Berg and Borensberg. For the truly ambitious, there is the Sweden Bicycle Route/Sverigeleden, from Stockholm to Göteborg – a distance of 2,620 km (1,630 miles).

Play golf at midnight

For golfers, Sweden offers some exciting landscapes, including golfing under the Midnight Sun in the north and winter golfing at Arvidsjaur. Sweden offers the most beautiful coastal locations for golfing, especially in Bohuslän, Halland and Skåne, which has the longest

Swedes get used to the idea of skiing from an early age. Even before they can walk, they're towed behind their skiing parents in a kind of pram-sledge, and once they've mastered the art of walking it isn't long before they start to get to grips with skis of their own. Almost everyone in Sweden owns a pair of cross-country skis.

Frankly, it makes getting about in the winter months so much easier. But it also opens up further opportunities to enjoy the countryside, or even city parks. Winter doesn't mean a shutdown of the great outdoors. It just requires a different approach.

In fact, one of the most unusual ways to tour the Stockholm archipelago in winter is

Tennis, Anyone?

Swedish tennis reached its zenith with Björn Borg – and Sweden has been waiting for his successor ever since.

It has all the makings of a Hollywood movie. Lone-wolf schoolboy from the frozen backwoods of northern Europe beats a tennis ball against a garage door from morning until night, battles his way to Wimbledon, sweeps to victory against all odds, and

Björn Borg, whose astonishing career still inspires Sweden's young tennis players.

retires at the age of 26 to become a multi-millionaire in Monte Carlo.

Recognise it? Of course you do: it's the Björn Borg story. And for tennis fans the world over, Borg's astonishing career still represents a golden era for the sport that will probably never be repeated. For, since 1983, when the quiet, willowy Swede with the steely eyes, the long, blond locks and devastating two-handed backhand abruptly disappeared from the world's centre courts, there has never been anyone quite like him. And even stories about his failure to build in later life on his early success have not dimmed the memories of those triumphs.

"It was obvious right from the start that Björn was something special," recalls Christer Hjärpe of the

Swedish Tennis Association. "He was simply one of a kind. I doubt if there will ever be anyone to take his place." Part of Borg's success was his famous charisma – the icy cool, the sexy stride, the hair and the headband, the three-day stubble, not to mention the Rolls-Royce, the bodyguards and the hordes of female admirers.

The Golden Age of Swedish tennis continued as Mats Wilander and Stefan Edberg won several Grand Slam tournaments in the 1980s and early 1990s. Between 1974 and 1992, the Swedes were America's main tennis rivals, winning 24 out of 76 Grand Slam events to the US's 25. Sweden's success was so remarkable that other countries sent representatives to study Swedish players and discover their secret.

But things have never again reached those dizzy heights. Following Edberg's defeat of Pete Sampras in the 1992 US Open, the country waited 10 long years for another triumph. It arrived when Thomas Johansson won a Grand Slam title in Melbourne in January 2002, and became a national hero. Since then, no Swedish player has won a major tournament.

After Borg won his first Wimbledon title in 1976 (he won it five times in a row), the Swedish tennis scene erupted. The game that had been widely dismissed as a "snob sport" suddenly shot to the top of the popularity polls, second only to ice-hockey.

Tennis was "in". And just about everyone wanted to have a go. To cope with the surge in demand for facilities, sports associations, local authorities, and clubs up and down the country began pumping money into the game. The national tennis association beefed up its operations. Individual club membership soared and a string of new tournaments got under way. Sweden also began to provide heavily subsidised training schemes for the thousands of youngsters who were queuing up.

Nowadays, there are not enough indoor and outdoor courts to go around, and Sweden's lack of international success is sometimes blamed on this shortage of court space. Others suggest that tennis is somewhat out of fashion with younger athletes, who do not remember Sweden's glory days, and have turned instead to golf and ice hockey to make their mark. The one ray of hope is Elias Ymer, who gave a creditable performance against Ivo Karlović at Wimbledon in 2015, aged just 19.

Tennis is still a popular spectator sport. The main tennis tournaments of the year are the Stockholm Open (a Grand Prix tournament in the autumn) and the Swedish Open (an international round-robin held in Båstad in late summer), with crowds of around 40,000.

to don a pair of long-distance skates, in which relatively long distances can be covered with very little effort. The reward is the chance to enjoy a fantastic Arctic-type landscape where you seldom encounter another soul.

Red cross routes

Whereas in summer the wilderness trails attract walkers, in winter they are covered by the parallel lines of skiers. Of course, the paths themselves are not visible, but to make sure people don't get lost, the paths are marked by red crosses mounted on poles. And to ensure

cross-country skiing facilities. The Alpine World Ski Championships were held in Åre in 2007, and the region is bidding to host them again in 2019, so there are hundreds of top-class, superbly groomed pistes served by high-speed lifts and cabins. Half-pipes and snow parks are available for snowboarding fanatics.

Dog-sledding

To enjoy the wintry wilderness in an entirely different way, try dog-sledding, which is offered by many firms up north, including in Åre and Kiruna. Drive the dog-sled yourself in or sit

Snowshoe hiking on a red cross route.

one cross can be distinguished from another in the height of a blizzard, they are spaced fairly closely together. On a clear day they make a strange sight, hundreds of crosses disappearing across a huge white expanse to the horizon.

Superb pistes

Downhill skiing in Sweden attracts a growing number of visitors thanks to the more reliable snowfall, the reduced risk of avalanches, when compared to the Alpine resorts, and the variety of slopes. As a result, Swedish downhill resorts attract skiers from all over Europe. Åre is Northern Europe's largest alpine sport resort, and Sälen is the most popular resort amongst Swedes themselves, with various Alpine and

back in the vast silence of the mountains and be driven by a team of huskies. Your guide will tell you how to take care of a sled dog and share bits of trivia, like the fact that the Sami have around 180 snow- and ice-related words. Dog-sledding, common in Greenland, is now well established in Sweden.

Climb a frozen waterfall

With such long winters, Swedes have added to their *smörgåsbord* of winter recreation with tobogganing, reindeer sleigh rides and lake fishing through the ice *(pimpling)*, common on most lakes and rivers. You can even go ice climbing. Many resorts have access to frozen waterfalls and equipment with guides to hire.

Water sports

A country that has some 100,000 lakes and countless miles of rivers is bound to be in favour with canoeists. There are canoeing centres all over Sweden, though the district of Värmland offers canoeing waters that are hard to beat: there are so many lakes with interconnecting rivers and creeks that you can work out a circular route avoiding the need to portage.

Because it is ideal for tours of the waterways, the open Canadian canoe is by far the most common. It's a stable craft capable of

Rafting on the Klarälven River.

carrying two people, and, just as important, it will take all the equipment needed for a week-long trip.

Some people can keep their equipment down to the minimum – some food, a couple of pots, matches to light a fire for cooking, a sleeping bag, and a shelter provided by their upturned canoe. Most though, prefer a few more home comforts, and perhaps a tent for shelter.

More popular than the canoe these days is the kayak, the enclosed type of canoe preferred for white water canoeing. Kayaks require a great deal of skill in handling, particularly over rapids, but they are also used on the coast. A favourite area for sea kayaking is around the Stockholm archipelago.

> *Thanks to Sweden's rich wildlife and varied landscape you can drift on a canoe and watch elk calmly grazing or follow reindeer as they migrate over the mountains.*

These days white water isn't only the domain of kayaks. Rubber dinghies add to the excitement of white-water rafting. Suitably clad in waterproofs and life-jackets, crews of half-a-dozen people or more descend raging torrents in large inflatable rubber dinghies.

Drifting down river

Down on the Klarälven River, though, there is a much more sedate form of rafting. Here an enterprising company, Vildmark i Värmland (Wilderness in Värmland), hit on the idea of charging people to build rafts out of logs and spend a few days on board drifting down river. Until 1991, the Klarälven was the only river in Sweden where logs were still floated down the forests to the sawmills. At the end of the rafting journey, the rafts were dismantled and the logs sent down the river to the sawmills at Skoghall, to be turned into pulp for paper. Nowadays, the logs for the mill are transported by truck, and the logs used to make the rafts are picked up at the journey's end by the tour operator to be used again.

It takes a couple of people several hours to build a raft, using ready-cut logs lashed together in three layers. One or two layers isn't enough because the logs don't have sufficient buoyancy to support the crew and equipment they need. When all is complete, camping equipment and provisions are placed on board and the crew paddle out to mid-stream to pick up the current. It's not a strenuous task because the current provides most of the power.

Then follow eight days of idyllic unwinding. The raft drifts along at a languid two kilometres an hour; its passengers relax on deck, fish or watch for shy beavers nosing through the water. The slightest sound and the beavers slap their broad tails and dive for cover beneath the surface. Occasionally, a little effort is called for, to paddle the raft out of the lazy gyrations of a small whirlpool, or to reach the shore to tie up for the night. The peaceful 100 km (60 miles) you travel is Sweden's longest stretch of river without factories, power plants, or other man-made obstacles. Just pure nature.

Fishing in the midnight sun in
Lapland.

CATCH OF THE DAY

No matter where you are in Sweden, you
will always be close to superb fishing
waters, even in the heart of the capital.

Fishing is a major recreational activity in
Sweden – two million Swedes cast a line
every year, and the industry is worth a
cool 5 billion kronor. The travel trade, too, is
bringing Sweden's fishing potential to a wider
international public by making it easy to book
packages which combine accommodation with
fishing permits for a particular area.

One of the most remarkable and most accessible places to fish is right in the centre of
Stockholm, in the fast-moving Strömmen channel which links the fresh water of Lake Mälaren
with the Baltic Sea. At one time the water here
was badly polluted, but a clean-up programme
has brought salmon and sea trout back to the
very heart of the capital. But big salmon and
sea trout can also be caught almost anywhere in
Sweden – in world-famous waters like the River
Mörrum in southern Sweden and, above all, in
the large and wild rivers of northern Sweden,
as well as along the coast when the fish are on
their migration.

The salmon season varies between rivers, but
it usually starts during the summer and continues well into the autumn. The sea trout tend to
arrive a little later. Both spinning and fly-fishing
can produce good salmon catches, but sturdy
tackle is recommended.

Trolling for large salmon and sea trout is also
popular in Sweden, and every year fish in the
15–30kg (33–66lb) bracket are caught. Lake Vättern, for instance, is popular for trolling enthusiasts with its unusual stock of fast-growing
non-migratory salmon.

Pike, perch and zander are regarded in some
countries as coarse fish that are not worth eating. But they are frequent and highly prized
catches in Sweden and are all regarded as fair
game for the table. Perch tend to be rather

A fine catch.

bony for some tastes, but the zander is a delicious fish. An unusual aspect about all three
fish is that they are caught not only in freshwater lakes and rivers but also in the brackish sea
water of the Baltic, including the Stockholm
archipelago. Västervik on the east coast, for
example, has some of the richest pike waters
in the world, with fish of around 10kg (22lb)
being common. Twice a year, in May and
October, around 100 participants come to the
area to take part in the prestigious Pike Open
fishing competition.

Game fishing

More conventional game fishing can be had in
virtually all of Sweden's 96,000 lakes, as well as

its countless streams and rivers. Apart from the migratory salmon, sea trout and whitefish (a member of the salmon family), there are wild stocks of brown trout, grayling and char, an attractive fish which some gourmets rate more highly than salmon.

There are also plenty of so-called "put and take" lakes with introduced stocks of rainbow trout and sometimes brown trout, too. All these game species are usually caught on light spinning tackle or fly, but in the winter they can also be caught by ice-fishing on frozen lakes with "jigging" or "angeldon" equipment. But restrictions on ice-fishing apply in some areas, so check locally before you start fishing.

Coarse fishing

Many visiting anglers head for Sweden's coarse-fishing waters, which provide some excellent sport, particularly in northern and central Sweden. Tench, bream, roach and common carp are just some of the species which can be tempted by a maggot, corn or other bait. Float-fishing is the most common method, but legering can also produce good results.

Sea fishing

Sea fishing is extremely popular along Sweden's 8,000 km (5,000 miles) of coastline, from the Norwegian border in the west to the Finnish border high up in the Gulf of Bothnia.

The west coast produces plenty of cod, haddock, ling, coalfish and mackerel, but there is also excellent fishing for garfish and migrating sea trout close inshore. A relatively new species to Swedish waters is the grey mullet, which has been attracted by the warm-water outlets from power stations in the south. The fishing season on the west coast lasts the whole year. Fishing for cod here is usually best in the spring and autumn, though large fish are caught in the Öresund strait in winter. A good way to enjoy a day's deep-sea fishing here is to go out on one of the many tour boats, whose experienced skippers will make sure that you attract some big fish to your hook. Tackle is often provided, or it can be hired for the day.

On the east coast the sea becomes less salty the further north you go, so you are more likely to catch freshwater species like pike, zander and whitefish. (See page 289 for more information on fishing in the far north.)

Making plans

If you are planning a fishing holiday, contact Sveriges Sportfiske- och Fiskevårdsförbund (the Swedish Angling Federation), also known as "Sportfiskarna", Svartviksslingen 28, 16739 Bromma, Sweden (tel: 08-410 80 600; email: info@sportfiskarna.se; www.sportfiskarna.se).

You can fish in the sea with rod and line free of charge around the Swedish coastline. Fishing is also free from the shores of the five largest lakes, Vänern, Vättern, Mälaren, Hjälmaren and Storsjön. Elsewhere, contact the local tourist office for information on permits, permitted equipment, close seasons, and minimum size and catch limits.

Fly fishing in the Torne River.

BALTIC CAVEAT

Though Sweden makes a priority of protecting its fishing waters, the Baltic Sea is bordered by some less considerate countries. Home of the herring – Sweden's national fish – the Baltic has been heavily polluted by Russian coastal towns and the Baltic States. Furthermore, the numerous troughs and ridges lining the Baltic's seabed slow the circulation of water. In some areas, such as the narrow strip between Sweden and Denmark, waters take up to thirty years to refresh. All these factors led to the EU banning the sale of Baltic catches abroad in 2002. However, they are still for sale in Sweden, as long as they are accompanied by a health warning about dangerous dioxins.

Ice-fishing on a frozen lake in Uppland.

Forest outside Vetlanda in Småland.

NATURE AND CONSERVATION

The Swedes combine a healthy appetite
for the fruits of nature with a passionate
concern for conservation.

Love of the land and their country is deeply rooted in Swedes. Even the national hymn *Du gamla, du fria* does not concentrate on glory, honour or warfare, but on a land of high mountains, silence and joyfulness.

Only three percent of the land is inhabited. From the air, you get a great sense of this virgin territory with its miles and miles of woods, forests (covering 69 percent of the country), and the twinkling eyes of many lakes – almost 100,000, great and small. Everywhere, it is a diverse landscape, from the fertile areas of Skåne to the tundra on the mountains of Lapland, known as Europe's Last Wilderness. In between is a land of small hills and valleys, rolling fields, small farms and clusters of red wooden cottages.

There are 8,000 kilometres (5,000 miles) of coastline, offering clean, if often chilly, water to swim in, and rocks to sun on (but few sandy beaches). The most spectacular seascape is the Stockholm archipelago, with its 24,000 islands, but nearly as thrilling are the waves crashing on the rocks of Bohuslän's archipelago.

A right to roam

"Everyman's Right" *(Allemansrätten)* is an ancient Swedish custom designed to guarantee every person the right to enjoy nature without undue restriction of access. You may pass over land, travel by boat over water, pitch a tent for 24 hours, and gather wild flowers (excluding those protected by law), berries and mushrooms as long as you respect the landowner's privacy and do not cause any damage to property or wildlife. The right does not extend to crossing or camping on a private plot such as someone's garden, or crossing cultivated farmland; and some national parks and

Keeping warm in the wild in northern Sweden.

nature reserves apply further restrictions. *Allemansrätten* gives Swedes a sense of collective stewardship: although you have right of access, you are responsible for behaving respectfully and leaving the land in the state in which you found it.

National parks

This respect for nature led to Sweden establishing nine national parks in 1909, Europe's first. Today there are 29 national parks, managed by the Swedish Environmental Protection Agency Naturvårdsverket (www.naturvardsverket.se), and over 4,000 protected nature reserves. The aim is that selected areas of superior natural value and beauty should be protected from exploitation, both in the interests of the natural environment and because of their value in human terms.

Padjelanta is the biggest national park in Sweden. The name comes from a Sami word that means "the higher mountain", and it is one of Sweden's most beautiful mountain areas, with rolling plains, gently rounded mountain massifs, and huge lakes, such as Vastenjaure and the beautiful Virihaure. Almost the entire park is above the tree line. There are many small streams, which the Lapps call *jokk*, and it has always been an important pasture for their reindeer herds. Here, it is safe to drink the stream water and to enjoy its own special, clean taste.

At the opposite end of the country and on a very different scale is Norra Kvill, a well-preserved virgin forest in the highlands of Små-land in southern Sweden. The forest has not been felled for over 150 years and some pines are more than 350 years old. The flora is sur-prisingly varied, and extremely rich in mosses and lichens.

Rich birdlife

If you want to study the herbaceous flora and listen to the birdsong, Dalby Söderskog near Lund in Skåne is at its best in the spring, while Store Mosse in Småland is worth a detour for birdwatchers: there are whooper swans, marsh harriers, cranes and many more rare species.

Countryside pursuits

The greatest proportion of Sweden is virgin country and for anyone from a densely popu-lated and polluted area, from north to south the whole country seems like a "green lung" – a place where you can breathe. In this wild coun-tryside, you can stroll for miles along tracks without seeing another human being, or drive a car on serpentine gravel roads and never pass another vehicle, or cycle through untouched land on the special bicycle trails.

The Swedes are dedicated to the countryside. Many families save for years in order to buy a *stuga* (cottage) in the country or on the coast. Others are lucky enough to have inherited their little spot in a meadow. Most Swedes are only a generation or two away from rural life and

Enjoying a brisk walk.

NEW NATIONAL PARKS IN DIVERSE LANDSCAPES

Söderåsen in Skåne, Fulufjället in Dalarna and Kosterhavet in Västra Götaland are Sweden's latest national parks. Söderåsen (2001), 30km (18.5 miles) east of Helsingborg, is one of the largest connected protected areas of decidu-ous forest. Deep ravines score the rolling hills, tumbling with streams and covered in rustling beech trees. The most visited part of the park is the Skäralid valley with its unu-sual jutting rock Hjortsprånget (The Deer Jump), where deer were once hunted by driving them over the cliff edge.

Further north is Fulufjället (2002). Its low-elevation mountains are rich in lichens, and hide Sweden's largest waterfall, Njupeskär, which makes a dramatic ice climbing site in winter. Another curiosity is a lone fir known as Old

Tjikko, thought to be the world's oldest tree at 9,550 years old. The bold Siberian jay is the park's symbol, and if you're lucky you may see golden eagles and the rare gerfalcon. One of the primary reasons for the park's creation was to protect the brown bears who live there.

Kosterhavet, Sweden's first national marine park, was inaugurated in September 2009. Its waters hide Sweden's only coral reef, where summer visitors can follow snorkel trails through brown algae forests and eelgrass meadows to look for sponges, brachiopods, ascidians, brittle stars and crabs. Delights include the green spoonworm *Bonellia viridis*, and the sponge *Geodia barretti*, known in Swedish as "svampdjur" (literally "mushroom animal").

many have relatives who still live in their original home districts.

The Swedes do not just enjoy the countryside and its fruits, they make use of them. At the first sign of spring nettles, the Swede rushes out, gloves on hands, with a pair of scissors and a paper bag to collect them. For, despite their stings, nettle broth is a fine start to a meal even at a first-class restaurant, and nothing beats the first nettle broth of spring, made from nettles picked with your own hands.

After that come sweet gale, and the tiny leaves of blackcurrant which Swedes use to spice the Christmas aquavit. Then comes the summer harvest: raspberries, cloudberries, wild strawberries, blueberries and, towards autumn, lingonberries, rose hips and blackberries.

To traditional Swedish families, no cultivated fruit can ever hope to compare with the wild ones they have picked themselves, even if they have had to fight off the mosquitoes to do so; and it is positively fashionable to appear in Stockholm on a Monday morning with the stain of berries still dark on your fingers.

The mushroom season begins with turbantops – now slightly suspect – followed by baskets of chanterelles, ceps, edible agarica, ringed boletuses and all the rest of the mushroom family which the nature-conscious Swede can find. Swedes take their fungi very seriously: there are organised excursions to look for mushrooms and berries, and classes to tell people what they can and cannot eat.

Conservation matters

It is no wonder that the Swedes are worried about dangers to the environment such as acid rain, which has already killed off some plants and over-encouraged others, and also damaged many of the fishing lakes. Particularly in the west, the lakes are clear, beautiful, and totally devoid of any water life, except for a strange white lichen-type plant on the bottom. Many fishing societies have taken an active part in trying to save these "dead" lakes and, with government co-operation, have organised programmes of liming the water. However, this is no more than a palliative which they have to repeat at regular intervals.

Millions of Swedes fish in their spare time, and all along the coasts and in the big lakes fishing with rod and line is free, though amateurs are expected not to disturb the activities of the professional fishermen.

Strict laws protect the rarer mammals such as the bear, wolf, wolverine, lynx, musk-ox (a late immigrant from Norway), Arctic fox, otter or whale. In any case, they are rarely seen. But other animals are very common – roe deer live in the forest and only in Scandinavia will you see the traffic sign which means "Danger, Elk". This is no joke: traffic accidents involving animals have increased as the number of cars has grown, especially at dusk and dawn when the elk are crossing the roads between the forests.

The Swedes are dedicated to protecting birds, particularly the more endangered spe-

Brown bears are protected.

cies. Rescue operations have been enacted to save the white-tailed eagle, the white-backed woodpecker, peregrine falcons, the gyr falcon and the Caspian tern, and there has been great success in saving the population of eagle owls. The biggest threat to birds and other animals is the continuing destruction of wetlands due to intense agriculture and over-use of pesticides.

The variety of the countryside offers suitable habitats for many rare plants, from the alpines of the high mountains to the rich orchid flora of the limestone areas. The months of May and June in particular bring out an army of botanists, but always just to look, never to touch – Sweden began to protect its plants as early as the beginning of the 20th century.

Eating outdoors, preferably near water, is an essential ingredient of summer life.

FOOD AND DRINK

Sweden has won international recognition for its
cuisine, based on an abundance of fresh fish,
wild berries and succulent mountain meat.

Perhaps the best testimonial to the high
standards of Swedish cuisine is the sight
of all those healthy looking tanned Swedes
you see in the summer, who certainly do not
appear to have succumbed to the junk-food culture, although inevitably most towns have their
fair share of fast-food outlets.

In the last 10 years, Sweden's chefs have discovered a new-found pride in the country's natural
resources, reinventing traditional ingredients and
finding fresh new flavours, all while subscribing to
the New Nordic cuisine ideals of "purity, simplicity, freshness and ethics". Dishes are usually simply
cooked, often over birchwood fires or smoked over
hay. There's never been a more exciting time for visitors to start exploring Sweden's gastronomic scene.

Gathering mushrooms and wild berries has
always been a national preoccupation in the
autumn, while favourite meat dishes include reindeer, venison or elk from the mountains and forests. Above all, the Swedes are great eaters of fish,
from both the sea and from the many rivers and
96,000-plus lakes. Freshwater fish like pike and
zander, usually thrown back by British anglers, are
much-prized items on restaurant menus. In the
west of Sweden, fishing villages along the coast
north of Göteborg make a religion of mussels,
oysters, crayfish, lobster, shrimp, crabs and squid.

A typical Swedish meal.

Smörgåsbord delicacies

Sweden is probably best known abroad for its
smörgåsbord. Translated literally, a *smörgås* is simply a slice of bread and *bord* is a table, but it is
definitely a misnomer to describe it as a "bread
and butter table".

Going back 200 years, an "aquavit buffet" was
the prelude to a festive meal in Sweden and it
was laid out on a separate table in the dining
room. Guests could indulge in a modest snack of
herrings, sprats and cheese before getting down
to the serious business – accompanied, naturally
enough, by a few aquavit (schnapps) sharpeners.

This buffet became more and more lavish over
the years as hosts and hostesses vied with each other
to provide the best spread, culminating in the giant
smörgåsbord, which had its heyday in the 19th century and even then was still regarded only as the
prelude to a "proper" meal. Nowadays, the Swedes
are gourmets rather than gourmands, so the *smörgåsbord* is a meal in itself; but the groaning table can
still present a daunting picture to the foreign visitor.

The secret of *smörgåsbordmanship* is to take
things gradually and not to overload one's plate.
Start with a few slices of herring prepared in all
kinds of mouth-watering ways – in a mustard

An Education in the Skål of Life

The Swedes comply to a rigorous protocol when it comes to social entertaining and, particularly, the drinking of toasts.

A visitor is more likely to be asked to a Swedish home for a casual meal than invited to a very for-

Skål!

mal dinner party, but, even then, there are quite a few social rules to bear in mind. It is firstly necessary to look at the etiquette for a formal party because it provides the basis for the more informal occasions.

To start with, arrive on time – punctuality is the norm in methodical, organised Sweden. Take some flowers or a box of chocolates for your hostess and, if there are a number of other guests, introduce yourself to them.

Once seated, you may find that a glass of schnapps or wine is already poured out. But on no account take a sip till the host has raised his glass for the first "*skål*" to welcome the guests. This first toast can also be a kind of communal *skål* in which you exchange greetings with your

fellow guests, particularly those seated close to you.

The most important part of toasting, whether formal or casual, is that you must establish eye contact, glass raised, with the other party or parties not only before you take your sip but also immediately after.

On a formal occasion, each male will *skål* the ladies, starting with the one on his right, then the one on his left. Men will also *skål* fellow guests at random throughout the meal, but if there are more than eight guests at the table it is considered polite not to *skål* your host or hostess, on the basis that an input of schnapps on that scale might well have dire consequences. Incidentally, the normal routine is to *skål* with schnapps, but not with wine.

The rules are naturally much less rigid if you are invited for an informal meal with Swedish friends. But again the first rule holds good: wait for your host to "*skål*".

The *skåling* tradition does not seem to have been especially affected by Sweden's tough laws against drinking and driving. Most people attending an evening party either take a taxi or one partner volunteers to stick to mineral water and drives home.

When the meal is over, and before you retire for coffee and liqueurs, you must do what every Swedish child is taught to do at an early age and say to your hostess: "*Tack för maten*" ("Thanks for the food", literally). At some stage your hostess will probably disappear into the kitchen and re-emerge with a tray of tea or beer, snacks and sandwiches. This is a tactful signal that the evening is coming to an end – although by the time you've quaffed your beer another hour will probably have passed all too rapidly.

Someone will eventually make the first move to depart, sparking off the ritual exclamations of "Is that the time?"

There then begins a round of farewells in which each guest shakes hands with the host and hostess and says "*Tack för i kväll*" ("Thanks for this evening"). All the guests will likewise shake hands with each other with mutters of "*Tack för trevligt sällskap*" ("Thanks for your pleasant company") or "*Det var trevligt att träffas*" ("It was nice to meet you").

If all this sounds rather daunting, just remember to say "*skål*" and "*tack*" in the right places and you won't go far wrong.

or horseradish sauce, maybe – accompanied by a hot boiled potato. If you're lucky, you may encounter *gravad lax*, thinly sliced salmon cured in dill, a delicacy which is now well known outside Sweden.

For the main course (or courses), you graduate to a bewildering choice of cold meats or fish and salad, or a typical hot dish like Swedish meatballs or "Jansson's Temptation" (a popular concoction of potatoes, onions and anchovies) before rounding off the meal with fruit salad or cheese.

The *smörgåsbord* is not such a dominant trend in Swedish cooking these days as it once was, but

Dish of the day

You can certainly stoke up for the day with a hearty Swedish breakfast – which would be a pity because the best-value eating out is to be had at lunchtime rather than in the evening. Particularly in the cities, you'll find restaurants offering an inexpensive *dagens rätt* ("dish of the day"), which includes a main course, salad, soft drink and coffee, and helpings are generous. Desserts or cheese are not often included on such menus, and it's worth paying a bit extra to sample some of Sweden's delicious wild berries such as the whortleberry, cloudberry or bilberry, served with a large dollop of cream.

Gravad lax at a restaurant in Dalarna.

it still prevails in the south in Skåne, where the good-living tradition is maintained most faithfully. You can also still find hotels that make a speciality of a lunchtime *smörgåsbord*, particularly on Sundays.

Breakfast feast

Perhaps the best value for visitors is the breakfast served in most Swedish hotels, which is really a mini-*smörgåsbord* in its own right. You will usually find several kinds of cereal, cheeses, herrings, boiled eggs, jams, fruit, milk and different types of bread (including the ubiquitous *Wasabröd* crisp-bread). Sometimes you may even find some scrambled eggs and sausages or bacon on the hot-plate.

NEW NORDIC CUISINE

In 2004, Scandinavia's finest chefs came together to devise the New Nordic Kitchen manifesto, focusing on slow food, local organic produce and foraged ingredients such as rosehips, chanterelles, sea buckthorn and cloudberries. Sweden, along with its northern neighbours, has come to appreciate Scandinavia's long, cool growing season, its abundance of fish and game, and its forests full of fungi, wild plants and berries. The manifesto was the start of a staggering resurgence in regional cuisine. Today you can experience the best of New Nordic cuisine in the restaurants of Stockholm, Göteborg and Malmö.

Dining out

Eating out in the evening is generally more expensive, although not necessarily prohibitive, so check prices before you venture into a restaurant. The price of wine in restaurants is high, so you may prefer to stick to mineral water (*Ramlösa* is the best-known local brand). The budget-conscious will find plenty of cafés and cafeterias in the larger cities, as well as fast-food outlets. For something more typically Swedish, try the *korvkiosk*, the nearest equivalent to Britain's "chippy"; it specialises in fast-food items like grilled chicken, hot dogs or sausage with French fries.

Smoked reindeer meat.

REGIONAL SPECIALITIES

Every region of Sweden has its own specialities. Skåne, in the far south, is a favourite region for gourmets with its eel feasts in the early autumn and goose dinners later on. Skåne is also the home of *spettkaka*, a tower-shaped confectionery of sugar, eggs and potato flour baked over an open fire. The west coast is ideal for seafood, particularly in Göteborg, where you can eat fish landed that very morning. On the island of Gotland smoked flatfish is a popular speciality, while other dishes include smoked lamb and stuffed pike with horseradish sauce. In the far north, you can enjoy Sami specialities such as smoked reindeer meat.

Foreign flavours

Cuisine in the larger cities is increasingly international as Swedish society becomes less homogenous, and many of the up-and-coming chefs have been influenced by immigrant owners. In a cosmopolitan city like Stockholm, for example, you can enjoy a Chinese, Japanese, Korean, Thai, German or Italian meal in addition to the home-grown Swedish fare.

Home-cooking

It's better to head for the rural regions to experience the more typical Swedish home cooking known as *husmanskost*, which produces strange combinations like pea soup with pancakes, traditionally eaten on Thursdays. The drink to accompany this is the lethal and deceptively sweet alcoholic *punsch*. Another favourite dish is *pytt i panna* (literally, "Put in the Pan"), a gigantic fry-up which is a good way of using up left-overs.

If you are in Sweden in August, you may be lucky enough to be invited to a *kräftor* (crayfish) party. These delicious freshwater shellfish are boiled in water, dill, salt and sugar and left to cool overnight and are then served with hot buttered toast and caraway cheese, accompanied by schnapps and beer.

What to drink

The Swedes themselves will admit that the most negative aspect of their gastronomy is the high cost of beer and spirits resulting from punitive taxes and excise duties.

Beer comes in three grades – Class I (light beer), Class II (ordinary beer) and Class III (export). Until recently, the choice was limited to bland big-brewery lagers, lacking in taste and character, but the new-found pride in Sweden's cuisine has spread to its drinks as well. Today a new generation of craft breweries has sprung up, producing solid, flavourful ales and lagers.

Lower excise duties usually apply to wine, which can be bought in the State-controlled *Systembolaget* at prices which are quite reasonable. But, as elsewhere, a three-fold mark-up will push up the price of wine at a restaurant.

It's worth splashing out on the odd *akvavit*, if only to assess which type is worth buying to take home. Skåne is the best-selling brand, but many connoisseurs prefer O.P. Anderson, which is flavoured with caraway, aniseed and fennel seed and goes well with herring dishes. Devotees of vodka will probably prefer to stick to Absolut, a 100-year-old brand now sold all over the world.

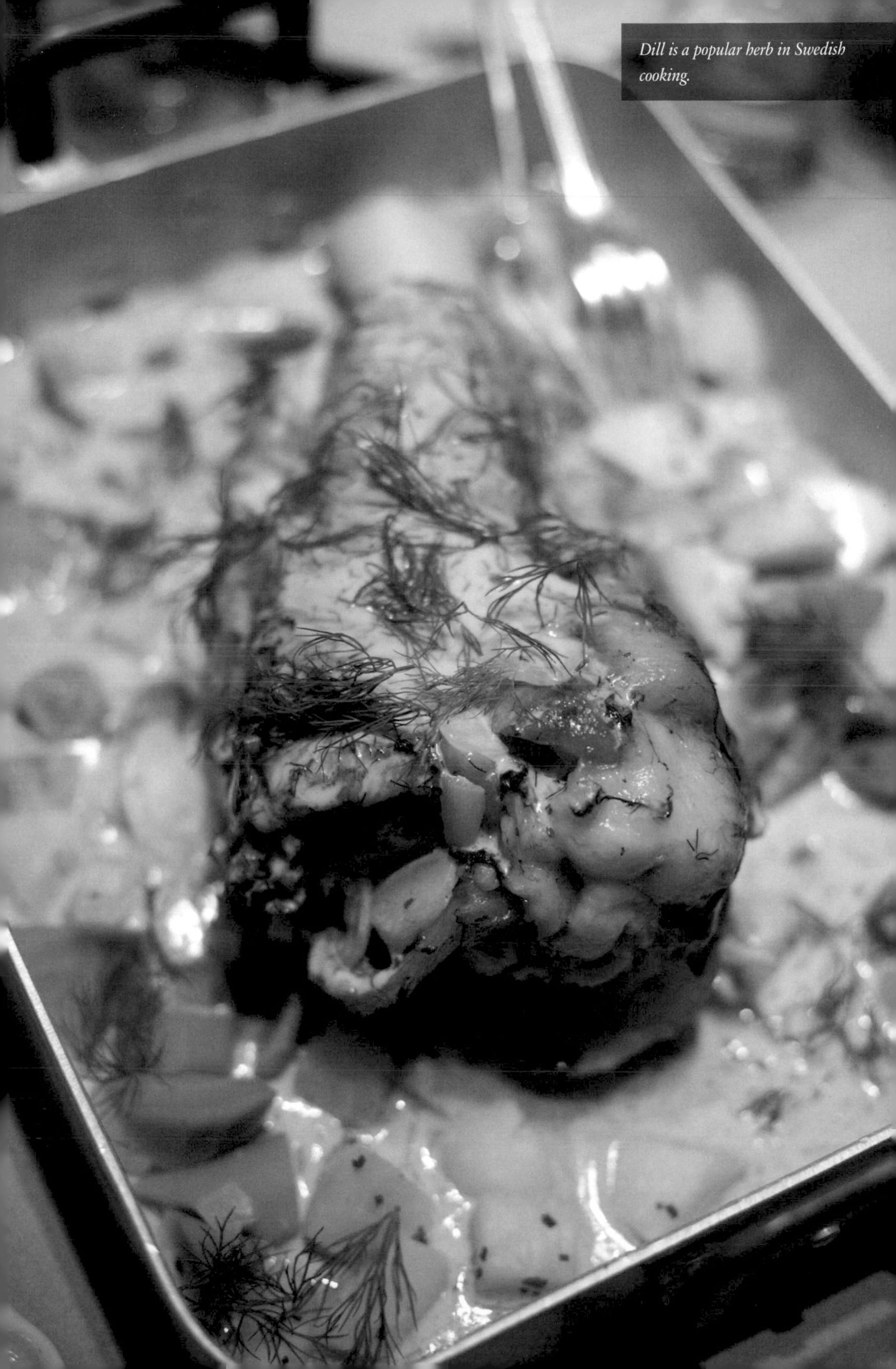

Dill is a popular herb in Swedish cooking.

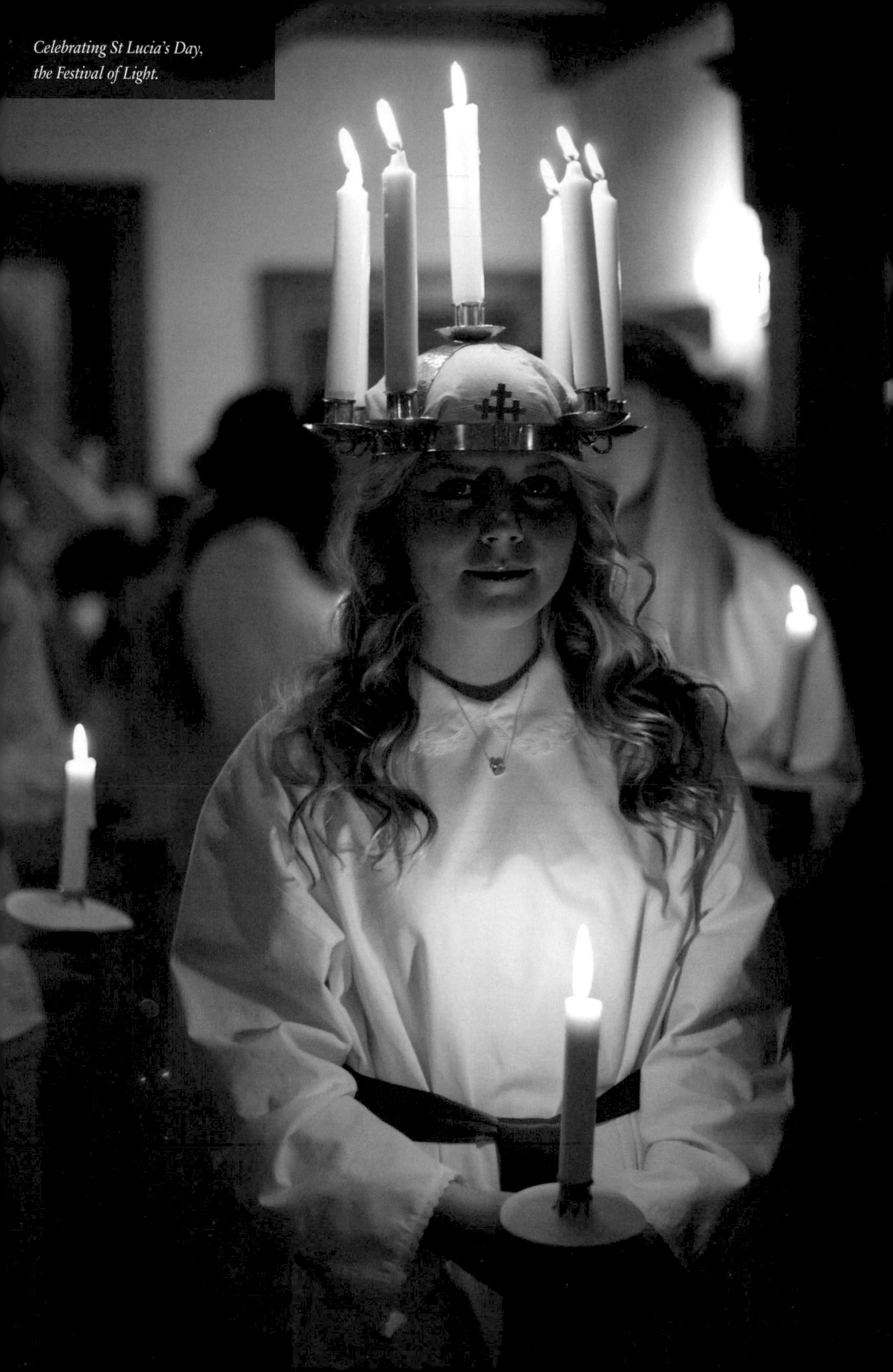

Celebrating St Lucia's Day,
the Festival of Light.

FESTIVALS

Pagan traditions, the Christian year and the sharp contrast between the seasons all contribute to a colourful festival calendar.

Church-going may be a minority pursuit in Sweden, but the vast majority of Swedes remain nominal Christians, even if they go to church only to be baptised, confirmed, married and buried. So perhaps it is not so surprising that the pattern of festivals and folk traditions throughout the year is still determined very much by the religious calendar, although some probably had their origin in the pagan festivals of old.

The dark days of winter coincide with the traditionally gloomy time of Lent, and although Catholic practices were outlawed in Sweden at the time of the Reformation, many people still keep up the tradition of eating heartily on Shrove Tuesday, just before the season of fasting begins.

Witches on broomsticks

Lent leads up to Easter, when many Swedes head for the mountains to ski. Both Good Friday and Easter Monday are public holidays, and a long weekend is a welcome break after the rigours of winter. But there are still plenty of traditions at Easter-time, like the eating of decorated hard-boiled eggs. Maundy Thursday in Swedish folklore was the day that witches flew off on their broomsticks to pay their respects to the Devil. Good law-abiding citizens used to protect themselves by lighting bonfires, letting off firearms and painting crosses on their doors.

Nowadays, Swedish youngsters still dress up as hags and pay visits to their neighbours on Maundy Thursday or Easter Eve, leaving a decorated card in the hope of getting sweets or money in return. Bonfires and fireworks are still part of the Easter tradition in some areas.

Children dress up as witches on Easter Eve.

Wild celebrations

The arrival of spring is celebrated on 30 April, at the Feast of Valborg, better known perhaps as Walpurgis Night. The wildest celebrations are in the university towns, particularly Uppsala, where thousands of students process through the streets in their white caps and sing traditional songs before dancing all night and seeing in the first dawn of spring. In some areas the spring celebrations are on 1 May although, as elsewhere in Europe, this is now a public holiday for Labour Day rather than a true spring festival.

Ascension Day is also a public holiday and many people mark the day by getting up early and going out into the countryside to hear the dawn chorus. Whitsun is another religious festival still marked in Sweden, with the Monday as a public holiday.

Sweden's National Day on 6 June is a normal working day, although there are parades and the flag is hoisted everywhere. The reason for the low-key celebration is probably that Midsummer is only just round the corner, and that has special significance in a country which is so influenced by the whims of the sun and the long dark winters.

Midsummer festivities

Midsummer Day is a slightly movable feast because it was decided in the 1950s that the celebrations should be on the weekend nearest to 24 June, the Feast of St John the Baptist, but in many areas people still observe the festival on 23 June.

On Midsummer Eve Swedes decorate their homes and churches with garlands of flowers and branches, and the dancing round the maypole goes on right through the night. Like Maundy Thursday, Midsummer has all kinds of supernatural connotations. Young Swedes traditionally picked flowers and placed them under their pillow in the hope of dreaming about their future bride or bridegroom.

After Midsummer, Sweden tends to pack up for a couple of months as people head off to the countryside or the coast for the summer, and there are no more public holidays until All Saints' Day at the beginning of November. This is when families lay flowers on the graves of their loved one, and it can be a moving sight to see the graveyards at dusk glowing with candles and lanterns.

Christmas lights

December rounds off the year with a bout of festivities, starting on Advent Sunday, when houses and streets are decorated with trees, garlands and lights for the Christmas season.

St Lucia's Day – the Festival of Light – is celebrated on 13 December, a throwback to the days when it was mistakenly regarded as the longest night of the year. In the present-day Lucia celebrations, a young girl dressed in a white gown and wearing a crown of lighted candles brings in a tray of coffee, ginger biscuits and mulled wine (*glögg*) for the guests, accompanied by girl attendants also dressed in white and boys wearing tall conical paper hats and carrying stars. As they process, the youngsters sing "Santa Lucia" and traditional carols.

Christmas is generally celebrated in Swedish homes on Christmas Eve rather than on the day itself. The festivities resemble Christmas elsewhere in Europe, with the traditional tree and the giving of presents, but after dinner there is a visit from the *tomte* or Christmas gnome, a benevolent sprite who was supposed to live under the barn and look after the livestock in bygone days. The *tomte* comes into the house loaded down with a sack of presents as a kind of substitute Santa Claus.

New Year's Day is a lower-key affair, but families tend to have a lavish meal on Twelfth Night (Epiphany), a public holiday. The last fling is one week after Twelfth Night, "Knut's Day", when the decorations are removed from the Christmas tree. The year's festivities may be over, but Shrove Tuesday is not far away.

Crayfish parties happen in August at the start of the season.

LOCAL FESTIVALS

Apart from the traditional seasonal events, a bewildering variety of local festivals are organised all over Sweden throughout the year, and particularly during the summer. Many have a musical theme, like the annual "Music on Siljan" festival in Dalarna, and there are also plenty of events for folk-dancers, fiddlers and accordion players. More offbeat happenings include an annual medieval week at Visby on Gotland, an apple fair in Kivik, and a potato festival in Alingsås (Västergötland). Christmas markets pop up all over Sweden in December, and winter is also the time for events like the famous *Vasaloppet* cross-country ski race between Sälen and Mora in Dalarna.

Dancing round the Midsummer maypole.

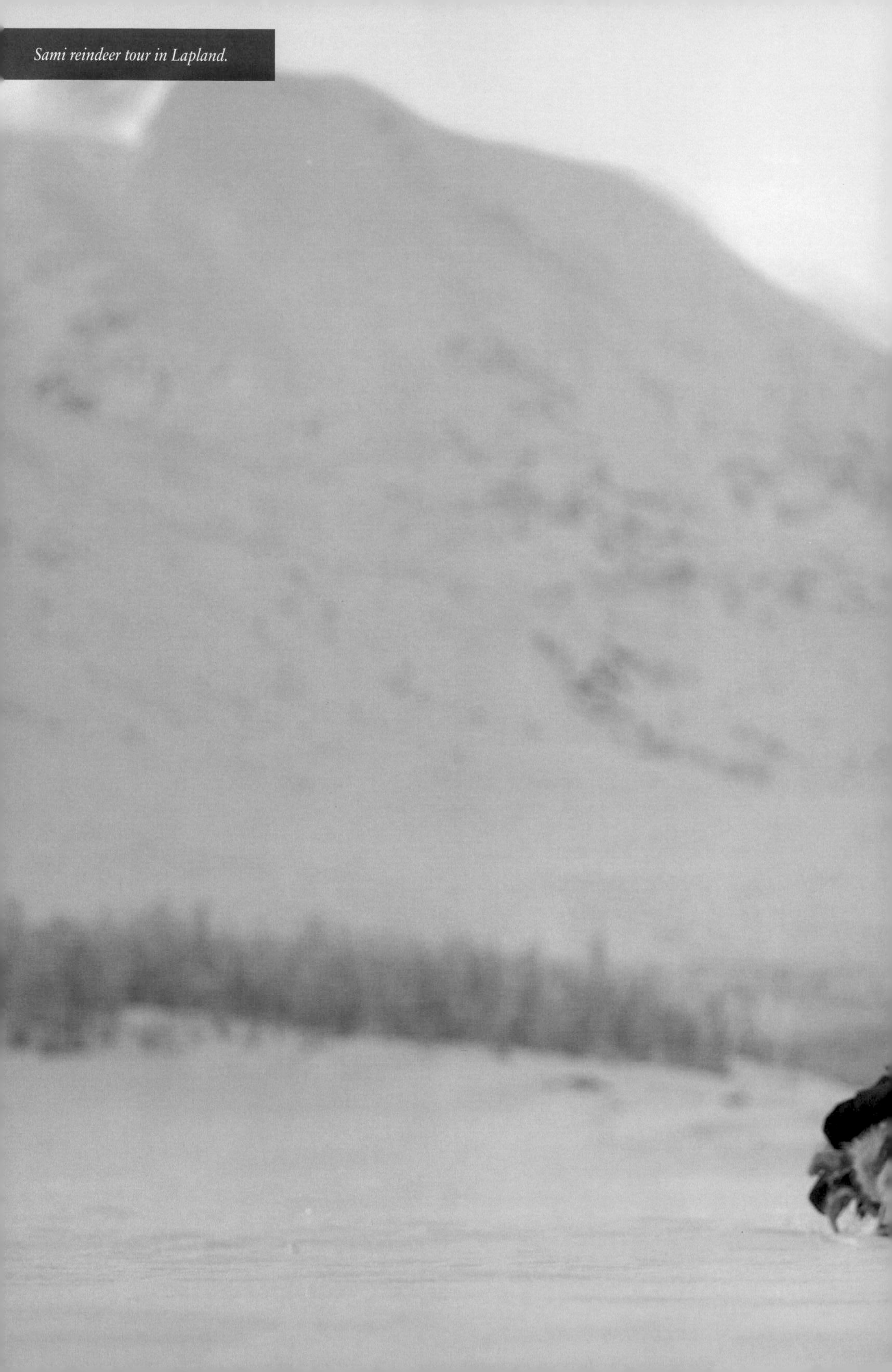

Sami reindeer tour in Lapland.

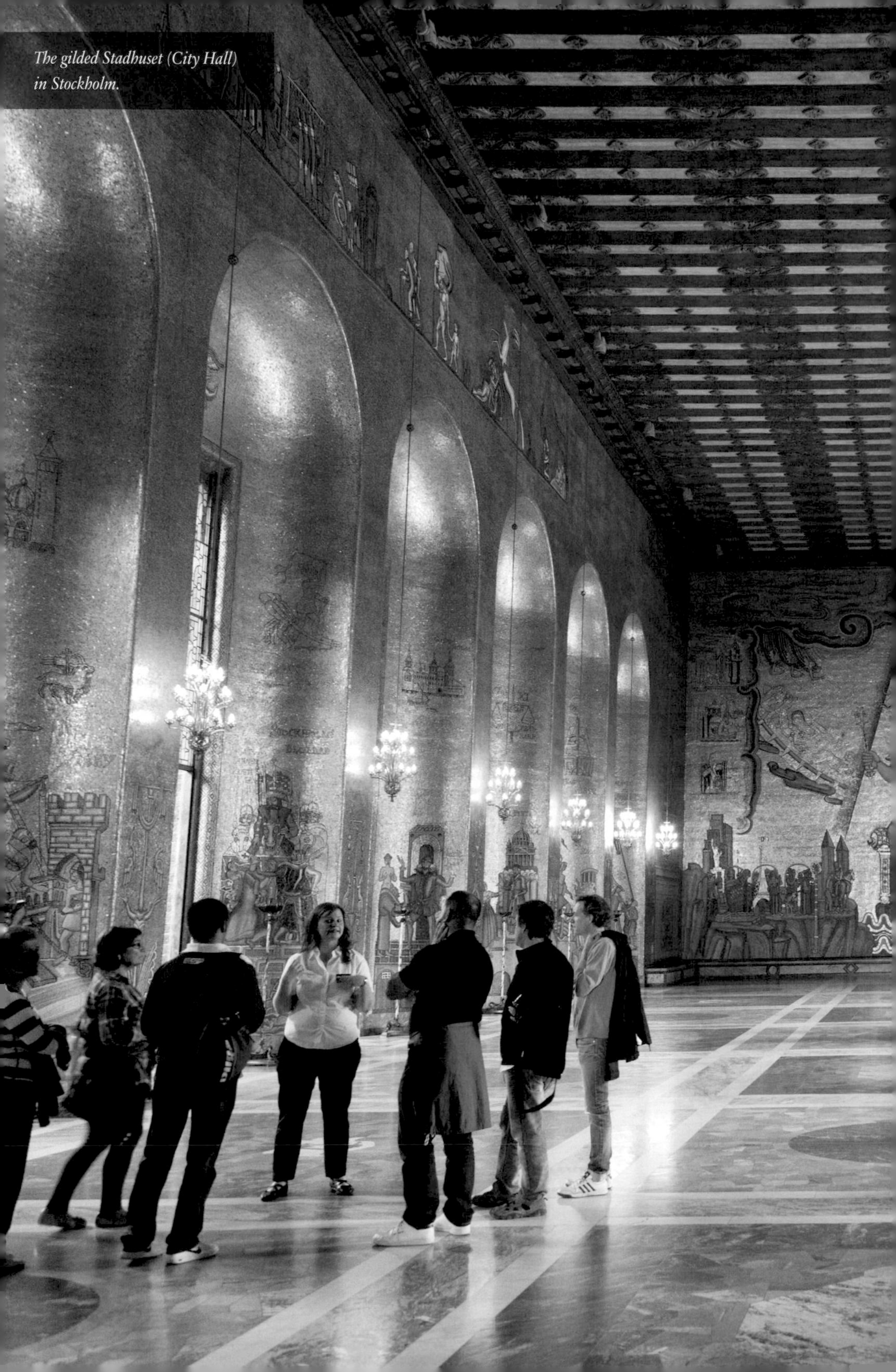

The gilded Stadhuset (City Hall) in Stockholm.

Fisherman's cottage along the
Bohuslän coastline.

INTRODUCTION

A detailed guide to the entire country,
with principal sites clearly cross-
referenced by number to the maps.

Dalarna horses.

I f you could pivot the whole of Sweden on the southernmost city of Malmö, it would stretch as far as Naples.
This long, narrow country is the largest in Scandinavia,
but its population of only 9.8 million makes it one of the
least crowded countries in Europe.

To fly over Sweden is to discover a land of forest, where
lakes glint among the trees. Even Stockholm, which covers
a much wider area than you might expect for its 900,000
population, is a city of sea, lake and open spaces, and never far from the
thousands of islands that form its archipelago, reaching out towards the
Baltic. If you arrive by boat from Western Europe, the magnificent west-
coast harbour of Göteborg (Gothenburg) is the first view. This is Sweden's second city, noted for its wide avenues and canals. The third main
city, Malmö, in the far south, is also a port; the gateway
to Denmark is just half an hour or so away across narrow
straits and is accessible by bridge and tunnel.

As well as these three principal cities, there are the two
university towns: Lund, near Malmö, and Uppsala, north of
Stockholm; the latter was the ancient capital of Uppland,
the cradle of Sweden and the home of the old pagan ways.

Outside the main centres, Sweden has miles and miles
of road through endless forest, a coastline spiked with rock
and smoothed by beaches, and unspoilt northern mountains ideal for summer walking and winter sports. The
southern provinces of Skåne, Blekinge and Halland (plus
Bohuslän on the west coast) were for centuries part of Denmark, and even today in Skåne the accent is faintly Danish.
Much of south-central Sweden is dominated by the great lakes, Vänern
and Vättern, the heart of a network of waterways that make it possible
to cross this widest part of Sweden by boat along the Göta Kanal, which
links Stockholm to Göteborg.

Picturesque Valholm.

Further north, the geographical centre of Sweden holds Dalarna, often
called the Folklore Province, where old customs linger. At the end of the
long road or rail route north are the mountains, many with a covering of
snow all the year round. This is the land of the Midnight Sun. It is also
the home of Scandinavia's indigenous people, the Sami, whose wander-
ings with their reindeer herds take little account of national boundaries.

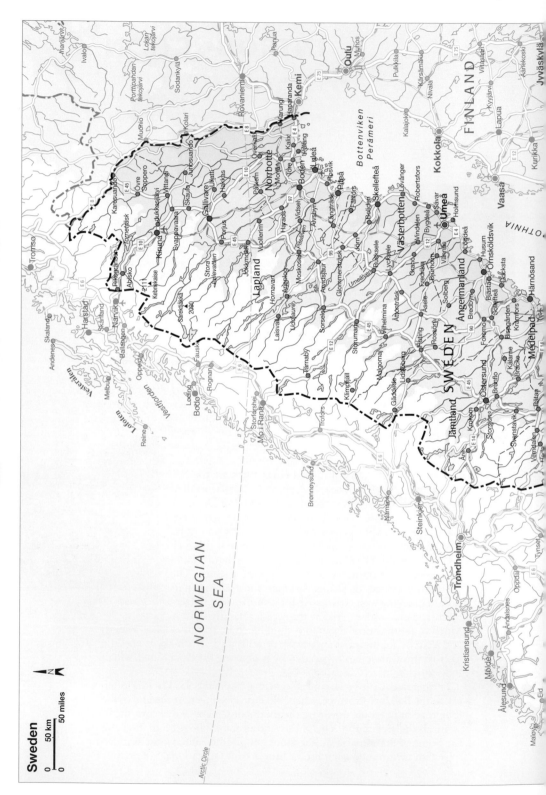

Sweden

0   50 km

0   50 miles

NORWEGIAN SEA

FINLAND

SWEDEN

Lapland

Norrbotte

Västerbotten

Ångermanland

Medelpad

Jämtland

Vesterålen

Lofoten

Vestfjorden

BOTHNIA

Bottenviken

Perämeri

Arctic Circle

Oulu

Kemi

Luleå

Umeå

Trondheim

Östersund

Härnösand

Kokkola

Vaasa

Jyväskylä

Tromsø

Narvik

Kiruna

Gällivare

Boden

Piteå

Skellefteå

Örnsköldsvik

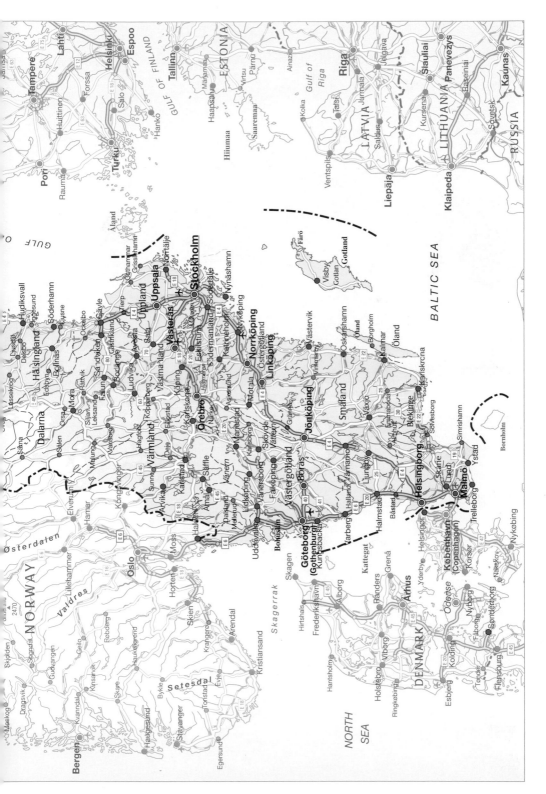

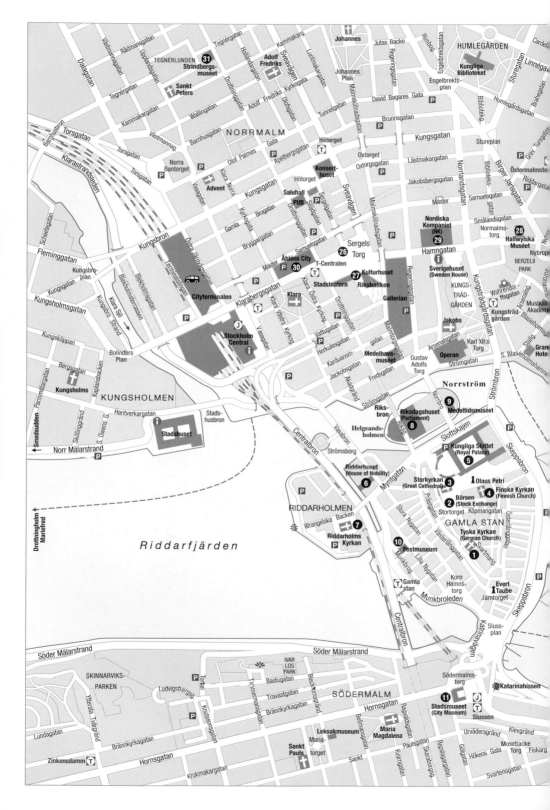

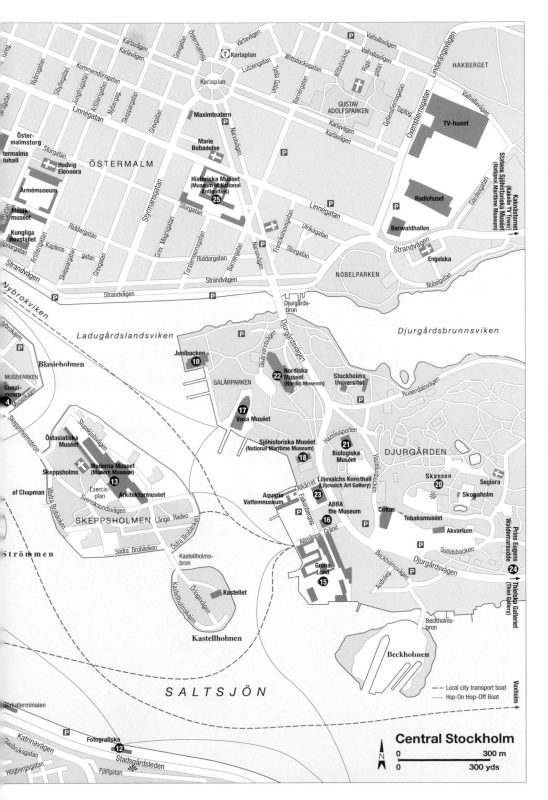

Karlavägen
Karlavägen
Karlavägen
Karlavägen
Östermalmsg.
Östgötagatan
Vårtavägen
T Karlaplan
Lutzengatan
Tyska Gatan
Wittstocksgatan
Valhallavägen
Valhallavägen
Riga-gatan
Wittstocksg.
Lindarängsvägen
HAKBERGET

Nybrogatan
Skeppargatan
Kommendörsgatan
Jungfrugatan
Artilligatan
Nybrog.
Skeppargatan
Grevgatan
Karlaplan
Barnängsgatan
Valhallavägen

Karlaplan

Linnégatan

Maximteatern

Narvavägen

GUSTAV ADOLFSPARKEN

Karlavägen
Karlavägen

Gyllenstiernsgatan
Tapitog.
Oxenstiernsgatan

TV-huset

Östermalmstorg
Storgatan
termalms luhall

Marie Bebadelse

Hedvig Eleonora

ÖSTERMALM

Valhallavägen
Gärdesgatan
Statens Sjöhistoriska Museet
(National Maritime Museum)
Kaknästornet (Kaknäs TV Tower)

Armémuseum

Historiska Museet (Museum of National Antiquities) **25**

Linnégatan

Radiohuset

Musik-museet

Styrmansgatan
Storgatan
Grev Magnigatan
Riddargatan
Riddargatan

Kungliga Hovstallet

Kaptens-gatan
Grevgatan
gatan
Torstenssonsgatan
Fredrikshovsgatan
Ulrikagatan
Narvavägen
Barnängtan
Storgatan

Ulrikagatan
Storgatan

Berwaldhallen

Strandvägen

Engelska

Strandvägen
Strandvägen
Strandvägen

NOBELPARKEN

Nobelgatan

Nybrokviken

Ladugårdslandsviken

Djurgårds-bron

Djurgårdsbrunnsviken

Nybrokajen

Blasieholmen

Junibacken
19

Djurgårdsvägen
Grönavägen

GALÄRPARKEN

Nordiska Muséet (Nordic Museum) **22**

Stockholms Universitet

Rosendalsvägen

MUSEIPARKEN
tional-
ueum
4

Museikajen
Skeppsholmsbron

17
Vasa Muséet

Östasiatiska Muséet

Slupskjulsvägen

Skeppsholms

Moderna Museet (Modern Museum) **13**

Sjöhistoriska Muséet (National Maritime Museum)
18

Hazeliusporten

21
Biologiska Muséet

DJURGÅRDEN

Hazeliusbacken

Skansen
20

Seglora

af Chapman

Exercis-plan
Svensksundsvägen
Västra Brobänken
Arkitekturmuséet

SKEPPSHOLMEN

Långa Raden
Östra Brobänken

Alkärret

Liljevalchs Konsthall (Liljevalch Art Gallery)
23

Falkenbergsg.

Aquaria Vattenmuseum

ABBA the Museum
16

Cirkus

Skogaholm

Tobaksmuséet

Akvarium

Prins Eugens Waldemarsudde

24

Thielska Galleriet
(Thiel Gallery)

Ström men

Södra Brobänken

Kastellholms-bron

Kastellet

Kastellholmsvägen
Örlogsvägen

Kastellholmen

Allmänna Gränd

Gröna Lund
15

Beckholmsvägen
Sollidsbacken

Djurgårdsvägen

Andréeg.

Beckholms-bron

Beckholmen

SALTSJÖN

Birkaterminalen

Katrinavägen
Fotografiska
12
Glasbruksgatan
Högbergsgatan
Stadsgårdsleden
Fjällgatan

--- Local city transport boat
—— Hop-On Hop-Off Boat

Vaxholm

Central Stockholm

N 0 ____ 300 m
0 ____ 300 yds

The City Hall dominates Stockholm's skyline.

STOCKHOLM

Sweden's capital is a city of islands, where palaces and peaceful hideaways line the shores, and where cobbled streets lead to chic shops, cafés and lively cultural attractions.

Spread across 14 islands set in a placid lake, Stockholm is "the city that floats on water". Boats and bridges link island to island, allowing visitors to wander at will from the cobbled streets of Gamla Stan (Old Town) to the buzzing cafés and clubs of Södermalm. Stockholm is a city for romantics: sail to enchanting Drottningholms Slott, slip back in time at the Viking-era settlement Birka, or visit the Vasa Museum to marvel at its glittering golden warship. Descend into the earth to explore the longest art gallery in the world; or take to the tower tops for panoramic views over the living city.

For the finest views over the rooftops of this low-rise city, take a trip to the dizzying observation platform on top of the **Kaknästornet** (Kaknäs Television Tower; Jan daily 10am–5pm; Feb–Mar Mon 10am–5pm, Tues–Sat 10am–9pm, Sun 10am–6pm; June–Aug: Mon–Sat 9am–10pm, Sun 9am–6pm; Apr–May and Sept–Nov: Mon–Sat 10am–9pm, Sun 10am–6pm; Dec: Mon–Sat 10am–9pm, Sun 10am–8pm), Ladugårdsgärdet, which rises 155 metres (508ft). Below, Stockholm spreads out in a glinting panorama of blue water and the red of old buildings against the stark white and glass of the new, cut through by green swathes of trees and grass. For the ultimate in high-altitude sightseeing, however,

Busy Gamla Stan.

why not drift over the city in a hot-air balloon? Stockholm is one of the few capital cities in the world that allows balloon trips within the city limits.

In winter, a white blanket lies over the city, fading the colours to pastel, and the summer ferries and pleasure boats are held fast in the solid ice of bays that cut deep into the heart of Stockholm. At that dark time of the year, only the icebreakers keep the more open stretches free of ice around the wharfs where ships for Finland and Denmark are docked.

Main Attractions

Gamla Stan (Old Town)
City Hall (Stadshuset)
Royal Palace (Kungliga Slottet)
Fotografiska
Museum of Modern Art (Moderna Muséet)
Vasa Museum
Skansen Open-Air Museum
Drottningholm Palace

Treasure islands

To the east are the thousands of islands of the archipelago, estimated at 24,000. The hundreds of small boats along the edge of the inlets and islands indicate the passion of every Stockholm family to own and sail a boat.

Fresh and salt water are separated by the island of Gamla Stan (Old Town) and the great lock gates of Slussen at the southern end. This island barrier is where Stockholm started some time before the 13th century. Today, half the city is on Lake Mälaren, the other on Saltsjön (Salt Lake), which leads out to the archipelago and the Baltic Sea, and the city continues to grow. From its small beginnings as a trading post and fort, Stockholm had no more than 75,000 inhabitants by the 18th century. Then came the late industrial revolution at the end of the 19th century, bringing Swedes by the thousands into the cities. By 1900, Stockholm had 300,000 city-dwellers. Now the population of the inner city stands at 912,000, while the Greater Stockholm region has more than 2.2 million inhabitants.

Vaxholm, one of the most popular islands in the archipelago.

Of late, Stockholm has rebranded itself the "capital of Scandinavia", causing hackles to rise in Copenhagen and Oslo. But there are reasons for Stockholm's confidence in its grand claims: it is the largest city in the largest country in Scandinavia, has the most multinational companies and the largest stock market, and receives the highest number of visitors from around the globe. The whole area is the powerhouse of Sweden, and accounts for more than one-fifth of the country's employment and a quarter of its total production. In many countries this would result in a noisy, industrial city, but Sweden's wide countryside means that the area covers some 6,500 sq km (2,500 sq miles) and has space enough for everyone and more.

From the high vantage point of Kaknäs, it is easy to understand why the Swedes were a seafaring people, and why the Swedish Vikings went east over the sheltered sea to Russia and down the great rivers to Constantinople rather than face the more perilous routes to the west. It reveals something about modern Stockholm, too. In this

city, life is still focused on the water, and, though nowadays Swedes may sail for pleasure rather than plunder, the affinity is as strong as ever.

Today, Stockholm is also considered a modern and sophisticated metropolis, famous for Scandinavian design in furniture, textiles and interiors and host to a number of international festivals. Once considered a place of *husmanskost* ("homely fare"), the city features some of the top chefs and most exciting cuisine in Europe. Stockholm's nightlife has exploded into an array of young, hip clubs and older, more sedate nightspots offering music and ambience for every taste. Infusing the old with the new is a speciality of today's vibrant Stockholm, as quick to seize on a new trend as Milan or Paris.

Gamla Stan

Stockholm's history starts in **Gamla Stan** (Old Town), one of the best-preserved medieval centres in Europe. Its interior forms a maze of narrow cobbled lanes where cars are banned, making exploration of its honey-coloured houses, shops and museums a pedestrian-friendly treat. Its winding alleys follow the same curves along which the seamen of former times carried their goods. No one restores a house or hotel in Gamla Stan without revealing the remains of an old fortified wall or an early workshop. Traces of even earlier times remain. At the corner between Prästgatan and Kåkbrinken, some bygone workman has casually repaired the wall with a Viking rune stone, probably the first stone that came to his hand.

These early years are shadowy, as is much early Swedish history, perhaps because the Vikings were too busy raiding and plundering to spend time writing more than the runes that decorate their memorials. In prehistoric times, this small islet between Lake Mälaren and Saltsjön was used by fishermen and hunters, but in the 12th century it became a base for German merchants from Lübeck who had begun to trade in iron, and an early king built a primitive watchtower.

The first mention of Stockholm is in 1252, when Birger Jarl, one of the regents in an age when kings died

Gamla Stan.

young and left infant heirs, built strong city walls and expanded the existing defences. Under the reign of Gustav Vasa, these defences grew into the grandest of royal residences, known as the Tre Kronor because of the three golden crowns (still a national symbol) that topped its keep tower. The castle burned down in a ferocious fire in 1697 – one eyewitness reported that within half an hour the entire edifice was ablaze. Today the present Royal Palace stands on the same site.

Stockholm was never a Hanseatic town, though one of the landmarks today is the graceful copper-clad spire and the bells of the **Tyska Kyrkan** (German Church) ❶, which at four-hourly intervals during the day alternate two hymn tunes. Other reminders of the Germans are Tyska Brinken (German Slope) and Tyska Skolgränd (German School Lane).

Today, Gamla Stan covers the original island of Stadsholmen, Riddarholmen (the island of the knights and nobles), Helgeandsholmen, occupied by the Riksdag (Parliament), and the tiny blob of Strömsborg, all so close that it is sometimes difficult to realise you have crossed from one to another. The best place to start a tour is **Stortorget**, the centre of the original city, from which narrow streets fan out in all directions.

Stortorget

Today, Stortorget is a peaceful square. In medieval times, it was a crowded, noisy place of trade, where German merchants, stallholders, craftsmen, and young servant girls and boys jostled and shouted. Along one side is **Börsen** ❷, the old Stock Exchange building. It housed Sweden's Stock Exchange until 1998, when the exchange moved into more modern premises in Frihamnen. Today, it's home to the Swedish Academy, who meet here to elect the winners of the Nobel Prize for Literature. It also contains the small **Nobelmuséet** (Nobel Museum; June–Aug daily 10am–8pm; Sept–May Tues 11am–8pm, Wed–Sun 11am–5pm; daily tours in English; tel: 08-534 818 00; www.nobelmuseum.se), dedicated to past Nobel Prize winners.

In the cobbled square, people laze on benches or sit at one of the outdoor

Statue of Birger Jarl, the founder of Stockholm.

A CITY AND ITS SYMBOL

From any part of Stockholm that lies south of Lake Mälaren, **Stadshuset** (City Hall) dominates the skyline. On the water's edge of Riddarfjärden, this is the master-work of architect Ragnar Östberg. The elegant building is made of decorated brickwork with an open-fronted portico facing the lake, and its delicate green copper roofs are topped with spires, domes and minarets. A massive square tower, around 105 metres (345ft) tall, rises from one corner of the central building. At its very tip gleam the Tre Kronor, the three golden crowns that symbolise the country.

Östberg began work in 1911 and devoted the next 12 years of his life to the City Hall. He used 8 million bricks and 19 million gilded mosaic tiles, the latter mainly used to stunning effect in the Golden Hall. This glittering ballroom is where the Nobel Prize guests dance the rest of the night away, after the ceremonial banquet held in the Blue Hall is over.

The interior of the City Hall is only accessible to visitors on a guided tour, available in English daily year-round on the hour from 10am to 3pm, subject to other events. You cannot pre-purchase, but must queue at the City Hall on the day of the tour to buy your ticket.

Even if you don't manage to explore the inside, anyone can enjoy the gardens. Look out for the statue of the 15th-century Swedish patriot Engelbrekt, who championed the cause of the peasants in Dalarna, on the southern terrace.

cafés, and it is hard to visualise that in 1520 the cobbles ran with blood during the Stockholm Bloodbath. Despite a guarantee of safety, the Danish king, Kristian II, known as The Tyrant, murdered 82 people, not only nobles but innocent civilians unlucky enough to have a shop or a business nearby. This gory incident triggered the demise of the Kalmar Union, which had united Sweden with Denmark and Norway for almost 125 years. The following year, Sweden's first heroic king, Gustav Vasa, put an end to the union and made Stockholm his capital.

More peaceful memories greet you if you follow **Köpmangatan** at the eastern corner of the square to number 11. Open the small door to the surprise of a gentle courtyard created in 1930 in what had been a dirty huddle of buildings. The work was carried out as an example of successful restoration and renewal by the St Erik Association, which has done so much to preserve Gamla Stan.

Back in the square, take the opposite Trångsund opening and you come to **Storkyrkan** ❸ (Cathedral; Jan–May and Aug–Sept: daily 9am–4pm; late May–early Aug: daily 9am–6pm; tel: 08-723 30 16). This awesome Gothic cathedral, parts of which date back to the 13th century, is the oldest church in Gamla Stan, and the scene of many royal occasions and coronations. The most recent was the wedding of Crown Princess Victoria to Daniel Westling in June 2010, for which the cathedral's interior was given an immense spring clean. Its high vaulted arches and sturdy pillars, stripped back to their original red brick, are still looking spruce. On Saturday lunchtimes from October to April, you can enjoy a recital on the magnificent organ, and then explore the church itself.

Storkyrkan's most famous statue is St George and the Dragon, the largest medieval monument in Scandinavia, a wooden sculpture carved by Bernt Notke in 1489, which somehow has retained its original colouring. Don't overlook the candelabra of various ages from the 17th century, or the plaque to the three generations of the Tessin family, who built the Royal Palace.

Inside the majestic cathedral.

Outside the cathedral, overlooking Slottsbacken and the front of the Royal Palace, is a **statue of Olaus Petri**, priest, writer, and one of the leaders of the Swedish Reformation. He was at one time sentenced to death by Gustav Vasa, apparently for failing to alert the king about an alleged plot against him, but received a royal pardon two years later. He looks like a man whom it would be dangerous to cross. The 22m (72ft) -high granite **obelisk** in front of him is considered to stand at the absolute centre of Stockholm.

If you feel like a rest between church and palace, cross over to the **Finska Kyrkan** ❹ (Finnish Church) opposite the palace gate. Behind it is Bollhustäppan (Ball Court Garden). This little courtyard has flowers, a small fountain and benches to welcome the weary sightseer and, most unexpectedly, Sweden's smallest statue, a seated figure just 15cm (6ins) high of a boy looking at the moon.

Royal Palace

Kungliga Slottet, the Royal Palace.

The present **Kungliga Slottet** ❺ (Royal Palace; tel: 08-402 61 30; www.

royalcourt.se; mid-May–mid-Sept daily 10am–5pm; mid-Sept–mid-May Tues–Sun 10am–4pm; daily tours) was built on the site of the Tre Kronor Palace, which burnt down in 1697, some say not without the help of Nicodemus Tessin the Younger, who had already built a new northern wing and who obviously relished the glory of rebuilding the palace to his Renaissance designs. His father, Nicodemus the Elder, had been architect to the old Tre Kronor palace, and the grandson Carl Gustaf was responsible for supervising the completion of the new palace many years later.

The palace is one of the biggest in Europe, with an astonishing 608 rooms, and still functions as the king's official residence. Various suites are open to the public – the stunning Royal Apartments are what most people go to see – and three museums show off the palace's history, sculptures and treasure. The palace is also famous for its tapestries, both Gobelin and of Swedish design, but the most evocative room is Oscar II's Writing Room in the Bernadotte Apartments. This has been kept exactly as the king left it when he died in 1907; even his desk is untouched. It is a comfortable, homely room, full of 19th-century clutter and family photographs.

In the old vaults (Skattkammaren) underneath the palace are the Crown Jewels, including 12 royal crowns, orbs and sceptres and other pieces of jewellery. They are immensely valuable and brilliantly lit so that they glow in the dim light of the vaults. Also below ground is the **Livrustkammaren** (Royal Armoury), including the stuffed remains of the horse of Gustav II Adolf, who extended the Swedish domain as far south as Poland until his death on the battlefield of Lützen in Germany in 1632. It's easy to see from his armour what a big man he was.

Lovers of pomp and circumstance can watch the 40-minute **Changing of the Royal Guard** (www.forsvarsmakten.

se; late Apr–Aug Mon–Sat 12.15pm, Sun 1.15pm, Sept–late Apr Wed and Sat 12:15, Sun 1:15), a colourful ceremony accompanied by brass band. The guards parade to the palace from various places, depending on the day and season – see the website for further information.

A noble island

To reach **Riddarholmen**, go west from Storkyrkan and then along Storkyrkobrinken through Riddarhustorget. Here you will find **Riddarhuset** ❻ (House of Nobility; tel: 08-723 39 90; www.riddarhuset.se; Mon–Fri 11am–noon), once one of four parliamentary estates. It is arguably the most beautiful building in Gamla Stan, with two pavilions looking out across the water. Inside, the erstwhile power of the nobles is matched by the grandeur of the Main Chamber, in which the nobles deliberated, watched from the ceiling by a painting of Mother Svea, who symbolises Sweden.

Riddarholmen is the silent island. Few live here, and most of the fine buildings are now government offices.

As you cross the bridge, straight ahead is **Riddarholms Kyrkan** ❼ (Riddarholm Church; tel: 08-402 61 30; mid-May–mid-Sept daily 10am–5pm; mid-Sept–Nov Sat–Sun 10am–4pm; closed Dec–mid-May), with its latticework spire and mellow red brick. Hard to imagine that in the days of the Franciscans who built it, the walls were painted bright red. Although the church is now used only on special occasions, its interior is as noble as the name of the island, because it holds almost all the graves of Swedish royalty since Gustav II Adolf.

On a summer evening, Riddarholmen is a pleasant place to stroll, past the quayside with a few pleasure boats and the graceful yacht *Mälardrottningen*, once the luxury yacht of the American millionairess Barbara Hutton and now a waterborne hotel, with the only restaurant on the island. There are no cafés or shops here, just slanting sun against the old buildings.

The idea of constructing the **Riksdagshuset** ❽ (Parliament; tel: 08-786 48 62; www.riksdagen.se; year-round; guided tours mid-Sept–mid-June:

FACT

Reconstruction of the old salmon runs, as well as salmon-stocking programmes, have increased the number of salmon and sea trout in the heart of the city. This is a fisherman's paradise.

Changing of the Guard at the Royal Palace.

Riddarholmen, the silent island.

Sat–Sun; mid-June–Aug: daily), on an island called "The Holy Spirit" (Helgeandsholmen), has a piquant charm. Do they speak in tongues on the chamber floor? The Riksdag and the old **Riksbank** (State Bank), now part of the parliament buildings, cover almost the whole of the island, with the parliamentary extension, a copper-clad, semicircular structure attached at the second level and following the curves at one side of the old building. Parts of the parliament buildings are open to the public, and there is a public gallery.

Archaeological discovery

The refurbishment of the Riksdag led to a remarkable archaeological find and a new museum. When the builders started to excavate the Riksdag terrace to form an underground car park, they discovered layer upon layer of the past, including part of the medieval wall and the cellars of an apothecary's shop. As good conservationist Swedes, the parliamentarians immediately forswore their claim to a car park. Stockholm's **Medeltidmuséet** ❾ (Medieval Museum; tel: 08 508 316 20;

www.medeltidsmuseet.stockholm.se; year round: Tues, Thur & Sun noon–5pm, Wed noon–8pm, closed Mon; free), on Strömparterren, Norrbro, incorporates the old wall and other treasures dug up during the excavations. It also includes the town gallows.

Gamla Stan is an ideal place for browsers and strollers. It always reveals something you have not seen before in the criss-cross of small lanes, hidden courtyards and unexpected nooks and crannies, and along the two favourite shopping streets, **Österlånggatan** and **Västerlånggatan**, which lie just outside the line of the first city walls. The Old Town is very much alive and working, and Stockholmers fight for the privilege of living in one of the tall houses that line the Old District's narrow streets.

Don't miss **Mårten Trotzigs Gränd**, the narrowest street in Gamla Stan, at the southern end of Västerlånggatan. It is more a stairway than a lane, less than a metre wide, which you can clamber up to reach **Prästgatan**, a route that more than any follows the lie of the island.

Only a step or two from Mårten Trotzigs Gränd, in **Järntorget**, is a statue not to miss. Evert Taube was a popular musician in the robust tradition of the Swedish troubadour, who died in 1976 much loved and in his 80s. The statue is so alive that, at first glance, the unpretentious figure almost seems to be Taube himself, ready to burst into song.

Close to the Gamla Stan metro station is the excellent little **Postmuseum ⑩** (Postal Museum; www.post museum.se; Tues–Sun 11am–4pm, to 7pm Wed; free for children), at Lilla Nygatan 6. The Postal Service has owned the gracious old building since 1720, and the collection includes the world's first stamp, from 6 May 1840, as well as an early mail coach, a train sorting office, and postal boat, which all indicate the rigours postmen endured in getting mail to Sweden's far-flung communities.

For those footsore from discovering the hidden treasures of Gamla Stan, the Old Town has an abundant selection of restaurants, jazz pubs and cafés. Many are in the same cellars where the merchants of old stored exotic imports: as you descend the stone steps or sit at one of the courtyard tables, history is still strongly in evidence.

The transformation of Södermalm

From the southern end of Gamla Stan it is worth making a detour to **Slussen**, where the lake is divided from the saltwater harbour by big lock gates, and on to **Södermalm**, the next island south. "Söder", as it is affectionately known, was once the great working-class area of the city. Today, it forms the bohemian heart of Stockholm, and is one of the hippest areas to live, work and socialise. Hornsgatan is Södermalm's main artery, with surrounding streets well worth exploring for their less mainstream shops. The inner circle of cool is the "SoFo" area (south of Folkungsgagatan), the place to head for fashion, food and nightlife.

Södermalm was the backdrop for much of the action in Stieg Larsson's best-selling *The Girl with the Dragon Tattoo*. From July to September, the city museum runs a two-hour

*Exploring
Gamla Stan.*

TIP

You can buy city maps such as the Millennium Map (SEK 40), which allows you to take a self-guided walking tour of *The Girl with the Dragon Tattoo*'s Stockholm.

Millennium walking tour (11.30am Sat, 6pm Thur) that points out landmarks from the books and films – contact the Medeltidsmuseum for tickets.

Stockholm's **Stadsmuséet** ⓫ (City Museum; www.stadsmuseum.stockholm. se), on Ryssgården, was closed for renovation at the time of writing. It was due to reopen in autumn 2017, with a new permanent exhibition focusing on stories of Stockholm, and extra space to display its extensive collection of items illustrating life down the centuries. While the museum is closed, you can get a flavour of Södermalm's industrial past at the former silk mill **Almgrens Sidenväveri** (tel: 08-642 56 16; www.kasiden.se; mid-June–mid-Aug Mon–Sat 11am–3pm; mid-Aug–mid-June Mon–Fri 10am–4pm, Sat 11am–3pm), at Repslagargatan 15, which wove fine silken goods and ribbons from 1833 until 1974. It's also one of the few places where you can see a working Jacquard loom.

The strange-looking 19th-century **Katarinahissen** lift, rebuilt in 1935, used to take visitors to the heights of Södermalm, but it is closed for renovation until 2019. However, if you've got the legs for it, you can still climb the stairs to the viewpoint for a great outlook over the lock gates, the waterside, and one of Stockholm's vibrant outdoor markets, bright with fruit, vegetables and the flowers beloved by Swedes for counteracting the darkness of their long winters.

From the top of Katarinahissen, east along the water's edge, you may well have spotted one of Stockholm's newer attractions, the fabulous **Fotografiska** ⓬ (daily 9am–11pm) exhibition space, which opened in 2010. Housed within the impressive Art-Nouveau Customs House (1906), Fotografiska puts on four major photographic exhibitions per year, and around 15 to 20 smaller shows and video installations. Previous exhibitions hosted within its superb industrial spaces have included everything from Martin Schoeller's close-up portraits to Brazilian photographer Sebastião Salgado's dreamlike shots of the natural world. Fotografiska is one of the few Stockholm attractions with late opening hours, and its popular café-restaurant terrace has beautiful views over the water.

Modern art and old masters

To the east of Gamla Stan lies the smaller island of **Skeppsholmen**. The sleek schooner moored off the island is the 100-year-old *af Chapman*, which is now used as a youth hostel. One of the highlights of Stockholm is the **Moderna Muséet** ⓭ (Museum of Modern Art; www.modernamuseet. se; Tues & Fri 10am–8pm, Wed, Thur, Sat–Sun 10am–6pm, closed Mon). The museum displays a collection of 20th-century art that is considered one of the finest in the world, with works by Dalí, Picasso and Magritte among many others, and parts of the collection can also be seen at other Stockholm art galleries and museums (see page 110). The museum's large restaurant-café boasts a beautiful panoramic view of the city skyline.

Vintage shop in Södermalm.

Skeppsholmen is linked by the Skeppsholmsbron bridge to the waterfront of **Blasieholmen**, where the big sumptuous building is one of Scandinavia's most famous hotels, the **Grand**. Nearby, on Södra Blasieholmshamnen, the stately **Nationalmuseum ⓮** (National Museum of Fine Arts; tel: 08-519 543 00; www.national museum.se) will open to the public again in 2018 after major renovation. Most of the permanent national collection, which includes several of the great masters from 1500 to 1900, is in storage, but the museum has temporary exhibition venues at Kulturhuset Stadsteatern and at Konstakademien (see pages 177 and 110).

Djurgården: Stockholm's playground

From Gamla Stan, it is just 10 minutes by boat (either the public transport SL ferry or the Strömma hop-on, hop-off sightseeing boat) across the harbour to the island of **Djurgården**, past the wharves where the big ferries leave for the Baltic, and Kastellholmen, now a military base. Once a royal deer park, much of Djurgården is still in its natural state, with paths and woods where you may spot an old hunting lodge or pavilion through the trees. There is fine birdwatching in the marshes and wetlands, and the forest reveals small creatures, both everyday and rare, such as hares and the occasional deer. The island is part of Ekoparken, the world's first city national park. A good way to get around is to hire a bike at the bridge which forms the road entrance.

As the boat slides into the Djurgården quay, there is no mistaking that this is an island that is entirely devoted to enjoyment. On the right past the quayside is **Gröna Lund ⓯** (tel: 010-708 91 00; www.gronalund.com; May–Sept and over Christmas: dates and times vary), an amusement park with 18th-century roots but some up-to-the-minute rides. The latest include Eclipse, a giant wave swinger built in 2013; and 2015's walk-through House of Nightmares, crammed full of animatronic horrors.

Just outside the amusement park, a new museum dedicated to Sweden's most popular band invites you

EAT

Restaurants often offer a good-value "dagens" lunch (dish of the day), which usually includes a soft drink and coffee.

Getting dizzy in Gröna Lund.

TIP

For a refreshing dip in wintry Stockholm, visit the Eriksdalsbadet (Mon–Thur 6.30am–9pm, Fri 6.30am–8pm, Sat–Sun 9am–6pm; www.stockholm.se/eriks dalsbadet), to the south of Södermalm. The city's largest swimming complex, it has five pools, including an adventure pool with slides, as well as a sauna and gym.

The Vasa warship, one of the most important shipwrecks in the world.

to 'Walk in. Dance out.' Fans of the flared-trousered, long-haired supergroup will do just that at **ABBA the Museum** 🔟 (www.abbathemuseum.com; daily 10am–6pm, Wed & Thur until 8pm), where you can view the costumes up close and sing along with the band's biggest hits.

Maritime treasure

The hop-on, hop-off sightseeing boat also stops at a quayside by the huge, oddly shaped, and utterly unique **Vasa Muséet** 🔟 (Vasa Museum; Galärvarvs-vägen 14; www.vasamuseet.se; Sept–May: daily 10am–5pm, Wed until 8pm; June–Aug: daily 8.30am–6pm), which houses the *Vasa* warship.

The magnificent ship was built in the 1620s for the Thirty Years War, on the orders of Sweden's warrior king, Gustav II Adolf, in honour of the founder of his dynasty, Gustav Vasa. Made from 1,300 tonnes of solid oak, with gold leaf on her poop and bow, guns of bronze, and decorated with 700 sculptures and carvings, her splendour was, however, short-lived. In 1628, she set off from Stockholm harbour on

her maiden voyage, watched by king, court and people. With her gun ports open for the royal salute, a sudden gust caught her, water flooded in, and the ship heeled over and sank, drowning most of those on board.

There she lay until 1956, when a Swedish marine archaeologist, Anders Franzén, found her and started planning her recovery. In 1961, the hulk of the great ship broke the surface again, and the long process of restoration began. More than 24,000 objects have been salvaged from the seabed, including skeletons, sails, cannon, clothing, tools, coins, butter, rum and many everyday utensils. The marine archaeologists also found thousands of missing fragments large and small of the vessel herself, which were painstakingly numbered and their positions recorded.

Over the next 30 years, *Vasa* was pieced together like a giant three-dimensional jigsaw puzzle, and regained her early splendour. The fact that she sank so swiftly without fire or explosion meant that most objects on board were recovered, and this valuable collection reveals a lot about life

on a 17th-century ship. To most people, these simple utensils that speak of everyday life are as fascinating as the structure and statuary – a sailor's *kista* (chest) which contains his pipe, his shoemaking kit and all the other necessities of a long voyage, as well as the admiral's cabin, where 12 officers slept in no great comfort.

Just south of the *Vasa* are two other interesting **museum ships** (daily 11am–6pm Jul–Aug; free). The *Sankt Erik* (1915) was Sweden's first large icebreaker and transformed winter trading in and out of the Baltic. The other is one of Sweden's last lightships, the *Finngrundet*, dating from 1903. They belong to the **Sjöhistoriska Muséet** ⓲ (National Maritime Museum; www.sjohistoriska.se; Tues–Sun 10am–5pm; free), whose main building, over the water in Östermalm, covers shipbuilding and merchant shipping as well as naval history.

Pippi & co.

Fans of Astrid Lindgren's children books should not miss **Junibacken** ⓳ (tel: 08-587 230 00; www.junibacken. se; Mar, Apr & Sept: Tues–Sun 10am–5pm; May, June, Oct–Dec: daily 10am–5pm; July–Aug: daily 10am–6pm), a children's attraction/theatre dedicated to her eccentric characters, with occasional guest appearances from other Scandinavian favourites such as the Moomins. An electrically operated indoor tram, with narration in English, allows the rider to experience *Astrid's World*, floating over miniature scenes from her books with moving figures, lights, and sound. This fanciful journey ends at Villa Villekula, the house of Pippi Longstocking, where you can ride her horse or play hopscotch in her garden. The exhibition also has a computer games room, a well-stocked book and toy store, and a waterfront café.

Another way of life

Where the island rises in steps to a hilltop is **Skansen** ⓴ (tel: 08-442 80 00; www.skansen.se; Jan–Mar and Oct–Dec: Mon–Fri 10am–3pm, Sat–Sun 10am–4pm; Apr daily 10am–4pm; May–mid-June and Sept: daily 10am–6pm; late June–Aug: 10am–8pm), the

Skansen open-air museum.

FACT

Stockholm is a city of summer festivals. Gamla Stan is the fitting setting for the Early Music Festival (www.semf.se) in June. In the same month, Skärgårdsbåtens Dag (Archipelago Boat Day) sees a procession of Stockholm's old steamboats sail from Strömkajen to Vaxholm. Stockholm Pride Week (www.stockholmpride.org) in July is the biggest Gay Pride celebration in Scandinavia. See www.visitstockholm.com for more.

oldest open-air museum in the world. In 1891, long before such things became fashionable, Artur Hazelius, who believed in practical education, decided to preserve the then familiar Swedish way of life, fast disappearing under a wave of industrial revolution that came late but fast to Scandinavia. He began to collect traditional buildings from different areas, and today there are some 150, including an 18th-century church, which is still in use for regular services and a popular place for weddings.

Many of the houses and workshops are grouped together to form the town quarter along a steep cobbled street. They include authentic workshops where tradesmen once practised their craft. During the summer, many of the buildings revive their traditional use, when Skansen employs craftworkers to carry on the old skills. In the shoemaker's house, where shoes have been made for more than 100 years, they still stitch and cut, and the engraver's workshop and the pottery demonstrate and sell their products. In the village shop, you can buy the

old handmade sweets that few stores stock today. Tempting smells draw you into the bakery, where Stockholmers queue up for their Sunday bread and tasty *bullar* (cinnamon buns).

Wildlife park

Skansen is not just a museum of life past; it also tries to give a picture of the Swedish countryside and wildlife today, so that you get a clearer view of an elk than you can hope for from a car, as the creature slips carefully back into the forest at dusk or dawn. This area, which is largely too informal and the surroundings too natural to be called a zoo, also holds a few more exotic beasts. Some are species once native but now extinct in Sweden, others such as monkeys and elephants are there to please children, and there is also **Lill-Skansen**, where children are allowed to handle and stroke small creatures.

About 300 metres (330 yds) north from the main entrance to Skansen is the **Biologiska Muséet ㉑** (Museum of Biology; www.biologiskamuseet. com; Apr–Sept: 11am–4pm; Oct–Mar: Tues–Fri noon–3pm, Sat–Sun 11am–3pm), also the first of its kind in the world, where Nordic animals are depicted against dioramas to give the illusion of their natural habitat. The dioramas were reproduced from works by one of Sweden's most distinguished nature painters, Bruno Liljefors.

Djurgården has music of many kinds, everything from chamber music in the old Skogaholm Manor at the heart of the island and nightly entertainment on the Main Stage at Gröna Lund, to rock concerts in the open air and folk dancing and special celebrations for Midsummer and other festivals. Against the green of the hill, the traditional costumes look as though they belong.

Bridal crowns

If you choose bus instead of boat and enter the island over Djurgårdsbron

Brown bear in Skansen wildlife park.

from Strandvägen, the first museum you come to is the ornate building that houses the **Nordiska Muséet** ㉒ (tel: 08-519 546 00; www.nordiskamuseet. se; daily 10am–5pm; Sept–May also open Wed until 8pm), which depicts Nordic life from the 16th century. Its collection of 1.5 million items includes peasant costumes, a special collection of bridal gowns and the traditional silver-and-gold crowns worn by Swedish brides. Other exhibitions explore Lapland culture, folk art, and more, to show how Swedes live and lived. The **Children's Playhouse** on the first floor is a fun place to dress up and experience life in the olden days.

Djurgården's art galleries

About 400 metres (440 yds) south from the Nordiska Muséet is **Liljevalchs Konsthall** ㉓ (Liljevalch Art Gallery; tel: 08-508 313 30; www. liljevalchs.sc; Tues–Sun 11am–5pm, Tues & Thur until 8pm, closed Mon), at Djurgårdsvägen 60. It is devoted largely to contemporary work, and the Spring Exhibition attracts many aspiring artists.

About 1.5 km (1 mile) southeast of Liljevalchs (a 15-minute walk, or accessible on tram 7) is what many describe as the most beautiful gallery in the city – **Prins Eugens Waldemarsudde** ㉔ (Prins Eugens väg 6; tel: 08-545 837 00; www.waldemarsudde.se; Tues–Wed, Fri–Sun 11am–5pm, Thur 11am–8pm, closed Mon; guided tours). It is the former home of Prince Eugen, the "Painter Prince" and brother to the late King Gustav V. When he died in 1947, the prince left his lovely home and garden as well as his collection, which includes many of his own impressive landscape paintings, to the nation. This gem of a gallery, looking south over Saltsjön, is not to be missed.

Another 2.5 km (1.5 miles) southeast, on bus 69 or by foot, is **Thielska Galleriet** (tel: 08-662 58 84; www. thielska-galleriet.se; Tues–Sun noon–5pm, until 8pm Thur), at Sjötullsbacken 6, designed by a popular architect of the time to house the collection of the banker Ernst Thiel. The marvellous range of pictures includes the work of Norwegian Edvard Munch,

STOCKHOLM'S GREEN SPACES

Stockholm is an amazingly green and leafy city: over 40 percent of it is green space, made up of recreational areas, nature reserves and around 8,000 kitchen gardens, cultivated by residents who rent them cheaply from the city.

In summer, many Stockholmers pack a picnic and head for an al fresco lunch in one of the 26 municipal parks. A particularly impressive choice is the huge Royal National City Park, known as **Ekoparken** (www.ekoparken.org), which is the world's first 'national city park'. This mighty set of green lungs stretches out in a 12km (7-mile) long arch from Djurgården (where the Vasa museum, Gröna Lund and Skansen are situated) to Ulriksdals Slott (Ulriksdal Palace) in the north. You need a full day of serious hiking to explore it, by foot during the warmer months or on skis or long-distance skates in winter.

The Ekopark incorporates three royal parks, Djurgården, Haga and Ulriksdal, with palaces to tour (Ulriksdals Slott, Gustav III's Paviljong, Rosendals Slott); tropical delights to admire, such as the butterfly house and the world's largest water lily in the Bergianska Botanical Gardens; and home-grown wildlife like herons, foxes and roe deer to spot. On

northern Djurgården you'll find greenhouses, a café serving excellent home-made food, and garden shops.

It may sound a little morbid, but one of the most beautiful of Stockholm's green spaces is the Unesco World Heritage site **Skogskyrkogården** (Woodland Cemetery; www.skogskyrkogarden.stockholm.se; open 24hrs, visitor centre June–Aug daily 11am–4pm, May & Sept Sun 11am–4pm; guided tours in English July–Sept Sun at 10.30am), in the southern suburb of Enskede. The work of two of Sweden's most important architects, Gunnar Asplund and Sigurd Lewerentz, this masterpiece of Modernist design took 25 years (1915–40) to create. Today Skogskyrkogården is a place of immense calm and beauty, where nature and architecture are blended into a seamless whole. Every detail was planned: for example, the 888m- (975 yard-) long Seven Springs Way, which brings mourners to the funeral chapel, is lined with trees that make the path increasingly dark and melancholic – a progression of weeping birches, pines and finally spruce. The cemetery is the resting place of many famous Swedes, including Greta Garbo and Asplund himself.

and Sweden's Anders Zorn, Carl Larsson and Bruno Liljefors, all part of the National Romantic Movement of the late 19th and early 20th centuries. The gallery even has some pictures by the playwright August Strindberg. In the early decades of the 20th century, Thielska Galleriet became a meeting place for artists, poets, and writers. When Thiel went bankrupt in the 1920s, the city bought the gallery.

Gold in Östermalm

North of Djurgården, the leafy green district of Östermalm commands the highest house prices in Sweden. It's mainly a wealthy residential area, but one visitor attraction is the **Historiska Muséet ㉕** (Museum of National Antiquities; tel: 08-519 556 00; www.historiska.se; Narvavägen 13–17; June–Aug: daily 10am–6pm; Sept–May: Tues–Sun 11am–5pm, Wed until 8pm), dedicated to Sweden's history from the Stone Age to medieval times. Here you'll find the world's largest collection of Viking-Age finds; a chilling exhibition about the Battle of Gotland; and the spectacular Gold Room, an underground vault designed for maximum security for the more than 3,000 prehistoric gold and silver artefacts.

Modern architecture

It's anyone's guess what John Tobias Sergel might have thought of the huge illuminated obelisk, modern fountain and square that bear his name, and of the modern city around it. He was a neo-classical sculptor, famed in Rome, who returned to the cultured court of Gustav III. Sergel sculpted many statues for Gustav, including one of the king himself and another, *Oxenstierna and History*, to commemorate the early statesman Axel Oxenstierna.

The heart of this modern business and commercial area is not large, but it sits somewhat uneasily with the rest. From **Sergels Torg ㉖** it is hard to miss the five towering office blocks on **Sveavägen**, which cast their shadow over the other buildings. In fact, they are visible from almost every part of the city.

In the 1960s, Stockholm City Council, like so many others,

The bright lights of Sergels Torg.

succumbed to the temptation to knock things down and build concrete-and-glass high-rise buildings, which are concentrated on Norrmalm's business area and around Central Station, where most of the big hotels stand today. The destruction of many fine old buildings continued until it threatened **Kungsträdgården** (King's Garden), with its famous statue of Carl XII on its southern side.

At this point the Stockholmers had had enough. Normally placid and biddable, they mustered in 1971 at the King's Garden, climbed the elm trees that were in danger of the axe, and swore that if the trees went so did the people. The City Fathers retreated, and Kungsträdgården survives to soften the edges of the new buildings and harmonise with the older buildings that are left. This is the place to stroll or sit beside the fountains on a summer day and enjoy a coffee at one of the outdoor cafés. In winter, part of Kungsträdgården is flooded with water and becomes a popular ice rink.

Kulturhuset ㉗ (The Culture House; tel: 08-506 20 200; www.kultur huset.stockholm.se; Mon–Fri 9am–7.30pm, Sat–Sun 11am–5pm) at the western end of Hamngatan is a popular venue for dance, theatre, music, films and art exhibitions. Housed in the same building, the **Stockholm Visitor Center** (tel: 08-508 285 08; www.visitstockholm.com; May–mid-Sept Mon–Fri 9am–7pm, Sat 9am–4pm, Sun 10am–4pm; mid-Sept–Apr Mon–Fri 9am–6pm, Sat 9am–4pm, Sun 10am–4pm) can give advice and help you book tours, travel and event tickets. This is also the place to buy a *My Stockholm Pass*, which gives free entry to 75 Stockholm attractions as well as free sightseeing tours by boat and bus.

A private palace

It's worth trying to catch a guided tour at one of Stockholm's most unusual museums, the early 20th-century private palace **Hallwylska Muséet ㉘** (Hallwyl Collection; Hamngatan 4; www.hallwylskamuseet.se; June–Aug Tues–Sun 10am–4pm, Sept–May

Statue of Carl XIII in King's Garden.

UNUSUAL TOURS

Stockholm is an unusual city, and visitors may want to explore it in unusual ways. If you've already climbed Kaknästornet television tower, seen the city from the platform of Katarinahissen, or soaked up the panorama from the top of City Hall, why not take things a step further with a fullblown rooftop tour? Takvandring (tel: 060-12 14 44; www.takvandring.com) offer vertiginous views of Gamla Stan from a series of ladders and catwalks on top of the Old Parliament Building on Riddarholmen.

If heights are not your thing, you can employ paddle power and investigate the city's watery routes by kayak, rowing boat, pedalo or canoe. Djurgårdsbron Sjöcafe (Galärvarvsvägen; tel: 08-660 5757; www.sjocafeet.se; Apr–Sept) is a central hire place, or contact Kanotcenter Svima Sport (Ekelundsvägen 26; tel: 08-730 22 10; www.svima.se) for more specialist equipment.

Once the lakes and canals have frozen, you can experience the nearest thing to flying by taking a skating tour. Although routes depend on which parts of the archipelago are solidly frozen, tours usually end with a skate through central Stockholm, right past the Stadshus (City Hall). ICEguide (tel: 08-33 60 01; www.iceguide.se) runs a five-hour introduction from January to March.

The World's Longest Art Gallery

For the price of a metro ticket, visitors to Stockholm can have access to the longest art gallery in the world.

Sculptures, mosaics, paintings and installations fill the cavernous stations of the city's underground system, instilling a sense of wonder in the passing crowds. In the subterranean halls, flowers bloom, a forest whispers, an arching ceiling becomes a boiling red sky. Travelling through the tunnels takes you into an artistic otherworld – an experience not to be missed.

Stockholm's underground railway, Tunnelbanan, is much more than a mere transport system. Down the escalators is a world of gleaming caverns full of colour, texture and shape. Booking halls, ceilings, platforms and track walls offer an endless variety of temporary and permanent artworks, spanning the 1950s to the present day.

Stockholmers can enjoy art on their daily commute; here at Akalla (line 11).

More than 150 artists have had a hand in this amazing endeavour, and to date at least 90 of the existing 100 stations are embellished.

The first metro line opened in 1950, but it was not until 1957 that the first works in this 110km (68-mile) -long visual feast were installed, largely down to a campaign by artists Vera Nilsson and Siri Derkert to bring art to the metro in conjunction with architects and engineers. T-Centralen, the hub of the network, became home to the first pieces, the winners of a national competition. Egon Möller-Nielsen constructed terrazzo sofas on the upper platform, while the track walls were decorated by Erland Melanton and Bengt Edenfalk's *Klaravagnen*, an abstract pattern of glass prisms in greens, blues and creams.

The best lines for art-spotting

Stockholmers argue about which is the best line for paintings, but the route out to Akalla (line 11) is a strong contender. The train leaves from T-Centralen's lower platform, and to go down the second escalator is to enter a deep mysterious cave. The platform and tracks have been tunnelled out of natural stone, left in its rough-hewn form, and covered with huge blue leaf fronds on a white-and-blue background.

As you pass the various stations, look also at Västra Skogen with an 18-metre (60ft) human profile in terrazzo, tile patterns and cobblestones. But the highlight on this line surely is Solna Centrum, which actually deserves a special stop. It has green hills and forests behind the rail tracks, silhouetted against red. The scene shows a man playing an accordion, and, the longer you look at the work, the more you find. This environmental theme, *Sweden in the 70s*, was completed in 1975 by Karl-Olov Björk and Anders Åberg.

On the other arm of this line (10) is Tensta, one of the larger immigrant communities, with some 30 different nationalities represented. Helga Henschen's 1970s paintings are a joyful tribute to Sweden's incomers, with blossoming flowers and phrases in many different languages. But many think the most interesting station on this line is Kungsträdgården, which has two beautiful entrances. Other more unusual exhibits are the *Green Bird* sculpture at Rågsved (line 19), the scientific, engineering and mathematical symbols of Tekniska Högskolan (Royal Institute of Technology, line 14), and the fantasy beetles in glass cases at Gärdet (line 13).

Tues–Sun noon–4pm, Wed until 7pm; guided tours in English: June Sat–Sun 12.30pm; July–Aug Tues–Sun 12.30pm; Sept–Dec Sat 1.30pm). The dedicated guides all have their own favourite stories of life in the palace; and you get to see the whole house, rather than just a few rooms.

The magpie collection of Countess von Hallwyl, who decided at a young age to transform her home into a museum, contains nearly 70,000 objects, including her furniture, personal knick-knacks (including a chunk of her husband's beard), her ornate piano and china, gathered from more than 70 years of extensive travels through Europe, Africa and Asia. The collection varies somewhat in quality, but never lacks in fascination; and the von Hallwyls spared no expense in designing and building their residence; even the facade is beautiful.

Shopping Swedish-style

Also on Hamngatan is **Gallerian**, a huge covered shopping arcade stretching all the way to Jakobsgatan. Further to the east is Sweden's equivalent of Harrods, **Nordiska Kompaniet** (NK) **㉙**. The illuminated rooftop sign, constantly turning, is visible from far and wide in the city. NK sells everything from shoes to sporting equipment, men's and women's clothing to glass, pottery and silver, jewellery and perfume; its services range from a pharmacy to a bank to a tailors and dry cleaners. **Åhléns City ㉚**, on the corner of Sergels Torg and Drottninggatan, has a similar range and quality to NK, and a visit to its food department is a sightseeing tour in itself.

Drottninggatan (Queen's Street), an old street which leads directly through the Riksdagshuset and over the bridge from the Royal Palace, is one of Stockholm's main pedestrian ways, with multi-coloured flags strung between the buildings. In summer, it is full of casual crowds strolling in T-shirts and shorts or sitting at one of the outdoor cafés.

Strindberg's Blue Tower

Not to be missed is **Strindbergsmuséet ㉛** (Strindberg Museum; tel: 08-411 53 54; www.strindbergsmuseet.se; July–Aug Tues–Sun 10am–4pm; Sept–June Tues–Sun noon–4pm), at Drottninggatan 85, housed in the top-storey flat of the Blåtornet (Blue Tower), where Sweden's greatest playwright spent his last years and wrote his last epic play, *The Great Highway* (1908).

August Strindberg's taste in room furnishing followed his ideas for stage sets, and the rooms in his flat are full of bright green, yellow and red. Even at the end of his life, Strindberg was astonishingly prolific, and he produced some 20 books in his four years in the Blue Tower. His study is just as he left it. The wreath beside a photograph of his daughter Anne-Marie was presented to Strindberg on the first anniversary of the theatre he founded, Intiman (the Intimate Theatre).

Islands by the thousand

It is a rare city that has 24,000 islands on its doorstep and 100 km (60

Shopping mecca NK department store.

miles) of lake at its heart, but this is Stockholm's eternal good fortune. Until the building of the Tunnelbanan, boats were often the only way of getting around these great expanses of water, and boats are still part of Stockholm life.

To maintain contact within the archipelago, Stockholm County Council's own shipping company, Waxholmsbolaget, subsidises boat transport to all the inhabited islands – thereby providing a valuable service for visitors who want to explore, as well as to the islanders themselves. The largest private company, **Strömma** (www.stromma.se), specialises mostly in transporting passengers across Lake Mälaren, and there are various other touring vessels that ply lake and sea. Between them, they provide a variety of craft, from beautiful old coal-fired steamers to modern ferries. Excursions vary from brief introductory tours to day-long excursions and evening cruises with dinner. The latter almost invariably involve music, allowing you to dance your way gently through the islands. (See also page 186.)

The state bedchamber at Drottningholm.

Mälaren stretches for more than 100km (60 miles) to the west, a lake of narrow straits and vast, sweeping bays, with beaches and rocky shores. You sail out past the modern buildings on **Norrmälarstrand**, but once the boat passes under the high arch of **Västerbron**, the shores change. On the left is the island of **Långholmen** and on the right a bathing beach, **Smedsudden**, one of 15 such beaches within the city limits. At the weekend and in the evenings, the lake is dotted with the sails of small boats.

Drottningholms Slott: home of royals

The most popular place to visit in the archipelago is the island of **Lovön**, to visit **Drottningholms Slott** 32 (Drottningholm Palace; tel: 08-402 62 80; www.kungahuset.se; May–Sept 10am–4.30pm; Oct Fri–Sun 11am–3.30pm; Nov–Mar: Sat–Sun noon–3.30pm; Apr daily 11am–3.30pm), a Unesco World Heritage site. The king and queen made it their primary residence in 1981 to give their young children a garden to play in – and what a garden! The palace is a

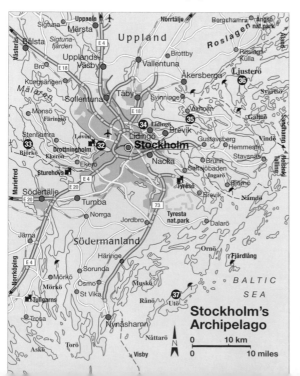

smaller version of Versailles, and looks out onto similarly formal stretches of fountains, statues, flower beds, box hedges and small dark trees, pointing upwards like green standing stones. The palace was built by the energetic Tessin family, headed by Nicodemus the Elder, and the gardens laid out by Nicodemus the Younger. Much of the palace is open to the public and there's a café serving coffee and waffles. The 17th- to 19th-century interiors are magnificent.

In the parkland stands the exotic pagoda of the **Kina Slott** (Chinese Pavilion; tel: 08-402 62 70; May–Aug 11am–4.30pm; Sept noon–3.30pm; guided tours May Sat–Sun noon, 2pm, 4pm; June–Aug daily noon, 2pm, 4pm; Sept daily noon, 2pm), built as a surprise birthday present for Queen Louisa Ulrika in 1753, when every fashionable European favoured *chinoiserie*.

Drottningholm Theatre

The island's other great treasure is undoubtedly the 18th-century **Drottningholms Slottsteater** (Drottningholm Court Theatre; tel: 08-556 931 00; www.dtm.se; Apr 11am–3.30pm; May–Aug 11am–4.30pm; Sept noon–3.30pm; Oct Fri–Sun noon–3.30pm; Nov–mid-Dec Sat–Sun noon–3.30pm; Teatermuséet, Duke Carl's Pavilion; guided tours in English every hour during opening times), which was opened in 1766 on the orders of the same queen.

Queen Louisa Ulrika's son Gustav III had two great loves – theatre and French culture (he could write the French language better than he wrote Swedish) – and it is said that he would have much preferred to be an actor or playwright than king. However, Gustav III was also a patriot who was determined to turn the country's French theatre tradition Swedish. He ejected the French actors from Drottningholm, replaced them with Swedes, and continued his aim of encouraging a Golden Age of the native arts.

Despite his enthusiasm for culture, Gustav's benevolent despotism was not popular with his unruly nobility. His assassination in 1792 at a masked ball inspired Verdi's *Un Ballo in Maschera*, a memorial Gustav himself might have approved of. On his death, the Court Theatre fell into disuse.

Drottningholm Palace, a mini-Versailles.

TIP

The site of the Viking town of Birka is open May–Sept. Strömma boats sail there in summer from outside Stadshuset (City Hall) on Kungsholmen. Ticket prices include the 7.5-hour round trip, a guided tour on the island, and entry to the Birka museum. Contact Strömma (tel: 08-587 140 00; www.stromma.se) for details.

Viking boat in Birka, on Lake Mälaren.

It was not until 1921 that the building once again came to life, after Professor Agne Beijer discovered it, complete and undamaged, just waiting for restoration. This unlikely set of circumstances makes it the oldest theatre in the world that still uses its original backdrops and stage machinery for productions today. Attending a performance here on a warm summer evening is like experiencing magic from an earlier age.

Trade and church

Further west is another Unesco World Heritage site. The elaborate trading routes of Viking-Age Europe are epitomised by the trading centres of Hovgården on Adelsö, and its more famous neighbour **Birka** on **Björkö** ③③ (see page 30). Between AD 800 and 975, Birka was the central trading hub for the 40,000 inhabitants of the rich Mälaren area, and the meeting point for traders from Russia and Arabia as well as from Central and Western Europe, at a time when the lake was still navigable from the Baltic.

This was also where Christianity first came to Sweden, when Ansgar, the Saxon missionary, landed in the early part of the ninth century. The Ansgar chapel, built in the 1930s, commemorates the missionary. Almost nothing is left of Birka above ground, but many archaeological digs have revealed the past at sites which include the old town, and the "sacrificial stones". Sadly for Ansgar, the sheer numbers of pagan graves show that he was largely unsuccessful in converting the island, and Sweden had to wait a further 200 years for Christianity to take a firm hold. A guide meets the boat at Björkö, which can only be reached by water. The **Birka Museum** (tel: 08-560 514 45; www.raa.se; May–Sept) features an interesting exhibition, although most of the archaeological finds are squirreled away at the Historiska Muséet in Stockholm. By changing boats in Birka, it is possible to continue west along Lake Mälaren to Västerås.

Baltic gateway

To the east, the islands of the archipelago seem endless, almost as though every Stockholm family could have

an isle of its own. A sense of freedom and distance begins the moment you start to skim through the skerries in a small boat or look down from the deck of a steamer.

Although now it is as easy to get there by underground (T-Ropsten) and bus, in summer you should grab the chance to take the boat to the island suburb of **Lidingö** ❸, where you can visit **Millesgården** (Carl Milles väg 2; tel: 08-446 75 90; www.millesgarden.se; Tues–Sun 11am–5pm), the summer home of the sculptor Carl Milles and his wife, the Austrian painter Olga Granner. Here, summer after summer, Milles patiently reproduced the statues that had made him more famous in his adopted country of America than in Sweden, though you can see a fine specimen in front of the Concert Hall at Hötorget. Milles's creations seem to evade gravity. They soar and fly, and step lightly over water, emphasised by their position on terraces carved from the steep cliffs of the island.

From Lidingö, the boat continues through the winding skerries as far as **Vaxholm** ❸, to the northeast. The urban area of Vaxholm is the trading centre for the 60 or so islands in this group, with rail and train links to the mainland as well as the more leisurely boat and car ferries to nearby islands. It is all part of an elaborate transport network that manages to keep a remarkable number of islands in contact with the city of Stockholm itself.

Elegance from centuries past

Vaxholm still has many traces of the mid-18th century, when the wealthier Stockholmers began to turn it into an ideal summer resort and build elegantly decorated wooden summer homes. The island already had a 16th-century fortress built under the supervision of King Gustav Vasa, now a museum. A walk round the town reveals the old customs house, the battery on the ramparts, and a 19th-century fisherman's cottage that holds **local heritage exhibitions** (Hembygdsgården; June–Aug: Sat–Sun noon–4pm).

Charming Vaxholm.

You can also sail, canoe, windsurf or swim at several good bathing beaches. Fishing for your own Baltic herring from the town's quayside is popular, but you could just sample them for lunch in the hotel near the harbour, or on one of the special herring picnics at **Vaxholm Fort**.

The journey out to Vaxholm takes about an hour and is an agreeable introduction to the archipelago. Though the Waxholmsbolaget boats are primarily designed to serve the islands, many have special day trips which allow you to stop, spend a day on an island and wait for the steamer's return.

The islands divide roughly into three areas which run parallel to the mainland: first, the big inner islands, then a belt of smaller skerries and, far out to sea, the isolated outer isles surrounded by pale, clear shallows. Each one is different, some wooded, some with heather, some scorched bare by the sea winds, and others steeped in silence and solitude. The bigger islands are ideal for cycling, and you can arrange a special excursion to Ljusterö **36**, an hour or so northeast from Vaxholm. Here you can rent a bicycle, make up a little picnic, and find out exactly what enticed artists like Bruno Liljefors here. In the evening the 100-year-old steamer SS *Storskär* returns for the journey to Stockholm, a beautiful trip in the long Scandinavian evening, winding in and out of the islands.

A similar cycling trip to **Utö 37**, in the southern part of the archipelago, reveals a hotel, restaurant, bakery, camping and bathing facilities; though central Sweden was the traditional home of the iron and copper industry in Sweden, Utö claims the oldest iron mine in Sweden, with a museum.

Many islands are rich in wildlife – elk and deer, otters, mink, fox, badgers and the occasional lynx. Others are a haven for birds and birdwatchers, with the rare white-tailed eagle, gulls, eiders, mergansers and velvet scoters, many wading birds such as turnstones and oystercatchers, with seabirds perching on the yellow lichen-covered rocks, and swans by the battalion.

Cycling in Utö.

The Eastern Archipelago

The further east you go in the seaward skerries, the more peaceful and unchanged the islands become. In spring and summer many are beautiful, with cowslips and wild pansies and orchids, and the scarlet of poppies. These outer islands are not always easy to reach, and the weather can be fickle, but they repay any difficulty in getting there. Three of the most beautiful are accessible from Stockholm.

Gällnö lies in the middle of the archipelago. It has a year-round population of farmers, and you will find youth hostels and camping sites which stipulate a maximum stay of two days, though it may be possible to stay longer. Waxholmsbolaget boats serve Gällnö.

Svartlöga is also on the scheduled route, via Blidö towards the northern end of the archipelago, and you can combine it with a visit to nearby **Rödlöga**. Svartlöga has a small general store, open in summer, and there is excellent bathing near the quay.

Bullerön, just south of Sandhamn, is one of the remotest islands in the archipelago, part of a nature reserve that takes in some 900 islands, islets and skerries. An exhibition in an old studio on the island gives information about island culture and nature. You reach it by taxiboat from Stavsnäs, on the inner island of **Fågeltrolandet**, or direct from Stockholm.

In all this remoteness, the bigger island of **Sandön** is a surprise, ideal for a short stay or a day excursion. For, though Sandön is on the outer edge of the archipelago, the village of Sandhamn is a lively place, with a restaurant, a museum and a large harbour stuffed with the masts of visiting boats. It is the headquarters of the **Royal Stockholm Yacht Club**.

Despite the influx, which swells the island's winter population of around 100 by an additional 100,000 people, on this island you feel you have really left the land behind. Sandhamn is part of the Baltic Sea, and a visit to the island will help you to understand what it was that from early times made the Swedes a maritime race, and what fires their present-day ambitions for a boat… and a star to steer her by.

Summer house in the Eastern Archipelago.

STEAMING OUT AMONG THE SKERRIES

When summer comes, the Swedes set off by boat to the thousands of idyllic islands that dot the waterways between Stockholm and the Baltic.

Every summer thousands of Swedes in boats navigate carefully through waters loaded with 24,000 islands, rocks and islets in the Stockholm archipelago. The brackish waters start in the centre of Stockholm and extend 80km (50 miles) out into the open Baltic Sea. Close to the mainland, the islands are larger and more lush, the bays and channels wider. Hidden here are idyllic island communities, farmlands and small forests. But as you travel further out, the scenery becomes more rugged, finally ending in sparse windblown islets formed by the last Ice Age.

Island retreats

In the middle of the 19th century affluent Stockholm families began to build their second homes along the shores of the various islands in the archipelago. Over the years, "commoners" had more money and leisure time and soon they, too, sought their way to the archipelago. The combination of wilderness, sea, fresh air and closeness to the city satisfied many leisure needs. Today, 20 percent of Swedes own a summer cottage. Others rent them, or tag along with family or friends to swim, sauna, fish, boat or immerse themselves in nature.

More than 50,000 second homes offering varying degrees of comfort are spread throughout Stockholm's archipelago.

There are plenty of ferries to help you get around.

A picnic on an islet in the archipelago. A bite to eat and something to drink out in the open, there's no better way to enjoy the archipelago before heading out on the water again.

Kayaking is a great way of exploring the archipelago.

A QUICK GUIDE TO ISLAND HOPPING

The archipelago can be explored on guided tours, which can be picked up from Stockholm's city centre, or by local transport boats run by Waxholmsbolaget (www.waxholms bolaget.se). The latter offers a handy five-day travelcard (also called the Island Hopping pass), which allows you to dart from island to island, including:

Sandön, with its attractive sailing-centre village of Sandhamn, sandy beaches and some good restaurants (a 6-hour round trip).

Fjäderholmarna, featuring a boat museum, aquarium, fish-smoking plant, restaurants and crafts shops (20 minutes by boat from Stockholm).

Vaxholm, with its famous fortress (1 hour by boat).

Utö, where a 12th-century iron-ore mine is the principal attraction. This is also a great place for bike-riding (3 hours by boat from the city).

Vaxholm fortress.

Arriving by ferry on an island in the Stockholm archipelago.

Sailing on Lake Mälaren; such is the importance of water to the Swedes that one in ten residents owns a boat.

Örebro Castle.

AROUND STOCKHOLM

Sweden's early history is firmly rooted around the sparkling waterways of Stockholm's hinterland, in close proximity to the ancient capital of Uppsala.

Three provinces – Uppland, Söder-manland and Västmanland – surround Stockholm, stretching from the ragged Baltic coastline to the interior, glinting with lakes and streams. Together they form the heart of Sweden, providing visitors with a synopsis of the country's past, its natural wonders and its cultural riches. The area is heavy with history: the Vikings once drew their religious strength from a great heathen temple at Uppsala, eventually replaced by the country's first cathedral. Sweden's wealth stems from the provinces' mineral deposits, which provided iron for the Eiffel Tower and copper for the roofs of Versailles. Along the banks of Lake Mälaren, castles, manors and palaces are reminders of hundreds of years of Swedish history.

Runestones and ruins

About 25km (16 miles) north of Stockholm is **Vallentuna ❶**, the birthplace of King Gustav Vasa. The shores of Vallentuna lake are studded with the greatest number of late Viking-Age rune stones to be found in Sweden – you can find a map of their locations at www.runriket.se. One runestone, telling of a shipwreck, is even built into the wall of the town's 12th-century church. About 4km (2.5 miles) east is **Angarnsjöängen**, a wetland area with the richest bird life in the Stockholm region.

Admiring Uppsala Cathedral.

Head 30km (18 miles) west into the plain of Uppland and where the sea meets the forest, you'll find **Sigtuna ❷**, Sweden's oldest town. In the 11th century this was the commercial centre for the Svea and Vandal tribes. Merchant ships from as far away as Asia dropped anchor here; monasteries and abbeys competed with one another in building glorious churches. Today, Sigtuna is a sleepy town on the edge of the sea, with crooked lanes, quaint wooden houses and a miniature town hall. The ruins of the medieval

Main Attractions

Uppsala
Industrial architecture, Norrköping
Kolmården Djurpark (Animal Park)
Gripsholms Slott
Örebro

FACT

Linnaeus's last home, Linnés Hammarby, just southeast of Uppsala, is a pretty 18th-century cross between a manor and a cottage (museum and café open May and Sept Fri–Sun 11am–noon, June–Aug Tues–Sun 11am–4pm, park open until 8pm; entrance fee; tel: 018-471 28 38; www.hammarby.uu.se).

monasteries provide a cultural focus, as do the summer evening concerts at the gazebo on the green.

Uppsala

Less than an hour's drive north of Stockholm on the E4 lies **Uppsala ③**, Sweden's ancient capital and today the seat of one of Europe's greatest universities. It is also the birthplace of Ingmar Bergman – he was born at No. 12 Trädgårdsgatan – and the setting for his film *Fanny and Alexander*.

Uppsala was once the north's foremost pagan centre. A few minutes north of the town lies **Gamla Uppsala** (Old Uppsala), one of the most important historical sites in Sweden. An excellent **museum** (tel: 018 23 93 12; Apr–Sept daily 11am–5pm, Oct–Mar Mon, Wed, Sat–Sun noon–4pm) explores the enigmatic landscape, dominated by three huge Iron Age grave mounds that rise above the misty fields. No-one knows the names of the dead who were buried there, but they were clearly important people: archaeological digs have unearthed the remains of an elaborate helmet,

golden jewellery, and the bones of a goshawk, symbols of the ruling class. Findings from the latest excavations of the area in 2012 and 2013 will be published in 2017.

As Christianity became the dominant religion, its leaders were careful to create a powerful symbol of their new religion here. A grand cathedral was constructed in the mid-12th century, possibly over the site of Scandinavia's last heathen temple, but burned down around 100 years later. The medieval brick-built **church** is all that remains.

After the fire, the Episcopal see was transferred to present-day Uppsala. Back in the town centre, you'll find the largest Gothic cathedral in Scandinavia, **Domkyrkan ④** (www.uppsala domkyrka.se; daily 8am–6pm). Its vaults house the shrine of St Erik, a king and the patron of Sweden, as well as the graves of other early monarchs (including Gustav Vasa and his three wives), bishops, generals and philosophers. The scientist and theologian Emanuel Swedenborg lies here in a huge red-granite sarcophagus, as does 18th-century scientist Carl Linnaeus, under a more modest slab.

Across the road at Akademigatan 3 is the **Museum Gustavianum ⑤** (www.gustavianum.uu.se; June–Aug Tues–Sun 10am–4pm, Sept–May Tues–Sun 11am–4pm), an ancient, onion-domed edifice that houses the university's small but interesting collection. Among the coins, mummies and Viking knickknacks, stand-out exhibits are the stunning Augsburg Art Cabinet and a 17th-century anatomical theatre built for the Renaissance genius Olof Rudbeck.

Across the town's lush parks stands **Uppsala Slott ⑥** (Uppsala Castle; www.uppsalaslott.com), a typically squat, dominating brick fortress from the days of the Vasa dynasty. Its halls were the venue of the abdication of imperious Queen Kristina, who preferred exile in Rome to "ruling a country of barbarians". Its

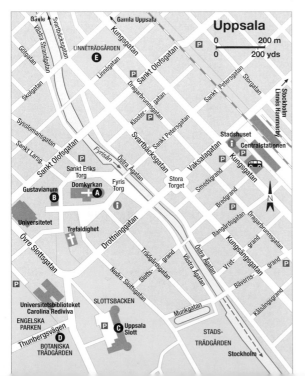

main use today is as a conference centre, although a portion of it is open to the public as the **Uppsala Art Museum** (http://konstmuseum. uppsala.se; Tues–Sun noon–4pm, Wed until 6pm, Thur until 8pm; free). Just below the castle are the university botanical gardens, the **Botaniska Trädgården** Ⓓ (Villavägen 8; tel: 018-471 28 38; www.botan.uu.se; May–Sept daily 7am–9pm; Oct–Apr daily 7am–7pm; free), with an orangery and small tropical greenhouse.

If you visit the town on the last day of April, you will witness Uppsala University students, decked in evening dress and white "student caps", engaged in Sweden's biggest student celebration *Sista April*, which welcomes in the spring. The day's fun starts with a champagne breakfast, followed by a wild raft race down the river. At 3pm the university rector makes a speech from the balcony of the library, after which everyone stampedes downhill to the beer barrels set up in the halls of the 16th- and 17th-century palaces, called *nationer* (student unions).

Linnaeus: father of botany

Uppsala University's most famous alumnus was Carl von Linné or Linnaeus (1707–78), the father of our system of botanical classification (see page 46). His residence in the heart of town at Svartbäcksgatan 27 is now the **Linnémuseum** (www.linnaeus.se; May–Sept Tues–Sun 11am–5pm). In front of the house, Linnaeus's botanical garden, **Linnéträdgården** Ⓔ (www. linnaeus.uu.se; May & Sept Tues–Sun 11am–5pm, June–Aug daily 11am–5pm), has been reconstructed according to the botanist's own plan. Like some latter-day Dr Doolittle, Linnaeus also kept a small menagerie in his home and garden, including a cockatoo that confused visitors by imitating his voice and a raccoon that stole food from the kitchen, inciting the wrath of the cook.

Around Uppsala

In summer, the narrow-gauge vintage steam train Lennakatten (tel: 018-13 05 00; www.lennakatten.se) runs from Uppsala station to **Faringe** ❹. It makes a sweet family outing, as you

FACT

Siggebohyttans Bergs-mansgård (Manor) near Lindesberg, 40km (25 miles) north of Örebro, gives a taste of the opulent life of the iron masters in Victorian days (tel: 019-602 8796; www.olm.se/siggebohyttan. html; June–mid-Aug Tues–Sun 11am–5pm).

The Linnaeus Garden in Uppsala.

can get on and off at the little stations along the route to swim, pet animals or eat ice cream.

At **Härkeberga** ❺, 30km (18 miles) southwest of Uppsala, medieval mythology is illustrated on the ceilings of Härkeberga Kyrka (Church), where Albertus Pictor, an ambulating vault painter in the 1400s, recorded the lives and hopes of the parishioners.

About 35km (22 miles) north of Uppsala lies **Örbyhus Slott** ❻ (Örbyhus Castle; www.orbyhusslott.se; entrance by guided tour mid-May–June & Aug Sat & Sun 1pm, July Tues–Fri 1pm & 3pm, Sat & Sun 1pm), a splendid baroque building. The dethroned King Erik XIV was imprisoned here for three years by his power-hungry half-brother Johan, who eventually assassinated him with a bowl of pea soup laced with arsenic. In the grounds are a "Turkish" orangery, stables and an extensive English-style park.

At **Älvkarleby** ❼, another 50km (31 miles) north, the River Dalälven tumbles into the Baltic over stunningly beautiful cliffs. This area is famous for salmon fishing and, despite the presence of a modern power station, the salmon still run thick here. There's an angling museum and a state game-fish research centre and hatchery at Älvkarleby.

Along the Baltic coast

About 60km (37 miles) northeast of Stockholm is the quaint fishing town of **Norrtälje** ❽. Roslagsmuséet (Roslags Museum; Faktorigatan

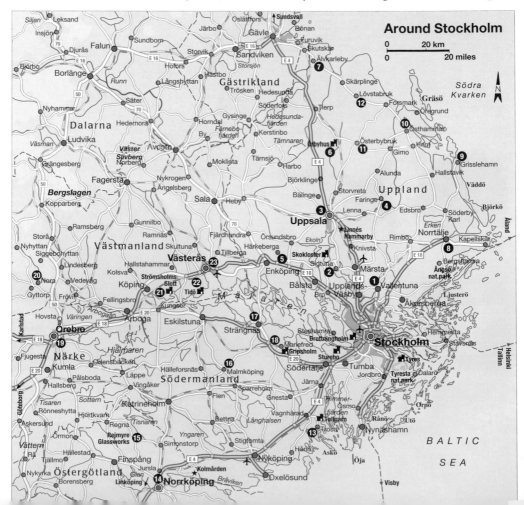

1; Mon–Fri 11am–4pm) shows life gone by in this island world. Try the nearby **Wallinska Gårdarna** (Wallinska Farm) for more heritage.

On a spit of land 30km (18 miles) north of Norrtälje, sticking even farther into the Baltic Sea, is **Grisslehamn** ❾, the departure point for Eckerö Linjen ferries to Finland's Åland islands. You can also try the freshly smoked whitefish that is the speciality in the fishermen's huts.

Neighbouring **Östhammar** ❿, and Öregrund to the north, are both summer retreats. Much of their 18th-century architecture is preserved. You'll get a good taste at the Frösåkers Hembygdsgård open-air museum at Vattentornsbergen in Östhammar (www.hembygd.se/frosaker) and along narrow Tullports Street.

Iron prosperity

Sweden grew rich in the 17th and 18th centuries on its iron ore. Scots and Belgian Walloons emigrated here to found thriving forges, smelting ovens and dynasties. Their estates, actually small foundry villages (*bruk*), are found where forest, swift streams and the Baltic supplied the right conditions for smelting metal.

About 30km (18 miles) west of Östhammar is **Österbybruk** ⓫, the oldest iron foundry in Uppland, dating from 1443. The original Vallonsmedjan (Walloon forge), the last of its kind, is preserved – several times a year, the waterwheel and hammers are set in motion so visitors can see it in action (tel: 0295 20220; entry by guided tour mid-June–mid-Aug daily noon and 3.30pm). From 1917 to 1932, the artist Bruno Liljefors lived here with his family, and his estate still manages the property: the manor house is now a hotel (http://gammeltammen.se).

Wealthy **Lövstabruk** ⓬, 20km (12 miles) north, was Sweden's largest iron producer in the 1600s. The foundry street is immaculately kept and gives an idea of the hierarchy of *bruk* society. The villagers resided in bungalows,

while directly across the street stretched the iron master's French parterres and, in the distance, his manor house, **Lövsta Herrgård** (www.lovstabruk.nu; mid-June–mid-Aug tours at 12.30pm & 3.30pm).

South to Södermanland

About 50km (31 miles) south from Stockholm you will find the seaside idyll of **Trosa** ⓭, where the attractions include the quaint, historic district, a handicrafts centre and town museum. A couple of hours' drive south on the E4 from Trosa brings you to **Norrköping** ⓮, with its tree-lined avenues, outdoor café society and trams. It was once the second largest industrial city in Sweden, full of wool and cotton mills – 70 percent of the country's textiles were woven here. Although the industry has long since disappeared, the town was far-sighted enough to preserve its unique industrial architecture, transforming the old factories into university buildings, a concert hall, exhibition spaces and offices. It's well worth a wander among the buildings and past

Sailing on Lake Mälaren.

the flowing waterfalls of the Motala River, which once powered this hive of industry.

Near Norrköping flows the Göta Kanal with its attractive cruise boats (see page 249). Around 20km (12 miles) northeast of town is the famous **Kolmården Djurpark** (tel: 010-708 70 00; www.kolmarden.com; May–Sept days and times vary – see website for details). This is Scandinavia's best zoo and amusement park, with large enclosures and a strong educational component. Don't miss the 'gondola safari', which flies you over habitats containing bears, lions and giraffes; but expect long queues.

About 25km (15 miles) north is **Reijmyre Glassworks** ⑮, (tel: 011-871 85; www.reijmyreglasbruk.se), the second-oldest glass furnace in the country. Its future looks a little uncertain, following the death of its owner in 2015, but his heirs are hopeful of finding a buyer.

Some 30km (18 miles) northeast you reach the market town of **Malmköping** ⑯ with its **Museispårvägen i Malmköping** (Tramway Museum;

The throne room in Gripsholms Slott.

www.muma.se; mid-May–early Sept Sat–Sun 11am–5pm; July–early Aug daily 11am–5pm), at Järnvägsgatan, full of colourful old trams.

Continue north past Lake Mälaren's bays and inlets to **Strängnäs** ⑰, a delightful small town dominated by a magnificent Gothic cathedral. The church's altar screens are worth a detour. Next to the church at Boglösa, 20km (12 miles) north, are hundreds of Bronze Age rock carvings.

About 15km (9 miles) to the east lies idyllic **Mariefred** ⑱ and **Gripsholms Slott** (Castle; tel: 0159-101 94; mid-Apr–mid-May and Oct–Nov Sat–Sun noon–3pm; mid-May–Sept: daily 10am–4pm; guided tours in English mid-May–Sept daily at 3pm). The impressive pile of the castle protects the royal portrait collections and a marvellous theatre from the late 1700s. Best of all is the architecture of this fortress, begun in the 1370s and continually updated: most of what you see today is the work of Gustav Vasa. Around the edge of the moat is a collection of rune stones – flat rocks carved in the deepest Dark Ages with

SKOKLOSTER SLOTT

Skokloster Slott (Skokloster Castle; tel: 08-402 30 60; www.skoklostersslott.se; May and Sept Sat–Sun 11am–4pm; June–Aug daily 11am–5pm; under-19s free) is what a castle is supposed to be: imposing, imperious, towered and abundantly endowed. Situated less than 70km (43 miles) from Stockholm and 45km (28 miles) from Uppsala, it was commissioned in 1654 by Field Marshal Carl Gustaf Wrangel. The banqueting hall remains unfinished to this day: Wrangel died in 1676 and the workmen downed tools in fear that they would never be paid!

The castle was left more or less empty and untouched after Wrangel's death, so everything you see dates from the 17th century. During his lifetime, Wrangel built up impressive collections of paintings, antiques, glass and silver, anthropologia, textiles and books, enlarged by gifts and purchases. Wrangel had a particular fancy for guns: the armoury (accessible only by guided tour) contains the largest personal collection of 17th-century military weapons in the world. There is no electricity in the castle, and it can get quite dark on gloomy days, so bring a torch.

Nearby is **Skokloster Kyrka** (Skokloster Church), an unusual three-aisled basilica with beautiful brickwork, dating back to the 13th century.

serpents, ships and magic inscriptions in the runic alphabet. Mariefred is a lazy, summer lake town, with cafés and restaurants to suit all tastes.

Mountain scenery

At the western end of Lake Hjälmaren lies bustling **Örebro** ⑲, capital of Västmanland and mountainous Bergslagen. In the city centre, on an islet in the river, is another splendid **castle** (accessible by guided tour only Sept–May Sat–Sun at 1pm) much enlarged by Gustav Vasa. This was where Swedish steel was born. The forests gave fuel, the rivers powered the trip hammers and the lakes provided transport for the swords, cannons and building materials produced by family-run forges. You can explore the town's history at **Wadköpings friluftsmuseum** (Wadköping Open-Air Museum; year-round; free), a collection of red-painted 17th-, 18th- and early 19th-century buildings, with exhibitions, craft workshops and a working blacksmith's forge. The preservation area also includes the house of the cookery writer Cajsa Warg, the Swedish version of Britain's "Mrs Beeton". For good views, take the lift up the **Svampen** (the Mushroom), a water tower 58 metres (190ft) high.

Karlslunds Gård on the outskirts of the town is a splendidly proportioned country house with 90 preserved 18th- and 19th-century buildings ranging from a cowshed to a tavern within its spacious grounds. The grounds are open to the public.

About 35km (22 miles) north is **Nora** ⑳, a village of wooden houses which preserves the feel of the old days in its shops and tea houses.

To explore the eastern section of Bergslagen, start with the splendid, baroque **Strömsholms Slott och Parker** ㉑ (tel: 0220-430 35; www.kungahuset.se; late May Sat–Sun and public hols noon–4pm; June–Aug daily noon–4pm, July until 5pm), a former royal residence and riding centre featuring a carriage museum, shop and restaurant. Nearby are the River Kolbäck and Strömsholm Canal water sports areas.

On the next peninsula to the east rises **Tidö Slott** ㉒ (tel: 021-530 17; www.tidoslott.se; May–June Sat–Sun noon–5pm; July–mid-Aug Tues–Sun noon–5pm), the 1625 castle home of Axel Oxenstierna, a regent of Sweden and feared warrior. The present owners have converted part of their home into a toy museum with 35,000 exhibits. The wooded grounds offer a deer park and an inn.

On an inlet of the lake, 20km (12 miles) east, **Västerås** ㉓ is a 1,000-year old settlement with a 13th-century cathedral and a fortress of the same vintage. A newer but very worthwhile attraction is the **Historiska Skeppsmuseum** (Historic Ship Museum; http://frosakersbrygga.se; June–mid-Aug Tues–Sun noon–7pm, late Aug Sat–Sun noon–5pm), where 25 beautiful reconstructions from the Viking Age and beyond float on the quayside – pride of the collection is a medieval cog.

At **Anundshög**, 15km (9 miles) east, are Sweden's largest Iron Age and Viking burial mounds and ship settings. Ferries run from here to Stockholm.

17th-century Örebro Castle.

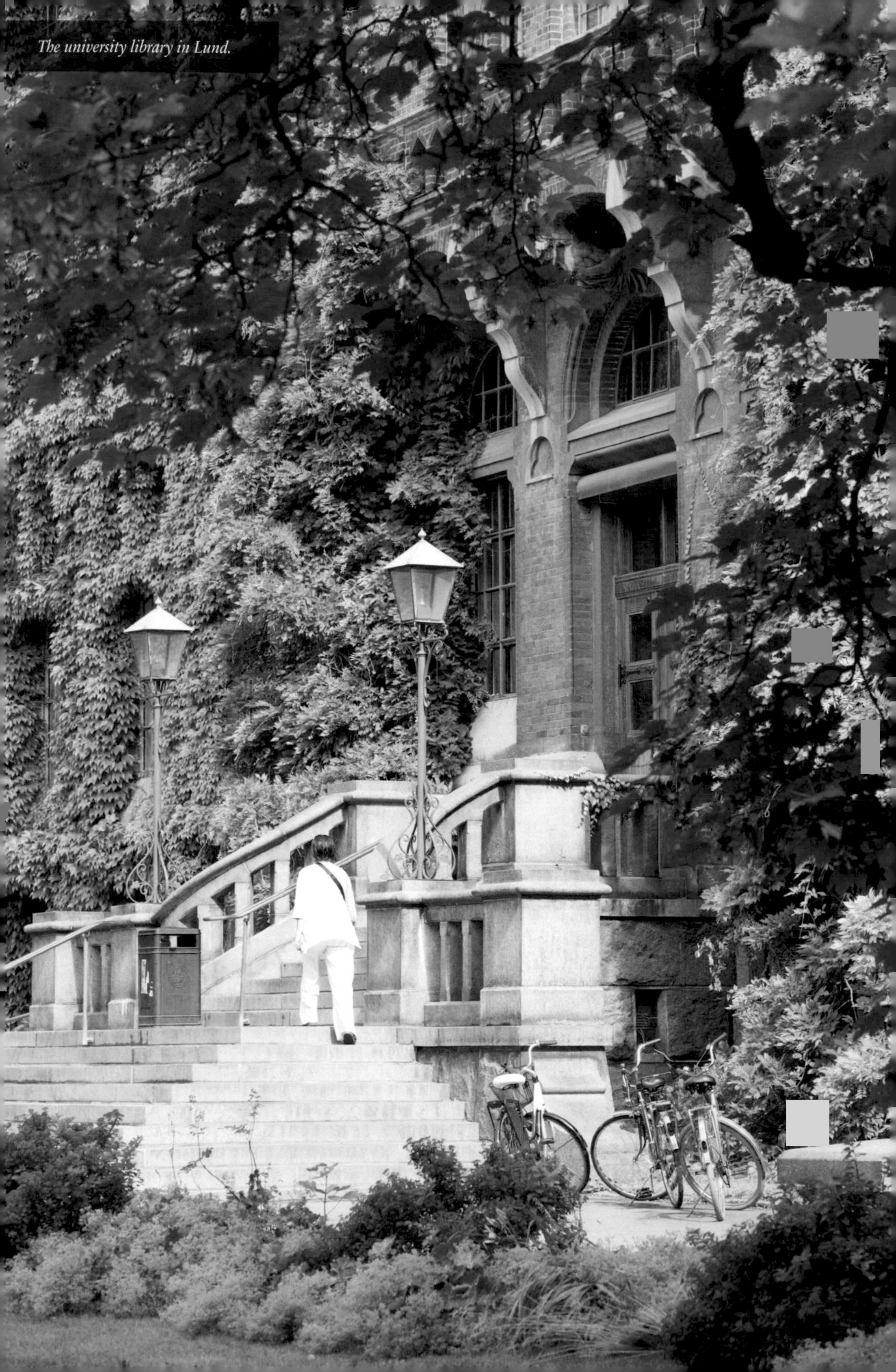

The university library in Lund.

SOUTHERN SWEDEN

Home to the vibrant city of Malmö, the garden landscape of southern Sweden has a peaceful charm. Castles and Stone Age sites abound, while bathers and birdwatchers head for Öland.

outhern Sweden has a faintly Danish flavour: historically, it was actually part of Denmark, and today it has strong ties with Copenhagen via the remarkable Öresund Bridge. Its "capital" Malmö, a former ship-building centre, is currently being rejuvenated by a brand-new university. The city's unusual architecture ranges from its 15th-century castle to the striking Turning Torso skyscraper and up-to-the-minute concert hall Malmö Live. Nestling in the silent Skåne countryside, Lund is a historic university town, rich with history and tradition. On the Baltic coast, Kalmar boasts a stunning castle, and is the gateway to the island of Öland, a paradise for birdwatchers.

Skåne is Sweden's most southerly province, so close to Denmark across the narrow sound that even the accent is faintly Danish. This isn't surprising, because for centuries Swedes and Danes fought over this area, along with the provinces of Halland and Blekinge, until Sweden established its sovereignty in 1658.

In May 2000, however, the two countries became one, joined by the Öresund Fixed Link, a combined 16-km (10-mile) bridge and tunnel that links Malmö and Copenhagen, the largest such connection in Europe. The project has prompted a renaissance for southern Sweden as a

centre of the Danish-Swedish Öresund region, with a total of almost 4 million people and the highest concentration of university-educated people in northern Europe, linking the four university towns and cities of Copenhagen, Roskilde, Lund and Malmö.

Skåne is often called Sweden's food store because of its rich farmland, mild climate and good fishing. Although many think of the landscape as flat, there is in fact a lot of variety. Along the coast it is undulating and lush and especially spectacular in the southeast

Main Attractions

Moderna Museét Malmö
Lund Cathedral
Karlskrona
Kalmar
Glasriket (Kingdom of Glass)
Öland
Utvandrarnas Hus, Växjö

Wheat fields in Skåne province.

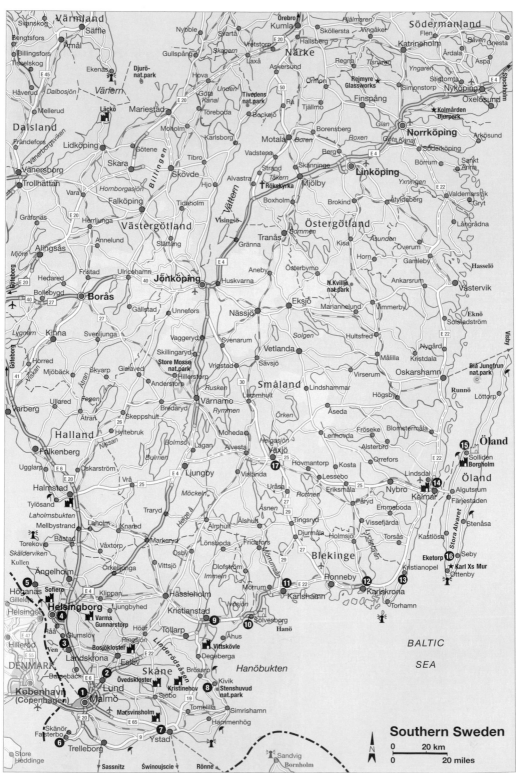

Southern Sweden

0 — 20 km

0 — 20 miles

corner, Österlen. Inland, there are three large ridges, Söderåsen, Romeleåsen and Linderödsåsen, with lovely walks and lakes.

History goes back a long way in Skåne: Stone Age burial chambers can be found at **Glumslöv**, at **Tågarp** and north of Kivik. The King's Grave at **Bredarör**, southeast of Kivik, dates from the Bronze Age and is famous for its rock carvings, different from any found in Sweden and the other Nordic countries from the same period. One of Harald Bluetooth's seven huge Viking ring fortresses can be found at **Trelleborg**, on the southern coast.

Castles galore

The affluence of Skåne is obvious when you consider the number of castles and manor houses. There are said to be 240 in the province. Most are still in private ownership and not open to the public, but it is usually possible to walk round the gardens.

Among the most interesting are **Vrams Gunnarstorp** (tel: 042-830 55), 8km (5 miles) northeast of Bjuv, built in Dutch Renaissance style; **Vittskövle**, between Degeberga and Åhus, another Renaissance beauty whose grounds are open to the public; **Bosjökloster** (tel: 0413-250 48; www. bosjokloster.se; May–Sept 10am–5pm) by Lake Ringsjön; and **Övedskloster,** (www.ovedskloster.com; Apr–Sept 9am–4pm; free) by Lake Vombsjön, north of Sjöbo, built in rococo style by Colonel Hans Ramel during the 18th century and still owned by the same family nine generations later. The courtyard and garden can be visited. **Sofiero**, 4km (2.5 miles) north of Helsingborg, was built in 1857, and King Gustav VI Adolf used it as his summer palace until his death in 1973. He was a keen botanist and made the gardens (tel: 042-10 25 00; www.helsingborg.se/sofiero; mid-Apr–mid-Sept daily 10am–6pm; mid-Sept–mid-Apr daily 10am–4pm) a real attraction. They have been voted Europe's most beautiful park, and are

particularly famous for their 10,000 rhododendrons, which bloom in the springtime.

Malmö: city of the south

Malmö ❶ is Sweden's third city, a lively place with a population of about 318,000. In the 16th century, Malmö competed with Copenhagen to be Scandinavia's leading capital, but in those days it was an important port on a major sailing route, not far from rich fishing grounds. Today, the Öresund bridge and tunnel has replaced the passenger ferries that once sailed to Copenhagen, although the port is still busy with freighters and cruise ships.

Malmöhus ⓐ, the dominating castle built by King Christian III when Skåne was still part of Denmark, is Scandinavia's oldest remaining Renaissance castle. It houses part of the **Malmömuséer** (Malmö Museums; tel: 040-34 44 37; www.malmo.se/museer; daily 10am–5pm), including historical and natural history exhibitions, and an aquarium. The other components of Malmömuséer are

Malmö's West Harbour and famous Turning Torso.

the **Teknikens och Sjöfartens hus** (Technology & Maritime Museum), where you can step aboard a U3 submarine; and the **Kommandants Hus** (Commander's House) **B**, both in Malmöhusvägen.

Built in the 14th century, but overlaid by a later, very attractive, Dutch Renaissance facade is **Rådhuset** (City Hall) **C**, which you will find in Stortorget, one of the largest squares in Scandinavia.

Northeast from Stortorget is **St Petri Kyrka** **D** (St Peter's Church; Göran Olsgatan 1; daily 10am–6pm), built in the Baltic Gothic style and dating from the early 14th century, although its towers were built in the 15th century and its copper spires in 1890. The church is elegant, and probably its most beautiful feature is the altar area, Scandinavia's largest, the work of several sculptors. In the 1800s it was painted over with grey oil paint, which has fortunately been removed in recent years.

Keep an eye out for the **Turning Torso**, a building twisting up a sculptural 190 metres (620ft) in the **Västra**

Hamnen area. This is Malmö's newest city district, and has replaced the old industrial harbour; cafés, restaurants and interior-design shops line its long beachwalk.

A short walk southeast of the harbour is an attraction solely for the (fool?)hardy – the **Ribersborgs Kallbadhus** (Ribersborg Open-Air Pool; tel: 040-260 366; www.ribersborgskallbadhus.se; May–Aug: daily from 9am, Sept–Apr: daily from 10am, closing times vary). This chilling open-air pool allows naturists to strip off and leap into the icy sea – it is divided into separate bathing areas for men and women. You can warm up again in the wood-fired sauna.

In the distance, soaring out over the waves is the stunning **Öresund Bridge**, a masterpiece of design. The 16km- (10-mile) long bridge and tunnel, a combined Swedish-Danish enterprise, took nine years to complete, from the signing of the agreement to its inauguration in 2000. It was given a starring role in popular Swedish-Danish crime drama series *The Bridge* (2011–).

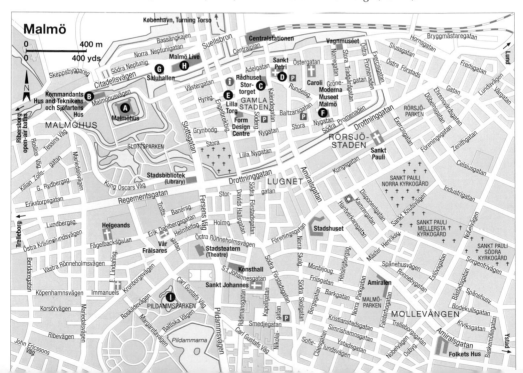

Malmö has a network of pedestrian streets, with many places to shop and coffee houses to sit awhile. A particularly idyllic place to sit and relax is **Lilla Torg** (Little Square) **E**, with its cobblestones, beautifully restored houses and 16th-century charm. Through an arch on the south side of the square is Hemanska Gården. Once a merchant's home and trading yard, it now houses the **Form Design Center** (Lilla Torg 9; www.formdesigncenter. com; Tues–Sat 11am–5pm, Sun noon–4pm), where Swedish design, textiles and furniture are displayed and sold.

Walking east from Lilla Torg, a rewarding visit can be made to **Moderna Muséet Malmö** **F** (Ola Billgrens plats 2–4; tel: 040-6857 937; www. modernamuseet.se/en/malmo; Tues–Sun 11am–6pm), a second branch of Stockholm's revered modern-art gallery. Part of the museum is based in a beautiful old brick-built electricity plant, whose turbine hall contains temporary exhibitions. Works from the Stockholm collection are also on display.

When you get hungry, head for the city's new indoor market **Saluhallen** **G**

(www.malmosaluhall.se; Mon–Fri 10am–6pm, Sat 10am–4pm), which opened in an old train-yard goods shed in summer 2016. Within its raw, industrial interior you can choose from fish restaurants, cafés, delicatessens and an abundance of fresh food if you want to prepare your own picnic.

Next door is another new structure, the swanky new concert hall **Malmö Live** **H** (Citadellsvägen 4; tel: 040-34 35 00; http://malmolive.se), opened in 2015, the home of the Malmö Symphony Orchestra.

After lunch, you can head southwest and stroll through **Pildammsparken** **I**, the largest landscaped park in Sweden, which houses Pildammsteater, a huge amphitheatre.

Lund: university town

Heading north from Malmö, before joining the coast road you should visit **Lund** **2**. Along with the University of Uppsala, north of Stockholm, Lund is one of the two ancient Swedish universities, both with their own traditions and customs. The town spreads out around the fascinating cathedral,

Cycling in Lund.

Kingdom of Glass

The traditional skills of glassblowing are highly valued in southern Sweden.

It's reassuring in a way that vandalism isn't just a present-day phenomenon. They even had the problem in 16th-century Sweden, when King Gustav Vasa's courtiers used to round off an evening of feasting and carousing by smashing as many expensive Venetian glasses as they could lay their hands on. The king, adopting a fatalistic attitude towards this medieval delinquency, invited Venetian glassblowers to his court, commenting that it would be cheaper in the long run to break home-blown glassware rather than the expensive imported variety. The first glass was melted in Sweden in 1556, but it was to be almost another 200 years before glassmaking really became established as an industry in Sweden.

A mighty glass-making company

The oldest works, Kosta, was founded in 1742 by Anders Koskull and Georg Bogislaus Stael von

At work at Målerås glassworks.

Holstein, provincial governors in Småland. Eager to make a little money on the side, they set up a glassworks, taking the first two syllables of their respective surnames to create "Kosta". The location was ideal, because the dense forests between Växjö and Kalmar provided vast supplies of timber to keep the furnaces going.

Kosta was a pioneer in the production of lead-crystal glass with what is claimed to have the highest lead content – up to 30 percent – of any produced in Sweden (to qualify for the "crystal" description, there must be at least 24 percent lead oxide in the glass).

In the 1970s, Kosta merged with neighbouring glassworks Åfors and Boda, and more recently with Orrefors to become the Orrefors Kosta Boda Group.

Orrefors is one of the best-known glass manufacturers and started in the glass business by producing window-panes and bottles, but in 1913 the works was taken over by Johan Ekman, an industrialist from Göteborg. Ekman was one of the first to involve artistic talent in the design of glass, and during World War I he recruited two artists who were to transform Orrefors into one of the world's most renowned glassworks: Simon Gate, a portrait and landscape painter, and Edvard Hald, a pupil of Matisse. They were followed by new generations of designers. It is their creative flair, coupled with the centuries-old skills of the glassblower, that has put Sweden in the forefront of worldwide glass design and production.

The nine major glassworks (including Kosta, Boda, Nybro, Målerås and Pukeberg), and several smaller ones in the area, are open to visitors for demonstrations; some will even let you have a go. The larger works have factory outlets where you can buy anything from simple tableware to complex art glass. For further information, see the Glasriket (Glass Kingdom) website, www.glasriket.se.

Herring evenings

Look out for an old glass-country tradition – the *hyttsill* ("glassworks herring") evening – which has been revived in recent years for the benefit of tourists by several of the larger glassworks. In bygone times the glassworks was also a social centre where the locals would gather for a chat and bake herrings and potatoes in the furnace, with music provided by an accordionist or fiddler. Reservations can be made on the spot.

Domkyrkan (http://lundsdomkyrka.se; Mon–Fri 8am–6pm, Sat 9.30am–5pm, Sun 9.30am–6pm), Sweden's most-visited religious building, with over 700,000 visitors per year. Built in the 12th century, the cathedral is packed with unusual details, from the great bronze doors and the astronomical clock to the mysterious Giant Finn, lurking in the crypt.

While in Lund, don't miss the fascinating **Kulturen** (Tegnérsplatsen; www.kulturen.com; May–Aug daily 10am–5pm; Sept–Apr Tues–Sun noon–4pm), an open-air museum that fills two blocks in the town centre with interesting buildings stretching from medieval times to the 1930s, with costumed craftspeople demonstrating their skills at certain times – see the website for details.

About 30km (19 miles) north along the coast, **Glumslöv** ❸ offers some very memorable views. From the hill above the church, on a clear day you can see 30 churches and seven towns: Helsingborg, Landskrona, Lund and Malmö in Sweden, and Dragør, Copenhagen and Helsingør in Denmark.

Potters and artists

The centre of **Helsingborg** ❹ is dominated by the remnants of an old castle, Kärnan, and with the 14th-century St Maria Kyrka and a bustling harbour. Half-hourly ferries ply back and forth across the narrow Sound to Helsingør in Denmark, often full of merry Swedes with clinking bags of cheap Danish alcohol.

Höganäs ❺, 20km (12 miles) north, is a town full of potters and artists, thanks to the geology of the area, which provides an iron-rich clay perfect for ceramics. The town has a small ceramics museum, where you can see examples of Höganäs stoneware.

About 40km (25 miles) southeast from Malmö are **Skanör** and **Falsterbo** ❻, once important towns but now summer idylls. **Skanörs Ljung** is popular with bird-lovers, particularly in September and October, when a large number of migrating birds gather for their flight southwest. It is considered northern Europe's prime location for watching birds of prey.

Beach huts in Skanör.

Viking heritage

Follow the coast road east and you reach Trelleborg, of interest to Viking enthusiasts as the site of one of Harald Bluetooth's ring fortresses, before touching Sweden's most southern point at **Smygehuk**.

The little town of **Ystad** ❼ is a pleasant enough place to stop for a coffee and a stroll of the cobbled streets; but for fans of crime literature, this is a serious place of pilgrimage. Ystad is the stamping ground of Detective Inspector Kurt Wallander, the creation of author Henning Mankell, star of 11 books and over 50 films and TV adaptations. In summer, Wallander visitors can hop aboard a vintage fire engine for a tour of his haunts.

Around 14km (9 miles) east of Ystad is Sweden's answer to Stonehenge, the mysterious **Ales Stenar** ship setting, composed of 59 standing stones and thought to date to 600 AD.

Heading north again, you reach **Kivik** ❽, famous for its three-day July market and its annual Apple Market (www.appelmarknaden.se) in September. Southeast of Kivik is **Bredarör** (Kiviksgraven), a cairn discovered by two farmers in 1748. Kivik's grave dates from the Scandinavian Bronze Age (1700–500 BC), and its large diameter (75 metres/246ft) suggests that it was constructed to house the remains of several members of a prominent family.

Kristianstad ❾ is where the Swedish film industry was born in around 1910. The original studio is intact and is now a museum, **Filmmuséet** (Östra Storg 53; tel: 044-13 52 56; Tues–Fri 8am–4pm), where you can watch some of the old films on video. The **Kristianstad Vattenriket** (Water Kingdom) is the name given to the catchment area of the River Helge with its rich wetland area, featuring a diversity of birds, wildlife and plants (www.vattenriket.kristianstad.se).

Along the coast

Blekinge is a tiny province with lovely sandy beaches along the coast and Sweden's most southerly archipelago. It is excellent for sea fishing of all kinds, from boat or shore. You can enjoy peaceful angling in some of the lakes, too, or good sport for salmon in the River Mörrum. Canoeing is also popular along the coast and on the rivers, and you can move from lake to lake by connecting canals. Driving to Blekinge from Skåne, you first reach **Sölvesborg** ❿, where the narrow streets and old buildings show their medieval origins and the ruins of 13th-century **Sölvesborg Slott** (Castle).

Mörrum, 30km (19 miles) north of Sölvesborg, is famous for its salmon fishing: at **Laxens Hus** (tel: 0454-501 23; Mar–Sept Mon–Sat 9am–5pm, Sun 10am–3pm; Oct–Feb Mon–Fri 9am–4pm), a salmon aquarium, you can see salmon and trout at different stages of their development. **Karlshamn** ⓫, about 10km (6 miles) to the east, is an old seafaring and market town with thriving industries. The Emigrants' Monument, entitled *Karl-Oskar and Kristina*, is a reminder of different times, when thousands of Swedes set off in search of a new life in the New World.

Skåne apples.

The biggest town in Blekinge is **Karlskrona** ⑫, a 17th-century naval centre that has made it onto the Unesco World Heritage list. The town was founded in 1680, when the navy relocated here from Stockholm to give Sweden's intimidating fleet a strategic advantage. Within 70 years, the town was at its peak, with 70,000 people living in a Baroque town of wide streets and impressive buildings, built from scratch according to the orderly vision of Karl XI. In the **Björkholmen** district you'll find quaint 18th-century cottages built by ships' carpenters. The town still has naval ties, hosting Sweden's only remaining naval base.

At **Hästhallen** in Möckleryd are fascinating rock carvings from the Bronze Age, while **Torhamn Point** is well known to ornithologists as the path taken by migratory birds, and is an excellent observation point. On the east coast of Blekinge is the village of **Kristianopel** ⑬, once a Danish stronghold on the border with Sweden. You can see the restored defensive wall and step-gabled church. These days it is more famous for its smoked herring.

Historic Kalmar

Kalmar ⑭, one of Sweden's oldest cities, was of great importance in the Swedish-Danish Wars. Sweden's best-preserved Renaissance castle, **Kalmar Slott** (Kungsgatan 1; tel: 0480-45 14 90; www.kalmarslott.se; daily, times vary – see website for details), was in fact begun in the 12th century but was completely renovated during the 16th century by the Vasa kings Gustav I, Erik XIV and Johan III. The castle's beautifully preserved coffered ceilings, panelled halls, fresco paintings and stonework have inspired the Renaissance Festival, held every July. This features tournament games, soldiers, craftsmen, a market, theatre and music, food and drink, and noblewomen and peasants walking the streets in costume.

Also worth a visit is the **Kalmar Länsmuseum** (county museum; Skeppsbrogatan 51; www.kalmarlansmuseum.se; Mon–Fri 10am–4pm, Wed until 8pm, Sat–Sun 11am–4pm), with more than 30,000 objects recovered from the sunken 17th-century warship *Kronan*, including Sweden's largest haul of gold coins.

FACT

The island of Öland is of great interest to botanists. Its limestone soil, warm summers, and long, mild autumns create plains full of blooming wildflowers. Its flora is reminiscent of that of the tundra, and there are 30 types of orchid. The symbol of the island is the Öland rockrose Helianthemum oelandicum.

Kalmar Slott.

Around Öland: an ornithologist's delight

Kalmar is the gateway to the island of Öland, one of the most heavily visited areas of Sweden. With its diverse landscape, it is a paradise for birdwatchers, nature-lovers, historians and sun-worshippers. The best beaches in Sweden are in northern Öland and attract some 2 million tourists a year.

Once you've crossed the Öland bridge from the coast of Blekinge, you soon see on the northwest coast the ruins of **Borgholm Slott** (Castle; open Apr and Sept: 10am–4pm; May–Aug: 10am–6pm; entrance fee; tel: 0485-123 33; www.borgholmsslott.se), rising above the main town of **Borgholm** ⓫, a once splendid residence from the 12th century. During the summer it is a venue for open-air concerts.

Solliden Slott (Castle; tel: 0485-153 56; www.sollidensslott.se; mid-May–mid-Sept daily 11am–6pm for park only), just outside Borgholm, is the king's summer residence.

Öland is fascinating not only to ornithologists and botanists but also to archaeologists. The island has many ancient burial places, and there are remains of 16 fortified dwellings from earlier times. The most interesting is **Eketorp** ⓰, in the south, an Iron Age fortress which has been partly restored. From mid-June to mid-August, costumed interpreters demonstrate weaving, forging, baking bread, archery and other skills and crafts from medieval times and earlier.

Sweden's prime birdwatching can be enjoyed at the **Ottenby bird station**, on the island's southerly tip, where 10,000 to 20,000 birds are ringed every year and more than 350 species have been recorded. Ottenby is managed by the Swedish Ornithological Society (www.sofnet.org), which has established a science centre and museum and offers tours of the bird station. In southern Öland you can also see **Carl X's Mur** (Carl X's Wall), impressive for its sheer size; it was built in 1650 to distinguish Ottenby's domain and keep out the peasants' animals. The entire island was a royal hunting park at that time.

Stora Alvaret, a great expanse of bare limestone soil covering 300km (186 miles) of central southern Öland, is an unusual and starkly beautiful landscape. It offers the beauty of rare flowers, flocks of cranes in the autumn, and a sense of the earth as it must have looked at the time of creation.

The emigrants

During the late 19th and early 20th centuries, Sweden's population exploded, and many families could no longer eke out a living on the land. So began the years of emigration to North America. Of the million who left, the majority came from Småland. Today, one of the most popular places to visit is **Utvandrarnas Hus** (House of the Emigrants; Wilhelm Mobergs Gata 4; tel: 0470-70 42 00; www.utvandrarnashus.se; Tues–Fri 10am–5pm, Sat–Sun 11am–4pm) in **Växjö** ⓱, about 70km (43 miles) west of Kalmar, which tells the story of the exodus.

Solliden Slott's manicured gardens.

Visby on a warm summer's day.

GOTLAND

Ingmar Bergman favoured the Baltic island of Gotland's northern outpost, Fårö, while holidaymakers are drawn to the beaches, and cyclists meander lazily past fields of wild flowers.

Blessed with more hours of sunshine than anywhere else in the country, the island of Gotland is a favourite summer holiday spot for Swedes. Its main town, Visby, is known as "the city of roses", and is the best-preserved medieval city in Scandinavia, and a renowned Unesco World Heritage site. It is especially lively during Medieval Week (Medeltidsveckan), held in August. The coast of the island is a wild place of fishing villages, long sandy beaches and jagged cliffs, zigzagged by hiking trails, while offshore are silhouetted strange sea-stacks, carved into eerie shapes by wind and waves. Film fans flock to the smaller island of Fårö, at the northeastern tip of Gotland, once the home of Ingmar Bergman.

Gotland is quite unlike the rest of Sweden. It is the largest island in the Baltic, a place of gaunt rocks, forests, wild flowers, cliffs and soft sandy beaches, with a milder climate than even Sweden's south. For a thousand years, the natives here spoke their own language, Gutnish, which the Gutamålsgillet (Gutnish Language Guild) keeps alive today. Although it belongs to Sweden, the island's position 90km (56 miles) off the east coast of the mainland, makes the Republic of Latvia its nearest neighbour to the east.

In the Viking Age the island was a busy trading post. Later, Visby, the principal centre of population, became a prosperous Hanseatic town. Its medieval walls are remarkably well preserved to this day, giving visitors a real flavour of the past. Despite its concentration on trade, Gotland could not escape involvement in the wars between Denmark and Sweden which ranged over the whole of the south of Sweden. In 1361, the Danish King Valdemar Atterdag conquered Gotland but, after some further changes in ownership, it finally became permanently Swedish in 1679.

Gotland was created over thousands of years as the animals and plants of

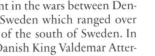

Main Attractions
Visby
Lummelundagrottan
Fårö

The rocky island of Fårö.

the ancient Silurian Sea slowly sank into the sediment that was to become the limestone platform of modern Gotland. Fossils millions of years old and the island's famous monumental sea-stacks *(raukar)*, carved out of the soft limestone by wind and water, can still be found around the coast.

Tourism is vital to Gotland, and during the relatively brief but hectic summer season, the normal population of 57,000 is swollen by more than 750,000 visitors – a number set to rise once the new cruise-ship pier is completed in 2018.

Medieval Visby

During the 12th century, the former Viking trading station developed into a leading commercial centre for trade with the Baltic. Great stone houses were erected in **Visby** ❶, churches were founded, and a wall was built to protect its citizens. Today, 3km (2 miles) of the medieval limestone **city wall** remain virtually intact, interspersed with 44 towers and numerous gates. The wall is one of the best-preserved in Europe and, because of its cultural value, Visby has become a Unesco's World Heritage Site.

One of Visby's superbly preserved medieval gates.

Within the walls, the town has many step-gabled houses and a network of little streets and squares, all of which contribute to its atmosphere. The original Hanseatic harbour, **Almedalen**, is now a park, while the **Domkyrkan** (Cathedral of St Maria) is the only medieval church in Visby that is still intact and in use. By contrast, only ruins remain of the old Gothic church of St Catherine, next to the market square.

One of the most interesting buildings to survive is **Burmeisterska huset**, the house of the Burmeister, who was a German merchant. The town also has a particularly fine historical museum, **Länsmuséet Gotland** (Historical Museum of Gotland; Strandgatan 14; tel: 0498-29 27 23; www.lansmuseet-gotland.se; mid-June–mid-Sept daily 10am–6pm; mid-Sept–mid-June noon–4pm). The museum houses rich collections of artefacts spanning most of the 8,000 years of Gotland's history.

The 450km (280 miles) of coastline are a mix of sand and shingle beaches with cliffs and meadows stretching down to the water. There's a good beach 20km (12 miles) south of Visby, at **Tofta** ❷.

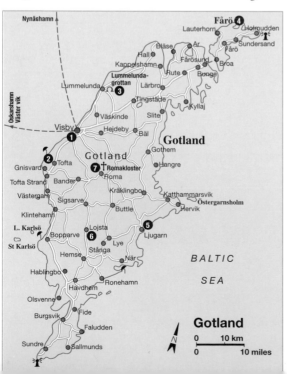

Limestone features

Once the summer season is over, Gotland is quiet. The brevity of the season has little to do with the climate, which is milder than anywhere else in the country. This kindly climate, and perhaps the limestone, is why many species of orchid, poppies and other rare plants can be found in Gotland.

Limestone has also created one of the island's major attractions – the impressive subterranean tunnels and stalactite caves of **Lummelundagrottan** ❸ (tel: 0498-27 30 50; www.lummelundagrottan. se; May–Sept for guided tours only, times vary – see website for details), 13km (8 miles) north of Visby, which should not be missed. Dress warmly, as it's always a cool 8°C (46°F) inside.

Bergman's hideout

About 50km (30 miles) north of Visby lies **Fårö** ❹, the "island of sheep". Take a free ferry (they run continuously and take just eight minutes) to the island from Fårösund, and enjoy sites such as **Gamlehamn**, a medieval harbour, and the ruins of a chapel to St Olof. You can also see one of Gotland's most bizarrely shaped *raukar* (rock stacks), called the Camel. Or, if you are in the mood for another of Gotland's best beaches, visit **Sundersand**. After you have been here a while, you should begin to understand why Fårö was the favourite place of Sweden's most famous film and theatre director, the late Ingmar Bergman. Learn more about the great man at the **Bergmancenter** (tel: 0498-22 68 68; http://bergmancenter.se; May–Aug 10am–5pm, first half of Sept noon–4pm), or during Bergman Week, held in late June.

Gotland ponies

If you travel about 80km (50 miles) southeast from Fårö, you come to **Ljugarn** ❺, an area often overlooked by visitors. This is Gotland's oldest seaside resort with its seaside villas and offshore *raukar*. The entire coastline also provides good opportunities for birdwatchers.

Sweden's most primitive horse, the Russ (Gotland pony), has lived in the forests of the island from time immemorial. Russ comes from Old Norse *hross*, and it is commonly thought that the horse is a descendant of the wild Tarpan. The oldest reference to the Russ is found in a legal code from the 13th century, where the "wild horses of Gotland" are mentioned. You can see these very small horses, 123–6 cm (46–52 inches tall), around the island. They are bred in **Lojsta** ❻ at Lojsthajd, 20km (12 miles) southeast of Klintehamn.

Ancient sites

Wherever you travel in Gotland you'll come across at least one of the island's 92 medieval churches. In the centre of the island is **Romakloster** ❼ (tel: 0498-500 57; www.romakungsgard.se; June–Aug daily 10am–6pm, Sept Thur–Mon 11am–3pm), 17km (11 miles) southeast of Visby, a ruined 12th-century monastery which is now an open-air theatre, crafts centre and café. There are many other relics of the past, including runic stones and burial mounds.

If you reach Gotland's southernmost tip, you'll be able to see some of the most impressive *raukar* on the island.

TIP

Don't miss Gotland's Medieval Week (www. medeltidsveckan.se), held in early August. You'll be transported back to the year 1361 and experience Visby as a mighty Hanseatic city. The entertainment includes a huge medieval market, historical plays, tournaments, parades, a battle re-enactment and typical food and handicrafts of the time.

Fårö is famous for its impressive sea-stacks.

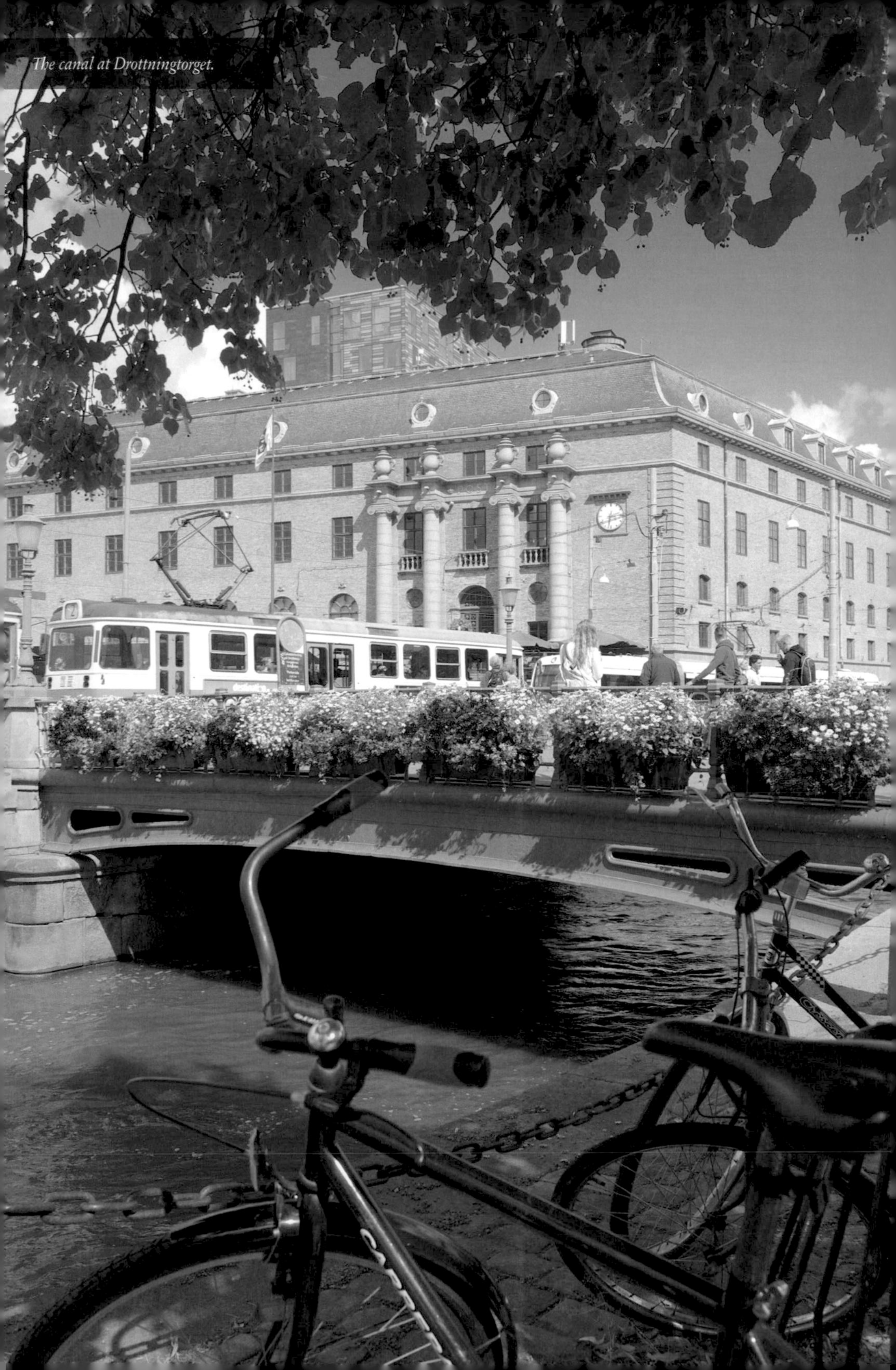

The canal at Drottningtorget.

GÖTEBORG

Southwest Sweden is home to the country's second city, with its café-lined boulevards, bustling harbour and a lively cultural and sporting scene.

Göteborg ❶ (Gothenburg), the "city by the sea", is a compact city ideal for sightseeing. Unlike airy-fairy, palace-filled Stockholm, Göteborg was always a hard-working industrial port, renowned for its shipbuilding industry. You can explore its fascinating maritime past at the floating ship museum Maritiman, or sail its stately Dutch built waterways on a Paddan canal tour. Today Göteborg has new strings to its bow, reinventing itself as a cultural centre, with a thriving music scene, some of the country's best seafood restaurants, and top-class museums and galleries such as the Göteborg Museum of Art and the Röhsska design centre. It's also a hub of family fun, offering Liseberg, one of Europe's biggest theme parks, and the fabulous nature and science centre Universeum.

Göteborg is Sweden's second city, with some 540,000 inhabitants, but many visitors are surprised by its apparent low profile. The city, situated at the mouth of the River Göta on the Swedish west coast, is built on a bed of clay 120 metres (400ft) thick in places. Said to have the consistency of microscopic cornflakes, it does not make the most suitable of foundations for construction, and high-rise buildings are few and far between in Göteborg.

Christmas time in the Haga district.

The city centre and its attractions are quite concentrated, but if you don't feel like walking, there is a comprehensive network of buses, ferries and trams – you can use the same tickets for each. The nature of the subsoil doesn't allow for an underground system.

Whether you arrive by sea or by train, one of the first buildings you'll notice is the mighty landmark of **Lilla Bommen** ❹, popularly known as "The Lipstick", an office block situated just beside the Götaälv Bridge. Reaching 86 metres (280ft) above sea

Main Attractions

Lilla Bommen
Maritiman
Paddan canal tour
Göteborgs Konstmuseum
  (Art Museum)
Trädgårdsföreningen
  (Gardens)
Nya Älvsborgs Fästning
  (Fortress)
Liseberg amusement park
Universeum

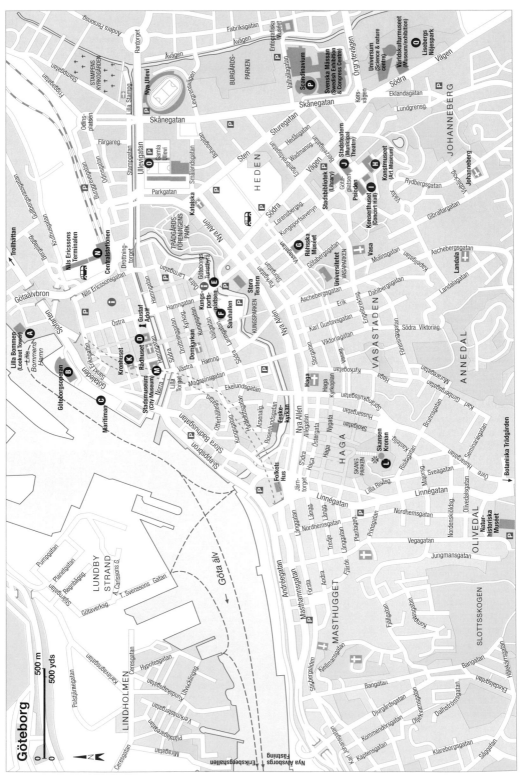

Göteborg

0   500 m
0   500 yds

N

Lilla Bommen (Lookout Tower) A
Göteborgsoperan B
Maritiman C
Konstmuseet
Rådhuset D
Stadsmuseum (City Museum)
Domkyrkan
Kungsports-platsen E
Saluhallen F
Göteborgs Turistbyrå
Rohsska Muséet G
Stadsteatern (Municipal Theatre) H
Konsthuset (Art Museum)
Konserthuset (Concert Hall)
Psalmen I
Stadsbibliotek (Library)
Universitetet
Nils Ericssons Terminalen N
Centralstationen
Gustaf Adolf

Nya Ullevi
Gamla Ullevi O
Scandinavium P
Svenska Mässan (Swedish Exhibition & Congress Centre)
Universum (Science & nature centre)
Världskulturmuseet (Museum/exhibition)
Lisebergs Nöjespark Q

LUNDBY STRAND
LINDHOLMEN
Göta älv
HEDEN
VASASTADEN
ANNEDAL
JOHANNEBERG
HAGA
OLIVEDAL
MASTHUGGET
SLOTTSSKOGEN

Skansen Kronan L
Haga
Feske-kyrkan
Folkets Hus
Botaniska Trädgården
Natur-historiska Muséet
Nya Älvsborgs-fästning
Eriksbergshallen

Trollhättan
Göteälvbron

level, this red-and-white-layered tower looks almost like a giant Lego construction. For a great view over the city and especially the harbour, take the lift (tel: 031-156 147; July daily 10am–4pm, Sept–June Mon–Fri 11am–3pm) to the café/viewpoint at the top of the building.

A favourable geographical position almost equally distant from the major population centres of Stockholm, Copenhagen and Oslo has helped Göteborg to become Scandinavia's second-largest seaport, handling over 37 million tonnes of freight per year. The city's two cruise-ship terminals, Frihamnen and Arendal, were visited by more than 70 cruise ships in 2014. It is in the harbour area that you will find the soul of the city. A good place to start your sightseeing is by following the quay westbound for a while.

A rejuvenated harbour

Just 200 metres (220 yds) west of Lilla Bommen stands the bold **Göteborg-soperan B** (opera house; Lilla Bommens Hamn; tel: 031-10 80 00; www.opera.se), inaugurated in 1994. Built in a bold, ship-like style, it is well worth a visit for its architecture alone.

A close neighbour of the Opera is Göteborg's **Maritiman C** (Maritime Centre; Packhuskajen; tel: 031-10 59 50; www.maritiman.se; May and Sept daily 11am–5pm; July–Aug: daily 10am–6pm). This floating ship museum has 13 impressive vessels that you can clamber aboard, including a claustrophobia-inducing submarine, a lightship, and the destroyer HMS *Småland*, the largest visitable warship in Scandinavia.

To see an interesting example of how a redundant shipyard area can be rejuvenated, follow the quay westbound for another 700 metres (765 yds) to Rosenlund and take the Älvsnabben ferry west along the River Göta to Eriksberg on the opposite bank. This ex-shipyard area is now the site of the Eriksbergshallen complex, containing concert and exhibitions

halls. There is still a shipyard of sorts here, which is where a replica of the East Indiaman which sank outside the city in 1745 has been rebuilt (tel: 031-779 34 50; www.soic.se; entry by guided tour, in English Sat at 1pm).

To explore the heart of Göteborg, take the Älvsnabben ferry back to the city and Lilla Bommens Hamn (harbour).

Civic architecture

Starting at the northern end of **Östra Hamngatan**, heading south you will pass **Östra Nordstan** (http://nordstan.se), one of Northern Europe's largest covered shopping centres containing a huge variety of shops, supermarkets and restaurants, as well as one of the two official **Göteborg Tourist Centers** (tel: 031-368 42 00; www.goteborg.com; Mon–Fri 10am–8pm, Sat–Sun 10am–6pm).

Gustaf Adolfs Torg (Gustaf Adolf's Square) is named after the city's founder, Gustav II Adolf. In the square around the statue of the old king, facing the canal, are several historic buildings, all with official uses. The **Rådhuset** (Town Hall) **D** was built in 1672 and

Göteborg's waterfront Opera House.

TIP

The Göteborg City Card allows unlimited travel on city buses and trams, a Paddan boat trip, and free admission to many museums and Liseberg amusement park (although note that ride tickets are extra) for 24, 48 or 72 hours. Buy one online at www.goteborg. com, at the city's tourist offices, at large hotels, at the airport or the central railway station.

Lunchtime outside Saluhallen.

extended in the early 19th century. It is now partly used as a courthouse.

Next is the **Wenngrenska Huset**, with the first two floors dating from 1759 and the top floor from 1820. Originally the home of a city councillor called Wenngren, it has come almost full circle and is now used as offices for the councillors. The **Stadshuset** (City Hall), built in 1758 as an armoury, was later used as a guardhouse and barracks for the city militia. It now houses the city council and administration department, which has spilled over into **Börshuset** (the former Stock Exchange, built in 1849) next door.

Cross Stora Hamnkanalen (Great Harbour Canal) and continue south to Kungsportsplatsen, where you can pop into the other **Göteborg Tourist Center** ❸ (tel: 031-368 42 00; www. goteborg.com; mid-June–mid-Aug daily 9.30am–8pm; mid-Aug–mid-June, see website for hours).

Across the street is **Saluhallen** ❺ (www.storasaluhallen.se; Mon–Fri 9am–6pm, Sat 9am–4pm), a large indoor marketplace built in 1886–9 and stocked with local specialities such

as seafood, cheese, game, sausages, fruit, Swedish lamb and turkey from Österlen. Other stalls offer more exotic wares, from Greece, Spain, Latin America and the Far East. This is a good place to sit and enjoy a cup of coffee, a light snack or a full lunch.

Kungsportsplatsen is also the place to embark on a 50-minute **Paddan canal tour** (www.stromma.se/Goteborg; Apr–mid-Oct two to three departures per hour, see website for days and times), on one of the flat-bottomed sightseeing boats that cruise through the old moat, under some 20 bridges, along canals built in the 17th century, out into the harbour and back again.

The city's cultural hub

From Kungsportsplatsen, cross the moat into Kungsportsavenyn – more commonly known as "**Avenyn**" (The Avenue). This, people claim, is Göteborg's answer to the Champs-Elysées – or how the Via Veneto used to be. The Avenyn, 40 metres (130ft) wide and just under 1 km (0.5 mile) long, is a boulevard lined with trees, restaurants, pubs and cafés as well as street

musicians and pedlars of fruits and trinkets. It is one of the few opportunities to experience the more open side of the Swedish character. Young people monopolise many of the watering holes and restaurants, but a certain tradition does prevail, as many of the establishments along the Avenyn have been the gathering place for successive generations of Göteborgers.

Halfway along the Avenyn, you are just a block away from the **Röhsska Muséet** Ⓖ (Vasagatan 37–39; tel: 031-368 31 50; www.designmuseum.se; Tues noon–8pm, Wed–Fri noon–5pm, Sat–Sun 11am–5pm), the Swedish museum for design and handicrafts. The collection includes a rich mixture of furniture, glass, silver, china and textiles and is well worth a visit. There is a good shop and an excellent café.

At the southern end of the Avenyn is Göteborg's cultural centre, **Götaplatsen**, with the imposing Poseidon fountain by the famous Swedish sculptor Carl Milles. Götaplatsen is flanked by the **Konstmuseum** Ⓗ (Art Museum; tel: 031-368 35 00; www.konstmuseum. goteborg.se; Tues–Thur 11am–6pm,

Wed 11 until 8pm, Fri–Sun and holidays 11am–5pm), with an extensive collection of Scandinavian art, including Carl Larsson, Anders Zorn, Albert Edelfelt and Karl Nordstrom, as well as works by Rubens, Rembrandt, Monet, Matisse, Van Gogh and others (see page 111).

On the west side of the square is the **Konserthuset** (Concert Hall) Ⓘ, home of the acclaimed Gothenburg Symphony Orchestra, and on the east the **Stadsteatern** Ⓙ (Municipal Theatre) and the Stadsbiblioteket (Municipal Library), which has over 400,000 volumes.

A city with a history

Göteborg has nothing to compare to Stockholm's Old Town; five major fires over the years saw to that. The city's historic centre within the confines of the moat, grand canal and the River Göta is an architectural hotchpotch of styles and periods. The first town called Göteborg, founded by King Carl IX, was actually on the other side of the River Göta in an area now called Hisingen. In one of the fierce internecine

FACT

Feskekörka (The Fish Church; www.feskekörka. se; Tues–Fri 10am–6pm, Sat 10am–3pm) in Rosenlundsvägen is a famous fish and seafood market. The 19th-century building, which also houses two top-class restaurants, resembles a church, hence the name.

The boulevard-like Kungsportsavenyn.

wars that broke out regularly among the Scandinavians, the Danes and Norwegians destroyed it in 1611 and cut Sweden off from the sea. A ransom of 1 million Riksdaler, equal to one year's grain harvest at that time, was eventually paid for the return of the Old Älvsborg fortress and an outlet to the sea.

To make sure it didn't happen again, in 1621 King Gustav II Adolf enlisted the aid of Sweden's first guest workers, the Dutch, who were more experienced than the Swedes at building defences. The Dutch engineers were well aware of the unstable subsoil and advised against having any structure more than two or three storeys high. Gustav II Adolf was, nevertheless, reported to be pleased with his choice of site, since the same clay would prevent his arch-rival, Denmark's King Christian, from assaulting the city with his heavy cannon.

The Dutch builders naturally gave Göteborg a typical 17th-century Dutch look, with canals and a moated fortress. The centre of Göteborg retains its distinctive Dutch character, even though two of the canals were filled in long

The Dutch-style Kronhuset.

ago and are now called Östra Hamngatan and Västra Hamngatan.

The day the king signed the Göteborg city charter, 2 June 1621, is not celebrated by the local citizens. Instead, they honour the day of his death, 6 November, by eating small cakes topped with the king's image in chocolate or marzipan.

Historical landmarks

Architectural remnants of Göteborg's very earliest days are few and include only Kronhuset, in the centre of town, the Bastion Carolus Rex at Kungsgatan and two small forts, Skansen Kronan and Skansen Lejonet.

Kronhuset  is Göteborg's oldest secular building, dating from 1643, and was originally the town's armoury. In 1660 it was briefly converted into the House of Parliament, so that the five-year-old Crown Prince could be sworn in as King Carl XI and succeed his father King Carl X Gustav, who died suddenly while visiting Göteborg. Enclosing a courtyard along with the facade of Kronhuset is **Kronhusbodarna**, a square of small buildings

---

THE GARDEN CITY

While Göteborg's canals and architecture reflect the early Dutch influence, its many parks give it an atmosphere reminiscent of 19th-century England. Göteborg has 20 parks, more than any other city in Sweden. At its heart, along the south and east side of the moat, is **Trädgårdsföreningen** (www.tradgardsforeningen.se; May–Sept daily 7am–8pm, Oct–Apr daily 7am–6pm; free). The locals call it "Trägår'n" and it is Göteborg's answer to New York's Central Park or London's Hyde Park. It may not be as large, but it does have the Palmhuset (June–Aug daily 10am–8pm, Sept–May daily 10am–4pm), a greenhouse for tropical plants, and a Rose Garden, best seen at the beginning of July and again during its second major blooming at the end of August.

Göteborg's other parks of note are all relatively close to the city centre. The largest is Slottskogen, which covers 137 hectares (338 acres) and is a complete recreation centre with sports facilities, zoo and restaurants, as well as small lakes and lovely areas for walking and picnicking. Across the Dag Hammarskjöld highway from Slottskogen is the Botanical Garden (www.gotbot.se; daily 9am–9pm, greenhouses open May–Aug daily 10am–5pm, Sept–Apr daily 10am–4pm). It is one of the largest of its kind in the world, containing 15,000 species of plants. It's hard to believe that this green city is also a highly industrialised centre.

that once served as warehouses and workshops for artillery makers, turners and saddlers. Today the buildings contain a small arts-and-crafts centre, including a chocolatier, potter, silversmith, leatherworker and clockmaker.

The squat little forts Skansen Lejonet and **Skansen Kronan** Ⓛ are picturesque buildings, topped respectively by a black lion and a golden crown, but both are privately owned and inaccessible to the public. The latter is situated on a hill in the city's Haga district, which was Göteborg's first suburb in 1640. As the city expanded it became the workers' district during the 19th century. During the 1980s and '90s, Haga was heavily rebuilt. Many of the old houses were demolished and, as the rents for the new flats were considerably higher, the impression of a workers' district faded. Still, some of the old atmosphere has been preserved, as the new buildings have been designed with the old architectural ideals in mind. Here, in the mainly pedestrianised streets you will find lots of small shops selling handicrafts and second-hand books, and a handful of small, cosy cafés and restaurants.

Göteborg became an economic force largely through the early efforts of the great merchant fleets and traders. Most notable was the Swedish East India Company, which brought great wealth into the city as early as the mid-1700s. Evidence of this wealth still exists today in the buildings along **Stora Hamnkanalen** (Grand Canal).

The East India House itself, built in 1750, houses the **Stadsmuseum** Ⓜ (City Museum; tel: 031-368 36 00; www.stadsmuseum.goteborg.se; Sept–Apr Tues–Sun 10am–5pm, until 8pm Wed) on Norra Hamngatan. It's worth visiting to see the lavish interiors, oriental exhibits from the glory days of the East India Company, and an exhibition of 20th-century industrial history.

Most of the city's more historic structures are now used by the local government, either as offices or for official functions as well as museums. Along the Norra Hamngatan side of the canal is the **Sahlgrenska Huset**, built in 1753 and, among other things, the office of the Municipal Secretariat

Trädgårdsföreningen, a park located at the heart of the city, boasts an elegant glass palm house.

for Trade and Industry and the Göteborg Region Promotion Office. Across the canal on Södra Hamngatan is the **Residenset**, built in 1650 for Field Marshal Lennart Torstensson, although its present appearance dates from an extension in the 1850s. It is now the official residence of the governor for Göteborg and Bohuslän.

Maritime traditions

If you arrive in Göteborg by ship, you can't help noticing the **Nya Älvsborgs Fästning** (Fortress) on an island at the mouth of the River Göta. It was built in the late 17th century in order to protect Sweden's western gateway against the Danes. Nya Älvsborg witnessed its last taste of fire against the Danish fleet led by Norwegian Peder Tordenskiold in 1717 and again in 1719. It was last used officially as a prison during the 19th century and now serves as a venue for meetings and banquets, as well as weddings in the chapel. It is one of the few Göteborg tourist attractions that is not within walking distance or a tram ride from the city centre. It can be reached in high summer only by **boat tour** (tel: 031-60 96 70; www.stromma.se/Goteborg; departure from Lilla Bommen four times daily Jul–early Aug).

Göteborg's relationship with the sea was the reason for its coming into being. Its importance during the 19th century was even proclaimed by Sweden's most famous dramatist, August Strindberg. A character in the 1886–7 drama *The Maid's Son* was to realise, after seeing Göteborg's busy harbour for the first time, that Stockholm was no longer the Scandinavian focal point and that Göteborg had taken the lead.

When Strindberg wrote those lines for the book, the city's harbour was alive with ships bound for, or returning from, the four corners of the earth. The outbound traffic was also human, for at that time the flow of Swedish emigrants to America was still in full swing. For most of the nearly 1 million Swedes who made their way to the promised land across the Atlantic, the last they ever saw of their homeland was Göteborg.

Several decades later, Göteborg was the port for the Swedish American Line luxury liners that used to bring

The River Göta.

dollar-laden American tourists, and some returning emigrants, to Sweden. These liners eventually gave way to fast air travel. The port of Göteborg has nevertheless survived as a gateway to Sweden for people and cargo.

Swimming in the city

Even though Göteborg is an industrial city, it takes pride in protecting its environment. The water in the River Göta is now as pure as it was 100 years ago, and fish such as salmon are thriving once again. As for swimming around Göteborg, there are bathing lakes just a few kilometres from the city centre, and the beach is less than half an hour away.

However, the very closest place to swim outdoors is at the **harbour pool and sauna** in Frihamnen, on the other side of the River Göta from central Göteborg, which opened in summer 2015 to the delight of Gothenburgers. The 20-metre pool allows swimmers to watch all the activity in the harbour as they swim, and is open May to September. The sauna is open year-round – book at www.timecenter.com/jubileumsparken.

Take tram 5 to Bögatan, 6km (4 miles) east of the centre. From here, a 15-minute walk brings you to the **Delsjön**, where you can sunbathe on the rocks before jumping in the water. You can also hire a canoe for an hour or two. Or you can go by trams 7 or 11 to terminus **Bergsjön**, the name of both the district and the lake, 10km (6 miles) northeast of the centre, to enjoy the rocks and the water.

If you prefer the sea, jump on the Rosa Express bus at the Nordstan shopping centre, across from **Central-stationen ⓝ** (Central Station), and go to the Askimsbadet (Askim Beach), 10km (6 miles) south of the city centre. Here you will find a lovely sandy beach with a jetty, café and kiosks.

Sporting Göteborg

Göteborg is the sports capital of Sweden. Football is the biggest sport, and the leading team is IFK Göteborg, well known all over Europe. In 2015, two out of Göteborg's four teams were riding high in *Allsvenskan*, Sweden's premier division. IFK Göteborg plays all its national games at **Ullevi ⓞ**,

Central Station.

which is situated just a few hundred metres southeast of the Centralstationen. Just a free kick away, you will find Nya ("New") Ullevi, the largest outdoor stadium in the whole of Sweden. Built for the football World Cup in 1958, today with a seating capacity of 43,000, this is not only the venue for many international sport events (including speedway, football and athletics), but also a conference centre and arena for international musicians and artists, musicals and concerts. Also here is **Valhallabadet** (Valhalla Swimming Complex; www.gotevent.se/valhallabadet), with various pools and spa facilities.

Some 600 metres/yards to the south of Nya Ullevi is **Scandinavium** ❶, a large indoor arena which seats 12,500 spectators and where Göteborg's ice hockey pride, the Frölunda Indians, play their home games. This arena's extraordinary flexibility is worth mentioning. Not only can it be used as a tennis arena, concert hall or for equestrian events; in 1997 a swimming pool was built for the world championship in short-track swimming. Two days after the final, it was back once more

The wooden roller-coaster at Liseberg amusement park.

to its normal use, with not a trace of the pool to be seen. Between Nya Ullevi and Scandinavium you will find the Heden grounds, where the annual Gothia Cup, the largest youth football tournament in the world, is played. 1,600 teams from 80 countries participated in the 2015 championships.

Just for fun

One of the main attractions for these young football players – and indeed for any visitor to Göteborg – is the **Liseberg** ❶ (tel: 031-40 01 00; www. liseberg.se; late Apr–Sept plus Halloween and Christmas, hours vary, check website), an amusement park which ranks as one of the largest tourist attractions in Europe, with more than 3 million visitors each year. Its top attractions are the wooden rollercoaster Balder, and AtmosFear, the highest freefall ride in Europe. Liseberg offers not only candy floss, popcorn and thrills for both adults and children; you can also see concerts from Swedish artists on the main stage as part of your entrance fee. The park has numerous restaurants, cafés and bars, a theatre and gardens.

For those in the mood to be further entertained, another big family attraction is the **Universeum** (tel: 031-335 64 50; www.universeum.se; daily 10am–6pm, mid-June–mid-Aug until 10pm), a seven-floor science and nature centre on the edge of Liseberg's extensive grounds. Visitors start with an investigation of Swedish wildlife at the top of the building, working their way down through a shark-filled aquarium, a fabulous rainforest zone full of chittering monkeys, colourful birds and caiman, and exhibitions on space travel and technology.

Nearby is the less youth-oriented **Världskulturmuseet** (Museum of World Culture; www.varldskulturmuseet. se; Tues–Fri noon–5pm, Wed until 8pm, Sat–Sun 11am–5pm), which offers changing exhibitions on current world events, set in an award-winning building.

Poseidon fountain on Götaplatsen, Göteborg's cultural centre.

The rugged Bohuslän coast.

THE WEST COAST

From the sandy beaches of Halland to the pink-tinged rocks and islands of Bohuslän, the west coast has long been a summer playground for the Swedes.

Map on page
226

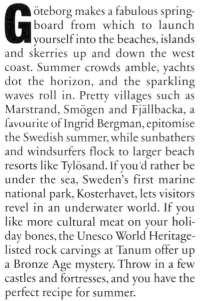

Göteborg makes a fabulous spring-board from which to launch yourself into the beaches, islands and skerries up and down the west coast. Summer crowds amble, yachts dot the horizon, and the sparkling waves roll in. Pretty villages such as Marstrand, Smögen and Fjällbacka, a favourite of Ingrid Bergman, epitomise the Swedish summer, while sunbathers and windsurfers flock to larger beach resorts like Tylösand. If you'd rather be under the sea, Sweden's first marine national park, Kosterhavet, lets visitors revel in an underwater world. If you like more cultural meat on your holiday bones, the Unesco World Heritage-listed rock carvings at Tanum offer up a Bronze Age mystery. Throw in a few castles and fortresses, and you have the perfect recipe for summer.

The west coast of Sweden, generously dotted with beaches and fishing villages, is 400km (250 miles) of glorious coastline divided in two by the city of Göteborg, see page 213. To the south is the province of Halland, where the best beaches lie. North of the city, in the province of Bohuslän, the coast is majestic: all granite rocks, islands and skerries. The Swedes discovered the west coast as a holiday spot early in the 20th century, and its popularity has never waned.

The E6 runs along the coast, separating it from the hinterland. Although the highway connects all the larger cities, you will have to take to the small coastal roads to discover the gems. Starting along the coast in the northwestern corner of the county of Skåne, a number of small towns offer views into the past. **Gamla Viken ❷**, about 15km (9 miles) north of Helsingborg along highway 22, is a picturesque old fishing village. Continuing up the coast, the furthest point out on the peninsula, **Kullen ❸**, offers a beautiful seascape. And **Mölle**, the town closest to Kullen, has a lovely summer bathing spot. **Torekov** sits at

Main Attractions

Tylösand Beach
Varbergs Fästning
Tjolöholm Castle
Marstrand
Tanumshede Rock Carvings
Kosterhavet Marine
   National Park

Smögen's wooded waterside boardwalk.

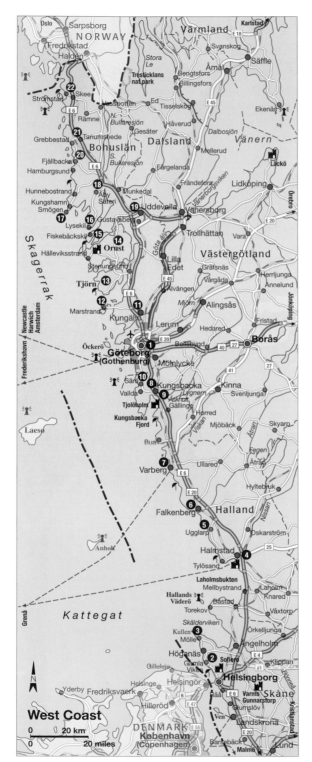

West Coast

0   20 km

0   20 miles

the tip of the next peninsula. Here, there is a seaside golf course (one of the oldest on the west coast), and Värdshus Hovs Hallar, a hotel surrounded by gentle countryside.

Abundance of sandy beaches

A ridge running inland from the coast forms a natural border between Skåne and Halland. This part of the coast has an abundance of sandy beaches, such as those at **Skummeslövstrand** and **Mellbystrand**, while inland, if you cross the busy E6, it is quietly pastoral, with woodlands, farms and winding rivers.

Halmstad ❹, the largest town in Halland, lies on the River Nissan and is the home town of 1980s rock duo Roxette. The river here is now a spawning ground for salmon. **Halmstads Slott** (Halmstad Castle), the provincial governor's residence, was built in the 17th century by the Danish king, Christian IV. It houses the town's small tourist office. Other sights include the remains of a city wall and St Nikolai, a 13th-century church. However, by far the most visitors – up to 40,000 each summer – head to the popular holiday resort of **Tylösand**, 6km (10 miles) west of town, with its 7km (4-mile) long sandy beach. Tylösand is dominated by the massive complex of the Nya Hotel Tylösand, which has all the trappings of a major modern holiday centre. There are lots of sports facilities, too, including two 18-hole golf courses. There are also good beaches at **Östra Strand**, **Ringenäs** and **Haverdals strand**.

The next town north along the coast, 25 km (15 miles) north of Halmstad towards Falkenberg, is **Ugglarp ❺**, where you will find **Svedinos Biloch Flygmuseum** (Car and Air Museum; tel: 0346-431 87; May and Sept Sat–Sun 11am–4pm; June and 17–31 Aug daily 11am–4pm; July–16 Aug daily 10am–6pm). It's a bit untidy, but is bursting at the seams with over 100 old cars and 31 old and new aircraft, which will delight the enthusiast and the engineer. The bigger, modern aircraft sit outside;

inside, the rest are crammed bumper-to-bumper and wingtip-to-wingtip. Treasures include such exotic names as a Bullerbilen car, which was built in 1897.

Salmon galore

Falkenberg ❻ is on the Ätran, a river famous for its salmon. The British were the first to enjoy the sport of angling here in the 1830s, when English and Scottish immigrants who had settled in Göteborg invited friends to join them for hunting and fishing. For many years in the 19th century the fishing rights on the river were leased to a Baron Oscar Dickson, who belonged to one of the best-known families in Göteborg.

A London solicitor, W.M. Wilkinson, was so moved by the quality of the fishing that in 1884 he wrote and had published privately a little book for the benefit of his Swedish and English friends. Called *Days in Falkenberg*, it reveals that the going rate for salmon was 3s. 6d. a pound (18p/25 US cents for 500g). One salmon smokehouse remains; it is now the local museum.

The old part of the town with its 18th-century wooden houses and cobbled streets is centred on the 14th-century St Laurenti Church. There is an old toll bridge *(tullbron)* from 1756 and the oldest pottery in Sweden, Törngrens Krukmakeri (Krumakaregatan 4; tel: 0346-103 54; www.torngrens-krukmakeri.se). It was run by the Törngren family from 1789 to 2014, when the final potter retired, although the shop was still open at the time of writing. Good beaches are found at **Olofsby** (north of the town) and **Skrea Strand** (south of the town).

Varberg: popular resort

Continuing 30km (19 miles) up the coast on the E6, the next large town is **Varberg ❼**, which, in contrast to the rather restrained atmosphere of Falkenberg, is a bustling sort of place combining spa, resort, port and commercial centre with a ferry service to Grenå in Denmark.

Looming impressively beside the water, its fortress, **Varbergs Fästning**, houses a youth hostel, restaurant, apartments and **Hallands Kulturhistoriska Museum** (tel: 0340-828 30; www.hkm.varberg.se; Sept–June Tues–Fri

Tylösand's popular sandy beach.

10am–4pm, Sat–Sun noon–4pm; July–early Aug daily 10am–5pm; entrance fee;) with 35,000 exhibits. Pride of place goes to the Bocksten Man, who demonstrates what the well-dressed 14th-century male should be wearing. He is the only preserved figure in the world to be wearing a complete costume from the Middle Ages. Another prize possession is the bullet (a button) which, according to legend, killed King Carl XII in 1718. There is also the Museum of Communications in King Carl XI's stables, which has a collection of carriages, boats and – from a somewhat different era – bicycles.

Varberg also has two reminders of its late 19th-century development as a Swedish holiday resort – and both are in use today. One is the 1883 **Societén** in the park, an elaborate wooden pavilion, which is now a restaurant and a site for free outdoor concerts in July. The second is the 1903 bathing section, where you can indulge in gentle sea- and sunbathing. A little bridge leads from the shore to a rectangular wooden stilted structure with the sea in the middle. Inside **Kallbadhuset bathing station** (www.kallbadhuset.se; mid-June–mid-Aug daily from 10am, see website for times rest of year) are changing huts and sun chairs where, after a quick plunge in this early version of a seawater swimming pool, the bathers relax naked (there are separate male and female sections) over coffee and waffles and enjoy the sun and sea air. More than once it has been suggested that the structure was an anachronism and should be demolished, but happily it still survives.

Around Varberg there are several more beaches. The gently shelving beach at **Apelviken** is safe for children, and is one of the country's top spots for windsurfing and kitesurfing. The island of **Getterön**, 5km (3 miles) to the north, has beaches, a nature reserve and bird sanctuary. It is reached by a bridge from the mainland.

North towards Göteborg

Heading north for Kungsbacka, you will pass what is probably the most out-of-character building along the entire coast. **Tjolöholm Castle** (tel: 0300-40 46 00; www.tjoloholm.se; garden open all year; house by guided tour only, in

English-style Tjolöholm Castle.

English daily Jul–mid-Aug, in Swedish at other times – see website for full schedule) was built at the beginning of the 20th century, but in an English Arts and Crafts style. It has often been used as a film set, perhaps most eerily in *Melancholia* (2011), directed by Lars von Trier and starring Kirsten Dunst. The castle stands at the centre of a large park on a private headland crisscrossed with walking paths, and has a splendid Art Nouveau interior. The original way of cleaning the inside of this architectural aberration was as unusual as the castle itself. Teams of horses dragged a huge and primitive vacuum cleaner up to the building, where cleaner, horses and all came in through the windows.

Kungsbacka ❽ is the most northerly town in Halland. Lying only 30km (18 miles) south of Göteborg, the town was inevitably reduced to becoming a dormitory for Big G. However, when it was established as a wooden city in the 13th century, Kungsbacka was a separate town with its own identity. In 1676, it briefly knew royal patronage when King Carl XI made it his headquarters during a war with Denmark.

Less than 10km (6 miles) inland from Kungsbacka, a high ridge runs parallel with the coast. It is called **Fjärås Bräcka**, and was the result of action by glaciers many thousands of years ago. From the top of the ridge, now a nature reserve, there are good views over the Kungsbacka Fjord. On the other side of the ridge is an equally attractive view of **Lake Lygnern** which, before the Ice Age, was part of the same fjord. Towards the southern end of the ridge there are some Bronze Age graves and about 125 menhirs (standing stones) from the Iron Age. The most impressive is the Frode stone, which gets its name from a Danish fairy king who, legend says, is buried there.

From Tjolöholm, along the E6/E20 towards Gällinge, signs indicate the route left to Fölanda i Gällinge and the hamlet of **Äskhult** ❾ (May–mid-June and mid-Aug–Sept Sat–Sun 11am–4pm, mid-June–mid-Aug daily 11am–5pm), a group of buildings from the 18th and early 19th centuries, gathered around a common courtyard. It is one of the few surviving examples of an undivided hamlet, and is now a museum. Take a

Grazing near Lake Lygnern.

minor road on your return to Kungs-backa and you pass **Gåsevadholm**, a privately owned castle built in 1757 by Niclas Sahlgren, then manager of the Swedish East India Company.

The moment you reach the little seaside resort of **Särö ⑩** (immediately north of Kungsbacka), you realise the coastline has changed. Apart from some small sandy coves, the beaches have gone, and instead, as you near Göteborg, a more dramatic landscape of rocks, inlets and islands takes over.

As early as the first years of the 19th century, Särö was a fashionable resort and, when it became popular with the Swedish royal family, its name was made. Both King Oscar II and the tennis-playing king, Gustav V, liked to spend time there each summer, and Gustav was a frequent player on the same tennis courts that you can use today. This was the resort where the wealthier inhabitants of Göteborg had their summer villas, charming wooden houses with verandas, balconies and an abundance of carved woodwork which still remain.

Fortunately Särö has resisted development and remains in something of a time warp with its turn-of-the-century atmosphere. You can walk along the Strandpromenaden and through **Särö Västerskog**, one of the oldest oak woods along the west coast. There is one small sandy beach on the south side of the town, otherwise it is smooth granite rocks. The pace is leisurely, and summer excitement is restricted to going out in a boat to fish or watch the basking seals.

The rugged coast

The province of **Bohuslän** begins on the north side of Göteborg, and already the coastal scenery has set a pattern that continues all the way to the Norwegian border: rocks, islands and skerries. There are few major towns in Bohuslän, but 10km (6 miles) north from Göteborg is **Kungälv ⑪**, an old Viking centre, which occupies a key strategic position on the River Göta. It is now within easy commuting distance of Göteborg and so, like Kungsbacka, it has become a dormitory town.

To start seeing the coast, head 15km (9 miles) west from Kungälv on road 168 past Tjuvkil, where you can catch a short ferry over to **Marstrand ⑫**. A

On board the ferry to Koster Marine National Park.

town without cars, Marstrand is a popular holiday resort and sailing centre. In summer it is also a good place to buy crafts. **Carlstens Fästning** (Carlsten Fortress), which is unfortunately spoilt by obtrusive radar equipment on its tower, dominates the town and offers the best views of the island. King Oscar II used to come here every summer to holiday, and his statue stands in front of the Societetshuset. As a link with the past, a quartet often plays in Paradisparken (Paradise Park) in season.

Beyond Marstrand lie two major islands, Tjörn and Orust, and a number of smaller ones. You reach Tjörn over a bridge near **Stenungsund**, 22km (13 miles) north of Kungälv. A second bridge links Tjörn with Orust and a third bridge gets you back to the mainland. This area is known as the Bästkusten ("Best Coast"), the heart of Bohuslän. **Tjörn** ⓲ is beautiful, with some barren areas inland, but a fascinating coastline. Off the southern corner of Tjörn is **Klädesholmen**, a tiny island, linked by yet another bridge (this area is full of examples of Swedish bridge-builders' skills).

Klädesholmen is a colourful jumble of tightly packed wooden houses that seem to cling to the rocky surface. Like the majority of these villages, they are not just pretty places for the holiday-maker but are working fishing villages, too. Views may be spoilt by industrial-style buildings connected with fish-processing or the repair of trawlers and their gear, but this is part of local life. A magnificent curved bridge, which provides good views in either direction, links Tjörn and **Orust** ⓮. This island, the third-largest in Sweden, has its quota of fishing villages, including Mollösund, Halleviksstrand, Gullholmen, Ellös and Käringön. Inland from the deeply indented coastline with its succession of rocks and coves, there is fertile farmland.

Crossing the fjord to Lysekil

As you cross yet another bridge, you have the impression that you are on yet another island, but it is in fact a long jagged promontory and part of the mainland. From the fishing village of **Fiskebäckskil** ⓯ a ferry crosses the Gullmarn, Sweden's only genuine fjord, to **Lysekil** ⓰.

FACT

Skärhamn, a pretty fishing village on the island of Tjörn, is the site of the Nordic Watercolour Museum (Södrahamnen 6; tel: 030-460 00 80; www.akvarellmuseet.org; mid-May–mid-Sept daily 11am–6pm; mid-Sept–mid-May Tues–Sun noon–5pm), which features a children's studio, exhibitions and a centre for research.

Fiskebäckskil.

Lysekil has been Swedish for 300 years; before that it was Norwegian. In the 19th century it became a summer resort, and its popularity has continued to the present day. During the summer it comes to life and is full of bustle and activity with boat excursions to the islands and sea-fishing trips. **Havets Hus** (Sea Aquarium; Strandvägen 9; tel: 0523-66 81 61; www.havetshus.se; daily 10am–4pm, mid-June–Aug until 6pm) is fun for kids. It contains Swedish sea life from Gullmarn and the Skagerrak, with the most impressive exhibit, the tunnel aquarium, holding 140,000 litres (31,000 gallons) of water and creatures such as rays, sharks, halibut and cod. The aquarium also runs a 1.5-hour boat trip to spot seals from the jetty outside (daily at 1pm from mid-June to mid-Aug).

North of Lysekil on the **Sotenäs peninsula** are yet more fishing villages. **Smögen** ⓱, another small bridge-connected island, is particularly attractive with its brightly painted houses near the water's edge. During the summer, this town's lovely small harbour is packed with leisure boats, pausing here

on their way up and down the coast. One of the main attractions of the town is the boardwalk, where you can shop, stroll and lounge. Here, numerous shops open just for the summer in the old wooden fishing huts, selling mainly clothing and souvenirs. The other attraction of Smögen is fresh shrimp. Smögen is a working fishing village, and it's worth watching a fish auction (www.smogens-fiskauktion.com; Mon–Fri 8am, Thur also at 4pm) and then going round the corner to buy some of the fresh catch from the fishmongers.

At **Åby Säteri** ⓲, about 17km (12 miles) northeast of Smögen on route 171, is **Nordens Ark** (tel: 0523-795 90; www.nordensark.se; daily, Apr–mid-June and mid-Aug–Sept 10am–5pm; mid-June–mid-Aug 10am–7pm; Oct–Mar 10am–4pm; last entry one hour before closing), a wildlife park featuring endangered species such as Amur tigers, snow leopards, wolverines, lynxes and wolves. All the animals are kept in large sections of the natural wooded habitat, so the walk is pleasant, but spotting the animals can be a challenge.

Inland from Lysekil, east of the E6, lies **Uddevalla** ⓳, the biggest town in the province. It was once a major ship-building centre, but like so many others in Europe, the shipyard closed and has been partially replaced by other industry. If the town has little to interest the visitor, then there is a place on the outskirts which has greater merit. **Gustavsberg** claims to be Sweden's oldest seaside resort, and it was mentioned by the botanist Linnaeus in his book *Westgötha Resa*, published in 1746. Like many of the other resorts, it has its **Societetssalongen** – another of these grand, richly ornamented wooden buildings – which lives on as a youth hostel, and this and other buildings are all set in a delightful park that leads down to the water's edge.

NEWS SET IN STONE

Concentrated around Tanumshede, in Bohuslän, is Europe's richest collection of Bronze Age rock carvings. They are included on Unesco's World Heritage list. These were the original tabloid newspapers: all the news in pictures and no text. The carvings show battles, ships, hunting and fishing scenes, warriors, sun-wheels, mating couples and footprints. These images hold many mysteries, but they also provide a lot of information about everyday life, beliefs and practices from 1500 to 500 BC. The abundance of ships, as well as the close proximity to the coast of all the carvings, indicates a reliance on the sea; and the ships are also believed to have been important as religious vehicles. There are numerous wedding and mating scenes, possible evidence that couples mated in public as part of the ceremonies. Many of the pictures are related to themes of fertility, spring and the afterlife. At nearby Vitlycke the carvings cover 204 sq metres (2,200 sq ft). **Vitlycke Museum** (tel: 0525-209 50; www.vitlyckemuseum.se; Apr Sat–Sun 11am–4pm; May–Aug daily 10am–6pm; Sept daily 10am–4pm; Oct Tues–Sun 11am–4pm; Nov–Mar by arrangement) provides information, exhibitions and tours. There is also a reconstructed Bronze Age village. Other carvings are at Fossum, Tegneby and Litsleby.

Towards Norway

As you travel north along this coast of smooth, pinkish granite rocks, the combination of fishing village and holiday centre is repeated. Actress Ingrid Bergman spent many a summer in the pretty little village of **Fjällbacka** 🈯, after her third husband bought the offshore island of Dannholmen, where Ingrid's ashes were scattered. Fjällbacka is also the birthplace of Swedish crime writer Camilla Läckberg – many of her books take place in and around the village.

Tanumshede 🈯, a small town on the E6 60km (37 miles) north of Uddevalla, lies inland from the fishing village of Grebbestad and has two claims to fame. One is **Tanums Gestgifveri**, an inn established by royal decree and which has been welcoming visitors since 1663. The modest-looking wooden building, painted in the traditional buff colour, belies an interior of cosy rooms and outstanding cuisine. Fish dishes naturally rank high on its list of specialities. Tanum's second claim to fame is of much greater historical importance, since nearby is Europe's largest collection of Bronze Age rock carvings (see box).

The last town before the Norwegian frontier is **Strömstad** 🈯. This old health resort was one of the first places in Sweden to provide saltwater and seaweed baths. Strömstad shrimps are considered by the local inhabitants to be in a class of their own. You can see the beasts in their natural habitat by taking a 45-minute boat ride from Strömstad to the Koster Islands, whose surrounding waters make up **Kosterhavet**, Sweden's first marine-based national park. The park contains the country's most species-rich seabed, which you can explore along marked snorkel trails – contact the visitor centre **Naturum Kosterhavet** (South Koster; www.kosterhavet.se; mid-June–mid-Aug daily 11am–5pm, mid-Aug–mid-June Thur–Fri 11am–5pm, Sat–Sun 11am–3pm) for details.

The Strömstad district has more than a touch of Norwegian about it, which is not surprising. In the past, the histories of Denmark, Norway and Sweden were inextricably linked, and for many years Strömstad was part of Norway. Today, the town remains overrun by Norwegians, especially on Saturdays, as they flock over the border to buy cheaper alcohol and food.

A guide explains the Bronze Age rock carvings at Tanumshede.

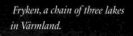
Fryken, a chain of three lakes in Värmland.

THE GREAT LAKES

At the heart of southern Sweden lie the two great lakes, Vänern and Vättern. In this region of forests, farmland and rivers, pretty villages, castles and painted churches abound.

Two great lakes, Vänern and Vättern, a mighty river and a network of canals dominate the landscape. As you might guess, many attractions here revolve around water and the historic mills and factories that it drove. Impressive 19th-century structures such as the Håverud aqueduct and the Trollhättan waterfalls show the element tamed and channelled for industrial use. The River Klarälven was once the centre of Sweden's logging industry, but today is a popular spot for rafting trips and beaver safaris. In April, visitors flock to Hornborgasjön (Hornborg Lake) to watch thousands of cranes dancing. Back on dry land – but only just – one of Sweden's most beautiful castles, the turreted Läckö Slott, dips its toe into Lake Vänern.

The larger of the two great lakes is Vänern, a vast stretch of water with an area of 5,585 sq km (2,156 sq miles). It is not only the biggest lake in Sweden but also the third-largest in Europe, and its western shore embraces two provinces, Dalsland and Värmland.

Dalsland is a province of neat farms and prosperous small towns and villages, with empty roads running through its forests. From a bus or car, you may be lucky enough to catch a glimpse of an elk sliding out of the trees. This gentle countryside with its sprinkling of lakes and rivers stretches from the fertile Dalboslätten in the

The scenic Fryken valley.

southeast to the northwest slopes of the Skogsdal. The nearer you go to the Norwegian border, the more barren it gets. No province in Sweden can be described as "small" but, by the standards of this large country, everything in Dalsland is on a modest scale – hence the title "Sweden in Miniature".

The greatest attraction in Dalsland is its nature and, thus, the most interesting activities are outdoors: namely, camping, hiking and canoeing. West of Mellerud is **Kroppefjällen ❶**, an upland area which is a nature reserve

Main Attractions

Håverud Aqueduct
Rafting the River Klarälven
Skara Sommarland
  (Waterpark)
Läckö Slott (Castle)
Trollhättan
Habo Church

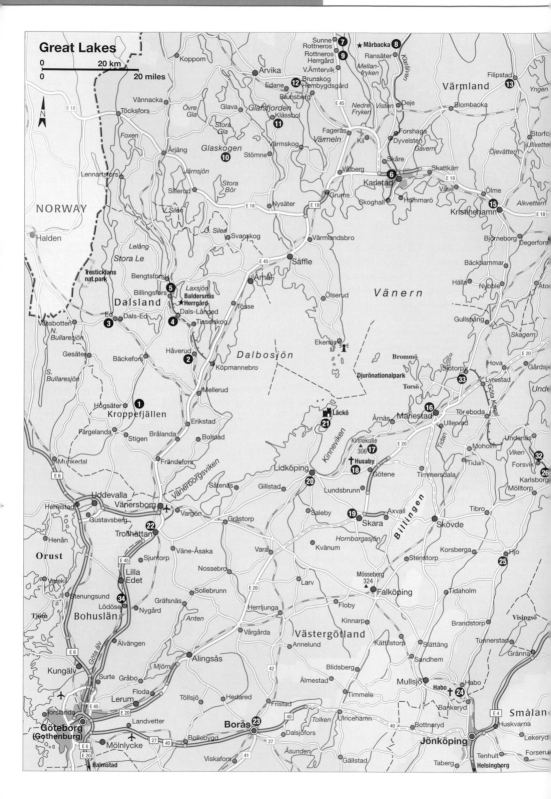

Great Lakes

0   20 km
0   20 miles

N

NORWAY

Halden

Tresticklans
nat.park

Dalsland

Vässbotten
N.
Bullaresjön

Gesäter

S.
Bullaresjön

Högsäter **①**
Kroppefjällen

Färgelanda

Munkedal

Uddevalla
Vänersborg

Herrestad
Gustavsberg

Orust

Henån

Varekil

Stenungsund

Tjörn

Bohuslän

Lödöse **③④**
Nygård

Kungälv

Surte   Gråbo

Lerum

Torslanda

Göteborg
(Gothenburg)

Mölnlycke

Halmstad

Koppom

Vännacka

Töcksfors

Övre
Gla

Foxen

Årjäng

Lennartsfors

Ed   Dals-Ed **③**

Bäckefors

Bengtsfors

Billingsfors **⑤**

③

Dals-Långed **④**

Håverud **②**

Köpmannebro

Bäckefors

Mellerud

Erikstad

Brålanda

Stigen   Bolstad

Frändefors

Vänersborg

Vargön

Trollhättan **㉒**

Sjuntorp

Lilla
Edet

Gräfsnäs

Gräfsnäs

Lödöse **㉞**
Nygård

Anten

Älvängen

Alingsås

Mjörn

Floda

Töllsjö

Hedared

Landvetter

Borås **㉓**

Bollebygd

Viskafors

Arvika

Edane

Glava   Glafsfjorden

Klässbol **⑪**

Glaskogen **⑩**

Stömne

Järnsjön

Stora
Bör

Sillerud

V. Silen

Svanskog

Ö. Silen

Leläng

Stora Le

Laxsjön

Baldersnäs
★Herrgård

Tisselskog

Dalbosjön

Ekenäs

Brunskög
Hembygdsgård **⑫**

Brunsberg

Värmskog

Valberg

Nysäter

Säffle

Åmål

Tösse

Ölserud

Sunne
Rottneros   **⑦**
Rottneros
Herrgård **⑨**

★Mårbacka **⑧**

Ransäter

V.Ämtervik

Mellan-
tryken

Nedre
Fryken   Visten

Deje

Fagerås

Värmeln   Kil

Skåre

Karlstad **⑥**

Grums

Skoghall

Värmlandsbro

Vänern

Gullspång

Skagern

Filipstad   **⑬**

Yngen

Värmland

Blombacka

Forshaga
Dyvelsten
Gävern

Storfors
Ullvette

Öjevättern

Skattkärr

Väse

Hammarö

Kristinehamn **⑮**

Ölme

Alkvettern

Björneborg   Degerfors

Bäckhammar

Hälla   Nybble   Åto

Djurönationalpark

Brommö

Torsö

Läckö **㉑**

Ärnäs

Kinneviken

Lidköping **⑳**

Gillstad

Såtenäs

Grästorp

Vara

Nossebro

Sollebrunn

Vårgårda

Annelund

Herrljunga

Västergötland

Blidsberg

Älmestad

Fristad

Dalsjöfors

Ulricehamn

Gällstad

Spötorp **㉝**

Hova

Gårdsjö

Lyrestad

Göta   Kanal

Unde

Mariestad **⑯**

Töreboda

Ullervad

Kinnekulle
306 **⑰**

✝Husaby **⑱**

Götene   Timmersdala

Lundsbrunn

Saleby

Skara **⑲**

Axvall

Hornborgasjön

Kvänum

Mösseberg
324
Falköping

Larv

Billingen

Skövde

Korsberga

Stenstorp

Tidaholm

Floby

Kinnarp

Slättäng

Sandhem

Mullsjö

Habo **㉔**

Timmele

Bankeryd

Tolken

Bottnaryd

 Åsunden

Tenhult

Taberg

Helsingborg

Moholm

Tidan

Tibro

Undenäs

Viken

Forsvik

Karlsborg
Mölltorp

㉜

㉖

Hjo

㉕

Visingsö

Tunnerstad

Gränna

Habo

㉔

Mullsjö

Jönköping

Huskvarna

Lekeryd

Forseru

Småland

㉓

E 4

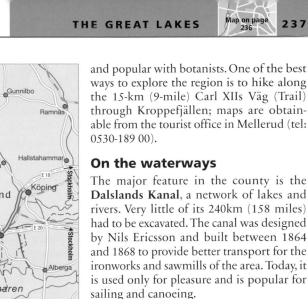

and popular with botanists. One of the best ways to explore the region is to hike along the 15-km (9-mile) Carl XIIs Väg (Trail) through Kroppefjällen; maps are obtainable from the tourist office in Mellerud (tel: 0530-189 00).

On the waterways

The major feature in the county is the **Dalslands Kanal**, a network of lakes and rivers. Very little of its 240km (158 miles) had to be excavated. The canal was designed by Nils Ericsson and built between 1864 and 1868 to provide better transport for the ironworks and sawmills of the area. Today, it is used only for pleasure and is popular for sailing and canoeing.

The most dramatic piece of engineering is the aqueduct at **Håverud** ❷, 14 km (9 miles) north of Mellerud. Made of iron and 33 metres (108ft) long, it carries the canal over the rapids of the River Upperud. Held together by 33,000 rivets, it is still watertight after 130 years. Apart from the aqueduct there are road and rail bridges and locks at Håverud, and the best view of this unusual combination is from the hill above the roadway. Håverud has a small Canal Museum, **Håverud Kanalmuséet** (tel: 0530-306 24; www.kanalmuseet.se; mid-May–mid-June and mid-Aug–Sept daily 11am–4pm; mid-June–mid-Aug daily 10am–6pm), which describes the various sets of locks.

King Carl's genius

Along highway 164, which runs between the two lakes Stora Le and Lelång (Big Le and Long Le), stand the twin villages of **Ed** and **Dals-Ed** ❸, nowadays so close that it is hard to tell where one ends and the other begins. The views of water and forest are lovely, and this has long been a popular holiday centre.

The area's earlier history was more dramatic because of its links with Sweden's 17th-century military genius, King Carl XII, and his final campaign against Norway (see page 238). If you're in the area, you might want to drop into the **Dals-Ed Älgpark** (www.dalslandsmooseranch.se; mid-June–Aug daily 11am–5pm, Sept–mid-June Sat 11am–1pm), a small elk farm where you can get particularly close to the creatures at feeding time (11am year-round, also 1pm and 3pm summer).

TIP

Trips on the River
Klarälven can be
arranged, May–Sept, from
Gunnerud (Hagfors) in
northern Värmland. You
can spend from one to
eight nights aboard,
sleeping at night either on
the raft or ashore, and
have a fine chance of
spotting beaver, elk and
deer. Contact the Vildmark
i Värmland, tel: 0560-140
40; www.vildmark.se.

Dals-Ed should not be confused with **Dals-Långed** ❹, which lies 23km (14 miles) to the east and is an art and handicrafts centre. About 4km (2.5 miles) south towards Håverud is **Tisselskog**, whose many Bronze Age rock carvings are the province's principal historical attraction.

North of Dals-Långed on Lake Laxsjön is **Baldersnäs Herrgård**, a manor set in a lovely Edwardian park. The original house was built in 1796 and then pulled down in 1910 when the present building, now a restaurant and hotel, was erected.

To the northwest are **Billingsfors** ❺, an area of pulp and paper mills (with a distinctive smell) and **Bengtsfors**, which has an open-air museum, Gammelgården (tel: 0531-126 20; May–Sept: Mon–Fri 11am–4pm; July: daily 11am–5pm, entrance by guided tour), devoted to local history and culture.

Along the River Klarälven

Holidaymakers building their raft on the River Klarälven.

An old parish register in western Värmland states: "Between Sweden and Norway lies Värmland", which shows a certain rugged independence that remains today, plus a slight Norwegian accent. A region with strong traditions, it has also produced a rich crop of writers and poets.

Spruce and pine forests cover 70 percent of the county and are often referred to as "Värmland's gold". Forests, fast-running water and the discovery of iron ore all played an important part in the economic development of the province, although the old ironworks are now just a part of history.

Värmland is criss-crossed with narrow lakes and rivers, and the River Klarälven can claim to be among its most beautiful. It begins turbulently enough in Norway, where it is called Trysilelva, but gradually becomes broader, winding and sluggish before emptying into Lake Vänern near the province's largest town, **Karlstad** ❻. The town is 400 years old and stands on the site of a trading post called Tingvalla. Karlstad has a cathedral (consecrated in 1730), a popular park, Mariebergskogen, and the award-winning local museum **Värmlands Museum** (www.varmlandsmuseum.se; Mon–Fri 10am–6pm, Wed until 8pm,

THE MYSTERY BULLET

Carl XII was one of Sweden's greatest military leaders. Considered invulnerable to normal bullets, some speculated he could only be killed with a bullet from his own coat. In 1718, during a battle in Sweden's last campaign against Norway, Carl XII was shot through the head while inspecting the trenches at the border fortress of Fredriksten. With no immediate witnesses, rumour took instant root; and the debate over whether he was killed by an enemy, a member of his own army, or even an assassin hired by his successor, Fredrik I, has never been satisfied.

A legend grew around a Varberg soldier who claimed to have found the deadly bullet, taking it home after the war, but later throwing it away. In 1924, a farmer found a strange object, the *kulknappen* ("bullet-button"), near Varberg and remembered the story. The object was made from a split brass button, formed into half spheres and filled with lead.

Although the legend and the *kulknappen* itself seem outlandish, some evidence supports it being the murderous bullet. It is the right size to have made the 20mm hole in Carl XII's (preserved) felt hat. It matches Russian and Polish army buttons; and Carl XII was known to cut the buttons from dead soldiers to put on his own clothes. And in 2001 a researcher recovered DNA from the *kulknappen*, with a sequence found in only 1 percent of the Swedish population – the same sequence found on bloodstained gloves worn by Carl XII on the night he died.

Sat–Sun 11am–4pm), with exhibitions on the history of the area, Japanese art and a hands-on science corner for kids. There's also an interesting little gallery (http://sandgrund.org; Tues–Sun 11am–4pm) that shows off the watercolours of local lad Lars Lerin, explorations of landscape, light and shadows.

From **Hammarö**, on the outskirts of Karlstad, you can follow the route of the pilgrims of old, up the valley of the Klarälven. They crossed Lake Vänern by boat to Hammarö, where they prepared themselves for the next stage of their journey. Then they set off on the road north, to follow the Klarälven throughout its 240km (168 miles) on their long pilgrimage to the grave of St Olav the Holy, at Trondheim, on the west coast of Norway.

At Ransäter, 83km (51 miles) north of Karlstad on the Klarälven, is a well-arranged heritage village, **Ilcm bygdsgården** (tel: 0552-303 43; May–mid-Aug: Mon–Fri 11am–4pm), which includes four exhibitions devoted to mining, forestry, agriculture and rural life. Together they provide a fascinating picture of the Värmland of yesterday.

Ransäter holds an annual festival with a local folk play in the open-air theatre.

The Klarälven was the last Swedish river used for floating logs. The practice ended in 1991, and now the river is used for pure recreation. One of the most popular ways to explore the river is by drifting along on a gentle current on a raft that you assemble yourself. It is regarded as an opportunity for overworked executives to become adventure-loving children once again (see page 238). See the Visit Värmland website (www.visitvarmland.se) for all the different rafting possibilities, which also include beaver safaris, evening dining on a raft and a sauna-on-a-raft.

Nobel Prize-winner

To the south, almost parallel to the river, are three lakes, Övre Fryken, Mellanfryken and Nedre Fryken, which together are 80km (50 miles) long. Between the first two is the little town of **Sunne ❼**, a convenient base from which to explore this area.

High on the list of places to visit is **Mårbacka ❽** (tel: 0565-310 27; www.marbacka.com; guided tours only, June

Rafting on the Klarälven.

and Aug daily 11am–4pm; July daily 10am–5pm; Sept Sat–Sun 11am–2pm; Oct–May Sat at 1pm; English tours July and Aug only, at 1.30pm), 10km (6.2 miles) southeast from Sunne. This is the manor house home of the Swedish writer Selma Lagerlöf, the first woman to receive a Nobel Prize (for literature), in 1909 (see page 120). Through her books, including the children's classic The Wonderful Adventures of Nils and the unconventional Gösta Berlings Saga, she made the Fryk valley and lakes famous. The house is exactly as it was when she died.

On Mellanfryken, 5km (3 miles) south of Sunne, is **Rottneros Park** ➒ (tel: 0565-692 95; www.rottnerospark. se; June–Aug daily 10am–4pm, July until 6pm), which appears as Ekeby in Selma Lagerlöf's Gösta Berlings Saga. One of Sweden's most beautiful parks, the 40-hectare (98-acre) grounds contain an arboretum and over 100 works by famous Scandinavian sculptors, including such luminaries as Milles, Eriksson and Vigeland.

At **Fryksdalshöjden**, on road 238 leading to Arvika, there is a bird's-eye view of the valley and lakes below. Midway along Övre Fryken, to the west, the mountain of **Tossebergsklätten** also gives wonderful and wide-ranging views. Further to the southwest is another region with a patchwork of lakes. This is where you will find **Glaskogen** ➓, a vast area rich in wildlife and with 300km (186 miles) of trails, where you can hike, fish, bathe, camp or go canoeing. Most of the area is unpopulated, and its forests are dominated by the Stora Gla and Övre Gla lakes.

Two other places of interest within this particular area are Klässbols Linneväveri and Brunskog Gammelvala. The linen mill at **Klässbol** ⓫ (tel: 0570-46 01 85; www.klassbols.se; Mon–Fri 9am–6pm, Sat 10am–4pm; also Sun 10am–4pm May–Sept) is a small traditional linen- and damask-weaving mill, the last of its kind in Europe. Among other things, the mill provides all the table linen for the Swedish diplomatic corps. Visitors are welcome and there is also a shop.

Brunskog Hembygdsgård ⓬ (entrance fee; tel: 0570-522 08; www.

Rottneros Park's elegant manor house.

varmland.nu) is a collection of 15 old buildings on a picturesque site located by Lake Värmeln. At the end of July, it comes to life during Gammelvala (Old World), a week-long celebration of traditional crafts and skills

The western part of the province is comparatively empty, except for elk – Värmland has Sweden's largest elk population.

Inventors remembered

North of Lake Vänern, the bedrock is rich in minerals – over 300 different types have been found at Långban, a former mine, making it the most mineral-rich place in the world. This area is strongly associated with Sweden's early industrial development, and is dotted with the remains of old disused ironworks.

Many Americans make the pilgrimage to **Filipstad** ⓭, home to the mausoleum of John Ericsson. Also along the lake are two cannons from the Monitor, the warship designed by this gifted inventor and engineer. The Monitor's greatest fame is that it is said to have won the American Civil War for the North. Ericsson also invented the ship's propeller, and his brother Nils was equally talented. They were born at Långbans Herrgård to the north of the town.

Björkborn Herrgård ⓮, near Karlskoga, was the home of another well-known Swedish inventor, Alfred Nobel. The manor house is now a museum, **Nobelmuséet** (tel: 0586-834 94; http://nobelmuseetikarlskoga.se; June–Aug: Tues–Sun, entry by guided tour only, on the hour 11am–2pm, at 1pm in English), while Karlskoga is dominated by Bofors, the armaments manufacturer. At **Kristinehamn** ⓯, 50km (32 miles) west of Karlskoga, a 15-metre (49ft) -high sculpture by Picasso is the most striking navigational feature on Lake Vänern.

Between the lakes

The region separating Lake Vänern from Lake Vättern is Västergötland, a province which extends beyond the lakes, spreading southwest until it diminishes almost to a point at Göteborg. It includes mountain tablelands overlooking the Västgöta plain, one of

Rottneros Park blooms.

Sweden's finest castles, Läckö, and the weavers' country centred on Borås. In 1746 the indefatigable Linnaeus said: "Truly no one could ever imagine such splendour as in Västergötland who had not seen it for himself." Such praise may be a little over the top, but nevertheless it is a pleasant area.

Heading south along the eastern shore of Vänern, you come to **Mariestad** ⓰, on the River Tidan. The silhouette of the town is dominated by the spire of the 17th-century Renaissance-style cathedral, one of the few churches of this period remaining in Sweden. There are interesting little streets around the cathedral, which conform to the 17th-century town plan.

About 30km (19 miles) southwest of Mariestad is **Kinnekulle** ⓱, which rises 306 metres (1,000ft) above the surrounding countryside and is known locally as the flowering mountain. As such, it attracted paeans of praise from Linnaeus. For good views, you can drive virtually to the summit.

Most Swedes learn at school that the king who first united the Svea and Göta tribes, Olof Skötkonung (*c.* 994–1022),

was baptised in 1008 at **Husaby Källa** (Husaby Spring) at the southern tip of Kinnekulle. In the eyes of many Christians, Husaby was the country's first bishopric and cradle of the Swedish church, although experts dispute the place, date and circumstances of Olof's conversion. **Husaby Church** ⓲ (Apr–Sept daily 9am–4pm, May–Aug until 8pm) has an imposing Romanesque stone tower with three spires, the only one of its kind in Sweden. At **Flyhov**, to the north, there are 350 rock carvings from the Bronze Age.

South of Husaby is the town of **Skara** ⓳. It has Sweden's second-oldest cathedral (after Lund) dating from the 11th century. **Västergötlands Muséet** (Provincial Museum; tel: 0511-260 00; http://vastergotlands museum.se; Tues–Fri 10am–4pm, Wed until 9pm; Sat–Sun 11am–4pm), at Stadsträdgården, includes the Skara-missalet (Skara Missal), a book written between 1100 and 1150 by monks in Sweden which describes Catholic church rituals and is probably the oldest book in Sweden.

However, in high summer, these cultural delights play second fiddle to **Skara Sommarland** (tel: 010 708 7000; www.sommarland.se; early June–late Aug daily 10am–5pm, July until 7pm), 8km (5 miles) from Skara on road 49. Scandinavia's biggest waterpark has more than 70 attractions for children, from slides, pools and wave machines to dryland dodgems and rollercoasters. For more relaxed pursuits, head 10km (6 miles) southeast of Skara on road 184 to **Hornborgasjön** (Hornborg Lake), a wildlife area that supports more than 100 species of birds. The biggest attraction is the annual mating dance of the crane, a graceful long-legged bird, best seen in April.

Porcelain and pottery in Lidkoping

Nestled into Kinneviken (Kinne Bay) is **Lidköping** ⓴, a town renowned for its porcelain and pottery. Rörstrand, the leading maker, moved its

Ready to race at Skara Sommarland.

production abroad in 2005, but the town features a pottery museum (tel: 0510-250 80; http://rorstrand-museum. se; Mon–Sat 10am–5pm, Sun noon–5pm; free) displaying the company's most famous porcelain, plus a large shop. The original town dates from 1446 when it was on the east bank of the River Lidan, but the present town on the west bank owes its existence to Magnus Gabriel de la Gardie. In 1670 he laid down a grid plan for the streets, an innovation at that time. The dominant feature is the large square with the old town hall in the centre, housed in a former hunting lodge.

For such a modest-sized town, Lidköping has several fine cafés. The best is **Garströms Konditori**, established in 1857, in the main square. The interior gives a real feel of café life in the early 20th century, and the selection and quality of goods are unbeatable (open daily). On the opposite corner of the block you can visit one of the finest millinery shops in Sweden.

Vänermuséet (Lake Vänern Museum; tel: 0510-77 00 95; www. vanermuseet.se; June–Aug Mon–Fri 10am–5pm, Sat–Sun 11am–4pm; Sept–May Tues–Fri 10am–5pm, Sat–Sun 11am–4pm) is away from the centre of town at Framnäsvägen 2, on the edge of the lake. The museum includes information and exhibitions about the environment and activities in and around the lake. The shore around Lidköping is very shallow and perfect for wading and bathing with small children.

Lovely Lacko, super Saab

Make the pleasant 20km (12-mile) drive from Lidköping north to the tip of the beautiful Kållandsö peninsula, which juts into Lake Vänern and ends in a fringe of islets and skerries. There sits **Läckö Slott** ㉑ (Castle; tel: 0510-48 46 60; www.lackoslott.se; May–mid-June by tour daily 10am–4pm; mid-June–Aug: daily 10am–5pm; Sept by tour daily 10am–3pm; guided tours on the hour), one of the most impressive castles in Sweden. Built in the 17th century in Baroque style, Läckö has 248 rooms. Now completely restored, it is an important attraction in this part of the country. Every summer it holds major exhibitions relating to Sweden's

The Baroque-style Läckö Slott.

TIP

On the east of Lake Vättern, historic sites of note include the stone of Rök at Rökeskyrka with its 800 runes (E4 north of Ödeshög) and Alvastra Kloster, Sweden's first Cistercian monastery (road 50, 15km/20 miles north of Ödeshög).

cultural heritage, as well as outdoor concerts and theatrical productions.

On the western side of the peninsula is the 5km- (3-mile) long **Hindens Rev** (Reef). It has a sandy beach and is a remnant of the glacial era that occurred 11,000 years ago.

Trollhättan ㉒ is 65km (40 miles) southwest from Lidköping along highway 44, and Vänersborg lies nearby, just within the borders of Västergötland at the southern tip of Lake Vänern. Trollhättan is the birthplace of Saab Automobile, which has a **museum** (tel: 0520-289 440; http://saabcarmuseum.se; Tues–Sun 11am–4pm) dedicated to it at the Nohab industrial area (where train engines were made), just south of the town centre. Next door there is a science and industry centre, **Innovatum** (tel: 0520-289 400; www.innovatum.se; Tues–Sun 11am–4pm), with lots of hands-on experimental activities for children.

Trollywood

Another of Trollhättan's claims to fame is as a film production centre – films made here by **Film i Väst** (West

Films) account for nearly half of Sweden's total movie output, leading to the town's affectionate nickname "Trollywood".

But Trollhättan was famous long before the invention of the motor car or celluloid because of the magnificent locks, canals and waterfalls of the River Göta. The water level drops by about 32 metres (105ft), and when the Göta Kanal was built, an impressive flight of locks was required to give ships access to Lake Vänern. Today, the river is diverted to generate electricity and the falls are silent. But during the summer (July and Aug daily at 3pm; May, June and Sept Sat at 3pm), the floodgates are opened and 300,000 litres of water per second torrent along the original river channel. During the annual **Falls Day** on the third Friday in July, it is released to music and illumination, providing an even more impressive spectacle. The best view is from Oscarsbron (Oscar's Bridge).

Borås: textile territory

The southern part of Västergötland was the heartland of Sweden's textile

Trollhättan in the summer, when the dam's floodgates are open.

industry, with the focal point at **Borås** ❷. This is not an elegant town but it does have factory shops, bargain stores and trendy boutiques, and a **Textilmuséet** (Textile Museum; tel: 033-35 89 50; http://textilmuseet.se; Tues noon–8pm, Wed–Fri noon–5pm, Sat–Sun noon–4pm). Around 15km (9 miles) south in **Rydal** is a well-preserved **spinning mill** (www.mark.se/rydalsmuseum; Thur noon–7pm, Fri–Sun noon–4pm; free, donations welcome), together with textile workers' houses, which tells the story of how this region became the textile centre of Sweden.

Borås Zoo (tel: 033-35 32 70; www.boraszoo.se; Jul–mid-Aug daily 9.30am–5pm, times vary rest of year – see website for details) features about 600 animals from 65 species, focusing on Scandinavian and African wildlife, in a natural habitat.

The buildings of Borås are at their most interesting in early September, when the **No Limit street art festival** (http://nolimitboras.com) literally paints the town red (and orange and yellow and green and…).

Industry at Vättern's tip

Lake Vättern, the second-largest lake in Sweden, covers an area of 1,912 sq km (738 sq miles). At its southern end, the twin towns of **Jönköping** and **Husqvarna** have a strong industrial past. Jönköping was known for its matchstick industry, started by two brothers, Johan and Carl Lundström, in 1844. The little town hit the big time after Johan replaced explosive white-phosphorous matches with his newly-developed safety match, a product that was exported all over the globe. The history of the match factory and its grim working conditions is explored in the **Tändsticksmuséet** (Match Museum; www.matchmuseum.se; June–Aug Mon–Fri 10am–5pm, Sat–Sun 10am–3pm; Sept–May Tues–Sun 11am–3pm).

Husqvarna is another worldwide success story – the Husqvarna company, which began life as a state-owned rifle factory in 1689, still supplies outdoor power tools to more than 100 countries. Its **museum** (http://husqvarnamuseum.se; May–Sept Mon–Fri 10am–5pm, Sat–Sun noon–4pm; Oct–Apr Mon–Fri 10am–3pm, Sat–Sun

Jönköping at nightfall.

noon–4pm) is a fascinating glimpse into how the company has adapted and survived over the centuries.

Habo's painted church

Travelling up the western side of the lake, **Habo Kyrka** ㉔ (Church; tel: 036-420 93; June–Aug Mon–Sat 8am–7pm, Sun 9am–7pm; Sept–May by appointment), just southwest of Habo village, is perhaps the most remarkable timber church in Sweden. Probably built in the 14th century, it was enlarged in the 1600s and then rebuilt in 1723. What makes this church so distinctive is the multicoloured interior, where every inch of the walls, ceiling, pillars and gallery are covered with the work of Johan Christian Peterson and Johan Kinnerus, both from Jönköping.

Between 1741 and 1743, Peterson painted the northern half and Kinnerus the southern half. Their paintings illustrate Luther's catechism, with the Ten Commandments on the walls (even numbers north side, odd numbers south side), the Lord's Prayer above the gallery and the Baptism and the Lord's Supper on the ceiling of the nave. There you will also find the Confession and Absolution. The church also has a 1731 organ built by Johan Niclas Cahman, a renowned Swedish organ builder, and there is a separate and elegantly proportioned bell tower.

Hjo to Askersund

Further north along the coast, the small lakeside resort of **Hjo** ㉕ has been popular since the early 20th century. It has some attractive preserved wooden houses in the centre of town, a pretty lakeside park, and a pool and beach area right by the marina. You can partake of the famous freshly smoked whitefish, tour the town sedately in a horse-drawn carriage, or cruise on the lake in the 1892 steamer, Trafik.

Karlsborg ㉖, on the western shore of Lake Vättern, 30km (19 miles) north of Hjo, is dominated by its huge fortress, **Fästning** (tel: 0505-45 18 26; www.fastningsmuseet.se; mid-May–mid-June daily 10am–4pm; mid-June–July 10am–6pm; Aug daily 10am–5pm; Sept–mid-May Mon–Fri 10am–3pm). In 1809, when the Swedes lost Finland to the Russians, they realised that a new defence strategy was required and decided to build two massive fortresses. These were to house the government and the treasury. The first, at Karlsborg, was started in 1819 and required 250,000 tons of limestone. It was quarried by prison labour on the eastern side of the lake and ferried across by boat. The castle has walls 2 metres (6ft) thick with 5 km (3 miles) of ramparts, but by the time it was finally finished in 1909 fortresses were out of fashion. The second castle was never built.

The other town of note in Närke is **Askersund** ㉗, a quiet little place at the northern end of Lake Vättern which was established by Queen Kristina in the 17th century. The **Landskyrkan** (Church) is worth visiting. Founded in 1670, it was designed by Jean de la Vallée, one of Sweden's most important Baroque architects, and Erik Dahlberg.

The peaceful Glaskogen nature reserve.

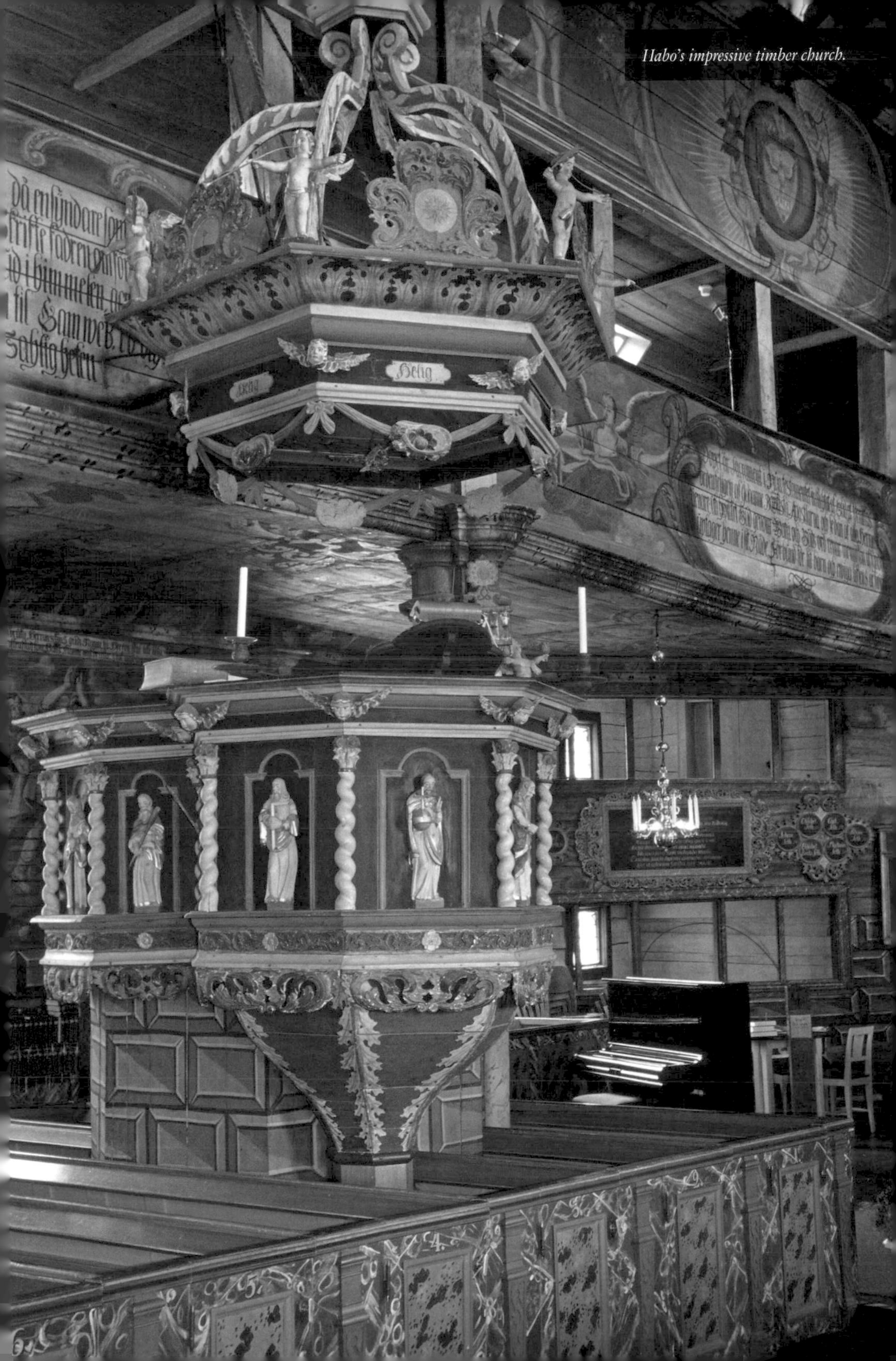

Habo's impressive timber church.

GÖTA KANAL

A leisurely cruise along Sweden's "Blue Band"
between Stockholm and Göteborg offers one of the
most relaxed ways of sampling the country's history.

Sweden's greatest feat of engineering, the Göta Kanal, had a short life transporting cargo until it was superseded by the railways. Today it has found a new niche as one of Sweden's most popular tourist attractions. Steamships ply its 190km (118 mile) length, crossing from Stockholm to Göteborg via the giant lakes Vänern and Vättern. It's a fabulous way to see some of the gems of Swedish history, from the medieval towns of Söderköping and Vadstena to the immense Karlsborg Fortress, completed in the 20th century. You can also travel the canal under your own steam, by kayak or canoe, or by cycling or walking along the broad towpath.

The challenge of linking the lakes and rivers through the interior of Sweden from Stockholm on the east coast to Göteborg on the west had exercised the minds of many industrialists, statesmen and kings before Baltzar von Platen actually succeeded at the beginning of the 19th century with the Göta Kanal.

The canal was intended to kickstart Swedish industry... and to avoid the Sound Dues that had to be paid to Denmark when transporting timber, iron, food and other goods by sea between the cities. For 22 years, 58,000 men laboured to build the Göta Kanal, many of them soldiers who worked with little to help them but steel-reinforced wooden spades. Assisted by the

prime movers of the day – one of the advisers to the plan was the famous Scottish engineer Thomas Telford – Sweden's greatest work of engineering was finally completed in 1832.

The canal stretches from Sjötorp on Lake Vänern to Mem on the Baltic, has 58 locks, and is 190km (118 miles) long. Of that distance, 87km (54 miles) is man-made. In 1998, the Göta Kanal was designated an "International Historic Civil Engineering Landmark", giving it the same status as the Statue of Liberty and the Panama Canal.

Main Attractions
Söderköping
Motala
Vadstena
Forsvik

The Göta Hotel along the canal.

FACT

A magical moment on the first night of the eastbound cruises, weather permitting, is when the boat inches through a tortuous channel towards the floodlit 17th-century Läckö Slott (castle).

One of the 58 locks along the canal.

A choice of ways

Today there is no commercial traffic, but many Swedes travel the canal each summer in their own boats. For the visitor there are many ways of seeing the Göta Kanal (open May–Sept). The classic way is to take a four- or six-day cruise between Stockholm and Göteborg on one of the vintage vessels operated by Göta Kanal Rederiaktiebolaget (the Göta Kanal Steamship Company). The oldest of the three vessels is MS *Juno*, built in 1874 and now the world's oldest registered passenger vessel with overnight accommodation. She is complemented by MS *Wilhelm Tham* (built in 1912), and MS *Diana* (1931).

There are also passenger boats which take you along part of the way, and small boats offering sightseeing trips at various points along the canal (tel: 0141-20 20 50; www.gotakanal.se). Along both sides of the canal there are towpaths, ideal for cycling; bikes can be transported across the lakes on the passenger boats and ferries.

Setting sail

Travelling along the canal gives you a whiff of Swedish history. The four-day westbound Göta Kanal Steamship Company cruises start from Stockholm at 9am and head down the Baltic coast for most of the first day before entering the first lock on the canal at **Mem** – where the canal was officially inaugurated in 1832 – in the early hours of the next morning. The first major town on the canal is **Söderköping** ㉘, a medieval trading town with a number of beautiful churches and a restored town hall. At lunchtime on the second day you reach **Berg** ㉙, with its impressive flight of seven locks, where there is time to visit the historic monastery church at nearby **Vreta**, once the richest religious establishment in Sweden.

Birds and more besides

The route crosses two picturesque lakes, Asplången and **Roxen**, where there are good chances of spotting ospreys and herons during the breeding season. After Lake Roxen the canal takes you through 15 locks in 3km (2 miles), lifting you 37 metres (120ft). You spend most of the next night moored at **Motala** ㉚, a town founded by Baltzar von Platen, who drew up the town plans and started the

now thriving engineering industry. The **Göta Kanalutställningen** (Göta Kanal Exhibit; tel: 0141-21 09 23; May and Sept: daily 11am–3pm; June–Aug: daily 10am–5pm) in Motala tells the story of the canal and its construction.

The schedules for the Göta Kanal cruises are constructed so that some sightseeing stops included on the westbound itineraries are not included on the eastbound route and vice versa. The eastbound cruises make a stop of several hours at **Vadstena** ㉛, 15km (9 miles) south of Motala, a delightful small town with wooden houses lining its narrow streets. The town is famous for its associations with St Birgitta, and grew up around a 14th-century convent. The abbey was built to the design of St Birgitta and consecrated in 1430.

Early next morning on the westbound cruise, you cross Lake Vättern from Motala to Karlsborg, site of a huge fortress built at the same time as the canal, and **Forsvik** ㉜, an old metalworking village and the site of the canal's oldest lock (1813). Vättern, the fifth-largest lake in Europe and the second-largest in Sweden, is deep and cold and rich in fish.

The Göta Kanal boats are often greeted at Forsvik by a local family singing hymns and offering passengers freshly picked wild flowers. This 100-year-old custom originated as a blessing for passengers as they embarked on what was then regarded as the hazardous crossing of Vättern.

For the rest of the day the route follows the western section of the canal, passing the towns of Tåtorp, which has the only manually operated lock, and Lyrestad. In the evening you reach **Sjötorp** ㉝, marking the beginning of Lake Vänern, which is Sweden's largest lake.

At the south side of Lake Vänern, you pass through **Vänersborg** before reaching the gorge at Trollhättan early the next morning. Once there were 11 locks here; today, there are only four. This is the last stage of your journey down the Göta, passing through the final lock at **Lilla Edet**. There is time to visit the Medieval Museum at **Lödöse** ㉞ (tel: 010-441 43 80; Tues and Thur 9am–7pm, Wed, Fri–Sun 11am–4pm), which depicts the area, its people and the crafts of early times.

Göteborg, with its four bridges, lies ahead. You have arrived on the west coast.

Vadstena Castle.

DALARNA

Dalarna is the country's ancient folklore region, as famous for its scarlet Dala horses as its Midsummer festivities. Artists have made their homes here, and industrialists their fortunes.

With its colourful traditions and evocative rural landscape, Dalarna is the centre of all that is classically Swedish. The red-painted *Dalahäst* (Dala horse), practically the national symbol, is made here. Two of Sweden's most beloved artists, Carl Larsson and Anders Zorn, drew inspiration from the region – today their homes inspire in turn thousands of admiring visitors. Gustav Vasa, who freed Sweden from the shackles of Danish rule, is honoured each year by the Vasaloppet cross-country ski race, held between Sälen and Mora. Much of Sweden's wealth derived from the great copper mine at Falun, now a Unesco World Heritage Site. The paint pigment that gives Swedish cottages their distinctive red colour is still extracted there.

Dalarna's legendary folklore and beauty attract an increasing number of visitors each year. The region can best be experienced in the twilight of the *fäbodar*, the old pasture cottages nestling in the Dalarnan hills; in the company of energetic musicians at a fiddlers' meet; or during the magic of Midsummer, when a young woman places nine different flowers under her pillow to dream of the man she will marry.

Music-making

Music is one of the most defining characteristics of Dala culture. **Falu Folk Musik & Dans** (www.falufolk

musikodans.se) keeps local traditions alive with concerts throughout the year, while **Musik vid Siljan** (Music on Lake Siljan; www.musikvidsiljan.se) is an annual festival in early July that attracts visitors from all over Sweden and abroad. Distinctly Dala are the *spelmansstämmor*, folk musicians' rallies, particularly the one held each summer in **Bingsjö ❶**, 30km (19 miles) east of Rättvik, where octogenarian fiddlers turn the classic polka into a musical performance that rivals any blues master.

Main Attractions
Dalhalla
Orsa Rovdjurspark (Orsa Predator Park)
Carl Larsson's house
Lake Siljan
Sälen ski resort
Vasaloppet Muséet
Falu Gruva (Falun Mine)

Painting the Dalarna wooden horses in Nusnäs.

An exotic setting for listening to music is **Dalhalla** (tel: 0248-79 79 50; www.dalhalla.se; guided tours available July daily at 11am, 1.30pm and 3.30pm), a cavernous outdoor concert arena set in the depths of a former limestone quarry near the town of **Rättvik ②**. The quarry, which was abandoned in 1990, was inaugurated as a music arena in 1994, with the first performance – of Wagner's *Der Ring des Nibelungen* – held two years later. The annual summer concerts, held between June and September, feature artists of international standing.

Pastoral scenes

For a change of pace, explore the gentle tranquillity of the region's *fäbodar*, which offer a taste of back-to-the-land living. These pasture cottages and surrounding buildings, dating from the 15th and 16th centuries, are found all over Sweden but are most often associated with Dalarna.

They constitute a living museum, where cows are milked, butter is churned, *messmör* (a type of goat's cheese) is made, and the classic *tunnbröd*

A tradional summer farm in Dalarna.

(thin bread) is baked, in the same way that it has been done for centuries. Many of the *fäbodar* are open for visits by tourists and sell local products or serve food.

The friendly farmer at **Prästbodarnas Fäbod** (book in advance; open early-June–early-Sept; tel: 0246-910 91), located 40km (25 miles) east of Rättvik, near Bingsjö, runs one-day courses where you can learn how to milk a cow and make dairy products. The farming life seems a natural accompaniment to the breathtaking scenery of the province, two-thirds of which is forested.

At the northern extremity of Dalarna is the deceptively gentle start of the mountain range which marches north, gaining height all the time until it culminates in the snow-topped peaks of the Kebnekaise range in Lapland. Dalarna is a transition zone between the softer landscapes of southern Sweden and the more dramatic, but harsher landscapes of the north. It is even divided within itself between the more densely populated area south and east of Lake Siljan

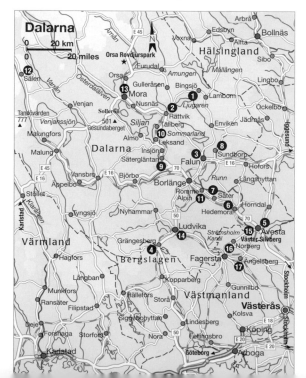

(dense by Swedish standards) and the relatively uninhabited zones to the north and west of the lake.

Industrial traditions

However, Dalarna is by no means an exclusively rural area. The provincial capital, **Falun ❸**, has been a centre of industry for probably 1,000 years, and is an attractive town, well worth a stroll to the central square. The **Bergslagen** area to the south has been a noted centre for mining for several hundred years and covers not just Dalarna but also parts of Värmland and Västmanland. This district is well worth exploring if you are interested in industrial archaeology (see page 260).

About 60km (37 miles) south, near Ludvika, is **Grängesberg ❹**, where a large iron-ore mining complex and the railway serving it were financed by capital from the City of London in the 19th century. Steam enthusiasts will not want to miss the **Lokmuséet** (Railway Museum; tel: 0240-204 93; daily mid-June–mid-Aug 10am–4pm) with its vintage locomotives which used to handle the iron-ore trains.

Fifty kilometres (31 miles) east is **Avesta ❺**, another centre with a long industrial tradition, this time dating back to the 14th century. It was once the home of the Swedish Mint, and the **Myntmuséet** (Mint Museum; tel: 0226-507 83; early June–mid-Aug Wed–Sat 1–3pm) contains what is claimed to be the world's largest copper coin, weighing almost 20kg (43 lb) and dated 1644.

Hedemora ❻, 20km (12 miles) north, claims to be the oldest town in Dalarna, with a charter dated 1459; its privileges as a market town go back even earlier than that, while parts of the church are 13th-century. The locals have devised Husbyringen (http://husbyringen.se), a 56km (35-mile) "museum trail" which you can take by car through the area northeast of the town to see a number of industrial archaeological sites.

About 10km (6 miles) further north, **Säter ❼** is claimed to be one of the seven best-preserved wooden towns in Sweden. But compared with Hedemora it is quite an upstart, with a town charter dated 1642. The ravines of the **Säter**

TIP

Orsa Rovdjurspark (tel: 0250-462 00; www.orsarovdjurspark.se; mid-Apr–mid-June and mid-Aug–Sept daily 10am–3pm, mid-June– mid-Aug until 6pm), 10km (6 miles) north of Orsa, is Europe's largest predator park. Its large northern-hemisphere carnivores include bears, lynx, wolves, wolverines, Siberian tigers and snow leopards, which roam in large, naturally forested enclosures.

The river Grövlan runs through the Dalarna province.

Around Lake Siljan

Lake Siljan, at Dalarna's heart, was formed when a giant meteorite crashed to earth 360 million years ago. Today it is a soothingly rural place full of quintessentially Swedish sights.

Around the edges of Lake Siljan, you can find some of the country's most well-known sights and symbols. The area is particularly renowned for its Midsummer celebrations, notably at **Rättvik**, where the long "church-boats" bring hundreds of villagers to church for the annual service, dressed in their local costumes. **Rättvik Kyrka** (Church) features folk-art paintings showing biblical scenes in a Dalarna setting.

Arts and crafts

About 20km (12 km) along the north shore, as you approach Mora, is the small village of **Nusnäs**, headquarters for the production of the brightly painted Dalarna wood-carved horses, which

Wedding party rowing to church on Lake Siljan; an age-old tradition in Dalarna.

became such a strong symbol of Sweden after they were shown at the New York World Exhibition in 1939. You can watch the horses being made and painted, or buy a kit and have a go yourself, at Nils Olsson Hemslöjd (workshop; www.nohemslojd.se).

Mora is a pleasant lakeside town. It is best known as the home of the Swedish artist Anders Zorn, who was a close friend of another Dalarna artist, Carl Larsson. Zorn's paintings are more varied in subject and treatment than those of Larsson, whose works usually reflect family life. Mora's **Zornmuséet** (tel: 0250-59 23 10; www. zorn.se; mid-May–mid-Sept: Mon–Sat 9am–5pm, Sun 11am–5pm; mid-Sept–mid-May: daily noon–4pm) is devoted to Zorn's work, and you can also visit his house and studio, **Zorngården** (tel: 0250-59 23 10; mid-May–mid-Sept by guided tour every half hour Mon–Sat 10am–4pm, Sun 11am–4pm; Sept–mid-May by guided tour every hour daily noon–3pm).

Heading 10km (6 miles) along the west side of the lake, make a detour to the island of **Sollerön**, which is said to have the sunniest climate in the region. The island is one of the places where church-boats (direct descendants of the Viking longships) are built.

Santa and local folklore

Back on the mainland is a good mountain-top viewpoint, **Gesundaberget**. On the slopes of Gesundaberget is **Tomteland** (Santaworld; tel: 0250-287 70; www.santaworld.se; mid-June–mid-Aug: daily 10am–4pm; Halloween and Dec Fri–Sun 10am–4pm). Children can meet Santa and see his animals, including the rare musk ox, and visit the toy workshops.

Leksand, at the southern tip of Siljan, is a bustling little community and the centre for many cultural attractions in summer, including a heritage play, *Himlaspelet* by Rune Lindström, which is performed in the local community theatre. **Leksands Kulturhus** (Culture House; tel: 0247-802 45; www.leksand.se/kultur; Tues–Fri 11am–4pm, Sat 11am–2pm) provides a spotlight on local folk culture.

One of the best-known resorts on Siljan is the village of **Tällberg**, 11km (7 miles) from Leksand, a typical Dalarna village, complete with maypole and timber buildings. A quiet stroll down to the lakeside here at sunset is a good a way to round off the day.

For further information, check the website at www.visitdalarna.se.

Valley were created at the end of the Ice Age and are of interest for their flora.

Larsson and the cradle of Swedish culture

Just 13km (8 miles) east of Falun is **Sundborn** ❽, a picturesque small village that was the home of a much-loved Swedish artist, Carl Larsson, in the early part of the 20th century. His work and that of his wife, Karin Larsson, a textile artist, still inspire the interior design of Swedish homes today, and their influence has spread internationally as well. About 60,000 people from all over the world visit **Carl Larsson-gården** (tel: 023-600 53; www.clg.se; entrance by guided tour only, with up to six tours per hour May–Sept daily 10am–5pm; Oct–Apr tour in Swedish only Mon–Fri 11am, Sat–Sun 1pm) at Sundborn each year. The house, beside a small lake, has been authentically preserved and is open for tours (it's best to phone ahead if you want a non-Swedish-language tour). Larsson's paintings reflect his happy family life and were strongly influenced by the local Dalarna folk-art traditions.

Local handicrafts

In the province that inspired the distinctive *Dalahäst* (Dala horse), a more readily recognised Swedish symbol than the flag, it is not surprising that the region is known for its abundance of carvers, potters, silversmiths, weavers, painters and bakers. This is a mecca for *hemslöjd* (crafts), all of which have their ancient roots in the farming culture.

At **Sätergläntan** ❾, 3km (2 miles) south of Insjön lake, **Hemslöjdens Gård** (tel: 0247-410 45; www.saterglantan.com) offers a wide array of handicrafts as well as week-long courses in blacksmithing, sewing, weaving and woodcraft. At **Nittsjö Keramik** (tel: 0248-171 30; Mon–Fri 10am–6pm, Sat 10am–2pm; June–Aug: also Sun 11am–3pm), 6km (4 miles) north of Rättvik, clay goods are made according to a 100-year-old tradition. You can save a great deal on the seconds, which have barely noticeable blemishes.

The province offers many attractions for families with children, including **Leksand Sommarland** ❿ (tel: 0247-138 00; www.sommarland.nu; June–Aug: 10am–5pm, closes later

Lake Siljan.

from end June), an adventure park on Lake Siljan's shores that combines a waterpark, bathing beach, fairground rides and a large go-kart track.

Cross-country ski challenge

Dalarna's ski resorts are the principal winter tourist attraction, both for cross-country skiing and downhill. **Romme Alpin ⓫**, (www.rommealpin. se), 10km (6 miles) south of Börlange, is Sweden's largest and most visited ski resort outside the proper mountain areas, with 13 lifts, 28 pistes and 62km (39 miles) of cross-country trails. **Sälen ⓬**, in northwest Dalarna, is the well-known popular resort in the higher mountains with longer and harder pistes. Together, Sälen and **Idre**, 100km (62 miles) further north, have almost half of Sweden's ski-lift facilities. There are also many other smaller resorts in the province.

Sälen is also famous for being the starting point for a 85km- (53-mile) cross-country skiing race to **Mora ⓭**: the **Vasaloppet**, the most popular sporting event in Sweden, held in March each year. It commemorates the beginning of a Swedish revolution: while fleeing from the Danish king, who had just murdered his father and brother in the Stockholm Bloodbath, Gustav Vasa tried to raise a rebellion in Mora. The villagers pondered; but with enemies hot on his trail, Gustav couldn't wait for a reply and fled on skis towards the Norwegian border. The villagers eventually decided to help, and sent their two best skiers after Gustav, who caught up with him at Sälen and brought him back to overthrow the king. Each year the race includes almost 34,000 competitors, who in the past have included the present king, Carl XVI Gustaf. The first Vasaloppet was run on 19 March 1922.

A victory in Vasaloppet is regarded by most of the world's best skiers as highly as a podium place in the Olympic Games or the World Championships. Nils "Mora Nisse" Karlsson won the race a record nine times. Women first began competing in the main race in 1981. In 1988, the 30km (19 mile) women's-only race **Tjejvasan** was inaugurated, and has grown to include some 10,000 female skiers each year. For more about the fascinating history of this race, stop by **Vasaloppet Muséet** (Vasaloppet Museum; mid-June–mid-Aug daily 10am–5pm; mid-Aug–mid-June Mon–Fri 8am–4.30pm, Thur until 3pm; free) in Mora, situated next to the finishing line.

In summer, walkers and cyclists can also follow the Vasaleden course: the cycle path is marked with green signage and the hiking path with orange. There are nine basic cabins in eight locations along the course, where you can spend the night for a nominal fee, payable in Sälen and Mora (for more information: www.vasaloppet.se).

The old mines of Dalarna

Few countries have preserved the places that laid the foundations of their prosperity like Sweden. In tracing the nation's industrial archaeology, you can follow a direct line that has led to what is today one of the most successful industrial countries in the world.

Snowboarders catching a lift at Romme Alpin.

The heart of Sweden's mining region forms a broad swathe across the centre of the country, from east to west, containing the majority of the nation's industrial archaeological treasures. The catalyst for this development was the 17th-century discovery of minerals, including iron, copper and silver, which, combined with an abundance of rivers (to provide water power) and timber (for charcoal), led to furious activity in the region. The manufacture of steel and other metals has continued, largely with the use of imported ores and powered by hydro-electricity.

Copper Mountain

A good place to start exploring the industrial treasures is Falun, Dalarna's capital and the jewel in the crown of Swedish mining history. The 1,000-year-old town was not just the centre of Sweden's copper extraction: at its peak, Falu Gruva (Falun Mine) was the largest copper mine on Earth, producing two-thirds of the world's copper. The importance of the mine and related workings in the area around the town were recognised by

Unesco in 2001, when Falu Gruva was added to the World Heritage List.

The most dramatic feature of the mine is the enormous **Great Pit**, 99 metres (325ft) deep and 396 metres (1,300ft) wide, which was created in 1687 when a huge area of the copper mine caved in. Miraculously, no one was killed, because it was Midsummer and all the miners were carousing, but production never returned to previous levels. Besides copper ore, the Stora Kopparberg mining company also extracted lead, zinc, silver and gold here until 1992 when the mine finally closed. However, red ochre, a by-product of the mine that is used as the pigment in 'Falu Red', the paint that gives Sweden's distinctive red cottages their colour, is still mined and processed in Falun.

You can descend into the earth on a **guided tour of the mine** (tel: 023-78 20 30; www.falugruva.se; May–Sept daily; Oct–Apr tours Tues–Fri at 2pm, Sat–Sun at 10.30am, noon and 2pm), which takes you down by lift (elevator) to the 55-metre (180ft) level and then along a tunnel to the oldest part of the workings, the Creutz shaft. The

The Great Pit at Falun.

shaft was opened in 1662 and is 207 metres (680ft) deep. All the shafts, drifts and chambers have names, such as the Christmas Gift, discovered at Christmas, and the General Peace, named after the short-lived peace treaty between Britain and France in 1801. The mine provides helmets and raincoats, but be sure to wear sturdy shoes and warm clothes: it's a chilly 5°C (40°F) inside.

There are also interesting buildings to see above ground, several peaceful walking trails and the **Stora Kopparberg Muséet** (early June–mid-Sept: Mon–Fri 10am–4pm, Sat–Sun 10am–3pm), with an interesting collection of exhibits of the industrial past.

Touring the mines

Sweden's biggest mining region was in Bergslagen to the south of Falun. Here, in the country's most important industrial region, the foundations for modern Sweden were laid. In recognition of this historical background, the Swedes have created the **Ekomuseum Bergslagen** (tel: 0240-66 30 82; www. ekomuseum.se), an award-winning eco-museum, covering some 60 cultural

and historical sites within a 150-sq km (93-sq mile) area. The area encompasses seven rural districts, two in Dalarna, five in Västmanland and two provincial museums. It is mainly concentrated along the River Kolbäcksån, where the **Strömsholm Kanal** links mines, blast furnaces and ironworks.

The eco-museum also includes workers' dwellings, homesteads, mansions, power stations, railways, canals, inns and restaurants – all in their historical settings. In order to see this area, your best bet is to hire a car and choose a few days in the summer when the sites are sure to be open. Also, make sure to pick up an Ekomuseum Bergslagen guidebook from one of the tourist offices in Ludvika, Smedjebacken, Norberg, Skinnskatteberg, Fagersta or Hallstahammar, and follow the map. Below are a few examples of what you can expect to see:

Ludvika ⓯: Ludvika Mining Museum, the first open-air museum of industrial history in the world.

Silvberg ⓯: Legendary Väster Silvberg silver mining district from the Middle Ages, 20km (12 miles) northeast of Ludvika; a varied cultural landscape, complete with hiking trails through valleys dotted with the ruins of abandoned mines, forges, cottages, mill ponds and furnaces.

Norberg ⓰: the most important producer of iron during the Middle Ages. Mossgruvan Mining Museum shows working life at a mine at the end of the 19th century. At the Svinryggen Mines is the famous Polhem's Wheel, an industrial invention that captured water to drive the mining pumps.

Ängelsberg ⓱: approximately 20km (12 miles) south of Norberg, the Engelsberg Ironworks is one of the world's most important remains of the early industrial era and is included on Unesco's World Heritage list. The blast furnace and forge are unique in that the water wheel, the crusher, the blower and the hammer are still in working order. Visitors will also find various industrial buildings, gardens, and the manor house from 1746.

Tour guide at the Falun copper mine.

Honouring the brave miners at the Falun copper mine.

Helpful sign in Jämtland.

THE CENTRAL HEARTLANDS

In an area where towns and villages are few and far between, the awe-inspiring landscape attracts numerous hikers, skiers and anglers.

Five provinces stretch across the immense central heartlands from the Bothnian coast to the Norwegian border, rising from sea-level to mountainous peaks. On the coast, tiny islands and fishing villages like Bönan burst into life in summer. Heading west, flat open farmland is dotted with impressive old Hälsingland farmhouses, several of which have made Unesco's World Heritage list. Further west still, open space and glorious silence become the main attractions. Take to the hiking trails on a mountain pilgrimage, fish the glittering rivers, hurtle down one of Åre's 100 ski runs, look for bears in Sweden's oldest national park Sonfjället, or search for the elusive monster hiding in Lake Storsjön, near Östersund.

Central Sweden is covered by five provinces: Gästrikland, Hälsingland and Medelpad in the east, which share the long coastline from Furuvik; and further inland come Härjedalen and Jämtland, stretching west to the Norwegian border, the land of lakes and coniferous or birch forests. Härjedalen marks the beginning of the great northern mountain ranges, and the further north you go, the more dramatic the scenery.

Gävle

The small province of **Gästrikland** has one major town, **Gävle ❶**, in

the southeast corner of the region. Though the history of this coastal town goes back over 500 years, on the surface this busy commercial centre is unexceptional. But don't let this note of discouragement overshadow Gävle's attractions. It has a castle built by Johan III (not open to the public), a town hall built by Gustav III, and a sizeable provincial museum, **Länsmuséet** (tel: 026-65 56 00; Tues–Fri 11am–6pm, Sat–Sun noon–4pm; free), which requires four floors to display its 16,000 varied exhibits. The top two

Main Attractions
Stenegård Manor
Inlandsbanen
Lake Storsjön and Frösön
Jamtli Open-air Museum
Jämtland hiking trails
Åre ski resort

Moose crossing the road.

are devoted to art, with works by Carl Larsson, the Göteborg Colourists and the Halmstad Group.

People from a wide area flock to Gävle for sporting events, shopping and theatre. It is also a place for a good night out.

The **Gamla Gefle** area has preserved wooden houses and an artists' quarter. Beside the River Gävle are the **Stadsträdgården** and **Boulognerskogen**, which together form one of the largest municipal parks in Sweden. A park of a different kind is **Furuviksparken** (tel: 010-708 70 00; www.furuvik.se; mid-May–mid-June daily 10am–5pm; mid-June–early Aug daily 10am–7pm), on the coast 10km (6 miles) south of the town, which combines extensive zoological gardens and an amusement park with variety of attractions for children.

The area's industries

Gästrikland is at the eastern end of the swathe of land which gave Sweden its early mining and smelting industries, and moving only a few kilometres inland to **Sandviken** you

are in an area which saw the development of the Swedish steel industry. Sandviken grew up with the development of the Bessemer process in the 1860s, and Sandviken steels are well known today.

Jädraås ❷, 80km (50 miles) to the north, is the starting point for a vintage railway with steam trains running for some 4.5 km (2.8 miles) to **Tallås**. This is typical of the railways used to haul minerals or timber, and it has the coach used by King Oscar II when he went hunting bears in Dalarna.

Only 10km (6 miles) northeast of Gävle and also on the coast, **Bönan** is famous for its golden-brown böckling (smoked herring), cured over spruce wood. **Engeltofta** is a good restaurant at which to sample it – in summer a little boat (tel: 073-701 1772; www.limötrafiken.se) zips between Gävle, Engeltofta, Limön and Furuvik. Grilled herring and potatoes with dill butter are favourites all along the Virgin Coast, which also has small fishing villages and working harbours such as **Skärså**, where catching the Baltic herring is still an important industry.

Houses in Gävle.

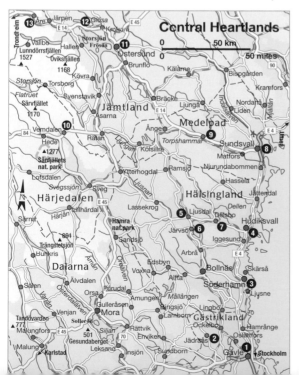

Choral tribute

The main highway north, E4, skirts two coastal towns in **Hälsingland**: Söderhamn and Hudiksvall. **Söderhamn** ❸, which is set between two hills, was founded in 1620 as an armoury for the Swedish army, and the museum is situated in part of what was the gun and rifle factory. Although a commercial centre, the town has an impressive town hall, plus a church to match, a pleasant riverside park and boat trips around the archipelago. On top of the hill on the eastern side of the town is **Oskarsberg**, a lookout tower built in 1895, which – for reasons not immediately apparent – was paid for by the members of the choral society.

Next to Gävle, **Hudiksvall** ❹ is the second-oldest town in northern Sweden; it celebrated its 400th anniversary in 1982. Some 100 years ago, when the timber industry was at its peak, the town had a reputation for high living. Today it has no buildings erected by unusual benefactors, but it does have a theatre of distinction, which was opened in 1882. It also has a group of the best-preserved 19th-century wooden buildings in Sweden, the **Fiskarstan** (Fishermen's Town). Strömmingsundet's wooden wharves and warehouses also merit a glance.

About 10km (6 miles) south of Hudiksvall is **Iggesunds Järnverk** (tel: 0650-28 565; Midsummer–early Aug daily 11am–5pm; free), an impressive former ironworks that has now become a heritage museum. The works were founded in 1685, but most of the surviving machinery – including the two blast furnaces – dates from the 19th century.

The interior of the province has the best scenery, particularly the valley of the Ljusnandalen (River Ljusnan), which is laced with lakes. West of **Ljusdal** ❺, where the Ljusnan meets the River Hennan, the forests begin. You can get a little closer to understanding the lives of the early charcoal-burners who lived here by spending a night in a cabin village that was reconstructed by author and environmentalist Albert Viksten – contact Lasse Krog (tel: 0651 850 55; www.lassekrog.se) for details.

In 2012, seven of Hälsingland's most splendid 18th- and 19th-century farmhouses, notable for their richly painted

Söderhamn at dawn.

FACT

Stenegård Manor at Järvsö is also a handicrafts centre featuring potters, silversmiths, glass-blowers, blacksmiths and woodworkers.

Järvsö.

folk-art interiors, were added to the Unesco World Heritage List. Three of them lie in the municipality of Ljusdal, including Bommars in Letsbo (www.bommars.se), open for guided tours in high summer.

Folk-dancing festival

About 12km (7 miles) south of Ljusdal, and halfway between the river's source and the sea, is **Järvsö** ⑥, a small town in farming and forestry country and a minor holiday and winter sports centre. Once a year, this peaceful routine is broken by an unforgettable festival: the **Hälsingehambo** (http://halsingehambon.com), a competitive event involving 300 folk-dancing couples and hordes of spectators. At dawn on a July morning, groups of competitors in traditional costumes begin to dance to the tune Hårgalåten, with the various stages of the competition continuing from Hårga to Arbrå, and finishing with the grand finale in Järvsö in front of **Stenegård** manor house (tel: 0651-34 00 21; www.stenegard.com; June–Aug daily 11am–7pm). The manor's gardens are planted up with greenery common to

19th-century Swedish farms, including 250 specimens of herbs, and there is an exhibition about the Unesco World Heritage-listed Hälsingland farmhouses.

The "Hambo" is a joyous event that celebrated its 50th anniversary in 2015, but the macabre story behind it is much older. Legend has it that a sinister fiddler stepped into the lodge at Hårga, and seduced the dancing couples there with his wild tunes. Lured by the music, the couples followed the devil – for it was him! – to the top of **Hårgaberget** mountain, where they danced until only their bones remained.

On an island on the river between the manor and village is the parish church. When it was built in 1832, it was the largest country church in Sweden, seating 2,400, which may say something about the piety of the local people of that era. Later this was reduced to 1,400. The pulpit comes from an earlier church, and the parsonage, built in 1731 and used until 1879, is now a museum.

Of the mountains around Järvsö, **Gluggberget**, 515 metres (1,689ft), has

a viewing platform at the summit, while **Öjeberget**, 370 metres (1,314ft), has the advantage that you can drive to the top.

To absorb this region you need to drive first along the minor road 30km (18 miles) east from Järvsö to **Delsbo** ⑦, which attracts an enormous number of folk fiddlers for the annual Delsbostämman, and then on the secondary road through Friggesund and Hassela and back to the coast. Surrounded by dark forests, this is Dellenbygden, rural Sweden at its best, and includes the Dellen lakes area, with boat trips and canoe and walking trails.

The most northerly coastal town of this central area is **Sundsvall** ⑧, across the border in the county of Västernorrlands, which has only a small area of coastline. Mainly industrial, Sundsvall still enjoys a fine location, partly on the mainland and partly on the island of **Alnö**, connected by bridge. It has a 13th century church and Hembygdsgård, an open-air museum with some 20 old buildings.

South of the town at **Galtström** is another restored ironworks, complete with blast furnace, works office,

chapel and forestry museum (daily; free). Drive 60km (37 miles) west on the E14, which starts at Sundsvall, and you will come to **Torpshammar** ⑨, which is claimed to be the very centre of Sweden.

Anglers' paradise

Together the provinces of **Härjedalen** and **Jämtland** are as big as Denmark. Though they cover an area of 50,000 sq km (19,300 sq miles), their population is only 137,000. Since 60,000 live in Östersund, the principal town of Jämtland, this means that outside the main towns people are few and far between. To the east and southeast are extensive forests with low hills, rivers and lakes. The higher mountains begin in Härjedalen and spread north and west.

This heartland has four main rivers, the Ångermanälven, Indalsälven, Ljungan and Ljusnan, all well stocked with fish, especially trout and grayling, and 4,000 lakes and watercourses make these provinces a fishing utopia. Perch, pike and whitefish are the most common in the forested regions, but many tarns have been stocked with trout in

FACT

The "Stone City" of Sundsvall, Medelpad, earned its nickname after a devastating fire – the largest in Sweden's history – destroyed the wooden town in June 1888. Architects from Stockholm were called in to rebuild Sundsvall in stone, with the fire insurance money used to pay for 600 fine new buildings. Today the town is one of the most complete examples of late-19th-century architecture in Sweden.

Ploughing the fields near Delsbo.

recent years. Most fishing waters are open to the general public, though you may need a permit, bought cheaply nearby or at the tourist offices. The vast tracts of near uninhabited territory are also home to wildlife such as bears, wolverines, lynx and the ubiquitous elk.

When tourism was in its infancy, Härjedalen was one of the first Swedish provinces to attract skiers, who still return to pit their skills against its varied terrain, and come back in the summer for mountain-walking. It is also the site of Sweden's first national park **Sonfjället**, created in 1909, today one of the most important bear habitats in Scandinavia.

The scenery is impressive, and, north of **Funäsdalen**, not far from the Norwegian border, the province has Sweden's highest road over the **Flatruet Plateau**, up to 1,000 metres (3,280ft) high. Close to the Norwegian border is the Rogen area, a remnant of the Ice Age with scratched and furrowed boulders.

For a driver, mile after mile of forest road stretching ahead can be mesmeric, and the art is not to fall asleep. But roads are not plentiful, apart from a few minor ones. At the cross of the north–south route, highway 45, and east–west, highway 84, is **Sveg**, a small town, but the province's largest at around 2,500 people. **Vemdalen** ⑩, 60km (37 miles) northwest, has an eight-sided wooden church with a separate onion-domed bell tower. Beyond the village, the road climbs steeply between two mountains, the Vemdalsfjällen, before crossing the provincial boundary.

Lakes and islands

Jämtland is by far the biggest province in central Sweden, a huge territory of lakes, rivers and mountains. Its heart is **Lake Storsjön**, the fifth-largest stretch of inland water in the country. At the centre of this network of water is the largest town, **Östersund** ⑪, connected by a bridge to the beautiful island of **Frösön**, which has been inhabited since prehistoric times. According to legend, it was dedicated to Frö, the god of fertility, a place of pagan sacrifice, and the most northerly spot where a rune stone has been found. Today, its oldest religious

THE INLAND RAILWAY

A trip on the Inlandsbanan (Inland Railway) is an enjoyable way of seeing some of Sweden's most dramatic scenery. The route stretches through the central heartlands from Mora in Dalarna to Gällivare in Lapland in summer (in winter, it only runs as far as Östersund). The idea of building such a long railway through a harsh and inaccessible landscape was first promoted in 1894, but it was to take another 40 years of hard labour before it was completed. The 1,100-km (680-mile) line was finally inaugurated in Jokkmokk in Lapland on 6 August 1937, and a monument was erected to commemorate the event. Today, the train often makes stops along the way so passengers can visit local artists and craftspeople or simply admire the views. Sometimes it has to stop to avoid running into herds of reindeer resting on the track. With luck, passengers may also see elk or bears on the trackside. It is possible to make stopovers along the route and stay for a night or two in local towns and villages to do some walking in the mountains, or just to enjoy the magnificent landscape. Those who crave more can continue the journey, looping up and round through Norway, before returning to Östersund in Sweden. Various packages are available combining rail travel with hotel accommodation, or trekking. For more information: Destination Inlandsbanan; tel: 0771-53 53 53; www.inlandsbanan.se.

building is of another faith, Christianity. The church dates in part from the 12th century, with a nave and porch added in 1610, the altar in 1708 and the pulpit in 1781. The separate bell tower is 18th-century, though one of the bells is 400 years older.

From the island there are magnificent views over countless lakes and waterways towards Norway. Five minutes' walk from the church you'll find **Stocke Titt**, which combines café, heritage centre and a good viewpoint.

The island was home to the noted Swedish composer and critic Wilhelm Peterson-Berger (1867–1942). This prolific composer produced a total of five operas, five symphonies and a violin concerto, as well as choral works, chamber music, piano pieces and songs. His most popular major work, the opera Arnljot, is performed every summer on the island.

Frösön also has a 21-hectare (52-acre) zoo, **Frösö Djurpark** (tel: 063-51 47 43; www.frosozoo.se; mid-June–mid-Aug daily 10am–4pm, July until 6pm), with 600 animals and a small amusement park.

All over Sweden you come across open-air museums which may be merely a handful of local buildings re-erected on one site, perhaps with a café, some indoor exhibits or traditional craft demonstrations. In a different league is **Jamtli** (tel: 063-15 01 10; www.jamtli.com; mid-June–mid-Aug daily 11am–5pm; mid-Aug–mid-June Tues–Sun 11am–5pm) in Östersund, one of the oldest and biggest open-air museums in the country. It contains 60 buildings and was established in 1912. In summer, local people perform bygone tasks using traditional implements and equipment, and visitors can also have a go. The buildings are from the 18th and 19th centuries, and include a fäbod (summer farm), a baker's cottage, a smithy and an old inn. The most amazing item in the museum's permanent indoor collection are the Överhogdal Tapestries, made in the Viking Age and rediscovered in 1910 in a church shed.

Sweden's lake monster

Lake Storsjön is reputed to have its own monster, a Swedish version of

Lake Storsjön.

the world-famous Scottish "Nessie", the serpent-like creature supposed to inhabit the depths of Loch Ness. Lake Storsjön's monster is said to vary in length from 3.6 metres (12ft) to 27 metres (90ft) and to have eyes like saucers, large ears, a tail and horns. Among its 40,000 exhibits, Östersund's provincial museum has traps with hooks and cables which were owned by a company set up in 1894 to find the monster. After failing to catch anything, the company went into liquidation and donated the implements to the museum. Present-day monsterseekers can take a cruise on the lake in the 140-year-old steamer SS Östersund (www.angaren ostersund.com; June–Sept).

Into Jämtland's mountains

The E14 is the main highway west from Östersund to the Norwegian border. It was the scene of frequent fighting between Norway and Sweden, marked today by the remains of some fortifications. In 1718 the Swedes suffered a major defeat along this route. When Sweden's great warrior king

Carl XII made his last fatal attack against the southern Norwegian fort of Fredriksten, he ordered his general Carl Gustav Armfelt to attack Trondheim from the north. It was a tragic failure. The king was killed at Fredriksten and, in the northern retreat, 3,000 men froze to death in a desperate attempt to withdraw into the safety of Sweden. You will find memorial stones to this disaster at Handöl, Ånn, Duved and Bustvalen.

In the 18th century, the area was the scene of frantic activity after the finding of copper – a boom period that lasted around 100 years.

Off the E14 as you travel northwest from Östersund, on the north bank of Lake Alsensjön at **Glösa ⑫**, are hällristningar. These primitive rock carvings, which may be Sweden's oldest, are unusual in their 60 depictions of elk and their internal organs.

In western Jämtland, the peaks rise to nearly 1,800 metres (6,000ft). It is a splendid area for trekking in summer and skiing in winter. Centuries ago, melting ice left many strange and unusual formations, such as the deep canyon between the Drommen and Falkfångarfjället mountains (the nearest road ends at Höglekardalen). An equally impressive Ice Age landscape is near **Vallbo**, at the end of a minor road from Undersåker. Western Jämtland is also rich in waterfalls, such as **Ristafallet** near Hålland, **Storfallet**, northwest of Höglekardalen, and **Tännforsen**, west of Åre.

Just before the Norwegian border is **Åre ⑬**, a popular winter sports resort. A funicular railway goes from the town centre part-way up the local mountain **Åreskutan**, and a cable car goes almost to the summit. Lakes and mountains on every side make a superb view.

Monotonous? Yes, to a degree. You need to be at ground level to absorb the immensity of the region: the brilliant blue lakes, their waters gently rippled by the breeze, the mysterious outlines of the distant mountains, the open space and the glorious silence.

Åre in autumn.

Sami tents under the Northern Lights.

LAPLAND

Under dancing Northern Lights and a golden midnight sun, Lapland beckons the traveller north to the land of the Sami, where the taxi service is by dog sled.

apland, Sweden's largest and most northerly province, is Europe's last great wilderness. It draws in those in search of solitude and breathtaking beauty, boasting 100,000 sq km (40,000 sq miles) of thundering rapids, glassy lakes, flowering alpine meadows and snow-covered mountains. In summer, the Laponia World Heritage area tempts, with four of the wildest of Sweden's national parks. In winter, the Northern Lights throw sheets of colour over Jukkasjärvi's Ice Hotel, where you can explore cross-country ski trails and dog-sled runs. Lapland is also the home of the Sami, the north's indigenous people, whose culture can be explored at the Arjeplog Silvermuséet, or in Jokkmokk at the Ájtte Svenskt Fjäll-och Samemuseum or the world-famous February market.

Baedeker's *Guide to Norway and Sweden*, published in 1892, said: "The vast Swedish Norrland is rarely visited by travellers, the points of interest being few, the distances great and the communications imperfect." Today this dismissive statement couldn't be further from the truth. Distances may be great, but modern communications are easy, with a rail link to the far north and good-quality roads. As for "the points of interest being few", what about the magnificent scenery? Lapland's uplands, lakes and mountains are among the finest in Europe, and

Sami herder.

remarkable enough to put any human attraction in the shade.

The best way to absorb the immensity of Lapland is to take the inland road – highway 45 – from south to north. In that way, this scenic extravaganza will build up like a highly polished piece of drama into a climactic grand finale.

Southern Lapland

Dorotea ❶, named after Queen Fredrika Wilhelmina Dorotea, consort of King Gustav IV Adolf, is at the

Main Attractions
Arjeplog Silvermuséet
Dog-sledding
Jokkmokk Market
Ájtte Svenskt Fjäll-och Samemuseum
Laponia
Ice Hotel, Jukkasjärvi
Kungsleden hiking trail

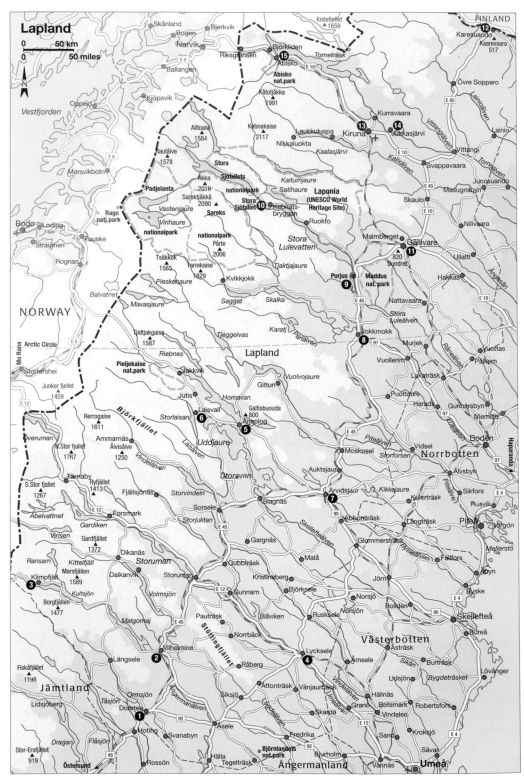

Lapland

0 — 50 km
0 — 50 miles

N

FINLAND

Skånland
Bjerkvik
Kistefjellet 1659
Karesuando
Kaarevaara 517

Bogen
Narvik
E 6
Riksgränsen
Björkliden
Torneträsk
15
Abisko
E 10

Ballangen
Abisko nat. park
Övre Soppero

Kjöpsvik
Kåtotjåkka 1991
Kurravaara
E 45
Lainio

Vestfjorden
Oppeid
Alitoaivi 1584
Kebnekaise 2117
Laukkuluspa
13
Kiruna
14
Jukkasjärvi
Lainio

Rautåive 1578
Nikkaluokta
Kaalasjärvi
E 10
Vittangi
Vittangi

Mørsvikbotn
E 6
Stora
Akka 2016
Sjöfallets
Kaitumjaure
Satihaure
Svappavaara

Padjelanta
Sarektjåkkå 2090
nationalpark
Laponia (UNESCO World Heritage Site)
Junosuando
Masugnsbyn

Rago natj. park
Vastenjaure
Sareks
Stora Sjöfallet
10
Kebnats-bryggan
Skaulo
E 10

Bodø
Loding
Virihaure
nationalpark
Ruokto
Nilivaara

Straumen
Fauske
nationalpark
Pårte 2006
Stora Lulevatten
Malmberget
Gällivare
11
Ullatti

Rognan
Tsåkkok 1565
Tarrekaise 1829
Tjaktjajaure
820 Dundret
Hakkas

Pieskehaure
Kvikkjokk
Porjus
9
Muddus nat. park
Nattavaara
E 10

Balvatnet
Mavasjaure
Saggat
Skalka
Stora Luleälven

NORWAY
Tjidtjakgaise 1587
Tjeggelvas
Karatj
Pärlälven
Jokkmokk
8
97
Murjek
Vuottas

Arctic Circle
E 6
Riebnes
Lapland
Vuollerim
Lakaträsk
Pälkem

Storforshei
Pieljekaise nat. park
Jakkvik
Vuolvojaure
Puottaure
Harads
Gunnarsbyn
Niemisel

Junker fjellet 1459
E 12
Jutis
Gittun
Galtisbuouda 800
E 45
Piteälven
Vidsel
Boden
97

Överuman
Rerrogaise 1611
Storlaisan
6
Laisvall
Arjeplog
5
Hornavan
Moskosel
Storforsen
Norrbotten

N.Stor fjallet 1767
Ammarnäs
Äivisåive 1250
Laisälven
Uddjaure
Auktsjaur
Älvsbyn
97

Tärnaby
Ryfjället 1413
Fjällsjönäs
Storvindeln
Storavan
Arvidsjaur
7
Ö. Kikkejaure
Sikfors
Rusvik
E 4

S.Stor fjallet 1267
Abelvattnet
E 12
Forsmark
Storjuktan
Slagnäs
Abborträsk
Långträsk
Piteå
Vargön

Virisen
Gardiken
Gardfjället 1372
Dikanäs
Sorsele
E 45
Gargnäs
Malå
Glommersträsk
Byskeälven
Fällfors
Mellerstö

Ransarn
Kittelfjäll
Marsfjällen 1589
Storuman
Gubbträsk
Jörn
Åbyn

Klimpfjäll
3
Borgfjällen 1477
Daikanvik
Storuman
Kristineberg
Björksele
Norsjö
Bollden
E 4
Byske

Fiskåfjället 1198
Kultsjön
Volmsjön
Pauträsk
E 45
Gunnarn
Bläviken
Ruskele
Norsjön
95
Skellefteå

Jämtland
Malgomaj
Vilhelmina
2
Norrbäck
Lycksele
4
Åmsele
Västerbotten
Åsträsk
Burträsk
Bureå

Lidsjöberg
Tåsjön
Ormsjön
Längsele
Råberg
Åttonträsk
Vänjaurbäck
Umeälven
Sikån
Lidsjön
Bygdeträsket
Lövånger

Dorotea
1
Åsele
Siksjö
Vänjaurträsk
Hällnäs
Robertsfors

Stor-Ersfjället 919
Dragan
Flåsjön
Hoting
Svanabyn
Fredrika
E 12
Skarda
Grano
Botsmark
Vindeln
E 4

Östersund
45
Rossön
Hälla
Tegelträsk
Björnlandets nat. park
92
Blurholm
Sävar
Kroksjö
Sand

Ångermanland
Vännäs
Umeå

Björkfjället
Stöttingfjället
Ångermanälven
Fredrika

heart of bear country – the animals sometimes wander into town in search of food.

Vilhelmina ② (which gets its name from the same queen) lies on the River Ångermanälven, 100km (60 miles) north, and is of greater interest. Off the main road on a hillside is its well-preserved church village; the church itself is imposing. The wooden houses now provide accommodation for tourists.

Sweden's lowest-ever temperature – a crisp –53.2°C (–63.76°F) – was recorded at Malgovik, 15km (9.25 miles) along a secondary road west of Vilhelmina. This road, running alongside Lake Malgomaj, eventually gives access to some splendid fell country, notably the **Kittelfjäll** region around **Klimpfjäll** ③. This is a largely uninhabited area, with untouched mountain scenery where the peaks rise to 1,375 metres (4,500ft).

Eventually the road crosses the Norwegian border at Skalmodalen and links up with the E6 near Mosjøen. The E6 runs up the Norwegian west coast and the east–west roads in Sweden all feed into it, allowing the itinerant traveller to criss-cross from one country to the other with few formalities.

Storuman, 120km (75 miles) north of Vilhelmina, is a more important road junction, where highway 45 is bisected by the E12, known as the **Blå Vägen** (Blue Highway) because it follows a succession of lakes and the River Umeälven. It starts on the Swedish east coast at **Holmsund**, on the Gulf of Bothnia, and passes **Lycksele** ④, where there is a zoo, **Lycksele Djurpark** (tel: 0950-163 63; www.lyckseledjurpark.se; June and Aug daily 10am–4pm, Jul until 5pm; times vary rest of year – see website for details), which concentrates on Nordic species including bear, elk, musk ox, wolves and reindeer. From Storuman the road continues through Tärnaby, where it joins the E6 at Mo i Rana (in Norway).

Sami heritage

At **Slagnäs**, 75km (47 miles) west of Arvidsjaur, there is a secondary road through glorious, peaceful lakeside scenery to **Arjeplog** ⑤, and this is an enjoyable alternative to the main road (highway 95). Arjeplog is one of Lapland's most interesting little towns, and it is almost surrounded by the waters of lakes Uddjaure and Hornavan, which at 221 metres (725ft) is Sweden's deepest lake.

The main attraction at Arjeplog is the **Silvermuséet** (Silver Museum; tel: 0961-145 00; www.silvermuseet.se; Mon–Fri 10am–5pm, Sat 10am–2pm). Housed in an old school, a typical beige-coloured wooden building, it provides a fascinating insight into the region's history and, above all, the lives of the Sami people. It owes its existence to Einar Wallqvist, "the doctor of the Laplanders", who came to the town in 1922. Besides his medical work, the remarkable Dr Wallqvist – a writer, lecturer, gifted linguist and sparkling wit – began to collect all kinds of cultural objects as a hobby. Later he decided to establish a museum in the old

Driving under the midnight sun.

FACT

Arjeplog's other claim to fame is as the capital of winter driving. Between January and March, the frozen Lake Udjaur is transformed into an enormous 1,250-acre ice-driving centre, where the major car manufacturers bring their latest models for winter testing. It's possible to hire a top-of-the-range sports car and try a circuit or two of the ice yourself – contact www. lapland-ice-driving.com.

schoolhouse, and today it has the finest collection of Sami silver in existence, plus a host of other artefacts relating to the life and times of the settlers and the Sami. The good doctor continued as the museum's curator until his death in 1986. Arjeplog's local church, which is 17th-century and quite impressive, was founded by Queen Kristina.

The Silver Road

Arjeplog is roughly halfway along highway 95, which is the historic **Silver Vägen** (Silver Road) stretching from Skellefteå on the Gulf of Bothnia to Bodø on the Norwegian west coast. In the 17th century there were silver mines around **Nasafjäll**, and the ore was transported, first by reindeer sleigh and then by boat, to the Swedish east coast. Not until 1972 did it become an asphalt-surfaced highway throughout its length, to open up an area of outstanding beauty.

About 60km (37 miles) west of Arjeplog and to the south of road 95 is the isolated community of **Laisvall** ⑥, where the inhabitants used to work in **Laisvallsgruvan**, one of the biggest

lead mines in Europe until its closure in 2006.

One of the finest viewpoints in this area is from the top of **Galtisbuouda**, 800 metres (2,624ft) above sea level. It is 15km (9 miles) north of Arjeplog, and there is a good road to just below the summit. The outlook is magnificent, with a network of lakes and range upon range of mountains stretching to infinity.

The wide main street of **Arvidsjaur** ⑦ has something of the atmosphere of a frontier town, which, to some degree, it is. Once a trading post, it is now a junction of both roads and railways, and has grown and expanded within the past 100 years. The major historic attraction is **Lappstaden**, an 18th-century Sami church village and the oldest surviving example in Sweden. It has nearly 80 buildings, including both the *kåtor*, the tent-shaped wooden huts, and the *härbren*, the distinctive wooden storehouses (tel: 070-379 76 37; mid-June–mid-Aug for guided tours). The village is still used from time to time by the Sami people, and is particularly worth visiting

Church in Jokkmokk.

during their celebrations over the last weekend in August.

In summer, Arvidsjaur is a tourist centre with all the essential adjuncts: hotels, chalets, camping site, swimming pool, putting green, tennis courts and sports ground. In winter, when it is intensely cold, it is taken over by Europe's vehicle industry, which uses the area to test the ability of its products to perform satisfactorily in sub-zero temperatures.

Across the Arctic Circle to Jokkmokk

The Arctic Circle is marked by a multilingual sign beside the road, 156km (97 miles) north of Arvidsjaur. At a nearby café you can buy a suitably inscribed certificate to prove you have crossed the line. Only a short distance further north is **Jokkmokk** ❽, which is the principal town in the *kommun* (localauthority district) of the same name.

The Jokkmokk *kommun* is the biggest in Sweden, covering an area of about 19,425 sq km (7,500 sq miles), equal to the whole of Wales, or Connecticut and Delaware put together.

The population, however, is a meagre 5,000, just over half of whom live in Jokkmokk itself.

Jokkmokk, meaning "a bend in the stream" in the local Sami language, is the only place where you will see nomadic Sami in summer, but the big event is the 400-year-old February market (www.jokkmokksmarknad.se). This attracts thousands of people, not so much to buy or sell but to experience the unique atmosphere (see page 283). If you need accommodation at the time of the fair you have to book at least a year in advance – and this is no time for camping out, with the temperature often dropping to -35°C (-31°F). Other smaller fairs take place in various parts of this country.

Jokkmokk is a centre for the Sami culture, which can best be studied at the **Ájtte Svenskt Fjäll-och Samemuseum** (Swedish Mountain and Sami Museum; tel: 0971-170 70; www.ajtte.com; mid-June–mid-Aug daily 9am–6pm, mid-May–mid-June and mid-Aug–mid-Sept Tues–Fri 10am–4pm, Sat–Sun noon–4pm, mid-Sept–mid-May Tues–Fri 10am–4pm,

Dog-sledding with Siberian huskies.

DOG-SLEDDING IN LAPLAND

Sweden's northern wilderness is an amazing area, particularly in winter, and dog-sledding is a fascinating way of exploring it. A dog team usually consists of five to 12 dogs, most of them Siberian or Alaskan huskies. The dogs enjoy the work: indeed, showing a sledge to a husky is like showing any other dog a lead and calling "Walkies". Once clipped in, they become extremely impatient to get going, leading to a crescendo of yelping until, at last, the driver releases the anchor and they're off like a flash. Most expeditions travel 25–50km (15–30 miles) a day, but the dogs can cover far greater distances. In one of the highlights of the dog-sledding season, the Tobacco Trail, dozens of teams compete in a 300km (186-mile) circular race from the Jukkasjärvi Ice Hotel to Saivomuotka and back to Kiruna. The fastest teams complete the course in about 15 hours, which includes several compulsory rest-stops.

Many settlements allow visitors to try dog-sledding (November to April depending on snow conditions), including at Kiruna, Jukkasjärvi and Abisko. Tours last anything from an hour to tougher multi-day tours through Sarek national park or along the Kungsleden. Passengers need to be well wrapped up against temperatures that could be -20°C (-4°F) or less. One operator is Jokkmokksguiderna (tel: 0971-122 20; www.jokkmokkguiderna.com; open by appointment), who run a kennel of 45 Siberian huskies.

TIP

There are around a quarter of a million reindeer in Sweden. Drivers in Lapland should keep a watchful eye out for them, as in summer, animals may wander unexpectedly into the road. Reindeer are regarded as currency to the Sami. It's bad manners to ask a Sami how many reindeer he owns, because it is like asking how much he earns a year.

Trekking near Kebnekaise, Sweden's highest mountain.

Sat noon–4pm), one of Sweden's most modern museums. As its name implies, the museum portrays not just the local culture but also the mountain world, placing mankind in a natural, cultural and ecological perspective. Geographically, it covers the whole of the mountain region and the areas where the Sami traditionally live.

The next stretch of highway 45 goes through a sparsely populated area to **Porjus** ❾, 75km (47 miles) north. It lies at the southern end of Lake Lulevatten and is a major centre for the generation of hydro-electric power. The original switchgear building is a monumental edifice, and today Porjus is the headquarters for the state-owned power stations which are on the upper part of the River Store Lule. From Porjus a very minor road follows Lake Lulevatten for 6km (3.7 miles) to **Stora Sjöfallet National Park** ❿, named after the Stuormuorkkegårttje waterfall that cascades in five silvery streams over a steep bluff. At Stora Sjöfallet is the **Naturum Visitor Centre Laponia** (tel: 072-587 6160; http://laponia.

nu; mid-June–Aug daily 9am–8pm, Sept Thur–Sun 11am–5pm), which opened in 2014 for all those eager to learn more about the breathtaking Laponia area. A unique combination of Sami culture and unspoiled nature, this immense Unesco World Heritage site covering 24,346 sq km (9,400 sq miles) is also home to four national parks, Padjelanta, Sarek, Muddus and Stora Sjöfallet.

Bear country

To the east of Porjus and the E45 is the wild, untouched **Muddus National Park** (tel: 0971-121 40; http://sverigesnationalparker.se), home of bear, lynx and wolverine. It is open to the public, but visitors are not allowed in some of the more sensitive areas of the park during the breeding season, which lasts from mid-March to the end of July.

A relatively short drive brings the bulk of the **Dundret Mountain** in sight, beyond which is Gällivare, one of the two major centres of population in northern Lapland. High on the side of Dundret is the bustling **Dundret Mountain resort** (www.

dundret.se), something of a culture shock after the peace and solitude of the area. But it gives you the chance to ride, walk, windsurf, fish, play golf, go white-water rafting, or even pan for gold; and in winter to ski, snowmobile and dogsled. Although the track is rough in parts, you can also drive right to the top of the mountain. At an altitude of 820 metres (2,690ft) the views are marvellous and, from early June to early July, this is the place to see the Midnight Sun. Like all of northern Lapland, in summer it also has rapacious mosquitoes with an appetite for foreign blood. Don't forget the insect repellent.

End of the line: Gällivare

Gällivare ⑪ owes its growth to the discovery of iron ore, and now has a population of 18,000. The main mining area is in its twin town of **Malmberget**, where most of the mineworkers live. Here, too, you find the contrast of a suburban small town at odds with the grandeur of the countryside all around it.

Gällivare is the end of the **Inlandsbanan**, a railway line that faithfully follows the E45, give or take a few miles, all the way from Östersund. Construction began in 1907, and the line was completed in 1937. At one time its future was in doubt, but the line was saved by a decision to turn it into a tourist route. Today, with new diesel trains, it has regained its youth as a useful alternative way into the far north.

Gällivare has a mining museum, a mid-18th century Sami church (**Lappkyrkan**), a park with some preserved buildings and a Sami camp that appears to exist purely for the tourists. The town is also the jumping-off point for treks into the vast Laponia area to the west, which includes the Padjelanta and Sarek national parks. Only a few minor roads penetrate into this enormous area, and it is very much for those who want to trek.

Beyond Gällivare, road 45 joins up with highway E10 and together they go north to **Svappavaara**, a former mining centre. Here the E45 goes off to the northeast to Karesuando, just short of the Finnish border. Many of the place names in northern Lapland owe more to Finnish than to Swedish: Kiruna, for example, where a fifth of the population are Finnish immigrants.

Across the tundra

Karesuando ⑫ has two main distinctions. It is home to the most northerly church in Sweden, 250km (155 miles) inside the Arctic Circle, and it also has the dubious honour of producing the coldest average winter temperatures in the country. All around the village is Sweden's only tundra scenery, and about 4km (2.5 miles) to the south is **Kaarevaara Mountain**. The summit is no higher than 517 metres (1,696ft), but from the top you can see Sweden, Finland and Norway. Better still, you can drive up there.

Distances in the far north between towns and settlements and places of interest are often great. Shared driving is a great advantage, particularly when

A snow-white reindeer.

the road runs mile after mile through an unchanging landscape. This happens beyond Svappavaara, where the E10 swings northwest through uninspiring scenery to **Kiruna** ⑬. With 23,240 inhabitants, this is the biggest centre of population in Lapland. Like Gällivare, it grew and developed through the discovery and extraction of iron ore.

A town on the move

Mining on a large scale began in 1900, and it is still Kiruna's main industry – the LKAB mine is the world's largest iron-ore mine, with more than 400km (248 miles) of two-lane underground roadways. Its workings are so deep and so extensive that Kiruna itself began to sink into the ground. In 2004, it was decided that the entire town should be moved to a new site three kilometres to the east. Evacuation of Kiruna will begin in 2018, with the new town to be completely settled by 2050. You can visit the mine that is causing all the fuss, descending 540 metres/yards to the **LKAB Visitor Centre** (daily tours in English at 3pm, minimum

Inside the Kiruna mine.

number required – book with Kiruna tourist office tel: 0980-188 80; www. kirunalapland.se).

Although most mining is now underground, there is also a huge opencast site. The mine led to the opening in 1903 of the town's railway line, to take iron ore either to the port of Luleå on the Gulf of Bothnia to the east, or across the Norwegian border to the ice-free port of Narvik on the Norwegian west coast. In 1903, this was an outstanding feat of engineering, and, until 1984 when Kiruna and Narvik were joined by road, the railway was the only cross-border link in this remote area.

Besides mining, Kiruna has diversified into tourism and scientific research. The **Swedish Institute of Space Physics** (**IRF Kiruna**), among other things, investigates the phenomenon of the Northern Lights, while on the banks of the River Vittangi is the **Esrange Space Center**, a rocket-testing station that launches around five to 10 research rockets and balloons into different layers of inner space every year. Kiruna tourist office can arrange trips to Esrange's small visitor centre.

Apart from a visit to the mine, try not to miss the small but informative **Samegård exhibition** (Brytaregatan 14; tel: 0980-170 29; year-round) in the basement of the hotel of the same name, which provides a glimpse of the life and history of the Sami.

A hotel made of ice

A secondary road just outside Kiruna takes you to the village of **Jukkasjärvi** ⑭, a centre for winter and summer excursions. In recent years Jukkasjärvi has acquired fame with its extraordinary **Ice Hotel**, which is sculpted entirely from ice and rebuilt every winter. In winter the dog-sledding is truly Arctic, in a snow-covered wilderness. In summer Jukkasjärvi provides the stomach-churning thrill of whitewater rafting through the rapids in an inflatable boat. You can choose from day and week-long trips using the rivers Torne, Kalix and Kaitum. The village also has a modest but quite interesting wooden church and a small open-air museum.

Tourism received its biggest boost in 1984 with the opening of road 98 from Kiruna via the Norwegian frontier to Narvik. This is the **Nordkalottvägen**, an outstanding piece of road-building which penetrates 170 km (105 miles) through one of Europe's last wilderness areas. It starts undramatically, but by the time you have **Lake Torneträsk** on the right with distant mountains, and even more impressive mountains rising up to 2,000 metres (6,500ft) on the left, the journey changes from interesting to spectacular. The clarity of the air sharply etches the outlines of the mountains, some snow-capped even in midsummer against the sky, while the lake is a brilliant blue.

The mountains to the southwest of the highway can only be reached on foot or by pony, and it is in this hinterland that **Kebnekaise**, Sweden's highest peak at 2,117 metres (6,945ft), reigns supreme.

The King's Trail

Abisko ⑮, 150km (93 miles) north of Kiruna, is a popular base from which to set out along the **Kungsleden** (King's Trail), a long-distance footpath which, for over a century, has enabled even inexperienced walkers to see something of the most mountainous region of Sweden. Abisko, Björkliden and Riksgränsen (the last place before the frontier with Norway) all have hotels.

This area presents wonderful opportunities for the angler, and an inexpensive permit allows you to fish in 3,000 lakes. Apart from walking and fishing, there are trips on Lake Torneträsk and sightseeing flights by seaplane or helicopter. From Riksgränsen the highway crosses the border and descends to meet the E6 at the edge of the Rombak fjord, and on to the coast at Narvik.

Despite these engineering feats, the abiding impression of Lapland must be that human achievements, however technologically advanced, are all upstaged by nature. This awe-inspiring combination of rivers, lakes and mountains cannot fail to leave its mark on the visitor.

The bar at the Ice Hotel.

ARTS AND CRAFTS IN THE FAR NORTH

Living in isolated communities across Lapland, the Sami have developed distinctive handicrafts using reindeer, wood and silver as raw materials.

Sami handicrafts have a long tradition. The raw materials are often derived from everyday items found in the mountainous northern landscape, such as birchwood. Antlers and skins from the reindeer herds are used to make knives, tools, clothes and decorative objects.

The products have developed from simple household items to the sophisticated handicrafts of today. Many objects are round, and this is because the Sami are a nomadic people who roam over wide areas with their reindeer herds, and angular items cannot be packed so easily.

Sami silver trail

A silver mine was established in Lapland in the 17th century, since when the Sami have become particularly noted for their silverware – including richly decorated drinking vessels, bowls and adornments. Today, their silverware is almost always made by silversmiths in the cities to Sami specifications. Embroidery is also used to exquisite effect in Sami handicrafts.

Sami products are sold in craft shops and markets in Lapland. Prices and quality vary, so be sure to hunt around before you buy.

Sami woman at the Jokkmokk winter market.

Sami reindeer herder in traditional costume at the Jokkmokk winter fair.

A pair of children's boots made from reindeer skin. Reindeer bones are used for sewing. The woven band is typically Sami and is tied around the boot.

Typical Sami textiles for sale at the Jokkmokk fair.

JOKKMOKK'S WINTER MARKET

The annual winter market in Jokkmokk (see page 277) takes place over the first weekend in February. This tradition started in 1605, and the market soon became a meeting place for the Sami and the merchants from the coastal communities. The merchants were generally looking for supplies of furs, in exchange for the everyday items that the Sami people needed for their harsh life looking after the reindeer herds.

Over time, the market became not just an occasion for buying and selling goods but also for special events such as weddings, baptisms and funerals. For many years it was staged over two weeks, but this was gradually shortened to a long weekend. During the 1930s, the market consisted of just 20 stalls; today, there are at least 500, and it is estimated that 40,000 people visit Jokkmokk during the market. It is still very much a Sami occasion, with the accent on traditional arts, handicrafts, music and food. For many visitors the most spectacular event is the reindeer race.

Sami-Christian altarpiece designed by artist Bror Hjort in the wooden church of Jukkasjärv.

The kåsan is the classic Sami drinking vessel, usually made from birchwood.

The Sami people have a long tradition of using pewter to decorate their garments and make jewellery, like these leather and pewter bracelets.

THE NORTHEAST COAST

The Bothnian coast of the northeast is Sweden's best-kept secret. Uninhabited islands, sheltered coves and historic towns await the traveller on the journey north.

This quiet corner of Sweden is still quite under-explored, allowing visitors to tuck the gems of the northerneastern coast away for themselves. They include two Unesco World Heritage sites– the 424 red wooden cottages huddled around the medieval church at Gammelstad; and the natural beauty and interesting geology of the Höga Kusten (High Coast), with its many little coves and islands. Sweden's old wars and Cold Wars with Russia have left interesting military remains, including Bodens Fästning and Hemsö Fästning, carved deep inside a mountain. The coast's sandy beaches are popular in summer; while inland the silvery rivers are an invitation to canoe, white-water raft and fish.

Bottenviken (the Gulf of Bothnia), the stretch of water that separates Sweden from its eastern neighbour, Finland, forms the common bond between the three provinces of the northeast – Ångermanland, Västerbotten and Norrbotten – that share its seaboard. For the most part, the coastline is low-lying and ranges from polished rock to sand and shingle beaches, and from wide bays to small coves and inlets.

All the major towns are on the coast, harking back to the days when the sea was the easy way to travel, compared to the dense forests and rolling hills further inland. Most of these coastal towns grew up as trading settlements, where fishermen would come to sell their pike and herring.

The coast is fringed with islands, which at times form an almost continuous archipelago. Only a handful are inhabited; and the boats you see today are not fishing vessels but the pleasure boats of holidaymakers, indulging the Swedish passion for sailing and the sea. Only the occasional small, simple chapel speaks of the past.

Main Attractions

Hemsö Fästning
Höga Kusten
Umeå
Gammelstad, Luleå
Torneälven fishing

Lighthouse at Holmön.

Northeast

0 _____ 50 km

0 _____ 50 miles

Inland, lakes provide tranquil blue oases in the dense forests, while river valleys cut swathes through the trees. The greatest charm of the area is its rich wildlife, with bears, lynx, elk and beavers in abundance.

Seafaring town

Starting in the south of this great stretch of empty land, the main coastal town of Ångermanland is **Härnösand** ❶, 50km (30 miles) north of Sundsvall in Medelpad. In 1585, King Johan III not so much granted as forced a charter on the old trading and seafaring centre. The king was looking for duties and taxes, and threatened the inhabitants with deportation to Russia if they did not agree to create a permanent trading centre. That threat was enough to turn Härnösand into a successful commercial town.

The town is part island, part mainland, with the major section on **Härnö Island**, 7km by 10km (4 miles by 6 miles). In the 17th and 18th centuries, it blossomed into the cultural and administrative centre of northern Sweden.

Although it is now a commercial and industrial town, its splendid location makes it attractive. The fine town hall, with its classic lines and impressive pillared entrance, was completed in 1791, and the equally handsome cathedral, **Domkyrkan**, built between 1843 and 1846, is in the same style. It replaces an earlier building which in 1721 was burnt down by marauding Russians during a turbulent time in Sweden's history. There are some well-preserved 18th-century wooden houses in **Östanbäcken**, but the rest of the town is modern.

Overlooking the town and harbour is **Murberget** (tel: 0611-886 00; mid-June–early Aug daily 11am–4pm, indoor museum also open early Aug–mid-June Tues–Sun 11am–4pm; free), which has one of the largest open-air historical museums in Sweden. The indoor section shows how people settled in the area more than 2,000 years ago, and displays the museum's collections of hunting weapons and medieval sculptures.

Visitors can glean fascinating insight into Sweden's Cold War with Russia at **Hemsö Fästning** (tel: 0611-690 02; www.hemsofastning.se; June–Aug daily 11am–5pm with guided tours every half hour), a top-secret 1950s military installation on the island of Hemsön, 20km (12 miles) north of Härnösand. The facility, carved 40 meters (130ft) down into a mountain, once housed 320 soldiers and was built to withstand nuclear attack.

About 40km (25 miles) northwest of Härnösand, on the River Ångermanälven, is **Kramfors ❷**, the home of the musician Frans Berwald, one of Sweden's best-known composers, and Kalle Grönstedt, a musician who made the town the country's leading centre for accordionists.

In the vicinity of Kramfors, near **Ytterlännäs** on highway 90, look out for a 13th-century church, regarded as an antiquarian wonder. The 16th-century golden Madonna is by Haake Gulleson; the ornate vaults and walls were decorated by an unknown farmer-painter in the 1480s.

The High Coast

One of the most important attractions along the E4 north of Härnösand is the spectacular **Höga Kusten** (High Coast) **Bridge**. It is 1.8km (1.1 miles) long and has a vertical clearance of about 40 metres (130ft). The bridge's supporting pillars stretch out 180 metres (590ft) over the sea. At its northern end there is a restaurant and visitor centre. It is an impressive structure, modelled partly on the Golden Gate Bridge in San Francisco, and is well worth a visit.

The bridge marks the start of the most beautiful stretch of coastline, stretching as far as Docksta, 60km (37 miles) to the north. The **Höga Kusten** was added to the Unesco World Heritage list in 2000 because of its exceptionally unusual geological uplift. Crushed flat by the weight of glaciers during the last Ice Age, the entire coastline has been rebounding ever since the ice melted, at a greater rate than anywhere else in the world.

Hoga Kusten Bridge at dusk.

TIP

The best way to explore the island of Norra Ulvön is to rent a bike in the village of Ulvöhamn, where the ferries tie up. Simple cabins are available for overnight stays, bookable on the island. Sailors arrive in force for the Ulvön Regatta, held in the first week of July.

The desolate beauty of the High Coast.

Its towering cliffs are now Sweden's highest, and are still rising at a rate of around 8mm (0.3in) per year. This impressive coastal landscape is one of Sweden's best-kept secrets, undervisited by Swedes and tourists alike.

The heart of the High Coast is the **Nordingrå Peninsula ❸**, where the bedrock is an intense red *rapakivi* granite – this word is Finnish and means "rotten stone", because of the way it weathers easily into gravel and shingle. To get to the High Coast, leave the E4 north of Härnösand and take the short ferry crossing over the estuary to **Nydal**. Coming from the north, you reach the peninsula by leaving the E4 at either Lockestrand or Sundborn. Offshore are several attractive islands, such as **Mjältön**, which achieves the record for the highest Swedish island with its peak at 236 metres (774ft).

The peninsula has a variety of scenic treasures – the wide sweep of Omne Bay, the villages of Måviken, Norrfällsviken and the view from the church over Vagsfjärden. Bönhamn is a tiny little place tucked away among the rocks, where Arnes Sjöbad (Arne's Boathouse) justifies its popularity as a rendezvous for meals of salmon or fresh grilled herrings and mashed potatoes. Also worth a visit is Mannaminne, near Häggvik, run by actor Anders Åberg. It provides lodging and sustenance, including a variety of home-baked delicacies, in addition to handicrafts, art exhibitions and musical evenings.

There are bathing places at Storsand, Norrfällsviken, Hörsång and Noraström.

The **Höga Kusten Trail**, a 129km (80-mile) footpath through the peninsula, starts at Hornöberget at the northern end of the High Coast Bridge and finishes at central Örnsköldsvik. The trail is well marked with orange markers, and there are hotels, guesthouses, hostels and primitive trail shelters along the route.

Skuleberget

On the inland side of the E4 is another surprise, the looming outline of the **Skuleberget**, 295 metres (968ft) above sea level. If approaching

from the north, it rises suddenly just before Docksta. At its foot is the **Naturum Höga Kusten visitor centre** (tel: 0613-700 200; www.naturu hogakusten.se; Apr daily 10am–4pm, May–mid-June and mid-Aug–Sept daily 10am–5pm, mid-June–mid-Aug daily 9am–7pm), with more information about the coastline and its unusual geology. The easy way to the top of the mountain is by chairlift, with fabulous views from the top. If you'd rather explore the mountain in a more hands-on way, Europe's biggest **Via Ferrata centre** (tel: 0613-405 00; http://viaferrata.se; May–Aug 10am–7pm, Sept 10am–5pm) is here. You can hire a helmet, harness and lanyard, and scramble up the rocky faces of the mountain on various fixed-cable routes, graded according to difficulty.

Behind Skuleberget is the **Skuleskogen National Park ❹**, noted for its birds, which include the rare white-backed woodpecker, grouse, Siberian jay and waxwing, as well as a whole range of mammals – elk, deer, lynx, fox, badger, marten, ermine, blue hare and squirrel (open all year).

Örnsköldsvik ❺, commonly called Övik, is the nearest town to the High Coast and is twice the size of Härnösand, with 55,000 inhabitants. The town itself is industrial, but there are some good views from the **Vansberget** hilltop (accessible by car), and it has a beautiful archipelago. In bygone years, many of the local people were fisher-farmers, combining the two jobs to make ends meet – the counterparts of the west-coasters. Örnsköldsvik is one of Sweden's leading winter-sports areas, particularly for ice hockey and ski jumping. There is also a good adventure swimming pool in the town centre.

Island hopping

There are two attractive islands to the south of Örnsköldsvik, **Södra Ulvön**, which is uninhabited, and **Norra Ulvön**. Södra has one of the oldest fishermen's chapels in Sweden, built in 1622. It has well-preserved paintings on the walls and ceiling. Another attractive island just to the north is **Trysunda**, a favourite with the sailing fraternity because

FISHING IN THE FAR NORTH

There is nothing quite like fishing against the impressive backdrop of Sweden's mountains. Creeping silently along a riverbank and trying to tempt a shy trout or grayling to the fly is an unforgettable experience. Fishing is well organised in the north. If you are driving along the northeast coast there are plenty of opportunities to fish along the route, especially in the rivers Piteälven, Kalixälven and Torneälven; just ask at the nearest tourist office. Further afield, the Tjuonajokk fishing camp on the River Kaitumälven in northwest Lapland, for instance, is renowned for its grayling fishing. The Miekak fishing camp, 100km (60 miles) northwest of Arjeplog (accessible by helicopter from Tjärnberg at Silvervägen, or by snowmobile in winter from Silvervägen), provides arguably the best char fishing in Lapland. At the northernmost extremity of Sweden, the fishing centre on Lake Rostujávri is renowned for its char and grayling. It is accessible in summer by seaplane or helicopter from Kiruna, or in winter by snowmobile.

Not surprisingly, transport can be expensive, but the cost of fishing permits is low compared with other countries. Permits can be bought at a number of outlets, including Tourist Information Offices and some petrol stations. The best month for fishing is usually August.

of its lagoon-like bay. Norra Ulvön can be reached by boat from Docksta and is linked by ferry to Trysunda.

Umeå: university town

Umeå ❻, on the River Umeälven at the junction of the E4 and E12 roads, is the principal town of Västerbotten and has a population of almost 120,000. It may be larger than Örnsköldsvik but, thanks to its layout, location and young, lively inhabitants, it is undoubtedly more attractive. Like so many towns in Sweden, it was founded by King Gustav II Adolf, in 1622. After a devastating fire in 1888 – a commonplace event in a country where virtually all the buildings were made of wood – the town planted avenues of birch trees as protective firebreaks, and these have created a gracious appearance that goes well with its riverside location. It was not always peaceful. Between 1808 and 1809, at the time when Sweden lost its 800-year-old rule over Finland, the Russians crossed the winter ice from Finland and attacked the town, which resulted in bitter fighting.

The town's main attraction is the **Västerbottens Museum** (www.vbm.se; Tues–Fri 10am–5pm, Wed until 9pm, Sat–Sun 11am–5pm; free), with permanent exhibitions on Sami culture and what may be the world's oldest skis, dating back to the Stone Age. There is also an open-air museum (mid-June–mid-Aug) whose farmhouses, cowsheds, barns and mills were gathered on the site in the 1920s.

Umeå was European Capital of Culture in 2014, which has left it with several new and interesting cultural curiosities. It has an acclaimed museum of contemporary art and visual culture **Bildmuseet** (www.bildmuseet.umu.se; Tues 11am–8pm, Wed–Sun 11am–6pm; free), housed in a modern seven-floor building on the Umeå University Arts Campus, with beautiful river views.

Music fans swear it's worth a trip to Umeå simply to visit **Guitars – The Museum** (www.guitarsthemuseum.com; Mon–Sat noon–6pm), one of the world's finest privately owned collection of guitars, gathered by twins Samuel and Michael Åhdén. A guided

Umeå old and new.

tour, explaining the story behind each instrument, is a must.

The 'Swedish Riviera'

An alternative to the main road along the coast from Umeå to the next place north, **Skellefteå**, an industrial centre, is to take the secondary road (364) inland, which is more interesting and very quiet. There are no dramatic panoramas, just a succession of pleasant rural views. You pass **Lake Bygde-träsket** and reach a smaller lake at **Burträsk ❼**, about 100km (60 miles) north of Umeå, which has an imposing village church and a very small open-air museum – "every community should have one" might well be the Swedish motto. Never mind: this museum serves good coffee and waffles (open in summer; free).

By now, you will have become so used to northern Sweden's quiet rural landscape that to arrive in **Piteå ❽** is something of a culture shock. It lies just north of the Vasterbotten-Norrbotten provincial boundary on a peninsula that dates back to the 17th century, and has a few narrow lanes

and wooden houses to recall the past. So far so good; but prepare yourself for the noise and people of the big holiday centre, **Pite Havsbad** (tel: 0911-327 00; www.pitehavsbad.se). It's a mass of self-catering cabins, camping sites and a large hotel complex, and entertainments include a waterpark, casino and golf course. Its 3.2km (2 miles) sandy beach has the warmest waves in Sweden, as the large dunes trap the sunshine and heat the shallow water. The Norwegians love it, and migrate there in great flocks from the austere calm of their northern fjords.

From Piteå, the road leads northwest and follows the course of the River Piteälven through Älvsbyn and on to Bredsel and **Storforsen ❾**, 90km (56 miles) away. This magnificent stretch of river rapids is one of the longest and most powerful in Europe, with a drop of 81 metres (265ft) over 5km (3 miles).

Luleå: World Heritage site

Back to the coast and it is not far to **Luleå ❿**, the most northerly major

The Bildmuseet in Umeå.

town in Sweden. Today, it stands at the mouth of the River Luleälven, bounded on three sides by water and fringed with islands. In olden times, the town was some 10km (6 miles) further inland. It had been given its own charter by King Gustav II Adolf in 1621, but in 1649 the crown decreed that trade had grown too large for that first small harbour and the town had to move.

The townspeople were reluctant to leave their homes, but the crown issued a decree forcing them to go. The king could not force the new town to develop quickly, though; and in 1742, when the intrepid botanist Linnaeus passed through Luleå on his Lapland journey, he dismissed it as "a pretty village".

The early shipyards closed when the first steamship appeared; then the discovery of iron ore in Lapland and the opening of the railways gave the town a chance to develop. The first steelworks were built in the 1940s, followed by a massive but stillborn project for a new steelworks on 250 hectares (618 acres) of reclaimed

Old farmhouse in Gammelstad.

land. It was due for completion in 1980, but by then overproduction of steel elsewhere made the new works a non-starter.

Though it has been dogged by a certain amount of misfortune, Luleå is today a pleasant town. Its museum, the **Norrbotten Museum** (tel: 0920-24 35 02; www.norrbottensmuseum.nu; mid-June–mid-Aug daily 11am–5pm, mid-Aug–mid-June Tues–Fri 10am–4pm, Sat–Sun 11am–4pm; free) in Herme-lin Park, provides a well-rounded picture of the county's history.

One happy legacy of the king's decision to move Luleå is that it left the old church town, **Gammelstad** (open all year; free; tel: 0920-45 70 10; www.lulea.se/gammelstad), on its original site. Now the church village and the church itself have been placed on Unesco's World Heritage list. It is a fascinating place to visit, with 400 small red-painted cottages surrounding the church. The cottages, built mainly in the 17th century, were used when people came in from the country to go to church at the major festivals, or when it was time to pay taxes to the sheriff.

Friendly, knowledgeable volunteers staff the small **visitor centre** (early June–Aug Mon–Fri 8am–6.30pm, Sat–Sun 10am–6pm; Sept–early June Mon–Thurs noon–4.30pm, Sun noon–3pm).

The 15th-century **church** (Mon–Wed 10am–2pm) at Gammelstad's centre has walls of red and grey granite. The altarpiece, carved in wood and gilded, was made in Antwerp, and the chancel frescoes date from the 1480s. The triumphal crucifix is a remarkable example of medieval art, while the sandstone baptismal font is even older than the church itself. The ornate pulpit in Baroque style was the work of a village joiner, Nils Fluur. The church is still used on important religious occasions. Close to the original harbour is an open-air museum with farm buildings, cottages, stables, a log cabin, a croft and a fisherman's dwelling. It also includes one of the typical haysheds which are a feature of the farming landscape in Norrbotten. Once a necessity, hundreds survive today as relics from the past.

Border country

About 35km (22 miles) inland from Luleå on the River Luleälven is a town once called the "Gibraltar of the North". **Boden** ⓫ is the largest garrison town in Sweden today, with military roots going back to the 19th century. In 1809, Sweden lost Finland to the Russians, a blow that left Sweden fearful of invasion from the east, and so "one of the strongest fortresses of Europe – that is to say in the whole world" – was built. **Bodens Fästning** is made up of 1,200 military structures that form a defensive ring around the town, including five huge artillery forts that were once manned by 500 soldiers apiece. In the summer, one of the five, **Rödbergsfortet** (www.rodbergsfortet.com; tours mid-June–early Aug daily at 11am, noon, 1pm and 2pm), is open to visitors. You can also learn more about Sweden's military history from the late 1800s to the present in the town's **Försvarsmuseum** (Defence Museum; www.forsvarsmuseum.se; Tues–Sat 11am–4pm, also Sun 11am–4pm mid-June–mid-Aug).

The road to Luleå in deep winter.

Even now, Sweden has remained sensitive about military issues, and a major slice of eastern Norrbotten is a defence area. This means restrictions on foreigners entering and staying in the designated area.

Sweden's easternmost town is **Haparanda** ⓬, which lies on the western side of the River Torneälven, and is another result of Sweden's losing the 1808–09 War. Along with Finland went the important Finnish town Tornio. To compensate for that loss, the Swedes built Haparanda opposite Tornio on the River Torneälven, which forms the border between the two countries for many miles. On the Swedish side it also skirts a largely uninhabited region of Norrbotten and Lapland. All these northern provinces, collectively called Norrland, have a distinctive northern terrain and, whether it be on mountain, lake or river, they offer endless outdoor pastimes, including canoeing, whitewater rafting and fishing.

This northern curve of the Gulf of Bothnia is a mixture of archipelago, rivers and wonderful scenery. It's worth taking road 400 to the north along the Torneälven on the Swedish side into the Tornedalen valley. Make a stop at the **Kukkolaforsen rapids**, 15km (9 miles) from Haparanda, where there are excellent visitor facilities close to the river.

Between Haparanda and Luleå lies **Kalix** ⓭, which has a medieval church from the 15th century, which was used as a stable by the Russian army in 1808. Earlier Viking graves lie nearby at Sangis.

This is Sami country, and 75 km (46 miles) inland from Kalix on the River Kalixälven is **Överkalix** ⓮, a typical Lapland township. There are fine views here from the top of the local mountain, **Brännaberget**, and, if you time your visit cleverly, you have the chance to see the glories of the Midnight Sun.

Come at the end of June and you can see the spectacular traditional netting of the whitefish. The locals build rickety, long jetties out into the rapids where they use traditional *haaf* nets to catch not only whitefish, but also salmon.

Fishing under the midnight sun.

Fiskebäckskil on the Bohuslän coast.

TRAVEL TIPS
SWEDEN

TRANSPORT

GETTING THERE AND GETTING AROUND

GETTING THERE

By air

The national carrier SAS Scandinavian Airlines is part of the Star Alliance airline partnership, whose members link many of the world's major cities to Sweden.

Sweden's main international airport is Stockholm Arlanda (www.swedavia.com/arlanda), 37km (23 miles) north of Stockholm, although budget airlines also fly in to Stockholm Bromma (www.swedavia.se/bromma; 8km/5 miles northwest of Stockholm), Stockholm Skavsta (www.skavsta.se; 100km/62 miles southwest of Stockholm) and Stockholm Västerås (http://vst.nu; 100km/62 miles west of Stockholm).

The other major cities of Göteborg and Malmö also have international airports, Göteborg Landvetter (www.swedavia.se/landvetter) and Malmö-Sturup (www.swedavia.se/malmo) respectively. In Göteborg, some budget carriers also use Göteborg City airport (www.goteborgcityairport.se).

It is also worth looking at flights into Copenhagen Airport, Denmark (www.cph.dk), and then taking the cheap, frequent train service to Sweden across the Öresund Bridge to Malmö.

From the UK and Ireland

There are direct flights from many airports in the UK and Ireland to Sweden, with a flight time of 2.5 hours.

Scandinavian Airlines (SAS) and British Airways operate direct daily flights from London Heathrow to Stockholm Arlanda and Göteborg

Landvetter. British Airways also flies direct to Stockholm and Göteborg from Manchester.

Several budget carriers also make frequent flights to Sweden. Ryanair operates flights from London Stansted to Stockholm's Vasterås and Skavsta airports. Ryanair also flies from Edinburgh and London to Göteborg; from London Stansted to Malmö; and from Edinburgh, Dublin and London Luton to Copenhagen, Denmark. Norwegian flies direct daily to Stockholm Arlanda from London Stansted, and several times per week from Edinburgh and Manchester. easyJet doesn't have flights directly to Sweden, but it does fly to Copenhagen from Edinburgh, Manchester, Bristol and several London airports.

Airline offices in the UK and Ireland
SAS, tel: 0871-226 7760; www.flysas.com
British Airways, tel: 0844-493 0787 option 2; www.britishairways.com
Ryanair, www.ryanair.com
Norwegian, tel: 0330-828 0854; www.norwegian.com
easyJet, tel: tel: 0330-365 5000; www.easyjet.com

From the US

Services between Stockholm and North America are operated by SAS, in connection with United Airlines and other Star Alliance members, with direct flights from Newark, NJ and Chicago to Stockholm Arlanda. At the time of writing, SAS were also advertising a new direct route from Los Angeles, starting in Spring 2016. There are direct SAS flights to Copenhagen, Denmark from Newark, NJ, Seattle and Washington, DC, with a new route direct from Boston starting in Spring 2016. In summer,

United Airlines have direct flights to Stockholm from Newark, NJ and Delta Airlines have direct flights to Stockholm from New York, JFK.

Airline offices in the US
SAS, tel: 1-800-221 2350; www.flysas.com
United, tel: 1-800-UNITED-1 (1-800-864 8331); www.united.com
Delta, tel: 1-800-241 4141; www.delta.com

By rail

The fastest rail route from the UK to Sweden is via the Eurostar service, through the Channel Tunnel from London St Pancras or Ashford International (Kent). You can head to either Brussels or Hamburg, where you stay overnight, before continuing the onward the following day to Copenhagen and then connecting services to Sweden.

For further information call:
Eurostar, tel: 03432-186 186; www.eurostar.com
International Rail, tel: 0871-231 0791, www.internationalrail.co.uk
Deutsche Bahn, tel: 08718 80 80 66; www.bahn.com
European Rail, tel: 020-7619 1083; www.etrains4u.com

By sea

There are no longer any direct ferry routes from the UK to Scandinavia. However, you can travel as a passenger on the DFDS cargo line between Immingham (near Grimsby) and Göteborg. For details tel: 01469-562 988; http://freight.dfdsseaways.com.

There are many ferry links from other countries in Europe to Sweden, including Denmark, Estonia, Finland,

Germany, Latvia, Lithuania, Norway and Poland.

By coach/bus

Eurolines is the leading operator of scheduled coach services in Europe, including 27 destinations in Sweden. Coaches depart for Sweden up to four times a week from London Victoria Coach Station, with changes in Amsterdam and Copenhagen. Eurolines offers competitive fares with reductions for children and young people as well as senior citizens.

For information call:
Eurolines, tel: 08717-81 81 81 (calls cost); www.nationalexpress.com; www.eurolines.dk

By road

The 16km- (10-mile) Öresund Fixed Link connecting Copenhagen with Malmö has eased the overland journey from the UK to Sweden and made touring the Scandinavian countries by car more practical.

GETTING AROUND

Sweden is an easy country to get around, with good-value trains, buses, boats and ferries, usually subsidised by the state. There is an excellent metro system in Stockholm; and a comprehensive tram service in Göteborg. Congestion is practically unknown on the well-maintained motorway and road network, although elk and reindeer are an unusual (but deadly) hazard that visitors need to be aware of.

A ferry plying the Stockholm archipelago waters.

The country's rail and road network is efficient and extensive, particularly in south and central Sweden. As you travel further north, distances become greater and services scarcer. To save time, many business travellers and tourists take to the air. There are a plethora of regional airports.

Hundreds of boats, vintage steamers and ferries link the country's many lakes, islands and canals.

To and from the airport

All three of Sweden's major international airports – Stockholm (Arlanda), Göteborg (Landvetter) and Malmö (Sturup) – have excellent links to their respective city centres.

From Arlanda, passengers can use the Arlanda Express (www.arlanda express.com) high-speed train which operates four times an hour to Stockholm Central Station in only 20 minutes. There are also frequent bus services from Arlanda's international and domestic terminals to the city Terminal at Klarabergsgatan above Central Station.

In Göteborg and Malmö, coaches operate from the airport to the cities' Central Stations.

A connecting bus meets all Ryanair flights at Västerås and Skavsta airports and goes directly to the Cityterminalen bus terminal in central Stockholm, taking around 1 hour and 20 minutes from both.

Taxis are always available. Get a price for your destination before getting into the taxi (you are not obliged to take the cab at the head of the taxi rank). At Arlanda airport, the larger taxi companies – Taxi 020 (www.

taxi020.se), Taxi Kurir (www.taxikurir.se) or Taxi Stockholm (www.taxistockholm. se) – offer fixed fares for rides into the city centre. These generally work out cheaper than a metered taxi ride, particularly during rush hour. At the time of writing, the cheapest fares were being offered by Airport Cab (tel: 08-25 25 25; www.airportcab.se).

By air

Air travel is part of everyday life in a country as large as Sweden, and all major cities and towns are linked by an efficient network of services operated mainly by SAS, which flies to 13 destinations from Stockholm Arlanda; and Malmö Aviation, which flies to 12 from Stockholm Bromma.

Cheap flights are available on selected domestic services all year, as well as standby flights for under 25s and special fares for senior citizens. But many of the best deals are during the summer peak season in July when few business executives are travelling.

For more information call:
SAS, www.flysas.com
Malmö Aviation, www.malmoaviation.se

By boat or ferry

For a country that boasts about its 96,000 lakes and countless rivers and canals, water transport plays a surprisingly small part in Sweden's public transport system. The main ferry links the Baltic island of Gotland and has up to 18 services per day from Nynäshamn and Oskarshamn, taking around three hours. For more information check with the local tourist office or call Destination Gotland, tel: 0771-22 33 00; www.destinationgotland.se

There are also innumerable commuter services in the Stockholm archipelago operated by the famous white boats of the Waxholm Steamship Company. Visitors can buy a 5-day or 30-day travelcard that gives unlimited travel on the Waxholm boats. For information call: 08-679 58 30, www.waxholmsbolaget.se.

Strömma Kanalbolaget's website also has information on sightseeing and excursions by boat in the canals and through the archipelagos of Stockholm and Göteborg: www.stromma.se.

By rail

Swedish State Railways, or SJ (tel: 0771-75 75 75; www.sj.se) operate an efficient electrified network covering the entire country and beyond, from Copenhagen (Denmark) in the south to Narvik (Norway) in the north. The route from Trelleborg in the south to Riksgränsen in the far north is reckoned to be the longest continuous stretch of electrified rail line in the world.

Swedish trains run at a high frequency, particularly on the main trunk route linking Stockholm with Göteborg, on which there is an hourly service. The high-speed train X2000 travels at up to 200kph (125 mph) and is a good choice if you want to travel long distances; the journey from Göteborg to Stockholm, for example, takes only three hours. There are also night trains between Malmö/ Göteborg/Stockholm and the far north, with beds in private rooms or in a 6-berth couchette.

Rail passes

Swedish state railways offer a wide range of fares for both business and leisure travellers. Conditions and prices may depend on whether you buy your ticket in Sweden or abroad. A number of discount fares are available, including the following passes, which must be purchased outside Sweden:

The **InterRail Sweden Pass** offers European travellers who live outside Sweden unlimited rail travel within Sweden for 3, 4, 6 or 8 days within any one month. Seat reservations must be made in advance. Check Interrail www.interrail.eu for details.

The **Eurail Sweden Pass** has similar terms, but is aimed at non-European travellers. See Eurail www.eurail.com for details.

Stockholm metro.

To get a *förköpsbiljett* (reduced rate ticket) in Sweden, you must book seven days in advance. Students, those aged under 26 and pensioners are also eligible for low-priced Last Minute tickets (students will need to show an ISIC card along with their ticket). For more information, prices and bookings call: 0771-75 75 75 or see www.sj.se.

Scenic train route

One very beautiful journey to take by train is the Inlandsbanan (Inland Railway), which runs for more than 1,300 km (800 miles) along the spine of Sweden from Kristinehamn in the south to Gällivare, north of the Arctic Circle. You can explore stretches of the route with point-to-point tickets, or purchase the Tågluffa (Inlandsbanan Card), which lets you hop on and off the train as much as you like within the 14-day validity period.

More information is available from Inlandsbanan AB, tel: 0771-53 53 53; www.inlandsbanan.se.

By coach/bus

Travelling by bus is usually cheap compared to rail but travelling time is longer. There are weekend-only services on a number of key routes.

An efficient network of express bus services links many major towns and cities, operated mainly by Swebus Express, which covers most of the south and centre of the country, and runs as far north as Umeå. Svenska Buss also runs a few services, from Stockholm south to Växjö and Malmö.

Svenska Buss, tel: 0771-67 67 67. **Swebus Express**, tel: 0771-218 218; www.swebus.se.

Stockholm

The local bus network in Stockholm is claimed to be the world's largest and is run by the Stockholm Transit Authority, SL, which also operates the underground and local mainline rail services, trams and some of the ferry lines in Greater Stockholm. The same tickets are used on all these services, and used according to which of Stockholm's three transport zones you are travelling in – most visitors to the city will travel within Zone A. You are allowed to travel freely within one zone on the bus, train and underground for an hour on the same ticket.

Tickets cannot be bought with cash on the bus, but must be bought in advance at SL travel centres, at the barriers in the underground or at newsagents' kiosks. You can buy a travel card, valid on all of SL's

routes, that you keep topping up with cash (like London's Oyster card); or alternatively, you can buy 24-hour, 72-hour or 7-day travel cards, which allow you to travel freely across Stockholm during those time periods.

Göteborg

Göteborg has a superior tram system, as well as a good network of bus routes.

By underground

Stockholm is justifiably proud of its underground railway, known as T-banan (the "T" stands for "tunnel" – all stations are identified by the "T" sign). The T-banan is spotless, with almost 100 stations covering 108km (67 miles). Work on new extensions is to start in 2016.

The commuter trains *(pendeltåg)* take you very quickly to the suburbs of Stockholm as well as down to Nynäshamn, where you can board the ferry to the island of Gotland.

By road

Main routes

Sweden's roads are uncrowded, with a good network of main highways, and thousands of kilometres of often picturesque byroads. There are tolls on the Öresund and Svinesund bridges, leading to Denmark and Norway respectively. Swedish citizens driving in Stockholm and Göteborg are liable for a congestion tax, but this does not apply to cars registered outside the country. Hire cars should have the tax included, or added on to the final bill – check with your rental company. Most Swedish roads are suitable for motor homes and caravans.

The main highways are part of the international E-road system, and cover around 6,700 km (4,160 miles). The E4 highway runs from the south of Sweden all the way to the Finnish border in the north, and the E20 from the Öresund Bridge north through Göteborg and then across the country to Stockholm. E22 goes from Trelleborg along the east coast to Norrköping, and the E14, E12 and E10 highways take you from the east coast to the northwest.

Rules of the road

Drive on the right
Everyone must wear seat belts.
Headlights are obligatory both day and night.
Traffic gives way to approaching traffic from the right, unless signs indicate

Cycling in the Koster Marine National Park.

to drivers to indicate where the next person is to be picked up.

Fares are steep. There is a minimum charge, and the meter goes on as soon as the taxi arrives at your address. If you are late, the meter starts at the time you ordered the taxi – even a five-minute delay can be costly. The bigger firms accept credit cards.

In Stockholm, some companies have a maximum fare for rides within the centre. This is good value if you want to travel, for example, from the north to the south of town or if there is a traffic jam.

Cycling

Many of Sweden's towns are ideal for exploring by bike – there are around 8,000km of good municipal cycle lanes around the country. Stockholm has a public bike scheme operating between April and October from 6am until 10pm, although you can return bikes up to 1am. You can borrow and drop off bikes at some 140 stands throughout the city by buying a three-day cycle card, available at various hotels, hostels, travel centres and newsagents' kiosks (tel: 077 444 24 24; www.city bikes.se). The card can also be used to borrow bicycles from four stands in Uppsala.

There is a similar bicycle rental system in Göteborg with 60 stations and around 1,000 bikes (tel: 031 227 227; www.goteborgbikes.se).

Cycling holidays are also popular in Sweden; a favourite among cyclists is the Sweden Trail *(Sverigeleden)*, which links a large number of tourist centres and all the ports. Another scenic and popular cycle route is alongside the Göta Kanal.

Bikes can be hired in most places; just enquire at the local tourist office. Costs are per day or per week.

On Foot

Sightseeing

All three of Sweden's largest cities, Stockholm, Malmö and Göteborg, are compact enough to sightsee on foot and are very pedestrian-friendly. Swedish pedestrians are disciplined, and respect red lights even when there is not a car in sight.

Hitchhiking

This is officially discouraged, and in any case finding a lift can be difficult in the holiday season, when every Swedish car seems to be packed with children, baggage and camping gear.

otherwise, and gives way to traffic already on a roundabout.

Drivers are not required to call the police after accidents but must exchange names and addresses. If you do not stop at all you may be liable to a fine or imprisonment. In the event of a breakdown, contact the 'Assistancekåren' service, toll-free 020-912 912. The emergency number 112 should be used only for accidents or injury.

Sweden's drink-drive laws stringent and are strictly enforced, with spot checks and heavy fines imposed. The blood/alcohol limit is 0.02 percent, which means that you can be prosecuted for drinking even the equivalent of a can of beer. It is illegal to use a mobile phone while driving.

Winter tyres are compulsory between 1 December and 31 March.

Drivers must stop at pedestrian crossings when a person is crossing or even indicates an intention to cross.

Swedes often forget to indicate when changing lanes, so be careful.

Parking

Cars can be parked only where there is a sign showing that parking is allowed. Parking is usually free from 6pm to 8am and on Sundays. Make sure you put money in the meter as Swedish traffic wardens are extremely efficient and on duty 24 hours a day. Avoid parking less than 10 metres (30 ft) from a crossing or a corner, or overnight when signs indicate that the street is due to be cleaned (with a no-parking symbol and times, such

as Måndag 0–6, Monday midnight– 6am); both incur a fine.

Speed limits

Motorways 110kph (70 mph)
Dual carriageways 90kph (55 mph)
Unsigned roads 70kph (43 mph)
Built-up areas 50kph (31 mph), or 30kph (19 mph) around school areas.

Over the last few years, municipalities have been given more freedom to set new speed limits to suit local road conditions better, so you may also see speed-limit signs for other speeds besides the ones listed above.

Swedish miles

NB: 1 Swedish mile = 10km
Many Swedes are unaware of the difference between the Swedish mile and the UK/US mile, so double-check distances if given in miles.

Car hire

All the major companies have desks at the airports, major railway stations and in the city centres, although it is usually cheaper to search out car-hire deals online before you travel.
Avis tel: 0770-82 00 82; www.avis.se
Budget tel: 0770-11 00 12; www.budget.se
Europcar tel: 0770-77 00 50; www.europcar.se
Hertz tel: 0771-21 12 12; www.hertz.se

Taxis

Swedish taxis are usually efficient, but rely more on the telephone than being flagged down. In larger cities, a computer system gives instructions

A – Z

A HANDY SUMMARY
OF PRACTICAL INFORMATION

A

Accommodation

Hotels

Swedish hotels are of a uniformly high standard, and can be expensive. However, hotel rates are usually lower at weekends, and come down on weekdays in high summer when the expense-account business travellers are on holiday. Big international hotel chains have made little impact. Accommodation is dominated by Scandinavian chains such as Scandic (tel: 08-517 517 00; www.scandic hotels.se), Sweden Hotels (tel: 0771-77 78 00; www.swedenhotels. se) or Elite Hotels (tel: 0771-78 87 89; www.elite.se). Away from the big cities, there are plenty of privately-owned hotels with the individuality lacking in chains. Many are converted manor houses or mansions in scenic rural settings. You can find some of the best on the Countryside Hotels Sweden website (www.countryside hotels.se). Swedish hotels share the same hotel classification system as many countries in Europe: hotels are assessed for 270 criteria and can be awarded between 1 and 5 stars.

Discounts

All the hotel groups run discount schemes during summer. Stockholm, Göteborg and Malmö also offer special discount packages at weekends year-round and daily in summer. These often include free public transport and free admission to visitor attractions.

Bed and breakfast

The bed and breakfast system is becoming more popular. Look for

the *Rum* sign. It means "room" literally and practically, i.e. it does not include breakfast. Ask at local tourist offices if any *rum* accommodation is available. Prices are very reasonable. There are also around 250 working farms across Sweden offering self-catering and B&B accommodation (www.bopalantgard.org).

Youth hostels

Sweden has 400 youth hostels (*vandrarhem*), ranging from mansion houses and medieval castles to renovated sailing ships, like the 100-year-old *af Chapman* moored in Stockholm harbour, and modern purpose-built hostels. These are mainly in southern and central Sweden. There are also plenty of youth hostels in the Stockholm archipelago. This is an excellent facility for an inexpensive holiday. Most have two- and four-bedded rooms or family rooms. The hostels have self-catering facilities, but meals or snacks are provided in some. Most hostels will charge extra for bed linen, so save money by bringing your own sheets and towels. Always book ahead in the summer. For details, contact the Swedish Tourist Federation (STF; tel: 08-463 21 00; email: info@stfturist.se; www.stfturist.se).

Motels

Sweden has a large number of motels, which are ideal for family touring holidays because they are easy to reach and are usually located on the outskirts of towns or in agreeable countryside areas. Many have family rooms with four beds at very reasonable rates. Check with the local tourist office for names and addresses.

Stuga

If you want to be truly Swedish, you could hire a *stuga*, a rustic cottage or cabin in the countryside. Some are found on campsites or in 'cabin villages', but the finest are in splendidly isolated spots where it's just you, the lake and the sauna. Cooking utensils and blankets are usually provided (but not sheets and towels). The family-oriented cabin villages have extra amenities such as a restaurant or swimming pool, as well as activities like tennis or badminton. Contact the local tourist office for more details, or two companies that offer holiday cottages for rent, Novasol (www.novasol.co.uk) with over 3,000 holiday homes in Sweden, and Eurocottage (www.euro cottage.com) with 2,000.

Typical stuga.

Camping

Camping is very popular among Swedes and there are about 1,000 sites, many in picturesque locations and of a high standard. Most are open from early June to the end of August, but some are also open, with more limited facilities, outside the peak season. Rates are claimed to be among the cheapest in Europe. You can also rent camping chalets and cottages, caravans and motor homes. For fast check-in and check-out plus comprehensive accident insurance for the whole family while staying at the site, as well as discounts on certain ferry crossings and the Öresund Bridge, you should get the Camping Key Europe (www.campingkey.com). You need to apply for it before you leave for Sweden. A great place to search for campsites is www.camping.se.

Admission charges

Admission to museums, galleries and palaces varies enormously, from free to around 120 kronor. Stockholm has phased out its tourist card, and Malmö's is perhaps of limited use; but the Göteborg City Card (www.goteborg. com) gives you free admission to various attractions, as well as free parking and travel on trams, buses and boats.

The arts

The musical scene in Sweden is busiest in the autumn, winter and spring, but there is still a lot going on in summer. In Dalarna, for example, several communities organise music festivals.

Stockholm, Göteborg and Malmö all have high regarded orchestras based in the cities' main Konserthus. Each city also has a dedicated modern opera house, offing varied programmes of opera, ballet and musicals. Most concert halls are closed in the month of July.

Classical music

Stockholm
The main concert hall is the Konserthuset (www.konserthuset. se), the home of the Stockholm Philharmonic Orchestra, whose season runs from September to May or June. The Berwald Concert Hall (http://sverigesradio.se) is the base for Swedish National Radio's musical activities, with regular performances by the Radio Symphony Orchestra. Stockholm's famous Kungliga Operan (Royal Opera House; www.operan.se)

hosts top international performances from mid-August to June.

Göteborg
The Konserthuset hosts the Göteborg Symphony Orchestra (www.gso. se), which is known worldwide and performs every week, often with guest artists, from August to June. The final concert in June is given outdoors. Göteborg's modern Opera House (www.opera.se) offers a varied programme from August to June.

Malmö
The city gained a new conference and concert centre, Malmö Live (malmolive.se), in 2015. It is home to the Malmö Symphony Orchestra, with a large concert hall seating 1,600.

Rock and pop

Stockholm
Globen (www.globearenas.se), the world's largest spherical building, is an arena for sports events and the biggest rock and pop concerts. EDM (electronic dance music) drives the city's music and clubbing scene – see Nightlife below for venues.

Göteborg
Lisebergshallen, the concert hall at Liseberg amusement park (www. liseberg.se), stages the biggest bands. Tribute bands and international singers can also be found at the Stora Teatern (www.storateatern.se), and there are other performances at Trädgår'n (http://tradgarn.se) in the heart of the city.

Malmö
Malmö's arts scene is strongly influenced by the multicultural nature of the city's residents, who have roots in more than 170 countries, and by Malmö University, founded in 1998, which gives the city a young and vibrant feel. Slagthuset (www.slagthus. se), a former slaughterhouse, houses some of the biggest rock, pop, soul and hiphop artists. Many clubs also have live music – see the app for nightlife listings.

Theatre

Sweden has a lively theatrical scene in the major cities, but many theatres close during the peak summer months. Performances are usually in Swedish.

Stockholm
The most prestigious theatre is the Kungliga Dramatiska Teatern (Royal Dramatic Theatre) (Dramaten; www.

dramaten.se) on Nybroplan, which contains eight stages. The most unusual theatre is Drottningholms Slottsteater (www.dtm.se) at Drottningholms Palace, founded by King Gustav III in 1766. More than 30 sets from then are still in use today, and in the summer it stages 17th- and 18th-century operas, attracting music-lovers from around the world.

There is a booth on Norrmalmstorg Square, Biljett Direkt, where you can buy last-minute theatre seats.

Göteborg
The two main theatres are Stadsteatern (www.stadsteatern.goteborg. se) and Folkteatern (www.folkteatern. se), both open from September to May. In summer, the Liseberg amusement park (www.liseberg.se) hosts many famous artists.

Malmö
The Stadsteater (www. malmostadsteater.se) is a modern building with three stages. Plays are in Swedish, but you can often catch an opera or musical performance.

Traditional plays

If you're in the right place during the summer, you may be able to see one of the country's traditional plays. Rune Lindström's play Himlaspelet (The Road to Heaven) has been performed in Leksand in mid-July since 1949. In Visby, on the island of Gotland, the atmospheric Medeltidsveckan (Medieval Week; www.medeltidsveckan.se) in early August features lively parades and theatrical performances.

Films

Virtually all foreign films are shown with their original soundtracks and Swedish subtitles (rather than being dubbed). Local newspapers have full details of programmes and times. In Stockholm, cinemas showing first-run international films include Filmstaden Sergel, Filmstaden Söder, Rigoletto, Biopalatset and Filmstaden Kista.

The film company SF (www.sf.se) has a website where you can book your ticket for any cinema around the country.

B

Budgeting for your trip

Accommodation: A double room with a shared bathroom in a cheap hotel costs around 500 SEK. A double in a moderate hotel is around 1,000 SEK, and a deluxe double anything from 1,500 to 3,000 SEK depending on the establishment.

Drinks: In a restaurant a glass of beer or house wine costs around 60 to 80 SEK.

Food: For a main course, expect to pay 70 to 90 SEK at a budget, 150 to 200 SEK at a moderate and anything from 300 SEK upwards at an expensive restaurant.

Transport: A single pre-paid transport ticket in Stockholm costs 25 SEK. The taxi journey from airport to Stockholm should cost 450 to 550 SEK, depending on the company and whether or not you have pre-booked. There is a set maximum fare of 675 SEK.

C

Children

Sweden is child-friendly and kids are encouraged to question, investigate and explore – this is the land of the headstrong Pippi Longstocking, after all. Swedes are good at devising attractions for the whole family, and there are some excellent amusement parks, water parks, zoos, vintage railways and the like. Museums are usually free to those aged 18 and under, and many have a good hands-on section aimed at children.

Most major hotels in Stockholm, Göteborg and Malmö offer a babysitting service.

Climate

Although the Arctic Circle slices right through the top fifth of the country, the Gulf Stream makes Sweden warmer than it has any right to be at this latitude.

Sweden has four distinct seasons (the Sami people would say eight). However, because it is such a long, thin country, their arrival times and effect vary from south to north.

If you divide the country into thirds, the southern section (including Malmö and Göteborg) has short, mild winters where snow is rare. Summer temperatures range from 15 to 25 ºC (59 to 77 ºF).

The central section (including Stockholm) has more snow, especially in the northwestern mountains bordering Norway where the biggest ski resorts are found. Summer temperatures are a few degrees cooler than in the south.

The northern section has long, cold winters, and year-round snow on the higher peaks. Summer is short, but temperatures usually hover around a pleasant 15 ºC (59 ºF).

When to visit

Summer (mid-June to mid-August): This is the peak time of year to explore Sweden – the Midnight Sun burns for 24 hours in the far north, while White Nights bless the rest of the country. All of Sweden's summery attractions are open, and most Swedes are on holiday and in a jolly mood. Sweden's weather is similar to Britain's in summer – and is just as unpredictable. In a good year some remarkably high temperatures can be recorded in the Arctic regions. The area around Piteå on the Gulf of Bothnia is known as the Northern Riviera because of its warmth.

Winter (November/December to February/March): Visitors can revel in the marvel of deep, crisp snow in the far north in winter, with chilly attractions like dog-sledding and skiing on offer. The aurora borealis (Northern Lights) are visible in winter, with the best time to see them being late March/early April.

What to wear

Sweden's weather is unpredictable, so plan for any eventuality. In summer, even in the Arctic north, you could have hot sunny days that call for shorts and T-shirts, or it could be one of those summers when the sun never appears and sweaters and rainwear are needed. Winters can be very cold, but this is "dry" cold, which is not uncomfortable. Still, you should take a heavy coat and warm headgear as well as sturdy footwear for the slushy streets.

Crime and safety

Sweden is generally a law-abiding country. Crime figures are low, and the streets are by and large safe. Lone female travellers rarely encounter problems.

Topless sunbathing is widely practised in all of Sweden's resorts, and in many places nude bathing is also acceptable.

A far less permissive attitude is, however, taken to drinking. Sweden's drink/driving laws are extremely strict (see page 300), and it is an offence to drink alcohol or to be found drunk in any public places. Drug trafficking is also a very serious offence, and carries heavy prison sentences.

For emergency assistance anywhere within Sweden (police, fire service or ambulance) dial 112. Calls are free from pay phones.

Customs regulations

There are no restrictions on importing/exporting goods for people travelling between Sweden and other EU countries, as long as the goods are for personal use and not resale; guide levels are 3,200 cigarettes, 400 cigarillos, 200 cigars, 1kg tobacco, 10 litres of spirits, 20 litres of fortified wine, 90 litres of wine and 110 litres of beer. Visitors travelling to/from non-EU countries can import duty-free 200 cigarettes/100 cigarillos/50 cigars or 250g tobacco, 1 litre of spirits or 2 litres of dessert wine (maximum 22 percent alcohol by volume), 4 litres of wine plus 16 litres of beer. You must be at least 18 years old to bring in tobacco, and at least 20 to bring in alcohol.

All travellers entering or leaving the EU with €10,000 or more in cash must declare the sum to Customs.

D

Disabled travellers

Access

Sweden has long been a pioneer in accommodating travellers with disabilities. Many hotel rooms and facilities are adapted for the needs both of people with mobility problems and those suffering from allergies. New public buildings are all accessible to people with disabilities, and toilets with the handicap symbol can be found almost everywhere.

In Stockholm, most buses are designed for easy access for people with wheelchairs and pushchairs. Mainline and underground trains have elevators or ramps.

For general information on travel for those with disabilities, and to request a guide to Swedish restaurants with disabled access contact:
DHR De Handikappades Riksförbund
Storforsplan 44, Box 43, 123 21 Farsta
Tel: 08-685 80 00
E-mail: info@dhr.se
www.dhr.se

Cinemas, museums, theatre

A guide to accessible cinemas, museums, theatres and libraries can be ordered from Kultur- och Idrottsförvaltningen in Stockholm. Tel: 08-508 00 000.

Stockholm cultural walking tours for the disabled "Kulturpromenader för personer med funktionshinder" by Elena Siré and Sten Leijonhufvud is a guide to Stockholm written in Swedish and English.
Order from www.elenasire.se
Tel: 08-85 73 85

E

Eating out

What to eat

Sweden, once known as the land of *husmanskost* (homely fare), is enjoying a culinary renaissance. Swedish chefs are in love with New Nordic cuisine, popularised by the world-famous Noma restaurant in Copenhagen, which focuses on simply-prepared food made from fresh, local organic produce and foraged ingredients.

There's a new feeling of joy and experimentation when it comes to the country's natural resources, whether that's reindeer, venison or elk; fish from the rivers, lakes and sea; or mushrooms and berries gathered in the forests and on the tundra of Sweden's far north, where the local Sami culture has a strong influence on the cuisine.

You will still find traditional dishes like *köttbullar* (meatballs served with tangy lingonberry sauce), *pytt i panna* (a fry-up of potatoes, onions, meat and sausage), *ärtsoppa* (yellow-pea and pork soup) and *Janssons frestelse* (a creamy baked dish of shredded potatoes, herring and onion). However, in New Nordic style, these are often reinvented with a new twist.

Sill (pickled herring) is an acquired taste but, served with new potatoes, is an essential part of Midsummer. Salmon is a common ingredient in Swedish cuisine, with less of a luxury connotation than in some other countries. *Gravad lax* (marinated salmon) and *rökt lax* (smoked salmon) are common components of the *smörgåsbord*.

Sweden is a nation of meat- and fish-lovers, but you can find vegetarian restaurants in the three big cities, and most eateries have one veggie dish on the menu.

Where to eat

Sweden's restaurant scene has exploded over the last 10 years. Although eating out can be pretty expensive, food is varied, high quality, and often sourced from local organic producers. Stockholm, Göteborg and Malmö boast their own superstar chefs with glittering Michelin-starred eateries.

Göteborg and the coast around it are a paradise for those who enjoy fish and seafood; for example, Smögen is known for shrimp, and Grebbestad for oysters. Malmö's restaurants, concentrated around Lilla Torg and Västra Hamnen, benefit from the city's location in Skåne, 'Sweden's granary'; and they are also strongly influenced by trends from nearby Copenhagen. Stockholm borrows the best from the rest of the country and abroad, making it a truly exciting city for gastronomic experiences.

A good place to seek out Sweden's best restaurants is the White Guide (www.whiteguide-sweden.com), which reviews over 600 restaurants annually across the country.

Travellers on a tight budget should look for the *dagens rätt* (dish of the day), which usually includes a main course, bread, salad and soft drink for a set price. It's also worth investigating the market halls in Malmö, Göteborg and Stockholm (eg Östermalmshallen and Hötorgshallen), where you can pick up delicious deli nibbles to make your own picnic.

Fast food outlets are everywhere, including the ubiquitous *korvkiosk* selling grilled chicken, sausages, hamburgers and *tunnbrödsrulle* (a parcel of mashed potato, sausage and ketchup wrapped in soft bread). Some also serve *strömming* (fried herring) and mashed potato.

See the app for restaurant listings.

When to eat

Swedes generally eat fairly early. Restaurants start serving lunch at about 11am and some small hotels, particularly in country areas, serve the evening meal at around 6pm and stop serving by 10pm.

Electricity

The normal electric current in Sweden is 220 volts AC 50 Hz.

Sweden uses the Europlug (Type C & F) for electricity, with two round prongs. Travellers should bring adapters for electrical appliances if the plug system is different in their country.

For laptops, check the label near the power cord to make sure it can cope with 100-240v and 50-60 Hz. Some laptops work on 110 volts only – you will need a transformer if yours is of this type.

Embassies and consulates

Swedish embassies

Australia
5 Turrana Street, Yarralumla, A.C.T. 2600, Canberra
Tel: 02-627 027 00
Email: ambassaden.canberra@gov.se
www.swedenabroad.com

Canada
377 Dalhousie Street, Suite 305
Ottawa ON K1N 9N8
Tel: 613-241 2277
Email: sweden.ottawa@gov.se
www.swedenabroad.com

UK
11 Montagu Place, London W1H 2AL
Tel: 020-791 764 00
Email: ambassaden.london@gov.se
www.swedenabroad.com

US
2900 K Street NW, Washington DC 20007
Tel: 202-467 2600
Email: ambassaden.washington@gov.se
www.swedenabroad.com

What to drink

The country's array of cosy cafés deserves its own special mention. Going for a fika is a very Swedish activity, involving curling up in a charming cafe with a steaming cup of coffee, a cinnamon bun and a couple of good friends to gossip the morning away. Gourmet coffee is a rising trend, with some cafes splashing out on their own roasting equipment.

Alcohol prices are prohibitively high. Outside restaurants, you can only buy wine, spirits and export beer through branches of the State-controlled monopoly Systembolaget. You must be 20 to buy alcohol from Systembolaget, and 18 from bars and restaurants.

Swedes drink more beer than wine. Commercial products tend to be bland lager-style beers, but craft breweries are increasingly popular. Sweden also has some excellent indigenous schnapps, usually drunk with herring. See page 139 for more information.

Tap water is safe to drink all over the country.

Embassies and consulates in Stockholm

Australia
Klarabergsviadukten 63, 8th Floor
Tel: 08-613 29 00
E-mail: reception@austemb.se
www.sweden.embassy.gov.au

Canada
Klarabergsgatan 23, 6th Floor
Tel: 08-453 30 00
Email: stkhm@international.gc.ca
www.canadainternational.gc.ca

Ireland
Hovslagargatan 5
Tel: 08-545 040 40
www.dfa.ie/irish-embassy/sweden

South Africa
Fleminggatan 20, 4th floor
Tel: 08-24 39 50
Email: embassy.stockholm@dirco.gov.za
www.dirco.gov.za/sweden

UK
Skarpögatan 6–8
Tel: 08-671 30 00
Email: Stockholm@fco.gov.uk
www.britishembassy.se

US
Dag Hammarskjölds Väg 31
Tel: 08-783 53 00
www.usemb.se
Note that there is no longer a New Zealand embassy in Stockholm. The closest one is in Brussels, Belgium.

Emergencies

Police, fire, ambulance: 112 (calls are free)

Etiquette

Swedes are meticulously polite to foreigners. But there are a few social traps for the unwary, such as the rituals involved in eating and drinking (see page 140). Punctuality is vital – always call and apologise if you are going to be late. It's common to take your shoes off when entering someone's home – if you're unsure, ask your host.

To get rid of queues, many shops and offices have a ticket machine hidden somewhere on the premises, theoretically by the door. To be served, take a ticket and then wait for your number to be shown on the display.

F

Festivals

Jan
Kiruna Snow Festival
www.snofestivalen.com

International artists make their way to Kiruna to express themselves in the medium of ice blocks, carved with chainsaws.

Feb
Göteborg Film Festival
Tel: 031-339 30 00; e-mail: goteborg@filmfestival.org; www.giff.se
This is the biggest film festival in the country, bringing films from all over the world to the west coast. The festival began in 1979 and has grown to treat over 30,000 visitors a year to a visual spectacle.

Mar
Vasaloppet
www.vasaloppet.se
The exalted cross-country ski race, held between Sälen and Mora, draws around 90,000 skiers and is watched by two million television viewers in Sweden alone.

Apr
Walpurgis Night
Across Sweden, parades, singing and bonfires mark the beginning of spring (30 April)

Jun
Midsummer's Eve
Sweden's biggest celebration is a joyful honouring of the longest day of the year, with more bonfires, plus maypoles, drinking and dancing.

Jul
Musik vid Siljan (Music by Lake Siljan)
www.musikvidsiljan.se
Held in the first week of July, this is a series of indoor and outdoor musical events ranging from organ concerts to jazz, held in Dalarna.
Bråvalla, Norrköping
www.bravallafestival.se
Sweden's biggest music festival is a three-day event with crowds of around 50,000, with past acts including Robbie Williams, Muse, Avicii, Deadmau5 and Kings of Leon.

Aug
Malmö Festival
Tel: 040-34 10 00; e-mail: info@festival.malmo.se; www.malmofestivalen.se.
The biggest festival in southern Sweden with art exhibitions, music, food and numerous other intercultural events. Mid-August.
Medeltidsveckan, Gotland
Tel: 0498-29 10 70; www.medeltidsveckan.se.
During Medieval Week, the town of Visby turns back the calendar

to 1361, when it was still a mighty Hanseatic stronghold. Mid-August.
Way Out West, Göteborg
E-mail: info@wayoutwestfestival.se; www.wayoutwest.se.
A three-day music festival, which draws crowds of around 20,000 to Göteborg. Headliners in 2015 included Florence and the Machine, Emmylou Harris and Patti Smith.

Oct
Stockholm Jazz Festival
E-mail: festival@fasching.se; www.stockholmjazz.se.
Great artists, both local and international, play at the city's best venues during this 10-day jazz extravaganza. Usually in mid-October.

Nov
Stockholm Film Festival
Usually mid-November. Tel: 08-677 50 00; e-mail: info@stockholmfilmfestival.se; www.stockholmfilmfestival.se.
Popular event with modern and innovative films from around the world.

G

Gay and lesbian travellers

Sweden is renowned for its liberal attitudes to sex, and its age of consent is 15 for heterosexuals and gays. Same-sex marriages have been legal in Sweden since 2009. But there is nevertheless little open affection between gay couples, and the gay scene in Stockholm is less apparent than in other capitals, although there are a couple of men-only, women-only and mixed gay clubs.

QX is an LGBT magazine that offers the most up-to-date information about clubs, restaurants, bars and shops in Stockholm, Göteborg, Malmö and Copenhagen (www.qx.se).

H

Health and medical care

Standards of hygiene in Sweden are among the highest in the world. No inoculations are needed, and tap water is safe to drink. Food poisoning or related problems are unlikely. However, in the far north of Sweden in high summer, precautions need to be taken against the vicious mosquitoes. Even the strongest insect repellents are not entirely successful.

People who do a lot of hiking and camping in southern Sweden and the northern coastal regions should check themselves carefully at the end of the day for ticks, which can carry Lyme disease or, rarely, tick-borne encephalitis (TBE). Remove any attached ticks carefully use tweezers or a tick plucker, and wash the bite with soap and water. If you develop a rash or fever after being bitten, seek medical attention.

Healthcare and insurance

Sweden has reciprocal agreements with the UK and other countries, under which visitors are entitled to the same medical treatment as Swedes. To qualify, EU nationals must obtain a European Health Insurance Card (EHIC; available in the UK free online at www.ehic.org. uk or by phoning 0300 330 1350), which allows visitors to pay the same fees as Swedes. Without this card you might have to foot the bill for the real cost of the treatment. For hospital visits, inpatient care is usually free, with just a small daily rate payable.

Visitors from outside the EU pay higher consultation fees, although these are modest compared with those charged in North America. Non-EU visitors also pay in full for hospital treatment, so it is important to take out adequate medical insurance coverage before your visit so that you can reclaim the money on your return.

Pharmacies and hospitals

Hospitals

Sweden does not have a GP system, so the place to go for any type of treatment is the nearest hospital. Casualty (Akutmottagning) deals with serious problems, but Vårdcentral or Husläkarmottagning out-patient clinics are a better option as you will normally be seen within an hour, compared with hours of waiting in Casualty. Take your passport and EHIC card with you.

There is a 24h non-emergency health helpline: tel: 1177.

Pharmacies

Chemists' shops (apotek) should be your first port of call for minor ailments. Generally, they are open from Monday to Friday 9am–6pm, although some also open on Saturdays 9.30am–1pm. The larger cities all have a 24-hour pharmacy. There is also one all-night pharmacy in Stockholm (C W Scheele, Klarabergsgatan 64, tel: 0771-450450).

Internet

Most airports, train stations, public libraries and hotels have free WiFi or computers with internet access. There are also cafes with WiFi or internet terminals in most cities. Stockholm is one of the most connected cities in the world, and was the first city in the world to introduce publicly available 4G.

M

Media

Newspapers and magazines

English-language newspapers are widely available at kiosks in larger cities, usually on the day of publication. Kulturhuset (the cultural centre) in Stockholm at Sergels Torg has a good selection of English newspapers and magazines that can be read for free, as does the City Library in Göteborg on the main square, Götaplatsen. For a wide selection of English-language magazines try a Pressbyrån store (there are 60 in Stockholm, including a one in the central station; www.pressbyran.se).

Books and maps

English-language books are widely available. In Stockholm, excellent bookshops include:

Akademibokhandeln, Mäster Samuelsgaten 32, on the corner of Regeringsgatan. www.akademibokhandeln.se

Hedengrens Bokhandel, Stureplan 4 www.hedengrens.se

The department store NK, Hamngatan 18-20, www.nk.se, also has a book department on the third floor.

There is a specialist map shop, Kartbutiken, at Mäster Samuelsgatan 54, www.kartbutiken.se.

Radio

Radio Sweden has programmes in English with news and information about Sweden on medium wave 1179 KHz (254m), and also in the Stockholm area on FM 89.6 MHz. Broadcast schedules are available at most hotels in Stockholm, check the Radio Sweden website: www.sr.se/rs.

BBC World Service programmes are also available on channel 89.6 FM.

Television

All foreign programs on Swedish TV are shown in the original language with Swedish subtitles. Sweden's state-run STV1 and STV2, and the commercial TV4, sometimes show English-language films, chat shows, sport, movies and soap operas. Plus there are many satellite/cable channels, featuring CNN, BBC and MTV, broadcast in English with subtitles.

Money

Leading credit cards (although some restrictions may apply to American Express) are accepted by most hotels, restaurants and shops throughout the country. You can draw cash out using a Visa, MasterCard, Maestro or Cirrus card in any "Bankomat" or "Uttagsautomat" ATMs.

Travellers' cheques can be exchanged without difficulty at banks all over Sweden. A foreign exchange service is also provided by post offices with the "PK Exchange" sign. Forex and X-Change, bureaux de change with branches in most major towns and airports, usually have better exchange rates than the banks and post offices and don't charge any commission.

Currency

The Swedish krona (plural kronor) is divided into 100 öre.

Sweden's banknotes and coins were all changing in 2015 and 2016. New 20-, 50-, 200- and 1000-krona banknotes became legal tender in October 2015. New 100-krona and 500-krona banknotes will become legal tender in October 2016, as will the new 1-, 2- and 5-öre coins.

The old 20-, 50- and 1000-krona banknotes will no longer be valid after 30 June 2016. The old 100- and 500-krona banknotes, and the old 1-, 2- and 5-krona coins will no longer be valid after 30 June 2017.

Tipping

In hotels and restaurants a service charge is included in the bill and a further tip is not expected, although it's usual to round up the bill to the nearest 10 or 20 SEK for an evening meal.

Taxi drivers are usually tipped. Cloakrooms at restaurants and clubs charge about 15–20 SEK.

Tipping for special services provided by hotel staff is fine but not expected.

N

Nightlife

As in other countries, there is an active nightlife in the larger cities but nothing particularly hectic in the smaller communities. Many of the hotels listed have bars, nightclubs and sometimes even live dance music. The university cities like Uppsala, Lund, Linköping and Umeå have quite a busy nightlife, at least for the students.

Swedes often combine dining and drinking on a night out. Many venues merge a restaurant with a bar, which might stay open until 1am at the weekend.

Skiing resorts like Åre and Sälen are also good for nightlife (mainly for younger people) during the season, from December to April. Après-ski is often very lively with bands playing covers of well-known tunes to packed crowds.

Out in the countryside and in smaller towns *dansband* music is very popular – Swedish-style country music to which people dance foxtrot and a kind of jive. If you like dancing this could be a fun thing to try and a chance to meet the locals. Dancing may not begin until midnight.

Outside the cities, Swedes tend not to drink during the week, but to save it for the weekend. Given the high cost of drinking in Sweden, a night out on the town can be expensive. Many younger Swedes visit the state-owned liquor store *Systembolaget* (open Monday to Friday 9 or 10am–6pm, Saturday 10am–2 or 3pm) to buy alcohol and 'pre-party' at home before hitting the town. The minimum age for buying alcohol is 20; take proof of your age if you are in your early 20s.

The best value is probably at one of the jazz clubs or piano bars, which offer a quieter and more relaxing environment for a late-night drink.

Opening hours

Nightclubs usually close around 3am (sometimes 5am in Stockholm). Unfortunately, numerous nightclubs have long queues outside after 9 or 10pm, even if it's not full inside. This is an irritating way of showing that the club is popular. Avoid the queue by getting there early or book a table and have dinner there, which also means that you avoid paying the entrance fee to the nightclub.

Age limits

If you're in your early 20s, you may not be able to get into some clubs. Some have remarkably high minimum age limits: the more upmarket clubs impose a minimum age of up to 26 for men and 24 for women.

Dress

Nightlife in Sweden tends to be a dressy affair. Look smart, or you may be refused admission to the more upmarket bars and clubs.

See the app for details and nightlife listings.

O

Opening hours

Shops on the whole open 9.30am–6pm on weekdays and until between 1 and 4pm on Saturdays. In larger cities many shops are open on Sundays as well, usually noon–4pm. Shops generally close early the day before a public holiday.

Department stores may remain open until 8pm or 9pm and possibly also on Sundays.

Banks Monday–Friday 9.30am–3pm (6pm in some larger cities), but closed on Saturdays. There are various currency exchange bureaux at Stockholm Arlanda airport – the one with the longest opening hours is SEB Exchange in the Terminal 5 arrival hall, open daily 5am–11pm.

P

Postal services

Post offices have been phased out and franchise postal services are now run by supermarkets, grocery stores and petrol stations. Stamps *(frimärken)* are also on sale at Pressbyrån newsstands, bookstalls and stationers' shops. Letters and postcards of up to 20 grams cost SEK 6 within Sweden and SEK 12 internationally. Mailboxes are blue for local letters and yellow for all other destinations. For more information, visit www.posten.se.

Public holidays

Sweden has several official holidays:
1 January New Year's Day
6 January Epiphany
March/April Good Friday and Easter Monday

IKEA

After exhorting people the world over to "chuck out the chintz", the Swedish behemoth IKEA will probably need no introduction to readers. The company's creative headquarters is based in Älmhult, in Småland – fans can stay in town at the Värdsjuset IKEA hotel (www.vardshuset.nu). IKEA stores are found across Sweden, usually on the outskirts of towns.

1 May Labour Day
May Ascension (usually second part of the month); Pentecost (10 days after Ascension)
6 June National Day
June Midsummer's Eve (around the 24th)
November All Saints' Day (usually at start of the month)
25 and 26 December Christmas
31 December New Year's Eve
Note: If the holiday is one day away from the weekend, offices tend to be closed the day between (known as *klämdag* or "squeeze day").

The whole of July seems to be a holiday, because this is the time when most office employees are on summer leave. It is virtually impossible to transact any business during this month.

R

Religious services

The Swedish State Church is in the Lutheran tradition. Stockholm has the widest range of places of worship, including a Greek Orthodox church, several synagogues and three mosques. Protestant services in English are usually held once a week in major cities.

S

Shopping

Sweden is famous the world over for its elegant design, and you will find plenty of good buys in glassware, stainless steel, silver, pottery, ceramics, textiles and leather goods. Department stores such as NK and Åhléns are noted for their high-quality, inexpensive kitchenware. Shopping in Sweden is rarely cheap, but it is always good value. For a bargain, the words to look out for are rea, which means sale, and extrapris, which does not mean extra, but special low price.

In Stockholm, the most exclusive shops are located in Östermalm, while Södermalm is the place for cool, creative clothes and design. Gamla Stan has some interesting little shops, but look around before parting with your money – Stockholm's most touristy area tends towards inflated prices.

Glass

The best bargains are found in "Glass Country" – Småland, in the southeast – where there are nine major glassworks and several smaller ones. The major glassworks like Orrefors (www.orrefors.se), Kosta-Boda (www.kostaboda.com) and Skruf (www.skrufsglasbruk.se) have shops adjoining their factories where you can buy seconds very cheaply. If you're only visiting Stockholm, you can buy flawless firsts at the city's big department stores.

Fashion

For cheap clothing, try Hennes & Mauritz (H&M), Lindex, JC and KappAhl. The best shopping area is probably Borås, near Göteborg, and the centre of the Tygriket (Weavers' Country). Knalleland (www.knalleland. se) is a large shopping centre in Borås where you can get bargains from the leading direct-mail companies.

Sami handicrafts (duodji)

Usually functional items made from natural materials, such as cups carved from reindeer horn or woven birch bags, Sami handicrafts make unusual presents. You can buy Sami arts and crafts in northern Sweden, for example, in the Carl Wennberg shop at Bergmästaregatan 2, Kiruna.

The centre of the fur business is Tranås in the province of Småland, where you can usually find bargains.

Markets

Stockholm has markets at Hötorget, Östermalmstorg and Medborgarplatsen, which are worth a visit, while Göteborg has its "Fish Church", a thriving fish market built in an ecclesiastical style.

Göteborg also has a fascinating market hall (Saluhallen) selling mainly food. Malmö's brand-new Saluhallen, with restaurants, cafés and delis, was due to open on Södra Neptunigatan in summer 2016.

Stockholm's suburbs contain what is claimed to be northern

Europe's largest flea market (www. loppmarknaden.se) at Vårberg, 30 minutes on the underground from the city centre. It's open daily, but Saturday and Sunday are the best days to go.

See the app for details and listings.

Local crafts

All over Sweden you can see craftspeople at work and buy their work at low prices. In the countryside, look out for Hemslöjd handicraft centres, where you can buy locally produced items. Women's and children's clothes are especially good buys, as well as furs and needlework. See the app for details and listings.

Design

If you're looking for shops selling contemporary Swedish (and international) design, you'll be spoiled for choice in Stockholm. See the app for details and listings.

Sport

Sweden is a health-conscious and outdoorsy nation, offering copious sports facilities nationwide and all kinds of opportunities to get out and enjoy the countryside. Visitors who wish to centre their holiday around sport can order the brochures Outdoor Activities, Summer Activities and Winter Activities from VisitSweden (www. visitsweden.com). See the app for details and listings.

T

Tax

Tax-Free shopping

Value Added Tax (called Moms) is included in the sales price of goods. If you live outside the EU, you are entitled to claim a tax refund of up to 19 percent on purchases of over 200 euros in shops displaying the Tax Free Shopping sign. When paying for your purchases, ask the shop staff for a Tax Free Form and to seal your bag as proof you haven't used the item. The refund is made at the airport on departure, at Stockholm Arlanda Terminal 5, Bromma, Gothenburg Landvetter, Haparanda or Malmö. For further details, see www.globalblue.com.

Telephones

Mobile phones are widely used across Sweden, although you can still find payphones on the street, at petrol stations and post offices. Most payphones no longer take coins – they operate only with credit cards (signposted CCC) or a telephone card (telia telefonkort). Telephone cards are widely available in Pressbyrån shops, kiosks, bookstalls, grocery stores and stationers' shops. As elsewhere, it is expensive to phone from hotel rooms. The telephone directory enquiry service is also expensive.

To call abroad, dial 00 followed by the country code (44 for the UK, 1 for the US and Canada, 353 for Ireland, 61 for Australia and 64 for New Zealand), then dial the number, omitting any initial 0.

Swedish mobile phones operate on the 900/1800 MHz GSM network – most European phones are compatible, although your phone must be unlocked in order to link up with the network. US phones work on a slightly different frequency, so US visitors should check with their phone company first regarding usability. The cheapest way to use your own mobile phone is to buy a Swedish SIM card from a newsagent or telephone operator; for example, Telia offer the IHaveLanded (www.ihavelanded. com) SIM with 12 months of data (0.5GB per month) and SEK 50 credit for 15 euros. Local mobile network operators include Tele2 (www.tele2. se), Telenor (www.telenor.se) and Telia (www.telia.se).

To make a call from your mobile phone, dial the area code (e.g. 08 for Stockholm) followed by the number. Don't rely on your mobile phones for emergencies – in certain isolated parts of Sweden, there might not be any coverage.

Useful numbers

Swedish directory enquiries 118 118
International directory enquiries 118 119
International dialling code +46

Time zone

Sweden conforms to Central European Time, which is one hour ahead of Greenwich Mean Time (GMT) and six hours ahead of Eastern Standard Time (EST). In summer Sweden moves to daylight saving time from the last weekend in March to the last weekend in October, which means that it is one

TRANSPORT

A – Z

LANGUAGE

hour ahead of Central European Time.

Tourist information

Local offices

Sweden has a country-wide network of tourist information offices, or Turistbyrå, in more than 300 cities and towns, which can be identified by the international "i" sign. They have multilingual staff, and can supply information about local sightseeing and sporting activities. Some are open during the summer only. About half of the tourist information offices sport a blue-and-yellow (rather than a green) "i" sign: these provide a more comprehensive service, with local *and* national information, and hotel booking systems (*rumsförmedling* or *hotellcentral*) that cover the whole country.

The main tourist offices are as follows:

Stockholm
Stockholm Visitor Center
Sergels Torg 5
Tel: 08-508 285 08
E-mail: touristinfo@stockholm.se
www.visitstockholm.com
This is the country's busiest tourist office. Run by the Stockholm Visitors Board (SVB), it can help you book sightseeing tours and tickets to events, and offers free WiFi.

Göteborg
Göteborgs Turistbyrå
Mässans gata 8
Box 29 401 20 Göteborg
Tel: 031-368 40 00
www.goteborg.com

Gotland
Donnerska huset, Donners plats 1, Visby
Tel: 0498-20 17 00
E-mail: info@gotland.info
www.gotland.com

Lapland
Swedish Lapland Tourism
Kyrkogatan 13
S-972 32 Luleå
Tel: 0980-188 80
E-mail: info@swedishlapland.com
www.swedishlaplandtourism.com

Skåne
Dockplatsen 26, Malmö
Tel: 046-75 30 01
E-mail: tourism@skane.com
http://visitskane.com

Småland
Södra Strandgatan 13, Jönköping, SE 55320
Tel: 0771-211 300
E-mail: turist@destinationjonkoping.se
www.visitsmaland.com

Tourist offices

UK & Ireland
VisitSweden
(no offices in the UK)
Voltvägen 32
SE- 831 48 Östersund
Tel: UK: 0207 108 6168
Tel: Ireland: 0124 75440
E-mail: info@visitsweden.com
www.visitsweden.com

USA & Canada
VisitSweden
P.O. Box 4649, Grand Central Station
New York, NY 10163-4649
Phone: +1 212-885 9700
Fax: +1 212-885 9710
E-mail: usa@visitsweden.com
www.visitsweden.com

Tour operators and travel agents

Brochures listing tour operators who offer holidays in Sweden are available to order or to download from www.visitsweden.com.

A selection of tour operators with interests in Sweden includes:

UK

Best Served Scandinavia
Tel: 020 7838 5956
E-mail: sales@best-served.co.uk
www.best-served.co.uk
Large range of packages, including city breaks, Göta Kanal cruises, cycling holidays and winter safaris.

Discover the World
Arctic House, 8 Bolters Lane, Banstead, Surrey SM7 2AR
Tel: 01737 214 250
E-mail: travel@discover-the-world.co.uk
www.discover-the-world.co.uk
Specialist in activity holidays, plus self-drive summer holidays and winter breaks to Lapland.

Nordic Experience
39 Crouch Street, Colchester, Essex CO3 3EN
Tel: 01206 708 888
www.nordicexperience.co.uk
Offers Stockholm breaks, Ice Hotel packages, husky mushing and winter holidays.

Simply Sweden
The Poplars, Bridge Street, Brigg, Lincolnshire DN20 8NQ
Tel: 01427 700115
E-mail: info@simplysweden.co.uk
www.simplysweden.co.uk
Offers tailor-made Swedish holidays including Ice Hotel stays, city breaks, log cabins, rafting etc.

US & Canada

There are numerous tour operators in the US, a list of which can be obtained from VisitSweden (see www.

Cruise to Finland

A popular outing – among young and old as well as conference parties – is to take the boat from Stockholm to Finland for a day's visit to Helsinki or Åbo (Turku). This takes about 40 hours and includes two nights on the boat and one day in Helsinki or Åbo. The boats have several dance floors, bars and a restaurant to entertain the captive audience. Contact Tallink Silja Line (tel: 08-440 5990; www.tallinksilja.com) or Viking Line (tel: 08-452 40 00; www.vikingline.se) for information.

visitsweden.com). The following is just a short selection:

Five Stars of Scandinavia
Tel: 1-800 722 41 26
http://5stars-scandinavia.com

Nelson's Scandinavia
Tel: 1-800 542 16 89
www.nelsonsscandinavia.com

Nordic Saga Tours
Tel: 1-800 848 64 49
www.nordicsaga.com

Visas and passports

A valid passport entitles EU and North American visitors to stay for a maximum of 90 days, and visas are not normally required. Sweden is part of the Schengen Area, and citizens of other Schengen countries should be allowed to enter without passports and if you arrive from another Scandinavian country, passports aren't usually checked at all. However, in January 2016 Sweden introduced identity checks for travellers from Denmark in an attempt to reduce the number of migrants arriving in the country. If you intend to stay longer than 90 days, you will need to obtain a resident's permit, which you can do once you are in Sweden. See www.migrationsverket.se for further information.

Weights and measures

Sweden uses the metric system.
Beware of the Swedish word mil, which is sometimes translated erroneously as "mile" – it actually means 10km (6.2 miles).

LANGUAGE

UNDERSTANDING THE LANGUAGE

THE ALPHABET

The Swedish alphabet has 29 letters; the additional three are å, ä and ö and come after the letter Z. To find Mr Åkerblad in the phone book, therefore, look at the end of the listings. (Note that the index in this guide uses the English A to Z alphabet.)

USEFUL WORDS AND PHRASES

toilet Toalett
gentlemen Herrar
ladies Damer
vacant Ledig
engaged Upptagen
no smoking Rökning förbjuden

GREETINGS

Yes Ja
No Nej
Hello Hej
Goodbye Hejdå
Thank you Tack
Please Tack/Var så god
Do you speak English? talar du engelska?
I only speak English jag talar bara engelska
Good morning God morgon
Good afternoon God eftermiddag
Good evening God kväll
Today Idag
Tomorrow I morgon
Yesterday I går
How do you do Goddag
What time is it? Hur mycket är klockan?
It is (the time is) Den är (klockan är)
Could I have your name please? Hur var namnet?

My name is Jag heter
Can I help you? Kan jag hjälpa till?
I do not understand Jag förstår inte
I do not know Jag vet inte

EATING AND DRINKING

breakfast Frukost
lunch Lunch
dinner Middag
eat Äta
drink Dricka
cheers Skål!
off-licence Systembolaget
Can I order please? Får jag beställa?
Could I have the bill please? Kan jag få notan?

MENU DECODER

starters Förrätter
main courses Huvudrätter, varmrätter
desserts Desserter
drink Dryck
blomkål **cauliflower**
blåmusslor **blue mussels**
bläckfisk **octopus**
bröd **bread**
bär **berries**
fisk- och skaldjursgryta **fish and seafood stew**
fläsk **pork**
grillad **grilled**
grädde **cream**
grönsaker **vegetables**
helstekt **roast**
hjortron **cloudberry**
hummer **lobster**
jordgubbar **strawberries**
kalkon **turkey**
kalv **veal**
kyckling **chicken**

kött **meat**
köttbullar **meatballs**
lax **salmon**
lök **onion**
mjölk **milk**
morötter **carrots**
ost **cheese**
ostron **oysters**
oxfilé **beef tenderloin**
potatis **potato**
purjolök **leek**
ris **rice**
rostbiff **roast beef**
rotfrukter **root vegetables**
räkor **prawns**
rökt **smoked**
smör **butter**
smörgås **sandwich**
soppa **soup**
stekt **fried**
svamp **mushroom**
tonfisk **tuna**
tårta **cake**
vitlök **garlic**
ägg **egg**
ärtor **peas**
ärtsoppa **pea soup**
öl **beer**

ACCOMMODATION

to rent Att hyra
room to rent Rum att hyra
chalet Stuga
sauna Bastu
launderette Tvättomat
dry cleaning Kemtvätt
dirty Smutsigt
clean Ren

ON THE ROAD

aircraft Flygplan
bus/coach Buss
car Bil

parking *Parkering, Garage*
train *Tåg*
How do I get to? *Hur kommer jag till?*
Where is ...? *Var finns...?*
Right *Höger*
To the right *Till höger*
Left *Vänster*
To the left *Till vänster*
Straight on *Rakt fram*

SHOPPING

entrance *Ingång*
exit *Utgång*
no entry *Ingen ingång*
open *Öppen/öppet*
closed *Stängt*
to buy *Att köpa*
department store *Varuhus*
food *Mat*
free *Ledigt*
grocery store (in countryside) *Lanthandel*
handicraft *Hemslöjd*
money *pengar*
shop *Affär*
clothes *Kläder*
overcoat *Kappa, Överrock*
jacket *Jacka*
suit *Kostym*
shoes *Skor*
skirt *Kjol*
jersey *Tröja, jumper*
How much is this? *Vad kostar det?*
It costs *Det kostar*
Do you have English newspapers? *Har du engelska tidningar?*

HEALTH & EMERGENCIES

chemist/pharmacy *Apotek*
Accident & emergency clinic *Akutmottagning/Vårdcentral*
hospital *Sjukhus*
doctor *Doktor*
police station *Polisstation*

DAYS OF THE WEEK

Monday *måndag*
Tuesday *tisdag*
Wednesday *onsdag*
Thursday *torsdag*
Friday *fredag*
Saturday *lördag*
Sunday *sön*

MONTHS OF THE YEAR

January *januari*
February *februari*
March *mars*
April *april*
May *maj*
June *juni*
July *juli*
August *augusti*
September *september*
October *oktober*
November *november*
December *december*
month *månad*
year *år*

NUMBERS

1 *en/et*
2 *två*
3 *tre*
4 *fyra*
5 *fem*
6 *sex*
7 *sju*
8 *åtta*
9 *nio*
10 *tio*
11 *elva*
12 *tolv*
13 *tretton*
14 *fjorton*
15 *femton*
16 *sexton*
17 *sjutton*
18 *aderton*
19 *nitton*
20 *tjugo*
21 *tjugoen*
22 *tjugotvå*
30 *trettio*
40 *fyrtio*
50 *femtio*
60 *sextio*
70 *sjuttio*
80 *åttio*
90 *nittio*
100 *hundra*
200 *tvåhundra*
1,000 *tusen*

FURTHER READING

Good books on Sweden are few and far between, but the best source of information on publications in English is the Swedish Institute, which itself publishes a good range of guides, available through its website.
The Swedish Institute (Svenska Institutet)
Slottsbacken 10, 103 91 Stockholm
Tel: 08-453 78 00
www.si.se (also search under Sweden bookshop; www.swedenbookshop.com)

HISTORY

A History of the Swedish People by Vilhelm Monerg Vols I & II. Iconoclastic view of Sweden's history by one of the country's greatest authors.
Sweden: The Nation's History by Franklin D Scott. Swedish history from its beginnings.
Swedish History in Outline by Jörgen Welbull.
The Vikings: Lord of the Seas by Yves Cohat. History of the Vikings, including accounts of their ships, weapons, artefacts and way of life, with excellent colour photography.
Vasa: A Swedish Warship by Frederick M. Hocker. A detailed examination of the history, archaeology, discovery and conservation of the 17th-century ship.

ARCHITECTURE

The Complete Guide to Architecture in Stockholm. A guide to over 400 of the city's buildings, plus detailed maps.
Great Royal Palaces of Sweden by Göran Alm. Presents a dozen castles, palaces and pavilions belonging to Swedish royalty over the past 500 years.

ART AND DESIGN

Carl and Karin Larsson: Creators of the Swedish Style by Michael Snodin and Elisabet Stavenow-Hidemark.

A profile of two of Sweden's most influential designers.
Scandinavian Design by Charlotte and Peter Fiell. Beautiful 704-page coffee-table book showing the best of northern European design.
A History of Swedish Art by Mereth Lindgren, Louise Lyberg, Birgitta Sandström and Anna Greta Wahlberg. A bird's-eye view of Swedish painting, sculpture and architecture from the Stone Age to the 1980s.
The Swedish Room by Lars Sjöberg and Ursula Sjöberg. Features some of Sweden's most classic interiors. Documents unique settings from the 16th to the early 19th centuries.

CHILDREN'S BOOKS

The Wonderful Adventures of Nils and *The Further Adventures of Nils* by Selma Lagerlöf. Old-fashioned travelogue of a boy who flies around Sweden on a goose, by a Nobel-Prize winning author.
Pippi Longstocking by Astrid Lindgren. The strongest girl in the world exasperates adults and befriends the kids next door in a children's classic translated into 70 languages.

FOOD

The Swedish Kitchen. A Culinary Journey by Lennart Hagerfors. A cookbook by one of the best-known chefs in Sweden, with 198 modern Swedish recipes from south to north.
The Swedish Table by Helene Henderson. A native Swede updates traditional dishes to suit a more modern palate.

FICTION

The Long Ships by Frans G. Bengtsson. The thrilling saga of Orm Tostesson, reluctant Viking, packed with historical detail and high humour.
The Emigrant novels by Vilhelm Moberg. A quartet of meaty historical

novels following a family's journey from Småland to a new life in America.
The Girl with the Dragon Tattoo, *The Girl Who Played with Fire* and *The Girl Who Kicked the Hornets' Nest* by Stieg Larsson. Larsson's best-selling Millennium trilogy about punk hacker Lisbeth Salander took the world by storm.
The Hundred-Year-Old Man Who Climbed Out of the Window and Disappeared by Jonas Jonasson. Freewheeling, farcical Swedish and international mega-hit, about the adventures of Alan, on the run from an old people's home.

Lovers of **crime fiction** should look out for Henning Mankell's Inspector Wallander books and Camilla Läckberg's crime novels.

Send Us Your Thoughts

We do our best to ensure the information in our books is as accurate and up-to-date as possible. The books are updated on a regular basis using local contacts, who painstakingly add, amend and correct as required. However, some details (such as telephone numbers and opening times) are liable to change, and we are ultimately reliant on our readers to put us in the picture.

We welcome your feedback, especially your experience of using the book "on the road". Maybe we recommended a hotel that you liked (or another that you didn't), or you came across a great bar or new attraction we missed.

We will acknowledge all contributions, and we'll offer an Insight Guide to the best letters received.

Please write to us at:
Insight Guides
PO Box 7910
London SE1 1WE

Or email us at:
hello@insightguides.com

TRANSPORT
A – Z
LANGUAGE

BIOGRAPHY

Strindberg – a Life by Sue Prideaux. The life and notoriously unstable personality of the dramatist Johan August Strindberg (1849–1912).
Abba: The Book by Jean-Marie Potiez. Meticulously researched profile of the prodigiously successful 1970s pop band.
Christina Queen of Sweden: The Restless Life of a European Eccentric by Veronica Buckley. Enjoyable recollection of Sweden's most intriguing queen.

OTHER INSIGHT GUIDES

Apa Publications' incomparable range of more than 400 Insight Guides, Insight City Guides, Insight Explore Guides and Insight Pocket Guides include the following titles relating to destinations in Scandinavia:
Insight Guide Norway provides a comprehensive guide to this Land of the Midnight Sun, complete with lively text and great photography.
Insight Guide Scandinavia brings to life the history, culture, politics and people of this sparsely inhabited landscape of fjords, lakes and mountains. It covers the whole region, from temperate Denmark to the land of the Sami, Greenland and the Faroe Islands.
Explore Guide Copenhagen is a route-based guide to the Danish capital showing places to eat, drink and shop en route.
Fleximaps Stockholm and **Copenhagen** combine clear cartography with useful travel information in an easy-to-fold, rain-resistant laminated finish.

CREDITS

Photo Credits

Alamy 52, 58, 113TR, 113BR, 227, 282/283T, 282BL, 283TR, 283BR, 284, 295
Aline Lessner/imagebank.sweden.se 59
APA/Insight Guides 233
Arild Vågen 7TL
Bengt Oberger 36R
Björn Tesch/imagebank.sweden.se 143, 146
Carolina Romare/imagebank.sweden.se 84
Cecilia Larsson Lantz/imagebank.sweden.se 62, 80, 94, 144
Christofer Dracke/Folio/imagebank.sweden.se 82
Christopher Drake/Frances Lincoln/Swedish Style 112/113T, 112BR, 112BL, 113ML, 113BL
Conny Fridh/imagebank.sweden.se 12/13, 186/187T
Corbis 102, 252
Eddie Granlund/Folio/imagebank.sweden.se 21
Elisabeth Edén/imagebank.sweden.se 100
Emelie Asplund/imagebank.sweden.se 6MR, 107
Erik Wahlström/Folio/imagebank.sweden.se 256
Faramarz Gosheh/imagebank.sweden.se 99
Francis Dean/REX/Shutterstock 67
Fredrik Broman/imagebank.sweden 16, 127, 131, 275, 277, 278
Friluftsbyn Höga Kusten/imagebank.sweden.se 288/289
Getty Images 4/5, 18, 22/23, 24, 25, 26, 27, 28, 29, 30/31T, 30BR, 30BL, 31ML, 31BR, 31BL, 32, 33, 34, 37, 38, 39, 47, 48, 49, 51, 56, 65, 66, 101, 116, 132, 133, 187ML, 208, 212, 216, 223, 244, 247, 255, 262, 263, 267, 268/269, 271, 293
Guillaume de Basly/imagebank.sweden.se 71, 136, 291
Göran Assner/imagebank.sweden.se 134, 213, 217
Helena Wahlman/imagebank.sweden.se 17B, 60, 125
Henrik Trygg/imagebank.sweden 10/11, 123, 124, 184, 185, 187TR

Hjalmar Andersson/imagebank.sweden.se 7ML
Håkan Vargas S/imagebank.sweden.se 137
iStock 9B, 40, 177, 218, 219, 221, 228, 229, 245, 266, 276, 292, 313L
Jacque de Villiers/Imagebank.sweden.se 257
Jan Simonsson/imagebank.sweden.se 7TR, 110
Janus Langhorn/imagebank.sweden.se 115
Jesper Anhede/Skara Sommarland 242
Jessica Lindgren/imagebank.sweden.se 103, 283BL
Johan Willner/imagebank.sweden.se 87, 89
John Sander/imagebank.sweden.se 203
Julian Love/Apa Publications 1, 6ML, 6MR, 7MR, 7BR, 8T, 8B, 9T, 17T, 31TR, 92, 118, 120, 128, 141, 150/151, 152/153, 154, 155T, 155B, 160, 161, 162, 163, 164, 165, 166, 167, 168, 169, 171, 172, 173, 174, 179, 180, 181, 182, 183, 186BL, 187BR, 187BL, 188, 189, 191, 193, 194, 195, 196, 197, 201, 205, 206, 207, 224, 225, 230, 231, 234, 235, 238, 239, 240, 241, 246, 248, 249, 250, 251, 253, 254, 259, 260, 261, 296, 298, 299L, 301L, 311
Justin Brown/imagebank.sweden.se 199
Jörgen Wiklund/imagebank.sweden.se 285
Kevin Kee Pil Cho/imagebank.sweden.se 111, 178
Kristin Lidell/imagebank.sweden.se 73, 91
Lena Granefelt/imagebank.sweden.se 119
Liseberg 6BL
Lola Akinmade Åkerström/imagebank.sweden.se 20, 104, 272, 273, 279
Magnus Liam Karlsson/imagebank.sweden.se 76
Magnus Skoglöf/imagebank.sweden.se 105, 142
Maria Emitslöf/imagebank.

sweden.se 14/15
Melker Dahlstrand/imagebank.sweden.se 70, 72, 74, 75, 77, 93, 138, 202
Mikko Nikkinen/imagebank.sweden.se 85, 122
Miriam Preis/imagebank.sweden.se 204
Niclas Vestefjell/imagebank.sweden.se 88, 90, 270
Nobel Media AB/Alexander Mahmoud 69
Ola Ericson/imagebank.sweden.se 78/79, 108, 147, 176, 302B
Per Pixel Petersson/imagebank.sweden.se 19, 57, 220, 243
Peter Grant/imagebank.sweden.se 281
Peter Thompson/Spectrum 35
Photoshot 126, 130, 283ML
Press Association Images 64, 98
Public domain 36L, 41, 42, 43, 44, 45, 46, 50, 53, 54, 55, 68, 106, 109
Sara Ingman/imagebank.sweden.se 135, 290
Shutterstock 7ML, 114, 264, 265, 287, 300
Simon Paulin/imagebank.sweden.se 61, 63, 96, 97, 186BR
Sofia Sabel/imagebank.sweden.se 95, 117
Sonia Jansson/imagebank.sweden.se 280
Staffan Widstrand/imagebank.sweden.se 148/149, 294
Stefan Berg/Folio/imagebank.sweden.se 81
Stig Kälvelid/Liseberg Amusement Park 222
Susanne Walström/imagebank.sweden.se 86, 139
Tina Stafrén/imagebank.sweden.se 140, 282BR
Torbjörn Skogedal/Folio/imagebank.sweden.se 215
Tuukka Ervasti/imagebank.sweden.se 170, 209, 210, 211
Ulf Lundin/imagebank.sweden.se 83, 129, 145, 302T
Viktor Gårdsäter/Folio/imagebank.sweden.se 121
www.visitfalunborlange.se 258

Cover Credits

Front cover: stuga *Shutterstock*
Back cover: wheat fields *Julian Love/Apa Publications*
Front flap: (from top) City Hall,

Stockholm *Julian Love/Apa Publications*; moose *Maria Emitslöf/ imagebank.sweden.se*; gravadlax *Julian Love/Apa Publications*;

Smögen *Julian Love/Apa Publications*
Back flap: Fryken lakes *Julian Love/Apa Publications*

Insight Guide Credits

Distribution

UK, Ireland and Europe
Apa Publications (UK) Ltd;
sales@insightguides.com
United States and Canada
Ingram Publisher Services;
ips@ingramcontent.com
Australia and New Zealand
Woodslane; info@woodslane.com.au
Southeast Asia
Apa Publications (SN) Pte;
singaporeoffice@insightguides.com
Hong Kong, Taiwan and China
Apa Publications (HK) Ltd;
hongkongoffice@insightguides.com
Worldwide
Apa Publications (UK) Ltd;
sales@insightguides.com
**Special Sales, Content Licensing
and CoPublishing**
Insight Guides can be purchased in
bulk quantities at discounted prices.
We can create special editions,
personalised jackets and corporate
imprints tailored to your needs.
sales@insightguides.com
www.insightguides.biz

Printed in China by CTPS

All Rights Reserved
© 2016 Apa Digital (CH) AG and
Apa Publications (UK) Ltd

First Edition 1989
Fourth Edition 2016

No part of this book may be
reproduced, stored in a retrieval
system or transmitted in any form or
means electronic, mechanical,
photocopying, recording or
otherwise, without prior written
permission from Apa Publications.

Every effort has been made to
provide accurate information in this
publication, but changes are
inevitable. The publisher cannot be
responsible for any resulting loss,
inconvenience or injury. We would
appreciate it if readers would call our
attention to any errors or outdated
information. We also welcome your
suggestions; please contact us at:
hello@insightguides.com

www.insightguides.com

Editor: Carine Tracanelli
Author: Fran Parnell
Head of Production: Rebeka Davies
Update Production: AM Services
Picture Editor: Tom Smyth
Cartography: original cartography
Gar Bowes Design, updated by Carte

Contributors

This new edition of *Insight Guide
Sweden* was commissioned and
edited by **Carine Tracanelli**,
Insight's Europe editor. The book
was comprehensively updated by
Fran Parnell, whose passion for
Scandinavia began while studying
Norse and Celtic at Cambridge
University. She has written guides
to Iceland, Denmark and
Scandinavia. It builds on previous

editions written by **Doreen Taylor-
Wilkie**, **Amy Brown**, **Debra
Williamson**, **Kathryn Boyer**,
Joanie Rafidi Oxhammar, **Peter
Birgerstam**, **Gert Frost**, **Pia
Helena Ormerod**, **Philip Ray**,
Caroline Bugler, **Inga Wallerius**,
Anita Oxburgh, **Terry Greenwood**,
Louis Borgia, **Jack Burton**, **H. J.
Hardy**, **Robert Spark**, **John Lloyd**
and **Elisabet Lim**.

About Insight Guides

Insight Guides have more than
45 years' experience of publishing
high-quality, visual travel guides. We
produce 400 full-colour titles, in both
print and digital form, covering more
than 200 destinations across the
globe, in a variety of formats to meet
your different needs.
  Insight Guides are written by
local authors who use their on-the-
ground experience to provide the

very latest information; their local
expertise is evident in the extensive
historical and cultural background
features. All the reviews in **Insight
Guides** are independent; we strive
to maintain an impartial view. Our
reviews are carefully selected to
guide you to the best places to eat,
go out and shop, so you can be
confident that when we say a place
is special, we really mean it.

Legend

City maps

	Freeway/Highway/Motorway
	Divided Highway
	Main Roads
	Minor Roads
	Pedestrian Roads
	Steps
	Footpath
	Railway
	Funicular Railway
	Cable Car
	Tunnel
	City Wall
	Important Building
	Built Up Area
	Other Land
	Transport Hub
	Park
	Pedestrian Area
	Bus Station
	Tourist Information
	Main Post Office
	Cathedral/Church
	Mosque
	Synagogue
	Statue/Monument
	Beach
	Airport

Regional maps

	Freeway/Highway/Motorway (with junction)
	Freeway/Highway/Motorway (under construction)
	Divided Highway
	Main Road
	Secondary Road
	Minor Road
	Track
	Footpath
	International Boundary
	State/Province Boundary
	National Park/Reserve
	Marine Park
	Ferry Route
	Marshland/Swamp
	Glacier Salt Lake
	Airport/Airfield
	Ancient Site
	Border Control
	Cable Car
	Castle/Castle Ruins
	Cave
	Chateau/Stately Home
	Church/Church Ruins
	Crater
	Lighthouse
	Mountain Peak
	Place of Interest
	Viewpoint

INDEX

Main references are in bold type